OUR PUNITIVE SOCIETY

Race, Class, Gender and Punishment in America

RANDALL G. SHELDEN
University of Nevada–Las Vegas

WAVELAND PRESS, INC.

Long Grove, Illinois

For information about this book, contact:
Waveland Press, Inc.
4180 IL Route 83, Suite 101
Long Grove, IL 60047-9580
(847) 634-0081
info@waveland.com
www.waveland.com

10-digit ISBN 1-57766-632-1
13-digit ISBN 978-1-57766-632-5

Printed in the United States of America

7   6   5   4

Contents

Preface

This book represents a good deal of my thinking about crime and punishment. I have been involved in the study of this subject matter for the better part of four decades, beginning in the early 1970s. All these years of research and thinking about the subject have informed the discussions in this book.

In general, I have reached the conclusion that you cannot possibly discuss in any honest way the subject of crime and punishment in the United States without reference to class, race, and gender inequality. Indeed, given the fact that this country has the highest degree of inequality among all industrialized democracies—a fact extensively documented in this book—what other conclusion can one make?

The French philosopher Anatole France once observed: "The law, in its majestic equality, forbids the rich as well as the poor to sleep under bridges, to beg in the streets and to steal bread." In other words, you cannot have equal justice in an unequal society. The way the law is written assumes that all citizens are pretty much equal and that people simply choose to commit a crime for no apparent reason, other than that they believe they can get away with it. This is one of the basic principles of the "Classical School" of Criminology that began with Cesare Beccaria's *On Crimes and Punishment* in 1764. This is part of the *deterrence* argument that says you prevent crime by making the punishment so severe, swift, and certain that people will think twice before they commit a crime. According to this line of thinking, the main instrument of the control of human behavior is *fear*, especially fear of *pain*. Thus, punishment, as a principal method of operating to create fear, is seen as necessary to influence human will and thus to control behavior. This theory can be said to be the very foundation of the criminal justice system. Two hundred and fifty years later we see the horrific results of this failed philosophy. Documentation of this failure is the impetus for this book.

I do not make any claim of originality, for I am, as the saying goes, "standing on the shoulders of giants." Many scholars over the past century have said some of the same things I am saying, and their work is cited repeatedly throughout this book.

The introduction discusses the first of several dimensions of the punitiveness of our society. It asks the important question: why is the United States so punitive?

Chapter 1 reviews recent trends in the use of incarceration. The incarceration rate in the United States is the highest in the world; it has increased fivefold in the past 25 years or so. Presently more than 2 million people are behind bars—either in jail or prison. Another 5 million are either on probation or parole, bringing the total to 7 million—an all-time high. This system is part of a much larger worldwide system of social control if we include the armed forces and our role in Iraq and elsewhere. The massive building of prisons in recent decades has resulted in what some have called a "Gulag" effect, whereby prisons are found just about everywhere, especially in rural areas. Additionally, military prisons are found in several parts of the Middle East, mostly hidden from public view and rarely discussed in the media.

Locking people up has become a booming business. The "Prison Industrial Complex" is the subject of Chapter 2, which provides a detailed discussion of the many dimensions of the profitability of this system from the building of prisons and jails to their daily operation. Literally hundreds of companies, both large and small, are reaping profits. (A partial listing is provided in an Appendix.) Also, supporting and benefiting from the existence of all these prisons are many professional organizations, including the American Correctional Association, various unions such as the California Correctional Peace Officer's Association, and others. All have a vested interest in crime and its control. In fact, as one writer commented, crime may not pay, but punishment certainly does. The basic thrust of this chapter is simply this: the current system of punishment cannot afford a significant reduction in crime because too much money is at stake.

Chapter 3 covers a key component of the penal system, the jail. The basic theme is stated in part of the title: "temporary housing for the poor." One of the themes of this book is that jails are the modern equivalent of eighteenth- and nineteenth-century "poorhouses." Jails serve as temporary holding facilities to control and manage the "rabble" or the "dangerous classes."

Chapter 4 is perhaps the most important chapter of all; it deals with the sensitive subject of race. As the title suggests, our penal system is little more than a new form of slavery. Penal institutions and slavery have paralleled each other throughout history. Many scholars have noted the similarity between the treatment of slaves and prisoners and in fact have documented the fact that both terms have been used interchangeably. One of the original forms of punishment was that of "galley slavery" and transportation to foreign lands. In early Roman society slaves and prisoners were essentially treated alike and helped build the Colosseum, the Pantheon, the Roman Forum, and many other famous edifices still visible in Italy. In the South, slaves turned quickly into convicts after the Civil War—in fact the oldest types of prisons in the South were called "Plantation Prisons" (some are still standing, such as the infamous Parchman and Cummins prisons). The chapter ends with a review of the recent incarceration trends that have resulted in a rate for blacks that is four or five times that of whites and even greater when considering drug convictions, which have been largely responsible for their greater numbers in prison.

Chapter 5 reviews the ultimate form of punishment: the death penalty. This is a form of "legalized homicide" inflicted almost exclusively on the poor. It is no accident that certain "legal" forms of execution began to increase just as a certain illegal form known as "lynching" began to decline. The racial factor has remained to the present day. What has also remained throughout the history of this form of punishment is the lack of a deterrent value and the fact that many innocents have been subjected to this punishment. A complete historical review is provided, with up-to-date statistics on the death penalty, including a review of key court decisions.

Chapter 6 provides an historical and contemporary look at a subject noticeably missing in most books on punishment. The incarceration rate of women has escalated a phenomenal 650% since the mid-1970s. The major cause of the unprecedented growth is the war on drugs.

Chapter 7 examines still another key dimension of our punitive society, namely, the punishment of young offenders. A significant segment of this chapter focuses on the excessively large proportion of minority of youth confined in both detention centers and "correctional" institutions. As with their adult counterparts, race and the war on drugs play a significant role. Black youths are five to seven times more likely to be confined in both detention and correctional facilities than their white counterparts. One segment of this chapter is devoted to the crisis in detention centers, which are filled to capacity with kids who do not really need to be there. One recent controversy centers on the mental health status of many kids—thousands are locked up in detention centers awaiting placement in mental health facilities. Conditions have become so bad that local, state, and national hearings have been held on the subject. Shelter care facilities face some of the same problems, and these are also discussed in this chapter.

Even after one is released from prison, the punishment continues in what some critics call a "recycling of prisoners." Chapter 8 discusses problems associated with re-entry and the many barriers that ex-cons face after they are released from prison. The chapter summarizes what has been written about the "collateral consequences" of our overuse of imprisonment. The parole system is set up almost as if those in charge want prisoners to fail. And fail they do, as national recidivism rates consistently hover around the 65%–70% mark.

Finally, chapter 9 provides some of my own—and others'—recommendations for alternatives to the current criminal justice response to crime and delinquency. An end to the drug war is recommended, starting with legalizing marijuana and treating it like alcohol. From there I move to a discussion of a variety of "diversion" programs that avoid the problem of "net widening"—including a program called DDAP that started in San Francisco, followed by a discussion of some broad-based national programs to address the more general problem of social inequality, plus a discussion of "restorative justice."

In closing I would like to draw on a quote from Richard Quinney, one of my mentors and arguably one of the most influential criminologists of the twentieth century. In a talk at the Midwest Criminal Justice Association meeting in Chicago in 2005, he commented on the connection between imprisonment and society:

> A society that separates people through the institution of the prison creates populations of incomplete and wounded lives, whether we are *inside* the prison or *outside* the prison. This is the dance of slave and slaveholder, inmate and captor, prisoner and non-prisoner. No one escapes the damage caused by the fact that the prison exists. The damage is pervasive—on levels economic, social and psychological, and ultimately spiritual.

One interpretation of what Quinney says is that our punitiveness damages all of us. This is one of the themes of this book.

Some final words of thanks are in order. Writers rarely if ever come up with original ideas. Most writing is a process of borrowing words and ideas from others and reshaping them in some other form. I have always considered myself as a kind of "assembler" who ingests ideas from many others and adds my own interpretation to them. Therefore, I would like to extend my thanks to all of the people who are cited in the endnotes to this book. Obviously they are too numerous to list here. However, the following people are those I have not only read but have personally met over the years; without them and their unique insights, this book would be little more than blank pages. They are, in no particular order of importance: Bud Brown, Richard Quinney, Noam Chomsky, Howard Zinn, Meda Chesney-Lind, Michael Hallett, and John Irwin.

I would also like to extend my thanks to my colleagues in the Criminal Justice Department at the University of Nevada–Las Vegas for their generous support over the years (especially Terry Miethe and Joel Lieberman) and to the university itself for granting me a sabbatical for the spring of 2009 that allowed me the time to put this book together.

A very special thank you goes to Carol and Neil Rowe of Waveland Press for their overwhelming support for this and previous books. It is a pure joy to work with both of you.

Finally, I wish to express my deepest thanks and love to my wife Virginia and stepdaughter Marcie for their unqualified love and support during this and previous book projects.

Introduction
Why Are We So Punitive?

In the east Texas town of Paris, amid allegations from black parents that the local schools and courts systematically discriminate against their children, a white judge sentenced a 14-year-old black girl to up to 7 years in a juvenile prison for pushing a hall monitor at her high school. The same judge sentenced a 14-year-old white girl, convicted of arson for burning down a house, to probation.[1]

In his videotaped confession to the police, the eight-year-old boy sits in an overstuffed office chair and calmly describes how he shot his father and his father's roommate to death with a rifle. . . . Prosecutors in Arizona, who could have sought to charge the boy as an adult, have charged him in juvenile court. . . . Only 16 states define an age at which a child is capable of forming criminal intent. . . . In North Carolina, the minimum age is six. Most of the other 34 states leave it up to prosecutors.[2]

[An ACLU report provides] the latest examples of a disturbing national trend known as the "school to prison pipeline" wherein children are over-aggressively funneled out of public schools and into the juvenile and criminal justice systems. . . . Students in Hartford, East Hartford, and West Hartford are being arrested at school at very young ages. . . . A majority of those arrested were seventh or eighth graders, but twenty-five were in grades four through six and thirteen were in grades three or below. Research shows that the earlier children are exposed to the criminal justice system, the more likely they are to commit crimes later in life. Relying primarily on arrests rather than other forms of behavioral intervention cements an unfortunate cycle of criminalization which, in the end, doesn't benefit our kids and doesn't benefit our communities.[3]

For years, courts have treated the mentally ill with the same dispassion accorded any other defendant. The results have been devastating. More than twice as many people with mental illness live in prisons as in state mental hospitals. When they are confined to tiny

1

cells, their conditions worsen, increasing their propensity to act out. As a result, the mentally ill face disproportionately harsher discipline than do other inmates behind bars.[4]

On October 15, 2008, the Mental Health Project (MHP) teamed up with groups across the country to file *Martinez v. Astrue*, a national class action lawsuit against the Social Security Administration (SSA) for revoking the retirement and disability benefits of over 100,000 poor, elderly, and disabled Americans under an arbitrary and unlawful benefit suspension policy. . . . Under a 1996 law, SSA must suspend the benefits of people who are "fleeing to avoid prosecution" for a felony. The law was enacted to prevent wanted fugitives from receiving benefits. Thousands of elderly and disabled Americans who are not "wanted," however, and indeed, who may have been completely misidentified, have been caught up in the crude computer dragnet SSA has used to implement the law.

For example, Rosa Martinez, a 52-year-old former nurse from Redwood City, CA, received a notice from the SSA last December that she was losing her only source of income—her disability benefits—because of a 1980 arrest warrant for a drug offense in Miami, Florida. Ms. Martinez, however, had never been to Miami, never been arrested and had never used illegal drugs. Nevertheless, SSA has refused to reinstate Ms. Martinez' $870 per month disability check.[5]

Razor wire topping the fences seems almost a joke at the Men's State Prison [in Hardwick, GA], where many inmates are slumped in wheelchairs, or leaning on walkers or canes. It's becoming an increasingly common sight: geriatric inmates spending their waning days behind bars. The soaring number of aging inmates is now outpacing the prison growth as a whole. Tough sentencing laws passed in the crime-busting 1980s and 1990s are largely to blame. It's all fueling an explosion in inmate health costs for cash-strapped states. . . . The graying of the nation's prisons mirrors the population as whole. But many inmates arrive in prison after years of unhealthy living. . . . The stress of life behind bars can often make them even sicker. And once they enter prison walls, they aren't eligible for Medicaid or Medicare, where the costs are shared between the state and federal government, meaning a state shoulders the burden of inmate health care on its own.[6]

This book is about punishment in the United States. The stories noted above are a small sample of the many cases of excessive punishments meted out in this society. The American system of punishment is filled with ironies. We spend more than $200 billion per year on the three major components of the criminal justice system: police, courts and the correctional system (which includes both probation and parole), plus several billion more in private security systems (security guards, gated communities, multiple variations of security devices, etc.). Yet the crime rate, especially violence, remains the highest in the world.

Simultaneously, our system of punishment is a source of rewards for those working within it and for those who build and maintain the system. Terms such as "crime control industry," "criminal justice industrial complex" and "prison industrial complex" describe the symbiotic relationship between criminal justice, politics, and economics. The prison industrial complex refers to the interactions among the prison system, the political system and the economic system.[7] Think also of the large number of lobbyists in the nation's capital.[8] Also, think for a moment about the building of prisons, jails, courthouses, and police departments—and furnishing them with everything they need to operate (from construction costs to furniture to toilet paper).[9] The end result is that punishment pays and pays very well.

The American Legislative Exchange Council (ALEC) demonstrates the connections between politics, economics, and the criminal justice system. The membership consists of state legislators, private corporation executives, and criminal justice officials. More than one-third of state lawmakers in the country (2400) are members. The Private Enterprise Board associated with ALEC includes some of the largest corporations in the United States: Coors, AT&T, UPS, Wal-Mart, ExxonMobil, Coca-Cola, Johnson & Johnson, Bayer, and State Farm, among others. Within ALEC is a "Criminal Justice Task Force," which drafts models of legislation on crime and punishment that members support. Examples include: mandatory minimum sentences, three-strikes laws, and truth-in-sentencing legislation. These kinds of laws contributed to the rapid increase in the prison population—creating larger markets for profits. The types of legislation sponsored are listed on their Web site.[10]

Politicians infrequently support prevention efforts, avoiding the risk of being labeled "soft on crime." Calls for more cops on the streets and more prisons resonate with public fears about crime and criminals. Those fears highlight an irony: in what is touted to be the freest and richest country in the history of the world, we are not just the most punitive; we are the most fearful. Indeed, despite all the measures taken and money spent for security, the fear of crime remains high.[11]

Embedded within the U.S. Constitution, the Bill of Rights, and the Declaration of Independence is the assumption that people should have freedom of movement and freedom in decision making. These are assumed to be "inalienable rights."[12] Punishment itself is not new, nor is the use of prison to produce pain for its inhabitants, which dates back as far as early Roman society.[13] What is new in modern societies is the length of prison sentences *as an expression of the deprivation of liberty.*

Today we incarcerate more people than any other country in the world. "The United States has less than five% of the world's population, but about a quarter of its prisoners. We have more prisoners than China—a country with a repressive government and more than four times the population of the United States."[14] In 1984 Japan's population was half the size of the United States; there were 40,000 sentenced offenders compared to 580,000 U.S. prisoners. Twenty-five years later, Japan's prison population was 71,000 compared to 2.3 million in the United States.[15] The U.S. incarcerates people in prison or jail at a rate almost five times higher than the average rate in other countries (see chapter 1). Combining those prisoners with the five million people on parole, on probation, or under some alternative sanction, approximately one in every 31 adults in the United States is subject to correctional supervision. How do we explain this?

David Garland provides an insightful analysis of what he describes as the "accelerating movement away from the assumptions that shaped crime control and criminal justice for most of the twentieth century."[16] He notes that

> As the character of everyday life changes, its changing habits and routines often have consequences for the structure of informal controls that can, in turn, cause problems for the functioning and effectiveness of the institutions of formal control. We have to bear in mind, therefore, that the field of crime control involves the social ordering activities of the authorities *and also* the activities of private actors and agencies as they go about their daily lives and ordinary routines. . . . A reconfigured field of crime control involves more than just a change in society's response to crime. It also entails new practices of controlling behavior and doing justice, revised conceptions of social order and social control, and altered ways of maintaining social cohesion and managing group relations. . . . Behind these new responses to crime, there lies a new pattern of mentalities, interests, and sensibilities that has altered how we think and feel about the underlying problem.[17]

He attributes the transformation away from the less punitive approach that had previously dominated thinking about crime to twelve indices of change, which are summarized below.

Indices of Change

First, there has been a rapid decline in the rehabilitative ideal.[18] The loss of faith in rehabilitation began in the early 1970s, based in part on a misunderstanding of a controversial work by Robert Martinson and his colleagues. In a summary of a study that reviewed evaluations of rehabilitation programs, Martinson said that while some programs showed promise of reducing recidivism, most of the evaluations lacked evidence of effectiveness and had been seriously flawed.[19] He never said "nothing works," but many commentators interpreted his findings to mean exactly that.[20]

The second index of change noted by Garland is the rebirth of very punitive sanctions and "expressive justice."[21] Use of the death penalty increased; chain gangs were reinstated; and prisoners once again were assigned striped uniforms. Public shaming and humiliation had been regarded as demeaning, but attitudes shifted toward embracing punishment for precisely that value. The open expression of vengeance and condemnation was accepted as a justifiable outlet for the angers and fears of the public.

The third index parallels the second and marks a change in the tone of discourse about crime and punishment. In the past, people vocalized commitments to treat offenders decently and humanely, but the tone shifted in the opposite direction beginning in the 1980s. Disgust and anger toward offenders became prevalent. While in previous years there had been concern about the various social and psychological causes of crime and delinquency, by the 1990s the rhetoric included terms like "super-predators," "dangerous" or "unruly" youth, and incorrigible "career criminals." Rather than seek to address the many causes of crime, the primary tone changed to "a collective anger and righteous demand for retribution."[22]

The fourth index reviewed by Garland is the "return of the victim."[23] The response to crime shifted rather dramatically from a focus on the criminal (and his or her shortcomings and prospects for reformation) to the victim. "Victim's rights" became a dominant theme, with many politicians attracting votes by expressing concerns over crime victims, even though nothing much was done to make them safer.[24] Laws were passed named for specific victims (e.g., Megan's Law, Jenna's Law, Brady Bill), and many crime bills were based on one or more popular cases ("three-strikes and you're out" legislation in California was enacted after the kidnapping and murder of Polly Klaas). Garland emphasizes that one outcome of basing legislation on cases receiving national publicity is that the victim is seen as someone whose experience is "common and collective, rather than individual and atypical." Widespread publicity serves as a sort of "it-could-be-you" symbol where the victim is "Everyman."[25] Many new laws with extremely harsh sentences are guided by exception-based policies and could be termed "legislation by anecdote."

The fifth index is the elevation of security as an urgent need exceeding all others, highlighted by such procedures as "community notification laws" (especially for sex offenders). Civil rights are deemphasized and become secondary to the search for security. People accept surveillance cameras on city streets and encroachments on procedural safeguards such as the exclusionary rule. "The call for protection *from* the state has been increasingly displaced by the demand for protection *by* the state."[26]

Garland's sixth index of change is the "politicization" of crime and a rise of a new form of populism.[27] Policy is decided under the glare of publicity and in political debate. Sound bites have taken the place of more careful analysis, with catch phrases like "three-strikes and you're out," "zero tolerance," or "do adult crime, do adult time." The opinions of experts and professionals are rejected in favor of the views of victims and the fearful public. Instead of relying on expert opinion and research, the emphasis shifted to "common sense" or "what everyone knows."

Seventh, there has been a "reinvention of the prison."[28] Incarceration is no longer viewed as a method of reforming criminals but rather as a means for incapacitation and punishment. The emphasis on the harshness of punishments satisfies a growing public demand to punish those who threaten public safety and to remove offenders from society.

Eighth, there has been a shift in emphasis within the field of criminology—a return to the "classical school" and its theme of "let the punishment fit the crime." Rather than stressing the importance of why people commit crime (underlying causes), there is a strong emphasis on *control theory*. Crime is not viewed as being caused by various forms of deprivation; rather, it is perceived as the result of inadequate controls. Crime is seen as "normal" and "routine," a "common occurrence" in modern societies.[29] Like the weather, there is nothing much in the way of prevention except to "batten down the hatches" or, like in the days of the "Wild West," guard the forts and hope that reinforcements come before the next attack. The assumption of these new theories (e.g., "routine activity," "rational choice") is that crime "just happens" since it is "normal." Crime will occur "naturally" as long as there are inadequate controls.

Ninth, there has been a tremendous growth in the infrastructure of crime control and community safety. "Today's most visible crime control strategies may work by expulsion and exclusion, but they are accompanied by patient, ongoing, low-key efforts to build up the internal controls of neighborhoods and to encourage communities to police themselves."[30] A host of components of this infrastructure has emerged, such as "community policing," "Safer Cities programs," and Neighborhood Watch—all of which are included in a rapidly growing crime control industry. A new set of priorities has emerged, including "prevention, security, harm-reduction, loss-reduction, fear-reduction," and the like.

The tenth index is "civil society and the commercialization of crime control."[31] This refers to an expansion of crime control beyond the normal state functions to citizen involvement and the involvement of entire communities and businesses. Public sector agencies have been remodeled to reflect the values of private industry. This development also includes a growing number of businesses and households investing in various forms of security devices and private security companies.[32] One of the fastest-growing industries is the private security industry. There are currently more than one million security guards employed in the United States, compared to around 650,000 police officers. The Bureau of Labor Statistics noted that employment of security guards is expected to increase by 17% by 2016, a faster than average increase for all occupations. "Concern about crime, vandalism, and terrorism continues to increase the need for security. Demand for guards also will grow as private security firms increasingly perform duties—such as providing security at public events and in residential neighborhoods— that were formerly handled by police officers."[33]

The eleventh index of change is the development of new styles of management and working practices by those involved in crime control efforts. Rather than an emphasis on social work practices and rehabilitation, agencies like prisons and departments of probation and parole focus on monitoring offenders. "Peace officers" are rewarded for catching violators rather than for helping offenders adjust to reentry. A more centralized form of management has taken over with an emphasis on the management of risks and resources.[34] Performance indicators and management measures reduce the amount of discretion available to employees. There is an emphasis on cost-effective management of risks and resources (i.e., hot-spots in policing).

Finally, Garland notes that there is a perpetual sense of crisis pervading the crime control establishment. He notes that the unrelenting upheaval in practices since the 1970s and the rapid change has exposed employees to sustained periods of uncertainty and disruption.

> Expertise of the professional groups that staff the system has tended to become discredited, both by others and by members of the groups themselves. . . . The public has increasingly lost confidence in criminal justice and politicians have become more and more unwilling to entrust decision-making powers to criminological experts or criminal justice personnel. . . . [The system is often seen as a] danger zone—a constant generator of risks and scandals and escalating costs—whose officials can no longer be entrusted with autonomous powers and grants of discretion.[35]

With Garland's analysis as background, we now return to the question posed earlier.

Why Are We So Punitive?

THE CONSERVATIVE PHILOSOPHY

The huge increases in imprisonment rates in this country beg for an explanation. Have the number of crimes increased exponentially? Have we legislated more laws defining specific activities as crimes? The "war on drugs" is one significant source of the rapidly expanding number of people sentenced to jail or prison. Two of the first questions to ask is why was such a "war" declared in the first place, and why have we become so punitive?

We need to look deep into the American culture to understand the tendency toward punitiveness. There is a strong cultural belief in "rugged individualism," accompanied by the belief that people succeed largely through their own efforts. Another strong image is that of the traditional nuclear family, often with overtones of patriarchy where the father is in control and sometimes is the major breadwinner. This pattern is usually marked by behaviors such as obeying the rules—in order to become a "good" and "moral" person a child must learn to respect authority. Proper behavior is taught through threats of punishment. Within such a system the exercise of authority is itself moral; that is, it is moral to reward obedience and to punish disobedience."[36]

Punishment, according to this philosophy, is the only way to become a self-disciplined and moral person. The system of rewards and punishments builds character and teaches children how to survive in a dangerous world. To be successful requires becoming self-disciplined. More importantly, rewarding someone who has not worked to earn the reward is immoral. Adherents to this philosophy reject various forms of welfare, affirmative action, and lenient punishments—believing that these programs and policies reward deviance and laziness.[37] There is an erroneous assumption that those who are rich and famous arrived there through their own efforts, with little or no help from others. Luck and the privileges of birth are often ignored within this philosophy.

Related to this worldview is a belief in a "morality of strength." The world is divided into "good" and "evil"; in order to stand up to evil, one must be morally strong; one becomes morally strong through a system of rewards and punishments that teaches self-discipline. A person who is morally weak cannot fight evil. If one is too self-indulgent, he or she is immoral. Crime and deviance are immoral and should be punished. Therefore, it logically follows that crime and deviance are the result of moral weakness. Teenage sex, drug use, and all sorts of other "deviant" behaviors stem from lack of self-control. A person with proper self-discipline should be able to "just say no" and those who do not must be and deserved to be punished.[38]

It should be pointed out that the entire criminal justice system (and to a somewhat lesser extent, the juvenile justice system) is based on a similar punitive philosophy, generally known as *deterrence*. Such a view argues that the best way to deter—that is, prevent—crime from occurring is the threat of punishment or the fear that one will be caught and punished. There are two kinds of deterrence. *General* deterrence is aimed toward the population as a whole. Thus, you punish one person in the hopes that others will "get the message" and refrain from committing crime. *Special* deterrence is the punishment of a specific individual in the hopes that he or she will "learn their lesson" from the punishment and never violate the rules again. It is based in part on the idea that all humans are rational with free will and will seek to minimize pain and maximize pleasure. Thus, the pleasure of committing a crime should be offset by the pain of punishment.

It can certainly be debated whether or not humans actually behave in this manner. What cannot be debated, it seems to me, is that increasing the punishments for crimes has not worked very well. Yet we seem to keep sounding the same horn, louder and louder—saying to those who might be tempted to commit crime "we're sending you a message that you will be caught and punished to the full extent of the law if you keep doing this."

The philosophy described above has become a more dominant force in American culture since the 1980s.[39] Underscoring this development has been the concomitant growth in the number of conservative "think tanks."[40] Part of this philosophy comes from religious teachings.[41] More specifically, it derives in part from the "Protestant ethic," which refers to a belief system that one must make sacrifices, be self-disciplined, be thrifty, and work hard in order to be successful.[42]

THE ROLE OF RELIGION

The earliest form of law in this country was shaped by puritan religious beliefs. In the Massachusetts Bay Colony, Governor John Winthrop expressed a desire to build "a City upon a Hill"—a society that would serve as "an example of godliness to the world." The Puritans viewed the state as legitimate "because it was a government confirming to what God had decreed," and they themselves were "chosen by God to represent Him on earth." More importantly, however, they viewed their leaders "as being ordained by God" and both the governor and the magistrates "were granted power through divine authority."[43] Many laws were taken almost literally from the Bible, including those prohibiting idolatry, blasphemy, bestiality, sodomy, and adultery, all of which were punishable by death. Even after the American Revolution, which stressed a separation of church and state, many religiously based laws remained on the books, some of which were known as "Sunday Laws" and "Blue Laws."[44]

According to one recent poll, Americans are far more willing to mix faith and politics than people in other countries. The poll, which also included Australia, Britain, Canada, France, Germany, Italy, Mexico, South Korea, and Spain, found that almost all American respondents "said faith is important to them and only 2% said they do not believe in God. Almost 40% said religious leaders should try to sway policy makers, notably higher than in other countries."[45] The most recent Harris poll (December 2005) revealed the following: 73% believe in miracles, 70% believe in heaven, 66% believe in the resurrection of Christ, 58% believe in the Virgin birth (Jesus born of Mary), 61% believe in the existence of the devil, and 59% believe hell exists.[46]

The *Los Angeles Times* ran a story entitled "Grooming Politicians for Christ."[47] The reporter discussed regular Monday meetings on Capitol Hill where aspiring politicians are taught by college professors and members of Congress to "mine the Bible for ancient wisdom on modern policy debates about tax rates, foreign aid, education, cloning, and the Central American Free Trade Agreement." One lecture was given by bioethicist Nigel Cameron, a professor at Chicago–Kent College of Law, who believes that federal law should be based on biblical precepts.[48]

Religious leaders were largely behind the passage of California's Proposition 8 to amend the state constitution to ban same-sex marriages. The Mormon Church donated a large sum of money to this effort, thus raising the question of whether or not their tax-exempt status should be repealed.[49]

Helen Ellerbe argues persuasively that orthodox religions are inherently punitive. In *The Dark Side of Christian History*, she writes that "orthodox Christianity is embedded in the belief in a singular, solely masculine, authoritarian God who demands unquestioning obedience and who mercilessly punishes dissent."[50] Those who adhere to this belief also believe that "fear is essential to sustain" a "divinely ordained hierarchical order in which a celestial God reigns singularly at a pinnacle."

With the fall of the Roman Empire, the Church took control and instituted what amounted to a reign of terror marked by the Crusades and the Inquisition. The Protestant Reformation terrified people "with threats of the devil and witchcraft." Submission to hierarchical authority was imperative. "Fear God, and keep His commandments: for this is the whole duty of man."[51] Christians were also taught to fear earthly rulers as they feared God. Mere mortals could only learn about the teachings of Christ from those appointed as successors to the Apostles. "This confined power and authority to a small few and established a specific chain of command."[52]

In the fourth century, St. John Chrysostom issued a statement that could easily provide the theoretical underpinnings of the Classical School of Criminology: without magistrates "and the fear that comes from them," entire nations would fall because there would be no one "to repress, or repel, or persuade them to be peaceful through the fear of punishment."[53] In short, people will coexist in an orderly fashion only through the threat of punishment.

Religion played a key role in the establishment of the first prisons. *Penitentiaries* derived their name from the desire of the Quakers and other religious groups in the late eighteenth and early nineteenth century, when crime was equated with sin, to confine prisoners in quarters where they could contemplate their crimes and seek penance. Prisoners were locked up in solitary confinement almost 24 hours per day, with nothing to read but the Bible; the only outsiders allowed to visit were members of the clergy. Going to prison was supposed to be a "monastic experience."[54] The "Pennsylvania model" has been reconstituted in "supermax" prisons where inmates are confined in single cells with no human contact (see chapter 3).

Vengeance and retribution are concepts common to many religions; they have also dominated discussions of crime control policies. Rational arguments against the death penalty, for instance, are often ignored because the crimes committed produce such strong feelings of vengeance. If members of the public focus on retribution—"an eye for an eye" in the Bible or "lex talionis" in Roman law[55]—the desire to punish will override the facts that the death penalty is not a deterrent, that it is more costly than life in prison, and that it discriminates against racial minorities.[56]

As will be discussed throughout this text, minorities suffer disproportionately from the punitive nature of society—from arrest to detention to imprisonment. It is much easier to impose severe punishments on people "with whom we have little in common or do not know in any personal sense . . . the more stratified a society, the easier it becomes for the well-off to advocate greater pain for those less fortunate."[57] Well over half of all of those imprisoned today are racial minorities, yet there is limited public debate about the disparity in treatment. Imagine if the police suddenly began arresting middle and upper-class white youths and placing them in prison in numbers approaching the arrest and conviction rates for blacks.

SOCIAL AND POLITICAL FACTORS

In *Thinking about Crime*, Michael Tonry reviews a number of possible explanations for the increase in punitiveness.[58] He sets the stage for his analysis by noting:

> The ways people think about contentious issues change slowly but predictably. Social scientists use the word "sensibilities" to refer to prevailing social values, attitudes, and beliefs, and show how sensibilities change slowly over time and shape and reshape what people think and believe. Current American crime control policies are to a large part an outgrowth of American sensibilities of the last third of the twentieth century.[59]

Attitudes toward crime in the United States are cyclical. Prevailing sensibilities affect what laws are passed and the policies pursued, as does the ongoing cycle of tolerance and intolerance.

Tonry notes that some people, including David Garland, point to economic and social disruptions as causing a postmodern angst— extreme concerns about the future accompanied by vast insecurity. This emotional state frequently prompts people to look for scapegoats. In Garland's words, punitive sanctions are adopted:

> Because the groups most affected lack political power and are widely regarded as dangerous and undeserving; because the groups

least affected could be reassured that something is being done and lawlessness is not tolerated; and because few politicians are willing to oppose a policy when there is so little political advantage to be gained by doing so.[60]

Tonry also discusses Theodore Caplow and Jonathan Simon's attribution of harsh punishment to "governing through crime."[61] The breakdown of broad-based political parties, the rise of "single-issue" interest groups (e.g., environment, civil rights, abortion, animal rights, taxation, gun laws), and an overall lack of public confidence in government programs created the necessity for politicians to find an issue to attract support without offending specific interest groups. Crime offered a point of consensus and a means of winning votes. Criminals were convenient scapegoats, along with welfare recipients and immigrants. "Criminals are among the most vulnerable and viscerally plausible scapegoats and politicians have tried to placate voters' discomforts and win votes by being tough on criminals."[62]

Tonry strongly suggests that race plays a major role in increased punitiveness. The vast differences in the rates of incarceration for blacks and for whites provide ample evidence of this factor. Linked to the factor of race is the drug war. Tonry argues that both drug and crime policies have been the result of "recurring patterns of tolerance and intolerance of deviance to produce widespread public susceptibility to calls for adoption of unprecedentedly repressive policies. The emotional force of ubiquitous mass media coverage of such events as the crimes of Willie Horton [suspension of weekend furloughs], the murders of Megan Kanka [sex offender registration and community notification laws] and Polly Klaas [California's "three-strikes" laws], and the crack overdose death of Len Bias [federal 100-to-1 crack cocaine sentencing law] produced moral panics that provided occasion for such calls."[63] During moral panics, people exaggerate the dangers of things they fear (e.g., fearing crime when crime is actually declining or when the odds of being a victim are extremely low) and they become more rigid and moralistic. Just look at the attitudes toward so-called "crack babies" and teen mothers expressed in recent years, with clear majorities believing the hype surrounding these two issues and wanting such individuals punished in the most severe way.[64]

> For two decades Americans "thought they wanted single-minded toughness and they got it. The question is why they thought they wanted it. "Moral panics" are part of the answer. They typically occur when horrifying or notorious events galvanize public emotion, and produce concern, sympathy, emotion, and overreaction. . . . Moral panics relating to crime lead to poorly considered and overly harsh reactions. In recent decades, moral panics have magnified the effects of longer term changes in values and attitudes.[65]

We're the Tough Guys

We live in what might be termed a "macho culture" marked by a belief that "might makes right." The history of the United States contains many examples of invasions of foreign countries, as thoroughly documented in William Blum's *Killing Hope: U.S. Military and CIA Intervention Since World War II* and his follow-up *Rogue State*.[66] Three other scholars—Chalmers Johnson,[67] Noam Chomsky,[68] and Stephen Kinzer[69]—have also addressed the topic of U.S. militarism. It seems to me that this mentality extends to our treatment of criminals (with the notable exceptions of corporate offenders and crimes of the state).

In *Harsh Justice*, James Whitman discusses the increasing divide between approaches to punishment in Europe and practices in the United States.[70] Europeans have moved away from the *degradation and humiliation* of offenders. They treat ordinary offenders of low social status with the dignity and honor formerly reserved for high status offenders. Meanwhile, the American system of justice has gone in the opposite direction. The United States practices "status degradation ceremonies" whereby the very "personhood" of offenders is ignored.[71] Europe distanced itself from the harshness and meanness of the ultra-authoritarian punishments associated with Fascism and Nazi Germany.

Whitman notes that it understates the complexity of the problem to say that American punishment is harsh and European punishment is mild. "The right way to describe the contrast is to say that, over the last quarter century, America has shown a systemic drive toward increasing harshness by most measures, while continental Europe has not."[72] He describes the factors he uses to analyze systems.

> Cultural differences in the perception of the "harshness" of particular acts of punishment are only the beginning. Deeper difficulties grow out of the fact that criminal justice systems are *systems*. Criminal justice is a complex machinery that begins with investigation and arrest; continues with trial, conviction, and sentencing; and ends only with the reintegration, or as the case may be, with the death of, the offender. . . . This machinery can operate in ways that are quite harsh in one respect, but quite mild in another. . . . [there are] ten different senses in which we can describe the workings of a given criminal justice system as relatively "mild" or "harsh": five forms of harshness in *criminalization*, three forms of harshness in *punishment*, and finally two important forms of mildness.[73]

Whitman's first measure of harshness is the degree to which various behaviors are "criminalized." [74] By this measure, the U.S. system is extremely harsh. Relatively minor offenses (especially those categorized as "morals" offenses) are prohibited by law. The second measure is the extent to which numerous classes of persons are subject to potential criminal liability. Examples of this abound, ranging from treating minors as adults via certification to violations of drug laws to various forms of "zero tolerance." A third dimension of harshness is *grading*—determining whether an offense is a felony or a misdemeanor. For example, in the United States many drug offenses are felonies, whereas in Europe they are misdemeanors. The fourth dimension is inflexible doctrines of criminal liability—for example, whether a criminal justice system treats ignorance of the law as an excuse. The U.S. system typically does not. The fifth dimension is *enforcement* of the law. Criminal justice systems where the police often ignore violations of the law are considered mild.

Whitman's first dimension for measuring the harshness of punishment is the *law of punishment* (the length of sentences). The second dimension of punishment is the *application* of punishment. Does the system maintain harsh conditions within prisons or administer rough treatment at the station house or on the streets? The third dimension is the *inflexibility of punishment*. A system that is very harsh tends to apply the same punishment regardless of individual circumstances.[75]

Whitman's ninth and tenth measurements are: respectful treatment and the use pardons, amnesties, and commutations.[76] Respectful treatment includes addressing prisoners in a dignified manner and avoiding undignified customs. A number of practices in prisons that are unquestioned (perhaps not even noticed) in the United States have been eliminated in Europe: keeping inmates in cells through which they are observed and all activities exposed; uniforms; prison regulations about personal grooming such as hair length and facial hair; restrictions on visitation, regimentation in when, where, and what to eat; deprivation of the right to vote; cell and strip searches; and letters censored.[77] Europe tends to be more respectful of its prisoners as well as exercising the discretion of pardons more frequently.

The movement toward determinate sentencing reflects the harshness practiced in the United States. People expressed anger that different offenders received different sentences for committing the same crime. The crime now determines the punishment, regardless of individual differences or circumstances. Determinate sentencing fits the goal of the classical school of criminology to make the system predictable and efficient.

Some Concluding Thoughts

Recently I came across a passage in Noam Chomsky's *American Power and the New Mandarins*. Chomsky was the first academic to challenge the conventional views about the Vietnam War and to put his views in writing. In the introductory chapter he expressed hope that the "struggle against racism and exploitation at home can be linked with the struggle to remove the heavy Yankee boot from the necks of oppressed people throughout the world." While the sentence resonated immediately, the next paragraph really caught my attention. His insights from more than 40 years ago apply to the subject of this book.

> Twenty years of intensive cold-war indoctrination and seventy years of myth regarding our international role make it difficult to face these issues in a serious way. There is a great deal of intellectual debris to be cleared away. Ideological pressures so overpowering that even their existence was denied must be examined and understood. The search for alternatives, for individuals, for American society, for the international order as a whole, has barely begun, and no one can guess where it will lead. Quite possibly it will lead nowhere . . . [because of] the dominance of a liberal technocracy who will serve the existing social order in the belief that they represent justice and humanity, fighting limited wars at home and overseas to preserve stability, promising that the future will be better if only the dispossessed will wait patiently, and supported by an apathetic, obedient majority, its mind and conscience dulled by a surfeit of commodities and by some new version of the old system of beliefs and ideas.[78]

At the time, Chomsky was hopeful that the radicalism of the times would bring about some important changes, and it did, at least for a while. But serious criticism of our involvement in Vietnam did not extend to a serious analysis of the values that got us involved in the first place. Part of the value system that created that war was the belief that "might makes right" and that you can change behavior through force or the threat of force. It is part of the same mentality that has created a prison system that confines more than two million people. It is part of a mentality that creates something of a "police state" that hovers over the daily lives of people, waiting to pounce on those who "get out of line."

The challenge that faces us today is the same one that faced us 40 years ago: create true "alternatives" in dealing with our problems, alternatives to the "might makes right" ideology. We need to remember also that the belief system that supported war in Iraq also wages a war here at home. The victims are similar: both are without much power to resist, but resist they must, for they have no choice, even if they are fighting against the most powerful war machine in the history of the world; whether you call it the military or the criminal justice system, it's essentially the same.

NOTES

[1] Witt, H. (December 26, 2007). "Three Towns: The Past, The Present, The Future." *Chicago Tribune.* http://www.chicagotribune.com/services/newspaper/printedition/tuesday/chi-122607racecoda-story,0,404932.story

[2] Searcey, D. (December 11, 2008). "Eight and on Trial: Young Defendants Throw Criminal Justice into Confusion." *Wall Street Journal,* p. A16.

[3] American Civil Liberties Union (November 17, 2008). "Report Reveals Arrests at Hartford-Area Schools on Rise." http://www.aclu.org/racialjustice/edu/37776prs20081117.html

[4] Emma Schwartz (February 16, 2009). "A Court of Compassion." *U.S. News & World Report* 144 (5): 39.

[5] Urban Justice Center. Litigation—Mental Health. http://www.urbanjustice.org/ujc/litigation/mental.html

[6] Associated Press (September 29, 2007). "Aging Inmates Straining Nation's Prison System: Soaring Number of Elderly behind Bars Sends Costs Skyrocketing for States." http://www.msnbc.msn.com/id/13415456/

[7] In 1993, Lilly and Knepper referred to the "correctional-commercial complex," which they describe as a "sub-governmental policy-making" system consisting of an alliance between government and private enterprise. Lilly and Knepper noted that this system is quite similar to the "military industrial complex," since it consists of patterns of interrelationships known variously as "policy networks," "subgovernment" or the "iron triangle." They argued that such a system may not be legally a form of government, but nevertheless may exert greater influence than more formal structures of the government. In comparing this system to the military equivalent they note that within the military subgovernment there is an "iron triangle" of the Pentagon, private defense contractors, and various members of Congressional committees (e.g., armed services committees, defense appropriations committees). They noted further that the decision-making within any given policy arena "rests within a closed circle or elite of government bureaucrats, agency heads, interest groups, and private interests that gain from the allocation of public resources." Lilly, J. R. and P. Knepper (1993). "The Correctional-Commercial Complex." *Crime and Delinquency* 39: 152.

[8] For documentation concerning lobbyists and the connection between politics and economics more generally, see Parenti, M. *Democracy for the Few* (8th ed.). Belmont, CA: Wadsworth, 2007.

[9] See Christie, N. *Crime Control as Industry* (3rd ed.). New York: Routledge, 2000; Shelden, R. G. and W. B. Brown (2000). "The Crime Control Industry and the Management of the Surplus Population." *Critical Criminology* 8 (Autumn): 39–62; see especially Herivel, T. and P. Wright, eds. *Prison Profiteers: Who Makes Money from Mass Incarceration*. New York: New Press, 2007.

[10] http://www.alec.org/AM/Template.cfm?Section=Criminal_Justice_and_Homeland_Security_Model_Legislation&Template=/TaggedPage/TaggedPageDisplay.cfm&TPLID=3&ContentID=5669

[11] Glassner, B. *The Culture of Fear*. New York: Basic Books, 1999.

[12] Bortner, M. A. and L. M. Williams. *Youth in Prison*. New York: Routledge, 1997, p. 175.

[13] Johnson, R. *Hard Time: Understanding and Reforming the Prison* (3rd ed.). Belmont, CA: Wadsworth, 2002, pp. 19, 27.

[14] Fathi, D. (April 1, 2009). "America's Prison Break: Lock 'em Up? It Costs You." *Chicago Tribune*, p. 27.

[15] Webb, J. (March 29, 2009). "Why We Must Fix Our Prisons." *Parade Magazine*, p. 4.

[16] Garland, D. *The Culture of Control*. Chicago: University of Chicago Press, 2001, p. 3.

[17] Ibid., p. 6.

[18] Ibid., p. 8.

[19] Martinson, R. L. (1974). "What Works?—Questions and Answers about Prison Reform." *The Public Interest* 35: 22–54.

[20] One of the best examples is the work of conservative criminologist James Q. Wilson in his 1975 book *Thinking About Crime*. New York: Vintage Books.

[21] Garland, *The Culture of Control*, p. 8.

[22] Ibid., pp. 10–11.

[23] Ibid., p. 11.

[24] For an excellent critique of the victim's rights movement see: Elias, R. *Victims Still: The Political Manipulation of Crime Victims*. Thousand Oaks, CA: Sage, 1993.

[25] Garland, *The Culture of Control*, p. 11.

[26] Ibid., p. 12.

[27] Ibid., p. 13.

[28] Ibid., p. 14.

[29] Ibid., p. 15.

[30] Ibid., p. 17.

[31] Ibid., p. 17.

[32] The Web site for a company called "Access Control & Security Systems" (http://www.securitysolutionsdirectory.com/) lists 16 specific categories of products and services representing more than 700 companies—one indication of the expansion of the private security industry.

[33] Bureau of Labor Statistics. "Occupational Outlook Handbook, 2008–09 Edition." http://www.bls.gov/oco/ocos159.htm

[34] Garland, *The Culture of Control*, pp. 18–19.

[35] Ibid., p. 20.

[36] Lakoff, G. *Moral Politics: What Conservatives Know that Liberals Don't*. Chicago: University of Chicago Press, 1996, p. 67.

[37] Ibid., p. 68.

[38] Ibid., pp. 74–75.

[39] Mauer, M. (2001). "The Causes and Consequences of Prison Growth in the United States." *Punishment and Society* 3: 9–20.

[40] Herman, E. (March/April, 1997) "Privatization: Downsizing Government for Principle and Profit." *Dollars and Sense*, pp. 10–12.

[41] In *Conservatives without Conscience* (New York: Viking, 2006), John Dean discusses the tendencies of conservative religious leaders to use fear to promote their agenda. They have very punitive attitudes and are strong supporters of the death penalty (pp. 102–108). Dean notes that most of those on the "religious right" could be described as belonging to a special category of the authoritarian personality. This category, called "Double Highs," is based on the research of Bob Altemeyer (The Authoritarian Specter. Cambridge: Harvard University Press, 1996). These individuals have such strong authoritarian traits that they score very high on two different but related scales of authoritarianism: "social dominance orientation" and "Right Wing Authoritarian." The "Double Highs" are extremely prejudiced, enjoy having power over others, are very dogmatic, "may think of themselves as being religious . . . but they believe in lying, cheating, and manipulating much more than" other religious people who regularly attend church, and "are brimming with self-righteousness and zeal, and are fain to give dictatorship a chance." Altemeyer noted that the traits resemble those of Adolph Hitler. Among religious leaders, for example, Pat Robertson would be classified as a "Double High." Altemeyer describes these people as "very scary" (pp. 59–72).

[42] Weber, M. *The Protestant Ethic and the Spirit of Capitalism*. New York: Scribner, 1958.

[43] Quinney, R. *The Social Reality of Crime*. Boston: Little, Brown, 1970, p. 61.

[44] Ibid., pp. 62–70. Many states, especially in the South, continued to be "dry" (various prohibitions against the consumption of alcohol) well into the 21st century, all heavily influenced by religion. As the author has found out, if you want to purchase wine and liquor in Utah you must go to a state operated liquor store. Curiously, you can buy beer at any grocery store.

[45] Zoll, R. (June 6, 2005). "Poll: Religious Devotion High in U.S." *Los Angeles Times*. http://wid.ap.org/polls/050606religion.html

[46] Harris Poll (December 14, 2005). "The Religious and Other Beliefs of Americans 2005." http://www.harrisinteractive.com/harris_poll/index.asp?PID=618

[47] Simon, S. (August 23, 2005). "Grooming Politicians for Christ." *Los Angeles Times*.

[48] For an analysis of the influence of fundamental religious organizations on politics see the following: Hitt, J. *Off the Road: A Modern-Day Walk down the Pilgrim's Route into Spain*. New York: Simon & Schuster, 2005; Hedges, C. *American Fascists: The Christian*

Right and the War on America. New York: Free Press, 2006; Danforth, J. (March 30, 2005). "In the Name of Politics." *Los Angeles Times*; Rich, F. (March 25, 2005). "The God Racket, from DeMille to DeLay." *New York Times*; Sugg, J. (November/December 2005). "A Nation Under God." *Mother Jones*; Prothero, S. (January 12, 2005). "A Nation of Faith and Religious Illiterates." *Los Angeles Times*; Simon, S. (January 31, 2006). "Evangelicals Branch Out Politically." *Los Angeles Times*; Simon, S. (October 1, 2006). "Pastors Guiding Voters to GOP." *Los Angeles Times*.

[49] McKinley, J. and K. Johnson (November 14, 2008). "Mormons Tipped Scale in Ban on Gay Marriage." *New York Times*. http://www.nytimes.com/2008/11/15/us/politics/ 15marriage.html?_r=1&partner=rss&emc=rss&pagewanted=all&oref=slogin. See also Riccardi, N. (November 17, 2008). "Mormon Church Feels the Heat over Proposition 8." *Los Angeles Times*. http://www.latimes.com/news/nationworld/nation/ la-na-mormons17-2008nov17,0,3771395.story.

[50] Ellerbe, H. *The Dark Side of Christian History*. San Rafael, CA: Morningstar Books, 1995, p. 1. Subsequent information is taken from this source.

[51] Ecclesiastes 12:13.

[52] Ellerbe, *The Dark Side of Christian History*, p. 9.

[53] Ibid., p. 5.

[54] Foucault, M. *Discipline and Punish: The Birth of the Prison*. New York: Vintage, 1979; Welch, M. *Punishment in America*. Thousand Oaks, CA: Sag, 1999.

[55] Shichor, D. *The Meaning and Nature of Punishment*. Long Grove, IL: Waveland Press, 2006, p. 26.

[56] Mauer, "The Causes and Consequences of Prison Growth," p. 16.

[57] Ibid., p. 15.

[58] Tonry, M. *Thinking about Crime: Sense and Sensibility in American Penal Culture*. New York: Oxford University Press, 2006.

[59] Ibid., p. 5.

[60] Garland, *The Culture of Control*, p. 132.

[61] Tonry, *Thinking about Crime*, pp. 42–45.

[62] Ibid., p. 24.

[63] Ibid., p. 60.

[64] Reinarman, C. and H. G. Levine. *Crack in America*. Berkeley: University of California Press, 1997.

[65] Tonry, *Thinking about Crime*, p. 5.

[66] *Killing Hope* was originally published in 1986 and the latest revision was published in 1995 by Common Courage Press. *Rogue State* was published by Common Courage Press in 2000. The subtitle of the latter is *A Guide to the World's Only Superpower*. All such interventions have at least two things in common: they were against countries (mostly in the Third World) that had rich resources that American corporations wanted and they were defenseless against the might of the American military. Most of these countries were in turn ruled with an iron fist by dictators more or less appointed by the American government. William Blum convincingly argues that four imperatives drive U.S. foreign policy: "(1) making the world open and hospitable for—in current terminology—globalization, particularly American-based transnational corporations; (2) enhancing the financial statements of defense contractors at home who have contributed generously to members of Congress and residents of the White House; (3) preventing the rise of any society that might serve as a successful example of an alternative to the capitalist model; (4) extending political, economic, and military hegemony over as much of the globe as possible, to prevent the rise of any regional power that might challenge American supremacy, and to create a world order in America's image, as befits the world's only superpower." *Rogue State*, pp. 13–14.

[67] Johnson, C. *Blowback: The Costs and Consequences of American Empire*. New York: Metropolitan/Owl Books, 2001; Johnson, C. *Sorrows of Empire: Militarism, Secrecy, and the End of the Republic*. New York: Metropolitan Books, 2004.

[68] Chomsky, N. *The Culture of Terrorism*. Boston: South End Press, 1988; and Chomsky, N. *Rogue States: The Rule of Force in World Affairs*. Boston: South End Press, 2000. Dozens of other examples could be listed, including Parenti, M. *Against Empire*. San Francisco: City Lights Press, 1995.

[69] Kinzer, S. *Overthrow: America's Century of Regime Change from Hawaii to Iraq*. New York: Times Books, Henry Holt and Company, 2006.

[70] Whitman, J. *Harsh Justice: Criminal Punishment and the Widening Divide between America and Europe*. New York: Oxford University Press, 2003.

[71] Harold Garfinkel used this phrase in 1956. See Garfinkel, H. (1956). "Conditions of Successful Degradation Ceremonies." *American Sociological Review* 61: 420–424.

[72] Whitman, *Harsh Justice*, p. 38.

[73] Ibid., p. 33.

[74] The five dimensions of criminalization are discussed on pages 33–35 in Whitman, *Harsh Justice*.

[75] The three dimensions of punishment are discussed on pages 35–36 in Whitman, *Harsh Justice*.

[76] Whitman, *Harsh Justice*, p. 36.

[77] Ibid., pp. 64–65.

[78] Chomsky, N. *American Power and the New Mandarins*. New York: The New Press, 2002 (originally published 1969), pp. 4–5.

1

The Punishment Business

The U.S. spends about $60 billion a year on incarceration. . . . The average annual operating cost for a prison bed—the amount it costs to incarcerate one person for one year—is about $24,000. That's a national average; in some states the annual cost is more than $40,000. That doesn't include capital construction costs, which add $65,000 per bed.[1]

The United States versus the World

The processing of offenders through the criminal justice system is a huge undertaking, beginning with arrests. In 2007 the police made an estimated 14,209,365 arrests.[2] While only a portion of those arrests result in time served in prison or jail, the incarceration rate continues to increase. As of June 30, 2008, the prison population was 1,610,584—a rate of 509 inmates in custody per 100,000 U.S. residents.[3] If we include jails, the number of people incarcerated totals more than 2.3 million, and the incarceration rate climbs to 762.[4]

The United States leads the world in producing prisoners, a reflection of a relatively recent and now entirely distinctive American approach to crime and punishment. Americans are locked up for crimes—from writing bad checks to using drugs—that would rarely produce prison sentences in other countries. And in particular they are kept incarcerated far longer than prisoners in other nations.[5]

The total number of prisoners in the world is 9.8 million. As noted in the introduction, the United States incarcerates almost 25% of the world's prisoners yet has only 5% of the world's population. The overall world prison population rate is 145 per 100,000; 59% of the countries in the world have rates below 150 prisoners per 100,000 population.[6] The next highest rates are the Russian Federation (626) and Rwanda (593). Canada's incarceration rate is less than one-sixth the U.S. rate despite relatively similar economic and political systems. As Nils Christie points out, there is one important difference: Canada has more of a "social safety-net" (various welfare benefits) than does the United States.[7] The crime rate in Canada has risen and fallen in the last forty years similar to the crime rate in the United States, but its imprisonment rate has remained stable.[8]

The United States has lower burglary rates than Australia, Canada, and the United Kingdom.[9] Yet the incarceration rate in Australia is 152, Canada 116, and the United Kingdom 152.[10] Several European countries would rank higher than the United States based on annual admissions to prison per capita. However, lengthy prison terms push the U.S. incarceration rate higher. Burglars in the United States serve an average sentence of 16 months in prison versus 5 months in Canada and 7 months in the United Kingdom.

Nonviolent criminals in most of the world are less likely to be imprisoned or to receive long prison sentences. The United States is, for instance, the only advanced country that incarcerates people for minor property crimes like passing bad checks.[11] Punishment for possession of illegal drugs is another major contributor to rising U.S. incarceration rates. In 1980, there were about 40,000 people in U.S. jails and prisons for drug crimes versus more than 500,000 today.

The gap between justice in the United States and its practice in the rest of the world continues to grow. The incarceration rate remained relatively stable from 1925 through 1975 (see table 1.1). If we go back farther in history, the United States served as a model for European governments, who sent delegations to study U.S. prison management. Alexis de Tocqueville toured U.S. penitentiaries in 1831 and remarked:

Table 1.1   The Growing Prison Population, 1925–2008 (rates per 100,000 in state and federal prison)

Year	Number	Rate
1925	91,669	79
1935	144,180	113
1945	133,649	98
1955	185,780	112
1965	210,895	108
1975	240,593	111
1985	480,568	202
1995	1,085,363	411
2005	1,462,866	391
2008	1,610,534	509
% increase (1975–2008)	569%	359%

Source: *Sourcebook on Criminal Justice Statistics*. Table 3.106.2007. West, H. C. and W. J. Sabol (2009). "Prison Inmates at Mid-Year 2008, Statistical Tables." Washington, DC: Bureau of Justice Statistics, March. Table 1, p. 2.

"In no country is criminal justice administered with more mildness than in the United States."[12] As Michael Tonry notes, prison sentences are now "vastly harsher than in any other country to which the United States would ordinarily be compared."

The introduction reviewed cultural, legal, and economic factors that contribute to excessive punitiveness. A *New York Times* reporter listed many of the same factors and added an observation about the contribution of democracy:

> harsher sentencing laws, a legacy of racial turmoil, a special fervor in combating illegal drugs, the American temperament, and the lack of a social safety net. Even democracy plays a role, as judges—many of whom are elected, another American anomaly—yield to populist demands for tough justice.[13]

Criminal justice professionals in Western nations are generally civil servants and less subject to public pressure motivated by fear of crime. In the United States, however, most state court judges and prosecutors in the United States are elected. Elected officials find positions that favor tough sentencing a means of gaining votes.

Tonry notes that English-speaking countries (Anglo-Saxon culture) tend to be more punitive. "It could be related to economies that are more capitalistic and political cultures that are less social democratic than those of most European countries. Or it could have something to do with the Protestant religions with strong Calvinist overtones that were long influential."[14] The American character with its tendencies to be judgmental, self-reliant, and independent also contributes to the punishment it endorses. James Whitman notes: "America is a comparatively tough place, which puts a strong emphasis on individual responsibility. That attitude has shown up in the American criminal justice of the last 30 years."[15]

Incarceration in the United States

The Pew Center on the States released a report in 2008 in which it found that one in one hundred U.S. adults is in prison or jail.

> Prison growth is not driven primarily by a parallel increase in crime or a corresponding surge in the population at large. Rather, it flows principally from a wave of policy choices that are sending more lawbreakers to prison and, through popular "three-strikes" measures and other sentencing enhancements, keeping them there longer. . . . As a nation, the United States has long anchored its punishment policy in bricks and mortar. The tangible feel of a jail or prison, with its surefire incapacitation of convicts, has been an unquestioned weapon of choice in our battle against crime. Recent studies show, however, that a continual increase in our reliance on incarceration

will pay declining dividends in crime prevention. In short, experts say, expanding prisons will accomplish less and cost more than it has in the past.[16]

Table 1.1 shows changes in the U.S. prison populations and rates during the past 80 plus years. The number of prisoners and incarceration rates vary significantly from one state to another. In 2008, California held 171,085 prisoners at a cost of $35,587 per prisoner. The average sentence was 49 months, and 18.2% of offenders were serving time for a drug offense; 29% were black.[17] Texas (171,790) surpassed California as the state holding the most prisoners followed by Florida (97,416), New York (62,620), Georgia (55,205), Ohio (50,730), and Michigan (50,326).[18] Florida's prison population grew by more than 4,400. In 1993, its prison population was 53,000 but legislation mandating that all prisoners serve 85% of their sentences and zero tolerance for any probation violations spurred the increase. Georgia and Kentucky each added more than 2,400 prisoners. Arizona added 1,900 while California's population decreased by more than 4,000.

In 2009, the Pew Center issued a follow-up report.

> The escalation of the prison population has been astonishing, but it hasn't been the largest area of growth in the criminal justice system. That would be probation and parole—the sentenced offenders who are not behind bars. With far less notice, the number of people on probation or parole has skyrocketed to more than 5 million, up from 1.6 million just 25 years ago. This means that 1 in 45 adults in the United States is now under criminal justice supervision in the community, and that combined with those in prison and jail, a stunning 1 in every 31 adults, or 3.2%, is under some form of correctional control.[19]

Thirteen states spend more than $1 billion a year on corrections. The yearly total for California is $8.8 billion.[20] Prisons consume almost 9 of every 10 state corrections dollars.[21] Five states (Vermont, Michigan, Oregon, Connecticut, and Delaware) spend as much or more on corrections as they do on higher education. For every dollar spent on higher education, California spends 83 cents on corrections; Florida spends 66 cents; Texas, Illinois, and Georgia spend equal amounts. In contrast, Minnesota spends 11 cents on corrections for every dollar spent on higher education.[22]

The Impact of Incarceration on Crime

There has been a considerable amount of research and commentary in recent years concerning the connection between the rise in imprisonment rates and the drop in crime. The overall crime rate (index crimes known to the police) dropped by 26% between 1990 and

1999; violent crimes went down by 28% (the murder rate dropped by 39%); property crime declined by 26%.[23] During the same period, the nation's incarceration rate increased by 56%.[24] Deterrent proponents have consistently argued that putting more people in prison is the best way to reduce crime.[25]

However, there is a tendency to use time periods that conveniently suit one's particular hypothesis. Consider this fact: during the 1980s the overall incarceration rate almost doubled, while the crime rate dropped by only 3% (in other words, virtually no change); during this same period of time the rate of violent crime *increased* by 12%, while property crime went down by about 5%.[26] In the 30-year period from 1971 to 2000, the overall crime rate increased until 1991 and then declined. In 2001 the crime rate for index crimes was almost identical to what it was in 1971. During the same time frame, the number of adults under correctional supervision went up by 357%, and expenditures on the criminal justice system increased by 366%.[27]

One obvious question comes to mind: why does putting more people behind bars lead to a drop in crime during one period, but not during another? Recent research has challenged the thesis that more prisoners equal less crime. Lynne Kovandzic and Tomislav Vieraitis began their study with the assumption that since most offenders commit their crimes close to where they live, the incarceration rates at the county level would be the most appropriate to use.[28] Using data on prisoners sentenced in each county in the state of Florida between 1980 and 2000 they found no statistically significant relationships between imprisonment rates and crime, holding constant several other variables (e.g., age, race, poverty rate, unemployment rate, female headed households). Prior research had estimated that increasing imprisonment rates would result in a range (from 3 to 187) of reduction in index crimes per year.[29] Most researchers, however, have questioned these high estimates, with most finding at best a modest effect.[30]

A very unique study looked at the incarceration rate and crime rate relationship involving both juveniles and adults. Mike Males, Dan Macallair, and Megan Corcoran examined both juvenile and adult incarceration rates and crime in the state of California. They noted that from 1980 to 2005 the juvenile incarceration rate declined by almost 60%. During that same period of time, juvenile felony arrest rates dropped by 57%. For adults, there was a 500% increase in imprisonment rates and a 13% increase in the adult felony arrest rate.[31] A study by Bruce Western showed that during the 1990s the 66% growth in the prison population led to about a 2–5% drop in the rate of index crimes (covering 1993 to 2001). Western also points out that the costs of reducing this amount of crime came to about $53 billion.[32]

Punishment as a Market for Capitalism

Part of the reason for the growth of the criminal justice industrial complex is reliance on a "technocratic" solution to crime—a combination of science and technology bolstered by the perception of science as systematic and infallible. In 1967 the President's Crime Commission noted:

> More than 200,000 scientists and engineers have applied themselves to solving military problems and hundreds of thousands more to innovation in other areas of modern life, but only a handful are working to control the crimes that injure or frighten millions of Americans each year. Yet the two communities have much to offer each other: Science and technology is a valuable source of knowledge and techniques for combating crime; the criminal justice system represents a vast area of challenging problems.[33]

Many observers have suggested that the criminal justice industrial complex has surpassed the military industrial complex.

For decades the United States has viewed crime as requiring the latest in high-tech equipment. According to the Office of Law Enforcement Technology Commercialization (part of the National Institute of Justice), annual sales for law enforcement technology total about $1 billion. "The hunger of companies for new customers in this post Cold-War era and the availability of government dollars have fueled a military-style buildup inside many of the nation's prisons."[34] Companies selling high-tech products use euphemistic terms such as "pursuit management equipment" (to track escapees) and "compliance technology" (to control unruly prisoners) as part of their sales pitch.

Several years ago, seven high-security federal prisons spent $10 million to purchase lethal electrified fences. A spokesperson for the Federal Bureau of Prisons stated that "This new technology will serve as new security and help us to deter potential escapes, allow us to operate more cost effectively by reducing the guard towers, the staffing at some of our guard towers." A representative of the Federal Prison Policy Project (a nonprofit prison reform group), Judy Freyermuth, questioned the alleged savings: "How many times have you read of an escape from a federal prison? None."[35]

Imprisonment pays, even when there is no longer a prison. "The Mock Prison Riot" is an annual event held at the defunct West Virginia Penitentiary (closed after the state Supreme Court ruled that conditions in the prison constituted "cruel and unusual punishment"). The event brings in about $650,000 into the local economy.[36] The former prison is now a tourist attraction with its own Web site.[37] As this example illustrates, the means of profiting from punishment are multiple.

Within a capitalist society there tends to be an insatiable desire to continue "converting money into commodities and commodities into money." Everything, it seems, is turned into a "commodity"—from the simplest products (e.g., paper and pencil) to human beings (e.g., women's bodies, slaves). Indeed, within a capitalist society "daily life is scanned for possibilities that can be brought within the circuit of accumulation," since any aspect of society that can produce a profit will be exploited. Life itself has been "commodified."[38]

Part of this drive for profits stems from the ideology of the "free market," a system of beliefs that undergirds the entire capitalist economic system. According to this ideology, every individual pursues his or her own personal interests, resulting in a collective good for the entire society. It is Adam Smith's "invisible hand" at work. Corporations are "free" to do whatever they want. The failure of this philosophy became evident in late 2008.[39]

This "free market" includes the criminal justice system. One can clearly see the size of this complex by first noting the annual expenditures of the three main components of the *criminal justice industrial complex:* law enforcement, courts, and corrections. In 1982 total expenditures were less than $36 billion, while the total in 2006 was more than $214 billion—a 494% increase.[40] The corrections portion alone increased from slightly over $9 billion to $68.7 billion.[41]

The American Correctional Association (ACA) is one of the largest criminal justice-related organizations in the country. It has 20,000 individual members plus 62 chapters and affiliated organizations.[42] ACA annual meetings draw hundreds of vendors, usually taking up an entire floor of a hotel or convention center. The "Advertise with Us" section of the ACA Web site urges participation to reach an enormous market:

> As thousands of people stream past exhibit booths at ACA's annual summer Congress of Correction and the Winter Conference, you do not want your company to be left out. These two annual events are the only international conventions that attract corrections officials from the county, state and federal levels, as well as from probation and parole and community corrections agencies.[43]

The marketing kit in the same section advises:

> The corrections industry is dynamic and evolving. If you have a product or service designed to keep corrections professionals on the leading edge, our members want to know about it. With an abundance of choices, how do you tap into this profitable market? ACA offers an array of possibilities for you to promote the latest technologies, trends and advances in your field.[44]

The advertising section of the ACA Web site includes the Corrections Marketplace.[45] Under 15 headings ranging from apparel/linens to training/education, more than 150 categories of products are listed selling everything from badges to batteries to insurance to cabinets to books to telephone systems to fans to modular buildings. Prisons are total institutions that must provide everything for the inmates incarcerated there. The market is vast and lucrative.

The ACA Web site also lists a "Buyers' Guide of Correctional Products and Services."[46] There are three drop menus (company, state, or category) where people can browse for products or services. The ad for the Bob Barker Company in North Carolina is representative:

> Bob Barker Company is the worldwide leader in delivering innovative products and services to correctional and rehabilitation customers. Our product categories include, but are not limited to, inmate clothing, footwear, personal care, bedding & mattresses, institutional furnishings, health care, laundry, food service, and our inmate transportation system—VanCell®. Bob Barker Company is family owned and operated, and has satisfied customers for over thirty years. Most orders are shipped same day.[47]

Telephone calls placed by inmates provide an informative look at the profits provided by the intersection of public and private interests. Telecommunications industry giants such as AT&T, Bell South, Sprint, GTE and MCI have found prisons to be an excellent market for long distance business. The more than two million "inmates in the United States are ideal customers: phone calls are one of their few links to the outside world; most of their calls must be made collect; and they are in no position to switch long-distance carriers."[48] Prisons receive a percentage of the revenues ranging from 10 to 55%. "At least ten states were taking in $10 million or more from prisoner calling, with California, New York, and the Federal Bureau of Prisons leading the pack with more than $20 million in phone revenues each."[49]

The revenue comes from various connection fees, surcharges and per-minute charges ranging from as high as 90 cents for local calls to $2.25 for long-distance calls; a 15-minute phone call can cost $20 or more.[50] MCI installed its inmate phone service (Maximum Security) throughout the California prison system free of charge and offered the Department of Corrections 32% of the profits. They levied a $3 surcharge for each phone call made. "When free enterprise intersects with a captive market, abuses are bound to occur. MCI Maximum Security and North American Intelecom have both been caught overcharging for calls made by inmates; in one state MCI was adding an additional minute to every call."[51] The bulk of the costs to "reach out and touch" a loved one in prison has been borne mostly by low-income and minority people.

Steven Jackson enumerated the harm done by overpricing a means of contacting families.

> (T)he ultimate effect of profit-sharing and what amount to price-gouging arrangements in the prison phone sector has been a long-term trend toward excommunication, making contact between prisoners and family members on the outside more costly and therefore

more difficult to maintain. But this goes directly against the findings of several decades of recidivism and community impact studies, some of which were used to justify the introduction of prison calling in the first place. Such studies have found a powerful predictor for reoffense is the failure to maintain family and community contact while under incarceration.[52]

It is almost as if those in charge of this system actually want high recidivism rates. As Jackson suggests, the likelihood of reoffending increases when released prisoners have almost no ties with the outside world. They return to their communities essentially as strangers because of lack of contact.

A nation-wide movement by such groups as Citizens United for the Rehabilitation of Errants (CURE), the Center for Constitutional Rights, and others who have filed lawsuits against this practice encounters fierce opposition from prison officials and telephone companies. It remains to be seen whether and to what extent these practices will continue. After several years of pressure, California reached an agreement with WorldCom to lower charges by 25% for adult prisoners and 78% for juveniles. However, the calls must be collect calls, and the state continues to receive a portion of the profits.[53] The "prison telephone monopolies remain firmly in place and ineffectively regulated throughout large parts of the country."[54]

Expenditures on the Criminal Justice System

Employment and career opportunities also benefit from the size of the criminal justice industrial complex. In 1982, there were 1.27 million justice system employees; in 2003, there were 2.36 million—an increase of 85%.[55] Corrections employees increased from 300,000 to 748,000 (149%). In 2007, there were 753,875 federal, state, and local corrections employees, with a payroll of almost $3 billion. The total of all justice system employees in 2007 was 2.27 million, with a payroll of almost $10.5 billion.[56]

California illustrates the growing power of employees working within the criminal justice system. In 1980 California had 22,500 prisoners, and the average salary of a prison guard was $14,400.[57] The California Correctional Peace Officers Association (CCOPA) is the union that represents correctional officers; it had 5,600 members in 1980. In 2009, California had more than 170,000 prisoners; and the starting salary for correctional or youth correctional officers was $45,288 with full benefits.[58] CCOPA has more than 30,000 members and is a potent political force in California. It spends more than any other law enforcement lobby in California. Of its $8 million yearly budget, 35% is spent on political activities, usually supporting harsher sentences for prisoners. "More prisoners mean more job security for prison employees."[59] In 1994, the CCPOA joined with the National Rifle Association to fund the "Three Strikes" initiative. In the last decade of the twentieth century, CCPOA-sponsored legislation was successful more than 80% of the time.[60] In 2008 the union helped defeat Proposition 5, which would have provided money to set up alternatives to prison for thousands of nonviolent offenders with drug problems. CCPOA spent several million dollars to defeat the proposition.

The chapter opened with a comparison of incarceration in the United States to other countries in the world followed by a discussion of the impact of incarceration on the crime rate and the budgets for criminal justice expenditures. The introduction identified harsher sentences ("mandatory minimums," "truth in sentencing," and "three strikes and you're out") and the war on drugs as the primary reasons for the exponential increase in the number of people incarcerated. The remainder of this chapter will discuss the impact of the drug war on incarceration.

The Drug War

The "war on drugs" has targeted mostly the poor and racial minorities and has helped to create a prison-industrial complex.

- In 1973, there were 328,670 arrests for drug law violations.[61] In 2007, there were 1,841,182 arrests—more arrests than for any other offense (13% of the total).[62] Of those arrests, 82.5% were for possession of a controlled substance, and more than half of those arrests were for marijuana; only 17.5% were for the sale or manufacture of a drug.[63]

- In 1980, there were 40,000 people incarcerated in prison or jail for a drug offense compared to 500,000 today. To place that increase in perspective, the number of people incarcerated for a drug offense is now greater than the number incarcerated for *all* offenses in 1980.[64]

- In 1980, the most serious offense committed by 19,000 people in state prisons was a drug offense. In 2005 the number was 253,300.[65] Of those incarcerated for a drug offense, 45% (113,500) were black and 20% (51,100) were Hispanic. Of women in state prisons, almost 29% were imprisoned for a drug offense.[66]

- More than 52% of the 204,000 inmates in federal prison are serving sentences for drug crimes.[67] Although two-thirds of regular crack cocaine users in the United States are either white or Latino, 80% of those sentenced in federal court for a crack cocaine offense are African American.[68]

- Many of the mandatory sentencing laws at both the state and federal level focus on drug violations. The New York legislature passed the harshest state drug laws in 1973 (the "Rockefeller" drug laws). Possession of four ounces of narcotics or the sale of two ounces received a 15-year prison term. Although modest reforms were enacted in 2004 and more substantial reform in 2009, these laws affected thousands for more than thirty-five years.[69]

- Under federal law, possession of five grams of crack cocaine (about 10 to 50 doses) carries a five-year mandatory prison sentence. To receive the same sentence for possession of powder cocaine, a defendant would have to have 500 grams (approximately 2,500 to 5,000 doses). This 100-to-1 sentencing disparity levels the same punishment for low-level crack cocaine sellers and high-level powder cocaine traffickers.[70]

- The increase in incarceration of drug offenders is costly to taxpayers. The American Correctional Association estimates that the average cost of incarcerating one person for one day was approximately $67.55. The bill for incarcerating drug offenders in state or federal prisons exceeds $8 billion per year.[71]

- Though the European Union has 200 million more inhabitants than the United States, the U.S. incarcerates nearly 10 times as many people for drug offenses.[72] Many European countries have found that criminalizing drug use aggravates the social problem because it increases the profitability of drug trafficking, leads to corruption of officials tempted by bribes, and results in lives lost to the violence associated with black markets. Those countries have decided that taxpayer dollars are spent more effectively on drug treatment than on police, prosecutors, and jail cells.[73]

These figures are just a sampling of the human wreckage resulting from the punitive policies used by the United States for more than three decades.

The manufacture and distribution of illegal drugs is a huge global enterprise. The United Nations calculated an illegal drug market in 2003 of $13 billion at the production level, $94 billion at the wholesale level, and $322 billion retail.[74] Profits are enormous, as evidenced by the increases in prices from the production level to retail. A kilogram of heroin in Pakistan sells for an average of $4,200 wholesale, while in the United States the wholesale value is $87,700.[75]

The profit potential is enhanced because drugs are illegal. Leonard Goodman, a criminal defense lawyer in Chicago and an adjunct law professor, notes:

> The United States should have learned its lesson from its failed experiment with alcohol prohibition in the 1920s. We also might have learned from the "war on drugs" over the past 25 years. In that time, illegal drugs have become more available, the violence associated with black markets has claimed countless lives, and the temp-

tation to take bribes has corrupted countless drug cops. In short, the war has proved more harmful than the drugs themselves. . . . In 1929 President Herbert Hoover assembled a panel of experts, the Wickersham Commission, to see how Prohibition could be saved. Instead, the commission cataloged the failure of Prohibition and set the stage for repeal. We need another Wickersham Commission. I have seen firsthand that the war on drugs consumes precious resources, promotes violence, takes thousands of lives and does nothing to make us safer.[76]

It has long been recognized that alcohol plays a huge role in criminal behavior. Alcohol use has been associated with assaults and sex-related crimes, family violence, and persistent aggression.[77] One survey found that about 40% of offenders under some sort of supervision within the criminal justice system (probation, parole, jail, prison) were using alcohol at the time of the offense for which they were convicted. This same survey found that about 60% of jail inmates said they drank alcohol on a regular basis during the year prior to their current conviction.[78] Alcohol is a legal substance. Unless consumed in quantities that exceed state limits, users are prosecuted only for their behavior under the influence—not for possession alone. This is clearly not the case with illegal drugs, since thousands are imprisoned every year for the mere possession of such drugs.

Why do we continue this drug war in the face of such obvious failure and human cost? My answer to this is not the standard answer and will no doubt surprise many. My answer is simply this: the drug war was never really intended to reduce drug abuse. The purpose was to do two things: control the growing population known variously as the "underclass" or the "surplus population" and to add to an already bloated "criminal justice industrial complex," increasing the profits of both private industry and agencies of the criminal justice system. Anti-drug legislation has consistently targeted drugs used almost exclusively by the poor and/or racial minorities (see chapter 4).

Some Concluding Thoughts

Proponents of deterrence theory maintain that increasing expenditures on crime control—especially expanding the prison industry and sending more people to prison—has resulted in a reduction in crime. The data do not support that belief. The crime rate is about the same as it was in the early 1970s despite constant annual increases in the incarceration rate. Locking people in prison or jail while spending enormous sums on the criminal justice system has had little impact on the crime rate. Many people might reasonably argue that the investment in the criminal justice system has not paid the expected dividend.

The death of Len Bias in June 1986 marked the start of the most repressive period of anti-drug legislation. The harm caused by most drug use pales in comparison to the harm caused by repressive laws. Literally millions have been rounded up and arrested, placed in jail or prison or both, and their families and communities forced to struggle with the hardships caused by their absence. The "collateral damages" from this "war" include wasted tax dollars, millions of children left without a parent, and several million who have lost the right to vote (to mention only a few) and disproportionately affect racial minorities and, increasingly, women.[79]

From a vastly different perspective, this war has been a resounding success. It has helped "dispose of" a growing surplus population while providing thousands of "career opportunities" to people who work in the system and adding billions of dollars to the bottom line of many suppliers of goods and services to the criminal justice industrial complex.

Notes

[1] Fathi, D. (April 1, 2009). "America's Prison Break: Lock 'em Up? It Costs You." *Chicago Tribune*, p. 27.

[2] Federal Bureau of Investigation (2008). Crime in the United States, 2007. Table 29. http://www.fbi.gov/ucr/cius2007/data/table_29.html

[3] West, H. C. and W. J. Sabol (March 2009). "Prison Inmates at Mid-Year 2008, Statistical Tables." Washington, DC: Bureau of Justice Statistics, table 1, p. 2.

[4] Ibid., table 15, p. 16.

[5] Liptak, A. (April 23, 2008). "Inmate Count in U.S. Dwarfs Other Nations'." *The New York Times*. http://www.nytimes.com/2008/04/23/us/23prison.html

[6] King's College London (2009). "News Highlights: 10 Million Prisoners in the World." http://www.kcl.ac.uk/news/news_details.php?news_id=993&year=2009

[7] Christie, N. *Crime Control as Industry* (3rd ed.). New York: Routledge, 2000, p. 31.

[8] Michael Tonry quoted in Liptak, "Inmate Count."

[9] Ibid.

[10] Walmsley, R. (2009). World Prison Population List (8th ed.). http://www.kcl.ac.uk/depsta/law/research/icps/worldbrief/wpb_stats.php?area=all&category=wb_poprate

[11] Liptak, "Inmate Count."

[12] Ibid.

[13] Ibid.

[14] Henry quoted in Liptak, "Inmate Count."

[15] Whitman quoted in Liptak, "Inmate Count."

[16] Pew Center on the States. *One in 100: Behind Bars in America 2008*. Washington, DC: The Pew Charitable Trusts, February 2008, pp. 3, 21. http://www.pewcenteronthestates.org/uploadedFiles/8015PCTS_Prison08_FINAL_2–1–1_FORWEB.pdf.

[17] California Department of Corrections. http://www.cdcr.ca.gov/Divisions_Boards/Adult_Operations/docs/Fourth_Quarter_2008_Facts_and_Figures.pdf

[18] Pew Center on the States, *Behind Bars*, table A-1, p. 29.

[19] Pew Center on the States. *One in 31: The Long Reach of American Corrections*. Washington, DC: The Pew Charitable Trusts, March 2009, p. 1. http://www.pewcenteronthestates.org/uploadedFiles/PSPP_1in31_report_FINAL_WEB_3–26–09.pdf

[20] Ibid., p. 11.

[21] Ibid., p. 4.

[22] Ibid., p. 14.

[23] Sourcebook on Criminal Justice Statistics (2007). Table 3.106. http://www.albany.edu/sourcebook/pdf/t31062007.pdf

[24] Ibid., table 6.28. http://www.albany.edu/sourcebook/pdf/t6282006.pdf

[25] Marvell, T. B. and C. E. Moody, Jr. (1994). "Prison Population Growth and Crime Reduction." *Journal of Quantitative Criminology* 10: 109–140; Muhlhausen, D. B. (February 12, 2007). "Changing Crime Rates: Ineffective Law Enforcement Grants and the Prison Buildup." Washington, DC: Heritage Foundation. http://www.heritage.org/Research/Crime/wm1355.cfm

[26] Sourcebook, table 3.106.

[27] Shelden, R. G., W. B. Brown, K. S. Miller, and R. B. Fritzler. *Crime and Criminal Justice in American Society: A Critical View*. Long Grove, IL: Waveland Press, 2008, p. 29.

[28] Kovandzic, T. V. and L. M. Vieraitis (2006). "The Effect of County-Level Prison Population Growth on Crime Rates." *Criminology and Public Policy* 5: 213–243.

[29] The high range comes from Zedlewski, E. W. *Making Confinement Decisions: The Economics of Disincarceration*. Washington, DC: National Criminal Justice Reference Service, 1987. The low estimate comes from Greenberg, D. F. (1975). "The Incapacitative Effects of Imprisonment: Some Estimates." *Law and Society Review* 9: 541–586. Other studies, showing varying estimates include the following: Levitt, S. D. (1996). "The Effect of Prison Population Size on Crime Rates: Evidence from Prison Overcrowding Litigation." *Quarterly Journal of Economics* 111: 319–351; Devine, J. A., J. F. Sheley, and M. D. Smith (1988). "Macroeconomic and Social-Control Policy Influences on Crime Rate Changes, 1948–1985." *American Sociological Review* 53: 407–420; Cohen, L. E. and K. C. Land (1987). "Age Structure and Crime: Symmetry versus Asymmetry and the Projection of Crime Rates through the 1990s." *American Sociological Review* 52: 170–183.

[30] See, for example, DeFina, R. H. and T. M. Arvanties (2002). "The Weak Effect of Imprisonment on Crime: 1971–1998." *Social Science Quarterly* 83: 635–653; Levitt, "The Effect of Prison Population Size on Crime Rates."

[31] Males, M., D. Macallair, and M. Corcoran. "Testing Incapacitation Theory: Youth Crime and Incarceration in California." In R. G. Shelden and D. Macallair, eds., *Juvenile Justice in America: Problems and Prospects*. Long Grove, IL: Waveland Press, 2008, pp. 63–81.

[32] Western B. *Punishment and Inequality in America*. New York: Russell Sage Foundation, 2006, pp. 186–187.

[33] President's Commission on Law Enforcement and Administration of Justice. *The Challenge of Crime in a Free Society*. Washington, DC: U.S. Government Printing Office, 1967, p. 1.

[34] Gonnerman, J. (2007). "The Riot Academy: Guards Stage Mock Prison Riots to Test the Latest High-Tech Gear," p. 229. In T. Herivel and P. Wright, eds., *Prison Profiteers: Who Makes Money from Mass Incarceration*. New York: The New Press, 2007, pp. 228–234.

[35] "7 Federal Prisons to Get Lethal Electrified Fences." (July 12, 2005). *Washington Post*.

[36] Ibid., p. 232.

[37] The Web site is: http://www.wvpentours.com/

[38] Heilbroner, R. L. *The Nature and Logic of Capitalism*. New York: W. W. Norton, 1985, p. 60.

[39] The financial crisis of 2008 illustrates this perfectly. "Free markets" faltered miserably. Trillions of taxpayer dollars were spent to "rescue" the markets, ironically resulting in socialism for the rich and free enterprise for everyone else. For a few examples of research on this crisis see the following: Cloughley, B. (October 3, 2008). "The Unacceptable Face of Capitalism." *Counterpunch*; Wolff, R. (November 7, 2008). "Capitalism Hits the Fan." http://www.alternet.org/story/105944/; von Hoffman, N. (September 12, 2008). "State Capitalism Comes to America." http://www.alternet.org/workplace/98168/state_capitalism_comes_to_America/; Benn, T. (2008). "What Went Wrong with the Capitalist Casino." http://www.zmag.org/znet/viewArticle/19141. AIG, Freddie Mac, and Fanny Mae have been given loans amounting to more than $1 trillion. As of 12/15/08 the "Big Three" U.S. automakers are begging for money, but Congress is resisting. On the auto bailout see the following: Puzzanghera, J. (December 12, 2008). "Senate Republi-

cans Kill Auto Bailout Bill." *Los Angeles Times*. http://www.latimes.com/business/la-fi-autobailout12–2008dec12,1,3325174.story. Some Republicans are using this as a way to reduce the power of unions: Puzzanghera, J. (December 13, 2008). "Auto Bailout's Death Seen as a Republican Blow at Unions." *Los Angeles Times*. http://www.latimes.com/business/la-fi-gopunions13–2008dec13,1,917540.story.

[40] Expenditure and Employment Statistics. Direct Expenditure by Level of Government. (December 2008). http://www.ojp.usdoj.gov/bjs/glance/tables/expgovtab.htm.

[41] Expenditure and Employment Statistics. Direct Expenditure by Criminal Justice Function. (December 2008). http://www.ojp.usdoj.gov/bjs/glance/tables/exptyptab.htm

[42] http://www.aca.org/Advertise/audience.asp

[43] http://www.aca.org/Advertise/exhibition.asp

[44] http://www.aca.org/advertise/Marketing2008/MarketingKit2008.pdf

[45] http://correctionsmarketplace.com/

[46] http://www.aca.org/advertise/buyers/

[47] http://www.aca.org/advertise/buyers/view.asp?ID=17&origin=results&QS='BuyersGuide06YMGHFRECompany_Name=Bob+Barker+Company&startrec=1&viewby=50&union=AND&top_parent=308.

[48] Schlosser, E. (December 1998). "The Prison-Industrial Complex." *The Atlantic Monthly*: 63.

[49] Jackson, S. "Mapping the Telephone Industry." In Herivel and Wright, eds., *Prison Profiteers*, pp. 236–240.

[50] Ibid.

[51] Schlosser, "The Prison-Industrial Complex," p. 63.

[52] Jackson, "Mapping the Telephone Industry," p. 241.

[53] Warren, J. (February 16, 2002). "Inmates' Families Pay Heavy Price for Staying in Touch." *Los Angeles Times*.

[54] Jackson, "Mapping the Telephone Industry," p. 248.

[55] Hughes, K. (April 2006). Justice Expenditures and Employment in the United States, 2003, p. 7. http://www.ojp.usdoj.gov/bjs/pub/pdf/jeeus03.pdf

[56] U.S. Census Bureau. (January 2009). Federal, State, and Local Governments. Public Employment and Payroll Data. Federal: http://ftp2.census.gov/govs/apes/07fedfun.pdf; State and Local: http://ftp2.census.gov/govs/apes/07stlus.txt

[57] Burton-Rose, D. with D. Pens and P. Wright, eds. *The Celling of America: An Inside Look at the U.S. Prison Industry*. Monroe, ME: Common Courage Press, 2002.

[58] http://www.cdcr.ca.gov/Career_Opportunities/POR/Pay.html

[59] Holwerda, D. A. (2006) "Prison Reform and the California Correctional Peace Officers Association." http://www.law.stanford.edu/program/centers/scjc/workingpapers/DHolwerda_06.pdf

[60] Macallair, D. (February 29, 2004). "Prisons: Power Nobody Dares Mess With." *Sacramento Bee*.

[61] Drug War Facts, Crime. http://drugwarfacts.org/cms/?q=node/34

[62] Federal Bureau of Investigation. Table 29. http://www.fbi.gov/ucr/cius2007/data/table_29.htmland

[63] Ibid. Arrest Table. http://www.fbi.gov/ucr/cius2007/arrests/index.html

[64] Mauer, M. (2009, April 29). Testimony before the Senate Judiciary Subcommittee on Crime and Drugs. Hearing on Restoring Fairness to Federal Sentencing: Addressing the Crack-Powder Disparity, p. 2. http://www.sentencingproject.org/userfiles/file/dp_crack_testimony.pdf

[65] *Key Facts at a Glance*. Number of persons under jurisdiction of state correctional authorities by most serious offense, 1980–2005. http://www.ojp.usdoj.gov/bjs/glance/tables/corrtyptab.htm

[66] West, C. and W. Sabol (December 2008). Prisoners in 2007. Table 10, p. 21. http://www.ojp.usdoj.gov/bjs/pub/pdf/p07.pdf

[67] Fields, G. (April 30, 2009). "Shorter Sentences Sought for Crack." *Wall Street Journal*, p. A3.

[68] Mauer, Testimony, pp. 3, 6.

[69] Mauer, M. *The Changing Racial Dynamics of the War on Drugs*. Washington, DC: The Sentencing Project, April 2009, p. 1. http://sentencingproject.org/Admin/Documents/publications/dp_raceanddrugs.pdf

[70] Mauer, Testimony, p. 5.

[71] Beatty, P., A. Petteruti, and J. Ziedenberg. *The Vortex: The Concentrated Racial Impact of Drug Imprisonment and the Characteristics of Punitive Counties*. Washington, DC: Justice Policy Institute, December 2007, p. 2. http://www.justicepolicy.org/images/upload/07–12_REP_Vortex_AC-DP.pdf

[72] Ibid.

[73] Goodman, L. (April 19, 2009). "Are We Winning Yet?" *Chicago Tribune*, p. 25.

[74] United Nations Office on Drugs and Crime (UNODC). *World Drug Report 2005*. Vienna, Austria: UNODC, June 2005, p. 127. http://www.unodc.org/pdf/WDR_2005/volume_1_chap2.pdf

[75] United Nations Office on Drugs and Crime (UNODC). *World Drug Report 2008*. New York, 2008, pp. 257, 258. http://www.unodc.org/documents/wdr/WDR_2008/WDR2008_Statistical_Annex_Prices.pdf

[76] Goodman, "Are We Winning Yet?".

[77] Quoted by Dilulio, J. L. (1996). "Broken Bottles: Alcohol, Disorder, and Crime." *The Brookings Review* 14: 14–17. See also U.S. Department of Justice. *Alcohol and Crime: An Analysis of National Data on the Prevalence of Alcohol Involvement in Crime*. Washington, DC: US Department of Justice, 1998.

[78] Greenfield, L. A. Alcohol and Crime: An Analysis of National Data on the Prevalence of Alcohol Involvement in Crime. Washington, DC: U.S. Department of Justice, April 1998.

[79] For one of the best assessments of the "collateral damages" of mass imprisonment in general, see Mauer, M. and M. Chesney-Lind (eds.), *Invisible Punishment: The Collateral Consequences of Mass Imprisonment*. New York: New Press, 2002.

The Prison Incarceration Boom
Bursting at the Seams

"In my mind there's no more recession-proof form of economic development. Nothing's going to stop crime."[1]

"There are no seasonal fluctuations, it is a non-polluting industry, and in many circumstances it is virtually invisible."[2]

"If crime doesn't pay, punishment certainly does."[3]

Chapter 1 looked at the business of punishment and reviewed some of the major factors contributing to the exponential increases in the numbers of people punished by confinement. In this chapter we look at the growth in the number of prisons—where, why, and by whom.

A Boom in Prison Construction

Prison construction has become a booming business. From 1975 to 2000, the number of state prisons went from under 600 to more than 1,000.[4] Viewing a longer historical trend, there were 61 state prisons in 1923; 150 in 1950, and 592 in 1974. Between 1979 and 2000, the ten states with the largest number of prisoners (Texas, Florida, California, New York, Michigan, Georgia, Illinois, Ohio, Colorado, and Missouri) increased the number of prisons by 63%.

During the last decade of the twentieth century, about 92,000 new beds were added each year, ranging in cost from $29,000 in a minimum-security prison to $70,000 in a maximum-security prison. The total cost of new prison construction alone was $3.88 billion; for every 92,000 beds added, there is an estimated additional cost of $1.3 billion per year.[5] During the 1990s a total of 371 new prisons opened. In 1999 alone, 24 new prisons were opened and 146 prisons added or beds renovated. The average cost of building a new prison came to $105 million and the renovation costs totaled $470 million. In 2000 another 29 institutions were under construction, while 137 existing institutions sched-

37

uled innovations or additions. The total costs came to more than $2.2 billion.[6] Many states publish reports on recent or upcoming construction projects.[7] The Web site for the North Carolina Department of Corrections lists prison construction since 1989. Twenty-six correctional facilities (including two for young offenders, two work farms and a women's prison) opened between 1989 and 2008.[8]

The construction of federal prisons has also increased substantially. In 1980 there were only 44 federal prisons.[9] In 2009 the Bureau of Prisons lists 180 facilities.[10] The most recent figures for the Federal Bureau of Prisons reveal that the budget in fiscal 2008 was $5.3 billion, up from only $330 million in 1980.[11] The Government Accountability Office (GAO) issues reports on federal prison construction projects.[12] In May 2008, the GAO reviewed increases in estimated costs for three new construction projects (located in Mendota, CA, Berlin, NH, and McDowell, WV), which had cost taxpayers $278 million (62%) more than initially estimated.

Searching the Internet produces multiple results for prison construction. One site listed ten planned prison construction projects around the country.[13] One of the companies advertising its services for prison construction on the Web was Kitchell. According to their Web site, they have built more than 110,000 detention and corrections beds in 17 states, including 42 state prisons, 30 adult jails, 30 juvenile facilities, four custody centers, two California Youth Authority schools, plus "police stations, courts facilities, camps and other justice-related projects."[14]

In 2005, there were a total of 1,821 state and federal correctional facilities, up from 1,668 in 2000 (a 9% increase). The number of private facilities increased from 264 to 415 (23% of all correctional institutions). The correctional institutions employed 445,000 people; 66% (295,261) were correctional officers.[15] There were 3,257 residential facilities for juveniles.[16] There are more than 5,000 confinement facilities for adults and juveniles in the United States—a huge and expanding industry.

Many of the new prisons are located in rural areas. My wife and I took a driving trip in the northern peninsula of Michigan, travelling through rolling hills and farms. We admired the serenity of the landscape, a throwback to an earlier era when farming was the dominant occupation in the United States. We arrived at the town of Newbury and noticed several businesses at the main intersection that leads into town. There were several motels, chain restaurants, gas stations, and minimarts, all of which seemed out of place. We decided to stay in one of these motels, but before checking in drove into the town itself. We noticed an old brick building surrounded by barbed wire, sitting on several acres of land. It appeared to be a prison. As we drove around the block, we saw prisoners in the yard—most of whom were African American. The facility had previously been a mental institution until it was closed in the 1970s. While driving along state route 29 the next day, we counted a total of five additional prisons before we left the state. I subsequently learned that there are four prisons and four prison camps in the Northern Peninsula of Michigan, and more than 90% of the prisoners came from Detroit and are primarily African Americans. Subsequent research confirmed the rural nature of the U.S. prison system, resembling in many ways Russian Gulags.

GULAGS AMERICAN STYLE

In *The Gulag Archipelago*, Russian author Alexander Solzhenitsyn discussed the existence of a network of prison camps spread throughout the Soviet Union, mostly in isolated areas like Siberia.[17] The term "Gulag" was a Russian acronym for the Soviet bureaucratic institution (translation: main administration of corrective labor camps) that operated the camps in the Stalin era. After the publication of Solzhenitsyn's book, the term was used more broadly to describe the entire Soviet forced labor penal system. The camps originated after the 1917 revolution, but the numbers grew exponentially during Stalin's campaign in the early 1930s to collectivize agriculture and to turn the Soviet Union into a modern industrial power.[18] The camps were also used for political dissidents.

Several authors have noted that the gulag phenomenon is not restricted to Third World or totalitarian societies. The "relocation centers" in the United States to which Japanese-American citizens were forced to move during World War II resembled gulags. In the early 1990s, Norwegian criminologist Nils Christie suggested that the "crime control industry" was beginning to look like the equivalent of the Russian Gulag.[19] Stephen Richards also used the term *gulag* to describe the modern prison system.[20] Mark Dow used the term in the title of his book about U.S. immigration prisons.[21]

Certain aspects of the American prison system share characteristics of gulags. As noted above, many prisons are now in rural areas. There are also human rights abuses in U.S. prisons, jails, and juvenile correctional facilities, including long periods in solitary confinement, extreme brutality, and violence. The forced labor is inexpensive and produces profits for corporations.

THE TEXAS, MICHIGAN, AND CALIFORNIA GULAGS

Texas institutional locations illustrate the scattered sites that prompted Solzhenitsyn to compare the Gulags to an archipelago.[22] Most of the locations are very rural, with populations of less than 6,500 in most of the towns where the institutions are located. The state has 120 correctional facilities, including 4 privately operated leased beds, and 5 parole confinement facilities.[23] As noted above, the U.S. incarceration rate is 509; the rate in Texas is 668—tied with Oklahoma for the third highest after Louisiana (858) and Mississippi (749). Thirty-seven percent of prisoners are African American, and 31% are Hispanic. Almost 20% are serving sentences for a drug offense.[24] The Texas Department of Criminal Justice spent almost $3.2 billion in 2008, including $1.35 billion on salaries and wages.[25]

Texas Correctional Industries (TCI) was established in 1963 as a department within the Texas Department of Criminal Justice. It manufactures goods and provides services to state and local government agencies, public educational systems and other tax-supported entities on a for-profit basis. TCI has five divisions (garment, graphics, furniture, metal, and marketing/distribution). It participates in The Prison Industry Enhancement (PIE) Certification Program, which allows a private company to employ offenders who have volunteered for the program. The private company pays the offenders; TCI takes deductions for room and board, dependent support, restitution, and contributions to a fund for crime victims. Through 13 years of participation, more than $12 million room and board deductions were deposited in the general revenue fund for Texas.[26]

Michigan reported 42 prisons and 7 prison camps in 2006. Of the 51,570 prisoners, 52% were black; the average minimum sentence was 8 years at an average annual cost per prisoner of $26,000. There were almost 54,000 people on probation, and 16,000 on parole. The Michigan Department of Corrections supervised 121,532 people with a staff of 16,940 and a budget of 1.87 billion.[27] As in Texas, the populations in the majority of towns where prisoners are confined range from around 1,000 to 10,000. The facility at Newbury (population 2,658) was opened in 1995 on the site of a former state mental institution.[28]

Prisoners in Michigan make a variety of products for sale to non-profit organizations and governmental institutions. The Web site for Michigan State Industries (run by the Office of Employment Readiness for the Michigan Department of Corrections) lists items from construction products to piers to furnishings to garments to janitorial to license plates to linens to signs.[29]

On the Web site for the Michigan Department of Corrections is a tab for programs and services. "Community Service and Public Works" is the first tab and describes the types of work performed by inmates: cleaning state parks; maintaining cemeteries; washing police cars; planting flowers in city and county parks; cleaning up vacant city lots; restoring bridges in recreation areas; improving county fairgrounds.[30] There is also a tab for "Hire a Skilled Worker," which instructs potential employers about how to search resumes to identify inmates for possible hire. Another listing is for "The Prison Build Program."

Under a pilot program in 1998, inmates constructed wall panels for houses for Habitat for Humanity. The Prison Build Program grew out of the pilot program. Prison Build completed its first home inside the perimeter of Saginaw Correctional Facility in March 2000. The house was moved to a location to house a single Hispanic mother and her 3-year-old son. Prison Build has participated in building a number of homes and added cabinetry construction to its offerings.[31]

The configuration of California correctional facilities also matches the Gulag description.[32] There were 33 state prisons in 2008 (compared to 12 in 1980[33]) plus 40 camps, 12 community correctional facilities, and five prisoner mother facilities. There were 316,229 offenders under the supervision of the California Department of Corrections and Rehabilitation; the total number of staff members was 63,050 (53,069 in institutions; 3,551 in parole, and 6,430 in administration). The budget proposal for 2009–2010 was $10.6 billion. Pelican Bay, the supermax prison facility, is located in Crescent City (population 7,242) near the Oregon border. Other remote locations include the two prisons in Susanville and Blythe.[34]

California produces a number of products for sale to government agencies. The California Prison Industry Authority (CALPIA) operates over 60 service, manufacturing, and agricultural industries at 22 prisons throughout California and provides work assignments for approximately 6,000 inmates. Its revenue comes from the sale of its products and services; it does not receive an appropriation from the legislature. CALPIA inmates contribute 40% of their wages to pay court-ordered restitution.[35]

Profiles of every other state in the country could be presented, showing basically the same formula: high number of prisons, youth facilities, parole agencies, camps, etc. spread throughout the state, many if not most located in remote rural areas.[36]

Rural Prisons: Uplifting Rural Economies?

Rural economies across the United States experienced serious problems in the 1980s. As we have seen, the population of prison inmates increased dramatically at exactly the same time. "The large-scale use of incarceration to solve social problems has combined with the fallout of globalization to produce an ominous trend."[37] There are more prisoners than farmers in the United States. Although most prisoners are from urban communities, many prisons are now in rural areas.

> It is remarkable that a public undertaking as far-reaching as the American prison expansion—which involves 50 state governments and the federal government, affects millions of incarcerated individuals, influences millions more family and community members, and consumes billions of public dollars—would receive so little empirical analysis and public scrutiny.[38]

State governments and communities embraced prison construction as a solution to economic woes. Rural areas had been the choice for about four new prisons per year in the decades of the 1960s and 1970s; the number increased to 16 per year in the 1980s and reached 24 per year in the 1990s.[39] During that decade, a new prison opened about every 15 days, and 60% of new prison construction was in rural areas.[40] Tracy Huling, who has done extensive research on the role of prisons in rural areas, commented on the tendency to lobby for more prisons.

> The tendency of states—including Texas, Arizona, New York, Pennsylvania, Illinois, Michigan, Colorado, Florida, and California, among many others—to "cluster" prisons in distinct rural regions has created dozens of rural penal colonies where prisons dominate the community's economic, social, political, and cultural landscape with myriad and profound effects.[41]

A disproportionate number of prisons in New York are located in the northern counties that border Canada.[42] Franklin County, New York, covers 1,678 square miles and is very sparsely populated; there are 19 small towns in the county. It has five state prisons and one federal prison. Depressed rural communities become dependent on prisons, often failing to attempt to attract other types of businesses. Residents in Franklin County depend on the prisons for jobs, and small businesses count on prison workers to patronize their stores. Inmate work crews clear snow from fire hydrants, maintain parks and hiking trails, mow the lawns at cemeteries, and unload trucks at food pantries. One resident remarked: "Everyone around here either works in the prisons, or has a relative who works in the prisons, or knows someone who works in the prisons. My kids were able to build their homes and raise their families here because of the prisons. If it weren't for the prisons, they would have had to leave the area." Huling commented: "What we've seen in New York and other states is that one prison led to another prison and led to another prison, creating the notion that there's no other economic development option than to build prisons to foster stability in rural areas."[43]

The increase in the number of prisoners in New York was primarily the result of the Rockefeller drug laws passed in 1973, which set severe punishments for drug offenders. Prison sentences have tripled since the passage of these laws and almost two-thirds (62.5%) were nonviolent drug offenders.[44] While rural communities hoped prisons would provide needed revenues and states could acquire land in those areas at much lower prices than in metropolitan areas, the families of prisoners suffered the collateral consequences, or "invisible punishment" as described by Marc Mauer and Meda Chesney-Lind.[45] Families and friends often must travel hundreds of miles to visit inmates. In fact, this necessity created another business. An ex-convict founded Operation Prison Gap (the Web site includes the description "Bringing Families Together"), which operates vans and buses from New York City to prisons in upstate New York on the weekends.[46]

EXPLOITING PRISONERS TO ENHANCE RURAL POPULATIONS: PRISONERS OF THE CENSUS

Prisons are also politically valuable. Since the first U.S. census in 1790, people serving sentences have been counted in the state and county where they are imprisoned—not in the community where they lived prior to their conviction.[47] One report refers to this as the "phantom" population of rural prisoners.[48] Before 1970 the numbers of prisoners was relatively small, and there were fewer disparities in the distribution of revenues or in drawing legislative districts due to census counts. Today, the 2.5 million people in prison represent a population larger than that of the four smallest states combined. Counting those people as living in the district where the prison is located is "a systematic inflation of the political power of districts with prisons" that diminishes the vote of everyone else."[49]

There are numerous examples, and Alamosa (Iowa) provides one of the most striking illustrations of the imbalance caused by the current census practice. There are four wards in the city, and each has a representative on the city council. In Ward 2, the council member won the last election by two write-in votes—one from his wife and the other from a neighbor. Each ward has about 1,400 people, but only 58 people in Ward 2 can vote. The other 1,300 "residents" are housed in Iowa's largest penitentiary located in the ward. Since none of those people can vote, the 58 voting constituents in Ward 2 have about 25 times more political influence. There are similar disparities in upstate New York, Tennessee and Wisconsin. As Nathan Persily, director of the Center on Law and Politics at Columbia Law School states, "There's no reason why a community ought to gain representation because of a large, incarcerated, nonvoting population."[50]

New York law requires each district to have around 300,000 residents. The 45th district in upstate New York extends to the Canadian border and covers more square miles than Rhode Island and Connecticut combined and carries the nickname "Little Siberia" because of the 13 prisons (12 state and one federal) located in four of the six counties in the district.[51] Without the 13,500 prisoners counted as residents, the district would have to be redrawn because it would not have the minimum population required for a seat in the state Senate. The practice of counting prisoners as residents skews the census results. Rural areas appear more populous than they actually are, while the urban areas where the majority of inmates lived previously appear less populated.

Adding prisoners to the Census count places many of these communities under the official poverty level, thereby qualifying for more federal funds. Gatesville, Texas (pop. 15,591), qualified for poverty status with its 9,095 prisoners, resulting in the town receiving $4.2 million in state grants, which it used to upgrade water lines and build new roads. Another irony to all of this is the fact that while these prisoners are helping towns qualify for large sums of federal dollars, they are not included in the official unemployment figures. According to one recent study, by including African Americans in the official unemployment figures, the unemployment rate for them increases to almost 40%, while adding about 2–3% to the official unemployment figures.[52] Minnesota's state demographer Tom Gillaspy estimates that the census "directs $2,000–$3,000 per person counted to any given community each decade, *not including additional census-based funding distributed to poor communities.*"[53]

In rural, upstate New York, the number of incarcerated African Americans in some counties is greater than the number of African Americans who have chosen to live in the area. Alice Green, founder and executive director of the Center for Law and Justice, noted that the practice of counting prisoners who cannot vote as constituents means that "they are not represented, and they are totally exploited."[54] Politicians profit from their numbers but do not represent the interests of the prisoners.

It is ironic that inmates are counted for purposes of aid or drawing congressional districts, while many have lost the right to vote because of a felony conviction. Suffrage laws vary by state and by felony. Maine and Vermont permit all felons to vote, including those still in prison. California, New York, and Colorado reinstate voting rights after felons are released from prison and are no longer on parole. Although 12 states have changed their laws since 2003, 1 in 41 adults (5.3 million people) have lost the right to vote because of a felony conviction. The numbers for African Americans are even more devastating: 1 in 8.[55]

The practice of counting people who cannot vote as residents of a district violates the principle of one person, one vote. As noted above, the political influence of those who can vote in districts where a large percentage cannot is greatly inflated. In addition, prisoners who cannot vote sometimes suffer a severe double punishment. Some of the politicians who are elected in districts that house prisons lead committees in charge of the legal code and what constitutes crime. In New York, many continue to support the Rockefeller laws that require long prison sentences for drug crimes. Kirsten Levingston, director of the Brennan Center for Justice, points out that the presence of prisoners "in the tabulation column expands the influence of those who have an incentive to keep them in prison, not those who need the resources to help keep them out."[56]

State tax dollars already support the districts by providing the funds for building, maintaining, and staffing the prisons. The census figures essentially allow otherwise thinly populated legislative districts to increase their political influence—essentially "double dipping" from state coffers.[57]

Because inmates are counted as local residents, larger populations mean more state and federal aid. Many inmates do not serve their sentences in the county in which they were convicted. As a result, the population gains in the county where the prison is located means a corresponding loss to the inmate's original county (often the most disadvantaged urban areas). Cook County Illinois will lose nearly $88 million in federal benefits over the next decade because residents convicted of a crime are serving their sentences downstate.[58] New York City has the same problem. Two-thirds of state prisoners in New York are from New York City, but 91% of prisoners are incarcerated in upstate counties. Because some states send inmates out of state to serve their sentences, the original state loses the benefits and the contracting state gains. Population counts that include inmates also affect the drawing of legislative and congressional districts.

In the 1990s rural prisons averaged thirty employees for every one hundred prisoners, providing employment for 75,000 workers at the end of the decade.[59] Corrections officials extol the economic benefits of a prison to local communities. One California official stated: "Prisons not only stabilize a local economy but can in fact rejuvenate it. There are no seasonal fluctuations, it is a non-polluting industry, and in many circumstances it is virtually invisible. . . . You've got people that are working there and spending their money there, so now these communities are able to have a Little League and all the kinds of activities that people want."[60]

Prison Town, USA provides a riveting examination of the unprecedented incarceration/prison-building boom and the unanticipated consequences when a struggling rural community views prisons as the means to revive the economy. The documentary "reveals the economic and political dynamics behind the prison-building frenzy that is changing the landscape of rural America, shedding light on some of the little-understood human costs of the nation's criminal-justice policies." It follows four families over two years in Susanville, located in the foothills of the California Sierras.

Susanville once thrived on logging, ranching, and agriculture. The local agricultural economy disappeared, much as it did throughout the United States. The language of California's penal code changed in the 1970s; punishment—not rehabilitation—became the primary purpose of prison.[61] A 1977 law established determinate sentencing for most crimes, and the 1994 "three strikes" law mandated a minimum of 25-year sentences for offenders with two previous convictions. When California needed new prisons, it promised jobs and a large institutional buyer for local services—and Susanville accepted. Susanville hosts three prison complexes housing more than 11,000 inmates—more than one-and-a-half times the number of local residents.[62]

Contrary to expectations, most prison jobs do not go to locals.[63] The majority of the jobs are awarded to those with seniority and educational backgrounds within the correctional field who meet professional certification requirements. One study found that in Missouri 68% of the prison jobs were filled by people living outside the county where the prison was located. The pattern holds in many other states, such as California and Washington.[64]

Because many prison workers drive long commutes from large urban areas, local businesses to not benefit from the purchases of new residents. In many places where prisons have been built, most of the locally owned businesses have closed, giving way to Wal-Mart, McDonald's and other chain stores. This happened in Tehachapi, California, a small town of just under 11,000 between Mojave and Bakersfield along Route 58. Two prisons are located there, and 741 local businesses failed in the 1990s and were replaced by chain stores.[65]

Although rural communities with high poverty and unemployment rates believe that opening a new prison will be economically beneficial, research has not found evidence of those benefits. The Sentencing Project reviewed 25 years of data from New York State rural counties. Looking at employment rates and per capita income, they found "no significant difference or discernible pattern of economic trends" between counties that were home to a prison and counties that were not home to a prison.[66] The Urban Institute found no significant positive economic impacts for smaller communities from the prisons located there. "Economic benefits of new prisons may come from the flow of additional state and federal dollars. In the decennial census, prisoners are counted where they are incarcerated, and many federal and state funding streams are tied to census population counts. . . . Within a state, funding for community health services, road construction and repair, public housing, local law enforcement, and public libraries are all driven by population counts from the census."[67]

A study by Clayton Mosher and his colleagues focused on the economic impact of prisons in virtually all counties in the United States between 1969 and 1994. They compared those counties that had built prisons with those that did not in both metropolitan and nonmetropolitan areas. The differences were rather stark. In both cases the impact was not as supporters claimed. For instance, counties without a prison had a much higher annual rate of growth, as measured by income, employment and other indicators. More importantly, in rural counties where the most prisons have been built the researchers concluded: "Neither established prisons nor newly built facilities made a significant contribution to employment grown in rural counties."[68]

As virtually every state is undergoing a budget crisis, cutting back on prison expenses has become one option, including closing some of them. States are finding that maintaining prisons is very expensive and they have taken steps to alleviate the problem.

- Several states have reformed "mandatory minimum" sentencing laws by returning sentencing discretion to judges, including Alabama, Mississippi, Michigan, Indiana, Connecticut, Louisiana, North Dakota and Utah.[69]

- Several states (e.g., California and Arizona) have passed special referendums concerning alternative sentencing for drug offenders.[70]
- Some states have instituted parole reforms, including early release.[71]
- Many states are cutting other costs, such as food and health services.[72]
- Some states have closed down entire prisons to save money.[73]
- Some states have put new construction on hold to save money and to find alternatives.[74]

Reversing the trend to ever-increasing imprisonment could begin with ending the warehousing of the mentally ill in correctional institutions, changing "three strikes" policies for nonviolent offenders, and eliminating draconian "truth-in-sentencing" laws. Money cut from prison spending could be allocated to alternative economic development in both the communities of the prisoners released and the communities surrounding prisons that close. Using dollars formerly spent on prisons to develop community-based alternatives to incarceration and economic development strategies in depressed communities could alleviate the drain of human resources. Connecticut is an example of a state that now devotes former prison dollars to economic development in the communities of the former prisoners; extending that aid to communities that have become dependent on prison dollars would be one means of improving both sides of the equation.[75]

The Privatization of Prisons: Profits for Private Industry

The majority of the criminal sentencing decisions that have decimated a generation of young people (particularly in minority communities) were made in state legislatures. Spending on prisons increased 529% over the last two decades. When budgets were strained, states turned to private prisons.[76] More than thirty years ago, researchers warned about the tremendous growth in privatization in general, especially within the private police industry. They quoted one source that called this phenomenon "creeping capitalism" or the transfer of "services and responsibilities that were once monopolized by the state" to "profit-making agencies and organizations."[77] Through privatization, states can get around voter resistance to prison construction bonds by having private corporations build the prison, who then turn around and send a huge bill to the state and thus taxpayers. This represents a classic case of "socializing the costs and privatizing the benefits."[78]

I had always suspected that there was a possibility that local police, prosecutors, or judges might be tempted to accept payments in return for sending offenders to privately owned correctional facilities. My suspicions were confirmed in 2009 when two judges in Pennsylvania pled guilty to receiving payments of about $2.6 million. It was found that at least 5,000 children over a period of five years were sentenced to a private detention facility for which one of the judges had helped negotiate the contract (worth $58 million). Under the plea agreement the two judges (both in their 50s) will serve 87 months in prison. Interestingly, the private juvenile detention centers, which are owned by Mid Atlantic Youth Services Corp., "are still operating and are not a target of the federal investigation, according to court documents. The company cooperated in the investigation, the documents said." The current owner of the business denied any knowledge of the kickbacks.[79]

As of June 30, 2008 (latest figures available), there were 126,249 prisoners in private facilities in the United States.[80] This represents an increase of almost 4,000% over the 3,100 prisoners housed in private facilities in 1987.[81] In eight years, the number of federal prisoners in private facilities more than doubled (from 15, 524 in 2000 to 31,310 in 2007), increasing to 15.7% of all federal prisoners. States confined 71,845 prisoners in private facilities in 2000 and 94,665 in 2007 (31.8% increase).[82] As of November 2008 the bulk of the prisons were being operated by CCA, the Geo Group, and Cornell Corporation.[83]

CCA is both the largest and perhaps the most controversial private prison corporation. One Web site provides an extensive list of the lawsuits against CCA (as well as Cornell and Geo).[84] Founded in 1983, the company is headquartered in Nashville, Tennessee. It confines 75,000 offenders in 60 facilities, 44 of which are owned by the company; it employs 17,000 people.[85] The company has had a checkered history, with its stock reaching a high of $45 in 1998 before plummeting to 18 cents per share. In 2009, it was trading at about $15. Its Web site advertises that it is the fourth-largest corrections system in the nation, behind only the federal government and two states.

The Geo Group is headquartered in Boca Raton. It operates 48 facilities (almost half in Texas) in the United States and has a number of international operations.[86] It appears to be doing a brisk business, even in the middle of a worldwide recession. One report noted that GEO reported quarterly earnings of $20 million at the end of 2008, plus an annual income of $61 million, almost doubling the $38 million in 2007. They also announced plans to add 3,925 new beds to immigration lockups in five locations around the country. They are being hired by the Immigration and Customs Enforcement (ICE) agency and the U.S. Marshals Service to operate these and other lockups. Business has been brisk in recent years as immigration enforcement has resulted in a 65% increase in the number of undocumented immigrants in federal jails between 2002 and 2008. The number of detainees was more than 31,000 as of February 2009. Charges of corruption, civil rights violations, and prisoner abuse have been leveled against GEO Group.[87]

The adult secure division began in 1984. Like its competitors, Cornell Companies emphasizes its cost-efficient services and programs that will save taxpayers' money.[88] The company has 70 facilities in 15 states (primarily the Southwest) and the District of Columbia with a capacity of just over 20,000 beds.

There have been numerous cases of serious problems with the privatization of prisons: Russell Clemens, an economist with the Department of Research for the American Federation of State, County, and Federal Employees, put the problem in perspective when he noted that the various "problems regarding security, staffing, and quality of services have plagued prison privatization from its inception."[89]

At least 31 states and the federal government (6.8% of all prisoners) contract with private prisons.[90] Corrections Corporation of America (CCA) runs two-thirds of the private facilities (see discussion below). Eleven states place more than one-fifth of their prison population in private prisons. Another irony in the prison boom is that state prison employees generally supported tougher sentencing laws that strained state budgets, and they now find their jobs disappearing to privatization through this two-step process. "The corporate prison industry helped enact 'tough-on-crime' policies in this country, at least partly by preying on the economic desperation of dying rural towns to build political alliances around the prison-industrial complex."[91]

The alliances, however, were sometimes fleeting. Hardin, Montana, and a neighboring town were convinced that a private prison would provide jobs for a hundred people and a steady source of income. The population in Hardin is 3,600 and its poverty rate is among the nation's lowest. They issued revenue bonds to finance the $27 million construction of Two Rivers Detention Facility. When it was completed in 2007, they hired a for-profit prison-management corporation to run the prison, intended to house 464 inmates. The former governor had told Hardin that the department of corrections needed more space, but the new governor did not issue a contract. Hardin tried to contact other states but learned that Montana law prohibited the incarceration of out-of-state prisoners. Although Hardin won a lawsuit in 2008 to eliminate the restriction, it still has no contracts. The town defaulted on the bonds in 2008. When it was announced that the U.S. detention facility at Guantanamo Bay would be closed, Hardin proposed using their facility. However, Montana's three congressional members opposed such use. Senator Max Baucus announced: "I understand the need to create jobs, but we're not going to bring al-Qaeda to Big Sky Country—no way, not on my watch."[92] The owner of a store in Hardin thought the wintry high plains of Montana "would be torture for some of those boys" and added, "Our city fathers wanted the economic benefits, but I guess they didn't foresee the political controversies."

The privatization of prison health care has become a $9.3 billion market.[93] America Service Group (Brentwood, Tennessee) is a publicly traded company that has two subsidiaries: Prison Health Services and Correctional Health Services. The company has a market value of about $139 million, and the price of its share tripled from 2008 to 2009. It provides care to 179,000 inmates in 23 states through 64 local and state government contracts. About 40% of all inmate medical care in America is now contracted to for-profit companies. Its major competitors are closely held companies, Correctional Medical Services and Wexford Health Sources Inc.

Private providers' services average 10% to 15% less than when governments provide the services. About half-dozen for-profit companies underbid each other to win contracts. Dr. Michael Puisis, editor of *Clinical Practice in Correctional Medicine*, describes the process: "It's almost like a game of attrition, where the companies will take bids for amounts that you just can't do it. They figure out how to make money after they get the contract."[94]

Prison Health Services is the largest for-profit company providing medical care in prisons and jails. It has contracts in 28 states to provide care for 237,000 inmates (about 10% of all prisoners). Based outside Nashville, the company promotes itself by suggesting that it can take the "messy and expensive job of providing medical care from overmatched government officials, and give it to an experienced nationwide outfit that could recruit doctors, battle lawsuits and keep costs down."[95] The *New York Times* researched the company's services for a year and found repeated instances of flawed and sometimes lethal medical practices.

> The company's performance around the nation has provoked criticism from judges and sheriffs, lawsuits from inmates' families and whistle-blowers, and condemnations by federal, state and local authorities. The company has paid millions of dollars in fines and settlements.[96]

In New York, the State Commission of Correction investigated 23 deaths of inmates in custody (see also chapter 6) and recommended that the state discipline Prison Health doctors and nurses. Since 2001, it has advised that Prison Health lacks any legal authority to practice medicine because business executives are in charge. Like many other states, New York "requires that for-profit corporations providing medical services be owned and controlled by doctors, to keep business calculations from driving medical decisions."[97] The company claimed it had two corporations run by doctors, but the commission called them sham corporations. Georgia hired Prison Health in 1995 but replaced the company two years later because of lack of staffing. Maine ended its contract in 2003 for similar reasons. In Alabama, one prison has only two doctors for more than 2,200 prisoners.

A former medical director for the Illinois prison system said problems arise when "You've got the professionals dealing with amateurs."[98] He noted that most government employees deciding on contracts aren't sophisticated enough to know what to demand until things go wrong. Laws requiring that contracts be regularly put out for bid and awarded to the lowest bidder complicate the issue. Even government clients who have been dissatisfied with services are reluctant to voice their complaints for fear that the company they drop will be the only bidder for the job the next year or that it will purchase competitors and, again, be the only choice available. Prison Health Services settles lawsuits quickly and then resigns so that they can claim that they have never been let go for cause.

Once governments decide to outsource services, they rarely return to providing services themselves.

> When cost-trimming cuts into the quality of care, harming inmates and prompting lawsuits and investigations, governments often see no alternatives but to keep the company, or hire another, then another when that one fails—a revolving-door process that sometimes ends with governments rehiring the company they fired years earlier.[99]

Privatization has become, in the words of Edward Herman, "one of the mantras of the New World Order. Economic, political and media elites assume that privatization provides undeniable benefits and moves us toward a good society." Movement toward privatization assumes efficiencies in the private market and inefficiencies in government-run programs. As Herman notes, "Part of the design of neoliberal politicians and intellectuals has been to weaken the state as a power center that might serve ordinary citizens and challenge the rule of the market."[100]

Some Concluding Thoughts

The introduction discussed the difference between specific and general deterrence. While the two million inmates have been deterred from committing crimes outside the prison, has their fate served as general deterrence for others? After legislatures passed laws that sent increasing numbers of people to prison, the focus switched to where to build the prisons to punish the convicted. Rural areas whose economies were deteriorating saw prisons as an opportunity, and states approved the construction of thousands of new prisons. The overriding issue of who we punish and how was lost in the frenzy to build enough prisons to meet the demand.

Federal, state, and local governments face a dilemma. On the one hand the demand to "get tough" on crime has not diminished, yet at the same time it is getting very expensive. Virtually every state is facing a huge financial crisis.[101] Some states—California is a prime example—are considering releasing a large number of prisoners in order to balance the budget.[102] Peggy Burke of the Center for Effective Public Policy believes high recidivism rates have prompted people to reconsider punishment. "In the past, it has been you are either for the victim or for the offender. It was a specious dichotomy. There is a conversation going on in all kinds of venues in this country, in governors' offices, state legislatures, courts, and state correction agencies on whether or not our incarceration strategies have been effective."[103] Paul Sutton, a professor of criminal justice at San Diego State University, notes: "The binge of the eighties and nineties was simply political, it was not correlated to crime or increases in the civilian population. Now why of a sudden does it stop? Once again it is not tied to a crime turnaround or people leaving the state, once again it's political. This time the politics driving the change is economics."[104]

NOTES

[1] City manager of Sayre, Oklahoma, which had just opened a prized new maximum-security prison. Kilborn, P. T. (August 1, 2001). "Rural Towns Turn to Prisons to Reignite Their Economies." *New York Times*; Street, P. (July/August 2005). "Race, Place, and the Perils of Prisonomics." *Z Magazine* online. http://zmagsite.zmag.org/JulAug2005/street0705.html

[2] A California Department of Corrections official explaining some of the benefits of putting a prison in a rural area. Quoted in Huling, T. "Building a Prison Economy in Rural America," p. 200. In M. Mauer and M. Chesney-Lind, eds., *Invisible Punishment: The Collateral Consequences of Mass Imprisonment*. New York: New Press, 2002, pp. 197–213.

[3] Duke, L. (September 8, 2000). "Prison Construction Boom Transforms Small Towns." *The Washington Post*.

[4] Lawrence, S. and J. Travis. *The New Landscape of Imprisonment: Mapping America's Prison Expansion*. Washington, DC: Urban Institute, 2004. http://www.urban.org/UploadedPDF/410994_mapping_prisons.pdf

[5] Shelden, R. and W. Brown (2000). "The Crime Control Industry and the Management of the Surplus Population." *Critical Criminology* 9 (1-2): 39–62.

[6] Camp, C. G. and G. M. Camp. *The Corrections Yearbook 2000: Adult Corrections*. Middletown, CT: Criminal Justice Institute, 2000, p. 76.

[7] The ACA Web site lists every state's Department of Corrections Web address: http://www.aca.org/research/stateadult/results.asp?union=AND&viewby=50&startrec=1.

[8] http://www.doc.state.nc.us/dop/list/newprisons.htm

[9] Johnson, K. (January 22, 2003). "Federal Prisons Packed with almost 165,000." *USA Today*.

[10] http://www.bop.gov/locations/weekly_report.jsp

[11] The latest figures are taken from the following Web site: http://www.usdoj.gov/jmd/2008summary/pdf/004_budget_highlights.pdf

[12] http://www.gao.gov/products/GAO-08-634

[13] http://www.reedconstructiondata.com/news/2008/05/twenty-large-upcoming-jail-prison-and-courthouse-construction-projects-may-/. This report also shows ten courthouse construction projects.

[14] http://www.kitchell.com/Markets/CriminalJustice.aspx

[15] Stephan, J. (2008). *Census of State and Federal Correctional Facilities, 2005*. http://www.ojp.usdoj.gov/bjs/pub/pdf/csfcf05.pdf

[16] Livsey, S., M. Sickmund, and A. Sladky (January 2009). *Juvenile Residential Facility Census, 2004.* http://www.ncjrs.gov/pdffiles1/ojjdp/222721.pdf

[17] Solzhenitsyn, A. *The Gulag Archipelago.* New York: Bantam Books, 1970.

[18] Conquest, R. (February 24, 1995). "Playing Down the Gulag." *Times Literary Supplement*; Harris, J. R. (1997). "The Growth of the Gulag: Forced Labor in the Urals Region, 1929–1931." *The Russian Review* 56 (2): 265–281.

[19] This is in reference to Christie's original edition of *Crime Control as Industry*, which was published in 1993.

[20] Richards, S. (1996). "Commentary: Sociological Penetration of the American Gulag." *Wisconsin Sociologist* 27 (4): 18–28.

[21] Dow, M. *American Gulag: Inside U.S. Immigration Prisons.* Berkeley: University of California Press, 2004.

[22] For details see their Web site: http://www.tdcj.state.tx.us/stat/unitdirectory/map.htm#map

[23] Texas Department of Criminal Justice. http://www.tdcj.state.tx.us/stat/unitdirectory/all.htm

[24] Texas Department of Justice. Statistical Report: Fiscal Year 2008, p. 1. http://www.tdcj.state.tx.us/publications/executive/FY08%20Stat%20Report.pdf

[25] Texas Department of Corrections. State Agency Search, 2008. http://www.window.state.tx.us/comptrol/expendlist/cashdrill.php

[26] Texas Department of Criminal Justice. Manufacturing and Logistics Annual Report Fiscal 2006. http://www.tci.tdcj.state.tx.us/info/pubs/ML_Annual_TCI001_2006.pdf. TCI has its own Web site, which lists all its products and services: http://www.tci.tdcj.state.tx.us/

[27] Michigan Department of Corrections. 2006 Annual Report, pp. 35–36. http://www.michigan.gov/documents/corrections/2006_Annual_Report_255078_7.pdf

[28] Since the "deinstitutionalization" movement, many people who would have been confined in mental institutions are now confined in prisons. Ironically, as in Michigan, the buildings are the same, but the purpose and administrations have changed.

[29] http://www.michigan.gov/msi/0,1607,7-174-23873-111809--,00.html

[30] "Michigan Offenders Perform a Wide Variety of Tasks." http://www.michigan.gov/corrections/0,1607,7-119-9741_9746-21080--,00.html

[31] Prison Build Program. http://www.michigan.gov/prisonbuild/0,1607,7-252-23507_24595---,00.html

[32] Gilmore, R. W. *Golden Gulag: Prisons, Surplus, Crisis, and Opposition in Globalizing California.* Berkeley: University of California Press, 2007.

[33] http://www.cdcr.ca.gov/Visitors/Facilities/index.html

[34] For a map of California prisons see this Web site: http://www.cdcr.ca.gov/Visitors/docs/20081124-WEBmapbooklet%202.pdf. The photos available at http://www.cdcr.ca.gov/Visitors/Facilities/index.html reveal the rural nature of many of the facilities.

[35] http://www.pia.ca.gov/GeneralInfo.html

[36] The following Web site provides links to most state prison systems: http://www.corrections.com/links/show/5

[37] Huling, "Building a Prison Economy in Rural America." In Mauer and Chesney-Lind, eds., *Invisible Punishment*, p. 197.

[38] King, R. S., M. Mauer, and T. Huling (February 2003). "Big Prisons, Small Towns: Prison Economics in Rural America." Washington, DC: The Sentencing Project, p. 2.

[39] Santos, F. (January 2008). "Plan to Close Prisons Stirs Anxiety in Rural Towns." *The New York Times*. http://www.nytimes.com/2008/01/27/nyregion/27prison.html

[40] Galloway, K. and P. Kutchins (2007). *Prison Town USA* [PBS documentary]. "About the Film." http://www.pbs.org/pov/pov2007/prisontown/about.html

[41] Huling, "Building a Prison Economy in Rural America," pp. 206–207.

[42] King, Mauer, and Huling, "Big Prisons, Small Towns," p. 30.

[43] Santos, "Plan to Close Prisons Stirs Anxiety."

[44] Duke, L. (September 8, 2000). "Prison Construction Boom Transforms Small Towns." *The Washington Post.*

[45] Mauer and Chesney-Lind, eds., *Invisible Punishment.*

[46] http://www.prisongap.org/

[47] Goldfarb, Z. A. (January 30, 2006). "Census Bureau, Activists Debate How and Where to Count Inmates." *The Washington Post*, p. A15. http://www.washingtonpost.com/wp-dyn/content/article/2006/01/29/AR2006012900775.html

[48] Prison Policy Initiative (2003). "Diluting Democracy: Census Quirk Fuels Prison Expansion." Springfield, MA. http://www.prisonpolicy.org

[49] Wagner, P. (December 12, 2008). "Three Timely Actions That Could Help End Prison-Based Gerrymandering." Northampton, MA: Prison Policy Initiative. http://www.prisonersofthecensus.org/news/2008/12/12/threeactions/

[50] Roberts, S. (October 23, 2008). "Census Bureau's Counting of Prisoners Benefits Some Rural Voting Districts." *The New York Times*. http://www.nytimes.com/2008/10/24/us/politics/24census.html

[51] Richburg, K. B. (April 26, 2009). "Before Census, a Debate Over Prisoners." *The Washington Post*. http://www.washingtonpost.com/wp-dyn/content/article/2009/04/25/AR2009042501403.html

[52] Western, B. and K. Beckett. (1999). "How Unregulated Is the U.S. Labor Market? The Penal System as a Labor Market." *American Journal of Sociology* 104: 1030–1060.

[53] Maynard, M. (2000). "Prison Math." *City Beat* 21 (www.citypages.com/databank/21/1039/), emphasis added.

[54] Richburg, "Before Census, a Debate over Prisoners."

[55] Dizikes, C. (October 27, 2008). "More Felons Learning—to Their Surprise—that They Can Vote." *Los Angeles Times*. http://articles.latimes.com/2008/oct/27/nation/na-felon27

[56] Ibid.

[57] Staples, B. (February 6, 2009). "The Census: Phantom Constituents" *The New York Times*. http://theboard.blogs.nytimes.com/2009/02/06/the-census-phantom-constituents/

[58] King, Mauer, and Huling, "Big Prisons, Small Towns," p. 3.

[59] Huling, "Building a Prison Economy in Rural America," p. 199.

[60] Quoted in Huling, "Building a Prison Economy in Rural America," p. 200.

[61] Miller, S. B. (June 20, 2005). "California Prison Boom Ends, Signaling a Shift in Priorities." *The Christian Science Monitor*. http://www.csmonitor.com/2005/0620/p03s02-usju.html

[62] Galloway and Kutchins, *Prison Town USA*.

[63] Huling, "Building a Prison Economy in Rural America," p. 201.

[64] Street, "Race, Place, and the Perils of Prisonomics"; King, Mauer, and Huling, "Big Prisons, Small Towns."

[65] Huling, "Building a Prison Economy in Rural America," p. 202. I have been to Tehachapi on numerous occasions over the years and have seen this development first-hand (my parents once lived there).

[66] King, Mauer, and Huling, "Big Prisons, Small Towns," p. 2.

[67] Lawrence, S. and J. Travis. *The New Landscape of Imprisonment: Mapping America's Prison Expansion*. Washington, DC: Urban Institute, 2004, p. 3.

[68] Mosher, C., G. Hooks, and P. B. Wood. "Don't Build It Here: The Hype versus the Reality of Prisons and Local Employment." In T. Herivel and P. Wright, eds., *Prison Profiteers: Who Makes Money from Mass Incarceration*. New York: New Press, 2007, pp. 90–97.

[69] Greene, J. and V. Schiraldi (February 7, 2002). "Cutting Correctly: New Prison Policies for Times of Fiscal Crisis." Washington, DC: Justice Policy Institute. http://www.justicepolicy.org/article.php?list=type&type=24

[70] Ibid.

[71] Ibid. See also Marks, A. (January 21, 2003). "Strapped for Cash, States Set Some Felons Free." *The Christian Science Monitor*; Butterfield, F. (December 18, 2002). "Inmates Go Free to Reduce Deficits." *New York Times*.

[72] Greene, J. and T. Roche (February 20, 2003). "Cutting Correctly in Maryland." Washington, DC: Justice Policy Institute.

[73] Ibid. These states include Florida, Illinois, Michigan, Ohio, Utah, and Virginia. Other states, like New York, Texas, and Nevada, have "downsized" unneeded prison space by closing prison housing units.

[74] Associated Press (January 8, 2003). "In Illinois, Pennsylvania and Wisconsin, Newly Built Prisons Remain Shut, as States Face Budget Crunch."

[75] Newman, N. *Governing the Nation from the Statehouses: The Rightwing Agenda in the States and How Progressives Can Fight Back*. New York: Progressive States Network, 2006. http://www.progressivestates.org/content/57/governing-the-nation-from-the-statehouses

[76] Ibid.

[77] Spitzer, S. and A. T. Scull (1977). "Privatization and Capitalist Development: The Case of Private Police." *Social Problems* 25: 18–29.

[78] Dyer, J. *The Perpetual Prisoner Machine: How America Profits from Crime*. Boulder, CO: Westview Press, 2000, p. 245.

[79] Chen, S. (February 23, 2009). "Pennsylvania Rocked by 'Jailing Kids for Cash' Scandal." CNN. http://www.cnn.com/2009/CRIME/02/23/pennsylvania.corrupt.judges/index.html; "Judges Sentenced Kids for Cash." Editorial, *Philadelphia Inquirer*, January 28, 2009. http://www.philly.com/philly/opinion/inquirer/20090128_Editorial__Judges_Sentenced.html

[80] West, H. C. and W. J. Sabol (2009). "Prison Inmates at Midyear 2008—Statistical Tables." Washington, DC: Bureau of Justice Statistics. http://www.ojp.usdoj.gov/bjs/pub/pdf/pim08st.pdf

[81] Ibid., p. 23; Austin, J. and J. Irwin. *It's About Time: America's Incarceration Binge* (3rd ed.). Belmont, CA: Wadsworth, 2001, p. 66.

[82] West and Sabol, "Prison Inmates at Midyear 2008."

[83] Chen, S. (November 19, 2009). "Larger Inmate Population Is Boon to Private Prisons." *Wall Street Journal*. http://online.wsj.com/article/SB122705334657739263.html

[84] Private Correction Institute. http://www.privateci.org/lawsuits.html

[85] Corrections Corporation of America. http://www.correctionscorp.com/about/

[86] http://www.thegeogroupinc.com/

[87] Rosa, E. (March 1, 2009). "GEO Group, Inc.: Despite a Crashing Economy, Private Prison Firm Turns a Handsome Profit." *CorpWatch*. http://www.corpwatch.org/article.php?id=15308.

[88] http://www.cornellcompanies.com/

[89] Dyer, *The Perpetual Prisoner Machine*, p. 203.

[90] West, H. C. and W. J. Sabol (December 2008). "Prisoners in 2007." Revised May 12, 2009, p. 23. http://www.ojp.usdoj.gov/bjs/pub/pdf/p07.pdf

[91] Newman, *Governing the Nation from the Statehouses*.

[92] Dawson, P. (May 18, 2009). "Postcard: Hardin." *Time*, vol. 173, no. 19, p. 6.

[93] Nolan, Kelly (April 7, 2009). "Prison Health-Care Provider Cushioned in Recession." *Wall Street Journal*.

[94] von Zielbauer, P. (February 27, 2005). "As Health Care in Jails Goes Private, 10 Days Can Be a Death Sentence." *The New York Times*. http://www.nytimes.com/2005/02/27/nyregion/27jail.html

[95] Ibid.

[96] Ibid.

[97] Ibid.

[98] Ibid.

[99] Ibid.

[100] Herman, E. (March/April 1997). "Privatization: Downsizing Government for Principle and Profit." *Dollars and Sense*.

[101] In 1973, James O'Connor wrote *The Fiscal Crisis of the State* (New York: St. Martin's Press), in which he discussed two contradictory functions of the state: accumulation and legitimation. "The state attempts to support the accumulation of private capital while trying to maintain social peace and harmony. . . . Both accumulation and legitimation are translated into demands for state activity. But while this implies an increase in state expenditures, the revenues for meeting these needs are not always forthcoming, since the fruits of accumulation (greater profits) are not socialized. This is the fiscal crisis." (quoted in R. Quinney, *Class, State and Crime*, 2nd ed., New York:

Longman, 1980, p. 90). Maintaining social peace and harmony is typically translated as spending on the criminal justice system. It remains to be seen how the current "fiscal crisis" will impact the prison system.

[102] Rothfeld, M. (May 15, 2009). "Schwarzenegger Outlines Drastic Budget Cuts." *Los Angeles Times*. http://www.latimes.com/news/local/la-me-budget15-2009may15,0,6045334.story; Furillo, A. (May 14, 2009). "If Budget Ballot Measures Fail, Governor May Release 38,000 Prisoners." *Sacramento Bee*. http://www.sacbee.com/capitolandcalifornia/story/1859909.html

[103] Quoted in Miller, "California Prison Boom Ends."

[104] Ibid.

3

Jails
Temporary Housing for the Poor

During the course of a year, around millions of people will be arrested and taken to jail. This characteristically American practice reveals the strong belief in "edifices" to enforce the law through coercion. The vast majority of those who end up in a local jail do not have access to a "get out of jail free card" as in the game of Monopoly. Most arrestees have little or no capital with which to secure their release; as an old saying warns: "those without capital get punishment."

Getting In and Out of Jail: It's Not like Monopoly

Virtually every large city and small town has at least one jail. Jails are ubiquitous features of modern life. Many old jails—dating back to colonial times—often remain standing as tourist attractions. The modern jail is a purely local institution (mostly city or county operated) that in effect provides "temporary housing" for the poor. Usually you will find four types of prisoners in jails: (1) those serving short sentences for misdemeanor convictions (normally "public order" crimes like disturbing the peace, drunkenness, vagrancy, loitering, as well as petty thefts and "contempt of court"—often failure to pay traffic fines), (2) those who have been convicted of a felony and are awaiting transfer to a prison, (3) those on hold temporarily for other jurisdictions (including federal offenders) and, (4) those awaiting their final court disposition. The latter group constitutes the largest category of jail prisoners. They have not yet been found guilty (although most will eventually plead guilty), but the majority are in jail because they cannot afford bail (usually a relatively small amount of about $500). Jails are the modern-day equivalent of eighteenth and nineteenth century "poorhouses." Ronald Goldfarb described jails as "the ultimate ghetto of the criminal justice system."[1]

A cursory look at the criminal court system reveals that social class and race play a major role. The bulk of cases coming before these courts, in sharp contrast to those coming before the civil courts, involve defendants from relatively poor and low-income backgrounds. Also, like the society that surrounds it, the American bar system is itself highly stratified, with the majority of criminal defense lawyers occupying the lowest position within this hierarchical system. Thus, it is the lowest status in the field of law defending and prosecuting the lowest status in the field of law violation and being judged by the lowest status in the judiciary (local judges in municipal or justice-of-the-peace courts rank the lowest on the judicial totem pole). However, the status of those being processed is the lowest in the hierarchy; those doing the processing come mostly from higher-status backgrounds (whether measured by income, education, or other advantages).

The Historical Context

The modern jail originated in England with the Norman Conquest in the eleventh century. Under Henry II the jail (or to be more precise, the English term *gaol*) began to take on characteristics and functions that exist today. Henry II sought to establish at least one jail in each county, under the control of a local sheriff. By the thirteenth century, all but five counties had a jail. It should be noted that the county sheriff was a royal appointment, "a functionary who upheld his master's interests against local powers."[2] Social control by the king was thus relegated to the local level, thereby masking the true sources of control.

From the beginning, jails were almost exclusively used to house the poor. It was ironic that the financing of local jails depended on fees paid to jailers by those confined there when the majority of jail prisoners were drawn from the poorest classes. "Control over the prisoners' bodies was an effective means of securing credit, since all accounts had to be settled before the guest could depart"—phrased another way, fees were extracted "from misery."[3] Corruption was rampant and efforts to control the problem essentially nonexistent. Then as now, much profit was to be made from the existence of crime. The jails of London functioned as "brothels, taps, criminal clubs, and asylums for thieves, robbers, and fraudsmen, and when their raw material—prisoners—threatened to run out, minions would bring false charges to replenish the supply."[4] The well-being of prisoners was virtually ignored, and many either starved to death or died from some disease.

By the middle of the fourteenth century London jails were used as a method to extract payment from those in debt; in fact, the term *debtors' prison* was used interchangeably with jail. Since most of the people sentenced to jail could not pay their debts (they were impoverished before the sentence and any possibility of earning money to repay the debt was eliminated by the fact of being in jail), the actual function of the jail was to serve as a threat to others. Some debtors elected to remain in jail until their death, since this would thereby cancel their debt and save their families from being charged.[5] Even though technically the jailing of people because of their debts ceased to exist by the nineteenth century, many still went to jail on the charge of "contempt of court"—failure to pay a fine.

Jails in the American colonies served similar functions. Eventually they became temporary holding facilities for those awaiting court appearances or confinement facilities for people serving short sentences. Most of those who could secure their release pending their day in court did so through the system of *bail*. The use of bail dates back to early English society (at least as early as 1000 AD) and was originally established to insure that an accused appeared for trial.[6] This practice was one of the mutual responsibilities of the collective whereby groups of ten families (under the control of the "tithingman") worked together to enforce obedience to the law. The families in effect "pledged" to ensure the defendant would appear in court.[7] Crime prevention in those early years was a collective responsibility, which was very practical in small, agrarian communities. Such a concept no longer applies in modern societies, characterized by much mobility and anonymity. Bail remains a pledge—now a monetary or property payment to guarantee an appearance by the defendant. The problem is that most accused people come from the poorest sectors of society.

For centuries, jails were synonymous with what were then called *workhouses* or *poorhouses*. This function of the jail can be traced directly to the *Ordinance of Labourers* passed in England in 1349 to control vagabonds. Vagabonds—people who could but would not work—were considered a threat to social stability. Their example could entice people away from laboring at their tasks, and travelling groups of vagabonds were perceived as dangerous and threatening. The Elizabethan Poor Law of 1572 enhanced the association of jails as workhouses and grouped the "unworthy poor" with people who refused to work for prevailing wages and petty criminals. Deterrents to idleness included corporal punishment, involuntary service, and hanging.[8] In time it became difficult to distinguish between the *pauper* (the common term for a person living in poverty) and petty criminals. Eventually, in the United States, these two terms were replaced by *welfare dependent* and *petty persistent offender*, and in time even the "mentally ill."[9]

Any understanding of the role of the local jail requires some knowledge of how this institution fits into the U.S. court system itself. In the criminal justice system, the bulk of criminal cases occur within the *lower* courts where the defendant appears following an arrest. Decisions about bail are made in these courts, which could be termed "poor people's courts" because the vast majority of people who appear there are working-class poor. Numerous studies of jail populations, bail procedures, and lower court processing of cases have found that between 75% and 80% of the defendants in the criminal courts are too poor to hire their own attorneys and thus have to be provided one by the court.[10]

Pretrial Detention and Bail

Bail is a form of security that a defendant pays to guarantee that he or she will appear in court at the scheduled time. A defendant can, in effect, *buy* his or her freedom. In most jurisdictions, bail is set on misdemeanor charges by a police official, usually a desk sergeant at the station house where the defendant was booked.

According to the Fifth Amendment to the U.S. Constitution, no person can be held, "nor deprived of life, liberty, or property, without due process of law." Also, according to legal principles, one is presumed innocent until proven guilty "beyond a reasonable doubt." There can be no punishment without conviction. The reality of criminal justice is often just the opposite. On any given day, thousands of people are held in jail awaiting court appearances (sometimes for several months). They have not been proven guilty; they are jailed because they cannot afford bail; many are locked up because they are deemed "dangerous."

In most courts there are clearly established procedures for releasing a defendant. If the charge is a minor misdemeanor, the individual is usually released almost immediately by posting bail at the police station according to a predetermined *bail schedule*, which provides a monetary amount needed to secure one's release.

For more serious misdemeanors and felonies, the accused stands before a judge during the *initial appearance*. According to the Sixth Amendment to the Constitution a defendant cannot be held for an indefinite period of time without a court appearance. In *Mallory v. United States,* the Supreme Court ruled that a suspect must come before a judge "as soon as possible" following an arrest.[11] In practice this usually means the next working day (or if the arrest was made on the weekend, the following Monday morning). The main purpose of this hearing is to arrange for some form of *pretrial release*. The judge usually refers to the bail schedule and sets bail accordingly. In more serious cases, the defendant along with his or her attorney and the prosecutor argue whether or not the individual should be released on bail.

There are four major ways to secure one's release following an arrest: (1) release on personal recognizance without having to post bond (usually reserved for persons charged with minor crimes or for prominent citizens of a community); (2) posting a cash bond for the full amount of the bail; (3) posting a property bond (e.g., a home) as collateral; (4) using the services of a bail bondsman. The defendant pays the bondsman a certain percentage (typically 10%) of the bond (which is usually not refundable) and is allowed to go free. Most defendants use a bail bondsman because cash bonds and property bonds require a sizable amount of cash and/or property, which most defendants do not have.[12] In 2004, felony defendants were most likely to be released on commercial surety bond (43% of all releases), followed by personal recognizance (25%), conditional release (16%), and deposit bond (9%).[13]

The amount of bail is supposed to be set according to the likelihood of the defendant's appearing in court and/or the seriousness of the crime. In most states the maximum and minimum amounts of bail are set by law for each type of crime (e.g., not less than $5,000 or more than $15,000 for robbery). Sometimes judges develop their own criteria for determining the amount of bail. The result is often a great deal of variation from one judge to another.

Some may argue that in addition to the seriousness of the offense, factors such as prior records, the strength of the case, and an individual's ties to the community (e.g., job, how long in residence) are considered when judges set bail. In the majority of cases, the real reason people are held in jail awaiting trial is that they simply cannot afford to post the bond, not because they are dangerous or are likely to commit further crimes.

An interesting study looked at compliance with a bail schedule. It examined whether or not the amount of bail required was below, above, or within the amount in the schedule. There were significant differences based on both race and gender. Whites and females were far more likely than minorities and males to receive bail that was below the schedule amount. Just over one-fifth of whites (21.3%) compared to only 12.5% of minorities received bail below the schedule (minorities were slightly more likely to receive bail in an amount above the bail schedule); more than one-fourth of the females (26.9%) had bail below the schedule amount, compared to only 15.5% of the males. This relationship remained regardless of other factors (e.g., seriousness of the offense, prior criminal record).[14] In a comparison of defendants brought to court on violent felonies in Detroit, it was found that 71% of African Americans compared to only 53% of whites were detained. The final outcome: 88% of those detained were sent to prison, compared to only 45% of those not detained.[15]

Race may at times interact with other variables that are themselves directly related to the amount of bail imposed. One study found that when comparing both African Americans and whites who had private attorneys, the amount of bail was greater for African Americans.[16] Many studies have shown that employment status is directly related to being out on bail—employed defendants are far more likely to be granted low bail or to be released on their own recognizance. A class-action lawsuit filed in New York City in the 1960s resulted in a detailed study of the granting of release, either on bail or on recognizance. Almost half (46%) of the employed defendants were released pending the outcome of their case, compared to just over one-fourth (26%) of the unemployed[17] A study conducted in the early 1990s found that African Americans who were unemployed were the most likely to be detained.[18] Still another study found that having a prior felony conviction more adversely affected African Americans than whites and that having more education and a higher income had a more positive effect for whites than African Americans.[19] This research highlights the functioning of jails as modern-day poorhouses.[20]

There are many cases in which bail could be equated to a ransom. For example, a Hispanic health-care worker in New York was charged with sexually assaulting the quadriplegic man for whom he worked. He was unable to raise the $5,000 for his bail. Because he refused to plead guilty, he spent 19 months in jail awaiting his trial. He was found not guilty; ironically, he spent more time in jail awaiting the disposition than he would have spent had he pled guilty to a lesser charge. A public defender eventually discovered that the alleged victim repeatedly had made complaints to the home care agency about workers hired for his care.[21] If the defender's caseload had not been so overloaded, he might have made the discovery earlier and saved his client the trauma of being jailed—guilty only of not being able to afford bail or a private attorney.

FREEDOM FOR SALE: THE BAIL BONDSMAN

Storefront offices with signs announcing "Bail Bonds, 24-Hour Service" or "Freedom for Sale" are commonplace around most courthouses and jails. The bail bondsman is often a shrewd businessman who profits from crime. He (or she) plays a role in deciding whether or not a defendant goes free. Once bail is set, the bondsman decides whether to lend the money to the suspect and what collateral to require to protect his investment.[22] The bail bondsman must contribute 10% of the premiums he collects to a reserve fund, and the company levies another 20% for posting the bond. That leaves the bondsman with a 70% profit on all premiums he collects from defendants.

Bail bondsmen have developed a close working relationship with others in the criminal justice system. They essentially help manage the population of arrested persons by screening defendants and releasing those they consider to be good risks—thus reducing congestion in the jails. This relationship appears to be reciprocal, since judges routinely do not pressure bondsmen to make good on bonds that are forfeited because the defendants did not show up for court. (The entire bond is forfeited and owed to the court if a defendant fails to appear for trial or other court appearance.) Bondsmen also have become part of the "courtroom workgroup" and are on a first-name basis with many of the court actors. They are sometimes financial contributors to judges' reelection campaign.[23]

Since only a small percentage of defendants fail to show up for court, bondsmen can make a lot of money. Companies advertise on radio and on billboards. "Bail Row" in Los Angeles is a "trash-blown block of downtown where the competition for freedom-buyers is as cut-throat as it gets."[24] In one block directly across the street from the downtown Los Angeles County jail complex (two huge jails that daily hold more than 20,000 prisoners) there are a dozen bond offices that "engage in a kind of urban combat for every dollar." Two other companies have found a very lucrative side business—towing illegally parked cars owned by people trying to bail out friends and family. During the past decade the number of bail bondsmen in California has doubled (to about 2,200), while the average bond in Los Angeles County has quadrupled from $5,000 to $20,000. Since a defendant must post 10% of the amount of the bond, they need between $500 and $2,000—totally out of the question for the majority of those arrested.

Many critics over the years have complained about the often shady practices of bail bondsmen, especially when they hire "bounty hunters" to track down those who skip town (there have been many cases of bounty hunters breaking into homes of suspected bail-jumpers, only to discover that they had the wrong address—in some notorious cases the occupants of the house have been killed). Bail bondsmen have been linked to many corrupt practices, such as paying "under-the-table" referral fees to lawyers, police, and sometimes judges who send them "business" (the "client" being offenders and their families and friends). Such practices have resulted in at least five states abolishing bail bonding for profit (Kentucky, Oregon, Wisconsin, Nebraska, and Illinois).[25]

LOCKING UP THE "DANGEROUS": PREVENTIVE DETENTION

One of the most controversial features of the criminal justice system is the practice known as pretrial preventive detention. This is the practice of refusing to grant bail to defendants who are declared "dangerous" and who present a clear danger to the community. The practice was introduced in 1970 as part of the District of Columbia Crime Bill.

Preventive detention is based on the unproven assumption that there is a way to predict who will and who will not commit a crime if released. Perhaps the most controversial part of this practice surrounds the term "dangerous." Who is dangerous and how do you objectively determine this trait? In one of the earliest critiques of preventive detention, the American Friends Service Committee asserted in the early 1970s that such a term has historically been reserved for those who in some way challenge existing power relationships. In *Struggle for Justice* the Committee wrote:

Those persons or groups that threaten the existing power structure are dangerous. In any historical period, to identify an individual whose status is that of a member of the "dangerous classes," the label "criminal" has been handy. The construct, criminal, is not used to classify the performers of all legally defined delicts [offenses against the law], only those whose position in the social structure qualifies them for membership in the dangerous classes.[26] National data provide support for the view that most jail inmates are not dangerous. Looking only at the most serious charges (almost 60,000 felony cases) filed in the nation's 75 largest counties in 2004, more than a third of the defendants (37%) were charged with a drug offense, and 31% were charged with a property offense (burglary 8% and larceny 8%). About 25% of the defendants were charged with a violent offense, usually robbery or assault. Less than 1% of defendants were charged with murder (0.6%) or rape (0.9%). About 10% of felony defendants were charged with a public-order offense (3% driving-related and 3% weapons-related).[27] The most recent report on jail inmates comes from a 2002 report comparing data from 1983 and 2002. The most significant change over this time period was with drug offenses—less than 10% of all offenders in 1983 versus 37% in 2002. Another noteworthy change was the decline in the violent offense category, dropping from about 31% to 25%.[28]

The majority of those booked into jail are released before the final disposition of their case. In 2004, 57% of felony defendants received a pretrial release prior to adjudication; of the 43% detained, 6% were denied bail. Murder defendants (88%) were the most likely to be detained, followed by defendants charged with motor vehicle theft (61%), robbery (58%), or burglary (54%). Defendants on parole (83%) were the most likely to be detained, and 58% of defendants with an active criminal justice status were more likely to be detained than those without such a status (33%). About 35% of released defendants committed one or more types of pretrial misconduct while in a release status. Among those released, 21% failed to appear in court as scheduled, and 21% were arrested for a new offense.[29] Despite the seriousness of some of these crimes, many of the defendants were released—which raises the question: Who is designated as dangerous and why?

SOME EFFECTS OF AWAITING TRIAL IN JAIL

Awaiting trial in jail has proven to have many disadvantages. Defendants cannot help find witnesses and/or evidence; attorneys face restrictions on the amount of time they can spend with their jailed clients; defendants are separated from their families and their jobs (if they have jobs, they may lose them). In addition, the inability to make bail is a form of sentence, or "punishment without conviction." Time spent in jail can count as time served—and can be used as an incentive to accept a plea. If a defendant with no means of posting bail has been jailed for two months, the prosecutor can offer a deal and request a sentence of time served. The arrestee is faced with a choice between pleading guilty and leaving jail immediately (although with a criminal record) or remaining in jail in hopes of proving his or her innocence.[30]

There is also a qualitative effect of not making bail, especially the image the defendant makes in court. Although his study is somewhat dated, Skolnick's observation of more than 30 years ago seems just as relevant today:

> The man in jail enters the courtroom under guard, from the jail entrance, his hair has been cut by the jail barber, he often wears the clothes he was arrested in. By contrast, the civilian defendant usually makes a neat appearance, and enters the courtroom from the spectators' seats, emerging from the ranks of the public.[31]

A more important disadvantage of awaiting trial in jail involves the sentence. Several studies, spanning four decades, have shown that those awaiting trial in jail receive longer sentences than those out on bail.[32] (Remember, making bail has little relationship to the seriousness of the offense. It depends almost entirely on the defendant's economic resources and race.) In a study conducted in the early 1960s it was found that of those convicted, 64% of those detained were sentenced to prison, compared to only 17% of those at liberty. It was also found that 47% of those at liberty were acquitted or dismissed, compared to only 27% of those detained.[33] The class-action suit in New York City mentioned above found that, even when controlling for such variables as prior record, current offense, employment status, and other factors, those who were detained fared far worse in the degree of punishment received than those released.[34] More recent studies have arrived at almost identical conclusions. A study in Detroit found that the incarceration rate for those detained was 88%, compared to only 45% of those released. A study in Connecticut arrived at similar conclusions.[35]

It should be obvious at this juncture that the "blind lady of justice" that graces most courthouses is not so blind after all. By the time the sentencing stage of the criminal justice process is reached, the defendants are primarily minorities and of lower socioeconomic status who have spent a considerable amount of time behind bars awaiting their fate in court.

Who Is in Jail?

In June 2007 there were 780,581 prisoners held in local jails; 62% (483,700) had not been convicted of a crime. Nearly 6 in 10 offenders in local jails were minorities: 301,900 (38.7%) were black and 125,600 (16.1%) were Hispanic. The incarceration rate was 259 per 100,000 population.[36] The jail population reported at midyear 2007 is based on "one-day counts" of prisoners in randomly selected jails around the country. Considerably more individuals see the inside of a jail during the course of a given year. An estimated 13 million people were admitted to local jails over the previous 12-month period.[37] About 10% of the adult population will spend some time in jail during the course of a year—and the percentage rises to almost 33% for African American males.[38]

At the beginning of the chapter, we discussed jails as the modern equivalent of poorhouses or as the "ghetto" of the criminal justice system." Some of the adjectives used to describe contemporary American jails include: degrading, filthy, inhumane, and human jungles. Many "blue-ribbon" commissions have documented terrible conditions over the years, and there have been exposes in newspapers and other media dating back as far as the 1930s.[39] Jails in other countries do not fare much better, as recent reports from England and Canada reveal.[40]

There have been a number of lawsuits filed on behalf of jail inmates for various conditions, including overcrowding, abuse, assaults, sexual harassment, and lack of access to legal help. Inadequate medical care is the most common complaint. A number of jurisdictions are under some form of court orders or consent decrees to limit the population and/or to improve conditions of jails and prisons.[41] In Pennsylvania, "many local jails are struggling to meet even minimum standards for safety, housing, food quality, and medical care."[42] Conditions have been so bad that states paid to confine prisoners from other states in local jails have been sued and ordered to return the prisoners to their original states.[43] Sixteen of the 50 largest local jail jurisdictions were operating over capacity in 2007. Maricopa County was at 130% and Denver County at 139.[44]

In many jails housing huge populations (such as Cook County Jail in Chicago, the Tombs in New York City, and the downtown facility in Los Angeles) gang rapes, assaults, suicide, and many other forms of violence are common. Officials cite lack of staff and overcrowding as the primary source of problems. "Overall, Los Angeles County has fewer than 3,000 deputies and civilian assistants to police a jail system with 21,000 inmates a day. Cook County has 2,900 correctional officers for 10,000 inmates."[45] Poor food, unsanitary living conditions, inadequate medical facilities, lack of recreational and educational opportunities, lack of treatment programs (especially for drugs and alcohol), harsh disciplinary practices, and abuse from staff are some of the more frequent problems in jails.[46]

In a 1997 consent decree, the Department of Justice detailed "numerous alleged constitutional deficiencies with regard to mental health care, including inadequate (1) intake screening and evaluation, (2) diagnosis, (3) referral to mental health professionals, (4) treatment plans, (5) administration of medications, (6) suicide prevention, (7) tracking and medical record keeping, (8) staffing, (9) communication, and (10) quality assurance in the Los Angeles jail system. The report also noted that Los Angeles had mistreated and abused mentally ill inmates, including using excessive force and improper restraint practices."[47]

Incidents continue to surface. In the winter of 2006, a series of riots occurred in the L.A. jails. The stabbing of a Latino prisoner at the main jail in downtown Los Angeles precipitated a lockdown of the entire county jail system. Two days later, a riot began at a jail housing 4,000 inmates in Castaic. One prisoner was killed, and at least 50 were seriously injured.[48] Fighting broke out the next day at the main jail downtown. Rioting involving 80 prisoners continued two days later at the Castaic facility. The next day 450 prisoners at another jail facility rioted. Because of overcrowding, officials had resorted to using dorm-like living conditions, with "violent inmates living in large, open rooms despite wide agreement nationally that such offenders should be held in cells."[49] As many as 100 prisoners are crowded into these dorms.[50]

Jail conditions have not changed much over the years. Almost 40 years ago Jessica Mitford reported on an experiment involving judges, prosecutors, policemen, and women, lawyers, and others who volunteered to spend a day and a night in Washington DC's Lorton Jail.[51] Mitford did her "time" in the Women's Detention Center. She found that the usual procedure during what is known as "reception" included vaginal checks (to look for contraband drugs), heads examined for lice, spraying with Lysol, and other degrading ceremonies. There were many petty rules and regulations (including one against talking "too loud"), and there were bed checks at odd hours. Infractions of rules resulted in disciplinary measures including being sent to "Adjustment" (a euphemism for "the hole" or "solitary").

Mitford concluded that jails such as Lorton are a "life of planned, unrelieved inactivity and boredom . . . no overt brutality but plenty of random, largely unintentional cruelty . . . a pervasive sense of helplessness and frustration engulfing not only the inmates but their keepers, themselves trapped in the weird complex of paradoxes that is the prison world."[52] One of the judges who participated in the experiment declared: "We wouldn't stand for having the bears in the zoo treated as we treat the men in Lorton."[53] Mitford discovered that few of the *women* at Lorton had been charged with serious crimes, the majority having been accused of prostitution and drug offenses. She wrote: "Is this not the essence of women's prisons, the punishment of unchaste, unwomanly behavior, a grotesque bow to long-outmoded nineteenth century notions of feminine morality?"[54]

The Bureau of Justice Statistics reports that approximately 64% of all jail inmates are suffering from a serious form of mental illness (for state prisons the percentage was 56). Among the major depressive or mania symptoms inmates suffered were "persistent sad, numb or empty mood," "insomnia or hypersomnia," "psychomotor agitation or retardation," "feelings of worthlessness or excessive guilt," and "persistent anger or irritability." Almost one-fifth (17.5%) suffered from delusions, and another 13.7% suffered from hallucinations. Well over half (60.5%) had symptoms of mental health disorders during the previous 12 months (major depressive disorder, mania disorder, and psychotic disorder); in contrast, only about 10% of the U.S. population suffered from such disorders. Those who suffered from these disorders were far more likely to have experienced physical and sexual abuse and to have abused drugs and alcohol than those without such disorders. Also, such prisoners had more prior experiences with the criminal justice system than those who did not suffer from such disorders. Few of them had received any treatment during the year prior to their most recent arrest.[55]

Psychiatrist Marcia Goin describes the deinstitutionalization of mental patients and the unintended consequences.

> Before the 1960s, people with mental illnesses were generally cared for in institutional settings, mostly state-run psychiatric facilities. Many advocates correctly saw this as "warehousing" people who could be cared for in less restrictive settings. Federal legislation and the courts powered a move toward deinstitutionalization, calling on states and counties to provide resources for social services, vocational rehabilitation and treatment services. . . . Deinstitutionalization has succeeded in decreasing the overall number of hospital beds, but an unforeseen consequence has been the proportional increase in the number of people with mental illnesses housed in the criminal justice system. Worse, once imprisoned, people with mental illness are shown to have much longer incarcerations than other inmates, primarily because a prison environment and lack of treatment aggravate the very illness that has led to their objectionable or antisocial behavior.[56]

Goin notes that the Los Angeles County Jail houses the largest psychiatric population in the country and comments: "That's not justice. That's emblematic of a national emergency."[57] She urges people to consider whether the justice system's role is solely to impose punishment that seeks retribution or whether justice would be better served in some cases through effective treatment and rehabilitation.

In effect, deinstitutionalization has been replaced by the "criminalization of mental illness" and these inmates receive little or no treatment. This view has been supported by numerous reports. Jamie Fellner, the director of Human Rights Watch, observes:

> Prisons now house three times more people with serious mental illness . . . [who] end up in prison because the community mental health systems are in shambles—fragmented, underfunded and unable to serve the poor, the homeless and those who are substance-addicted as well as mentally ill. Nationwide, half of the state inmates with mental health problems were convicted of nonviolent

offenses, primarily low-level drug and property offenses. Alternatives to incarceration may have been appropriate, but the court's hands are tied by mandatory sentencing laws. Once behind bars, the mentally ill find themselves ill-equipped to handle the stresses and rules—formal and informal—of prison life. They are more likely to be victimized and more likely to be injured in a fight than other inmates. They are more likely to break the rules. They are more likely to behave in ways that annoy, disgust and even enrage security staff who have scant training in how to recognize, much less cope with, symptoms of mental illness. Moreover, prison mental health services across the country are woefully deficient, crippled by understaffing, insufficient facilities and limited programs, and swamped by the sheer number of prisoners who need them. Lacking resources and options, prison officials put problem prisoners, including the mentally ill, in segregation, where by virtue of being locked up around the clock they cause less trouble.[58]

Reports from virtually every part of the country confirm the seriousness of the problems. In Lawrence, Kansas, for example, the local jail faces continuing demands on its limited resources. Undersheriff Kenny Massey stated: "We've become the mental health unit of Douglas County. We deal with a lot of people here who really ought to be dealt with somewhere else. We're not set up for this." When inmates with mental health problems are released, they often have no place to go, no support system, and usually still suffer from the conditions that caused the behavior leading to the original arrest; the jail is a revolving door in this persistent downward cycle.[59]

HIV/AIDS is 2.5 times more prevalent in inmates than in the general population. "About one-fourth of all people living with HIV in the United States in a given year pass through a correctional facility in that same year."[60]. For the prison population as a whole,[61] 20,450 state prisoners were HIV positive or had confirmed AIDS in 2006 (a decrease from 21,084 in 2005). Half of all cases were in the South, nearly a third in the Northeast, and about a tenth in both the Midwest and the West. The Northeast reported the largest percentage of HIV/AIDS (3.6% of its custody population). Sixteen states and the federal prison system reported a decrease in the number of HIV-positive inmates; 25 states reported an increase.[62]

> Despite the growing realization that HIV/AIDS among inmates represented an important public health as well as correctional or criminal justice problem, many of the issues surrounding HIV/AIDS in correctional populations have been almost from the beginning and still remain controversial. These include the extent of HIV transmission among inmates and related policy choices, the acceptability and advisability of mandatory or routine HIV testing, the appropriateness of making condoms available to inmates for use in correctional facilities, access to medical treatment and related HIV/AIDS

services, and the importance and elements of discharge planning and transitional programs for inmates with HIV being released to the community.[63]

The Functions of Jails: Managing the "Rabble" Class

The typical jail population has been described variously as "catchall asylums for poor people," the "social refuse," "social junk," "riffraff," "social trash," "dregs," and many other degrading, descriptions.[64] After a detailed study of the San Francisco City Jail, John Irwin concluded that most jail prisoners have two essential characteristics, which he calls *detachment* and *disrepute*. He suggests that the prisoners are detached in the sense that they are not well integrated into mainstream society; they are not members of conventional social organizations; they have few ties to conventional social networks; and they have unconventional values and beliefs.[65] Irwin uses disrepute to mean that prisoners are perceived as "offensive," "irksome," and often threatening. While the public impression is that jails hold dangerous people, Irwin points out that most of the people in jail are not predators. Rather, they are poor, undereducated, unemployed, and minorities. Society often uses terms such as "street people" or the even more degrading "social trash." Irwin chose the term *rabble* to describe those from the lowest classes whose detachment and disrepute often lead to being jailed.

The characteristics of detachment and disrepute play a significant role in who is arrested and convicted in addition to the crime committed. "Society's impulse to manage the rabble has many sources, but the subjectively perceived 'offensiveness' of the rabble is at least as important as any real threat it poses to society."[66] The most serious of this class—those who commit serious violent and property crimes—are eventually sent to prison. "Usually the more violent and rapacious rabble are arrested, convicted, and sent to prison; the merely offensive are held in jail. The jail was devised as, and continues to be, the special social device for controlling offensive rabble." In addition, the jail functions as a "subsidiary" of a much larger "welfare system" that serves to "regulate the poor."[67]

Irwin emphasizes that he is not suggesting crime is not an issue but that he believes that culpability, in the words of Egon Bittner, has "restricted relevance."

> It is not simply the fact of theft that provokes arrest; it is who commits the theft and what type of theft it is. Our society—like its predecessors, chiefly England—has been quicker to criminalize covetous property accumulation by the rabble than by other classes. The police are always on the lookout for purse-snatching, theft from cars, and shoplifting, but they almost never patrol used-car lots or

automobile repair shops to catch salesmen or repairmen breaking the law, and they never raid corporate board rooms to catch executives fixing prices. The difference between these crimes is not seriousness or prevalence, it is offensiveness, which is determined by social status and context.[68]

Jerome Miller conducted a similar study in Jacksonville, Florida.[69] Miller had been appointed by a federal court to monitor jail overcrowding in Duval County. He had access to police summaries of every arrest and to the criminal histories of jailed prisoners, allowing him to analyze who was jailed for what crimes.

> The best face one could put on these patterns was that the criminal justice system was being inappropriately applied to the wide range of personal and social problems that afflict the cantankerous poor and minorities. It all gave validity to sociologist John Irwin's unhappy characterization of jails as places of "rabble management.[70]

In both Jacksonville and San Francisco, the majority of the offenses committed by jail prisoners were rather petty in nature. Irwin conducted extensive interviews with many of these prisoners. Using a seriousness scale devised by several prominent criminologists,[71] Irwin determined the degree of seriousness of the charges against those confined in the jail. He determined that only a very small percentage of crimes could be categorized as "serious" (around 4%), while the vast majority were "petty" (scoring from 0 to 5 on a seriousness scale that goes as high as 35.7). In fact, the average seriousness score from Irwin's sample was around 3.[72]

Irwin then classified the prisoners according to one of several types, the most common of which were what he termed "petty hustlers," who represented 29% of his felony sample. This type was followed in frequency by "derelicts" and "corner boys" (each at 14%, for a total of 28%), followed by "aliens" (9%), "junkies," "gays," and "square johns" (each constituting 6%), and "outlaws" (really serious types, 4%), "lowriders" (4%), and "crazies" (4%). Most of these individuals (57%) represented a mild degree of offensiveness and committed mostly petty crimes.[73]

Miller introduced his study with the following comments:

> Most of the frenetic criminal justice handling in the country is concerned with minor incidents, many of which could be dealt with in manner far short of arrest and jailing. Often this has less to do with the seriousness of the behavior or the dangerousness of the alleged perpetrator than it has to do with some other vague point like "upholding the integrity of the system" [nontechnical violations of conditions of misdemeanor probation]. . . . The fact that there were a host of alternative strategies and tactics immediately at hand by which defendants could be encouraged to fulfill these legal obligations seemed not to matter. It mattered even less as the potentially arrestable moved down the socioeconomic ladder. (p. 1)

Some Concluding Thoughts

Miller summarized his findings about the Jacksonville jail with these comments: "Despite its pretensions, modern criminal justice is no more about crime control than it is about rehabilitation. Nor is it about deterrence. None of that matters. Rather, it is increasingly about identifying and managing unruly groups."[74]

Clearly, most jail prisoners do not fit the popular image of the "dangerous felon" so often portrayed by the media and politicians. In 2007, 15.5% of arrests (2.2 million) were for index crimes. Ten million people were arrested for nonindex crimes, including vandalism, prostitution, gambling, disorderly conduct, and suspicion—and almost 2 million more for drug violations (13% of all arrests).[75] Too frequently, local campaigns to expand jail capacities and to build more jails are based on misconceptions of dangerousness, often advanced by those with vested interests in building new jails.[76] Many of the people confined in jail will be released within two to three days, including some charged with serious crimes, such as homicide, rape, robbery and assault—once again suggesting that "dangerous" is defined and redefined to suit a particular purpose.

The chapter began with a brief history of the jail and its description as a debtors' prison. The subheading of an article in 2009 suggests times have not changed radically: "Shades of Charles Dickens, critics say the controversial measures create debtors prisons."[77] The measures included charging jail inmates $45 per night in the new $27-million jail in Taney County, Missouri; charging $60 in Springfield, Oregon; billing $1.25 daily for meals in Maricopa County, Arizona; proposals to charge daily fees of $10 to $15 in New Jersey and Pennsylvania; and a $30 booking fee for medical charges in Richland County, Ohio. While states and counties face mounting deficits, critics say the idea of expecting prisoners to pay is absurd. Sean O'Brien, formerly the chief public defender in Kansas City, Missouri, and now a law professor, says the idea of user fees for jails may sound appealing in the abstract but unfairly affects struggling families. "They're typically poor people anyway from poor families, and when you take $45 a day from them that's money that doesn't go for groceries or rent. . . . Really it's a poor person's tax."[78]

NOTES

[1] Goldfarb, R. *Jails: The Ultimate Ghetto of the Criminal Justice System.* New York: Doubleday, 1975; see also Goldfarb, R. *Ransom: A Critique of the American Bail System.* New York: Harper & Row, 1965.

[2] McConville, S. "Local Justice: The Jail," p. 299. In N. Morris and D. J. Rothman, eds., *The Oxford History of the Prison.* New York: Oxford University Press, 1995, pp. 297–327.

[3] Ibid., p. 300.

4 Ibid., p. 301.

5 Ibid., p. 301.

6 Goldfarb, *Jails.*

7 McConville, "Local Justice," p. 311. See also Shelden, R. G. *Controlling the Dangerous Classes: A History of Criminal Justice in America* (2nd ed.). Boston: Allyn & Bacon, 2008.

8 Ibid., pp. 313–314.

9 For a detailed discussion of the law of vagrancy, see Shelden, *Controlling the Dangerous Classes*, chapter 1; and Chambliss, W. (1964). "The Law of Vagrancy." *Sociological Analysis of Social Problems* 12: 67–77.

10 Reiman, J. H. *The Rich Get Richer and the Poor Get Prison* (8th ed.). Boston: Allyn & Bacon, 2007, pp. 129–131; Cole, D. *No Equal Justice: Race and Class in the American Criminal Justice System.* New York: The New Press, 1999; Chiricos, T. G. and W. Bales (November 1991). "Unemployment and Punishment: An Empirical Analysis." *Criminology* 29; Wice, P. B. *Chaos in the Courthouse: The Inner Workings of the Urban Criminal Courts.* New York: Praeger, 1985.

11 354 U.S. 455, 1957.

12 Shelden, R. G., W. B. Brown, R. Fritzler, and K. Miller. *Criminal Justice in American Society.* Long Grove, IL: Waveland Press, 2008, p. 183.

13 Kyckelhahn, T. and T. H. Cohen. *Felony Defendants in Large Urban Counties, 2004.* Washington, DC: Bureau of Justice Statistics NCJ 221152, April 2008, p. 2.

14 Patterson, E. B. and M. J. Lynch. "Biases in Formalized Bail Procedures." In M. J. Lynch and E. B. Patterson, eds., *Race and Criminal Justice.* New York: Harrow and Heston, 1992, pp. 36–53.

15 Walker, S., C. Spohn, and M. DeLone. *The Color of Justice: Race, Ethnicity, and Crime in America* (4th ed.). Belmont, CA: Wadsworth, 2007, p. 130.

16 Farnworth, M. and P. Horan (1980). "Separate Justice: An Analysis of Race Differences in Court Processes." *Social Science Research* 9: 381–399.

17 Single, E. (July–August 1972). "The Unconstitutional Administration of Bail: *Bellamy v. The Judges of New York City.*" *Criminal Law Bulletin* 8 (6): 459–513.

18 Chiricos, T. G. and W. Bales (November 1991). "Unemployment and Punishment: An Empirical Analysis." *Criminology* 29.

19 Albonetti, C. A., R. M. Hauser, J. Hagan, and I. H. Nagel (1989). "Criminal Justice Decision Making as a Stratification Process: The Role of Race and Stratification Resources in Pretrial Release." *Journal of Quantitative Criminology* 5: 57–82.

20 For an excellent study of poorhouses see Wagner, D. *The Poorhouse: America's Forgotten Institution.* New York: Rowman & Littlefield, 2005, p. 3. In this study Wagner found that many American institutional settings evolved from the poorhouse, including prisons and jails, orphanages, mental institutions, and the like.

21 Finder, A. (June 6, 1999). "Jailed Until Found Not Guilty." *The New York Times*, pp. 33–34.

22 Dill, F. (1975). "Discretion, Exchange, and Social Control: Bail Bondsmen in Criminal Courts." *Law and Society Review* 9: 639–674.

23 Shelden et al., *Criminal Justice in American Society*, p. 184.

24 Pringle, P. (March 25, 2005). "It's Brutal in the Bail Business" *Los Angeles Times.*

25 Shelden et al., *Criminal Justice in American Society*, p. 184. See also Wice, *Chaos in the Courthouse.*

26 American Friends Service Committee. *Struggle for Justice.* New York: Hill & Wang, 1971, pp. 77–78.

27 Kyckelhahn and Cohen, *Felony Defendants*, p. 2.

28 This report is obviously dated, but it was the most recent available as of the summer of 2009 when this chapter was written. The report can be seen at: http://www.ojp.usdoj.gov/bjs/pub/pdf/pji02.pdf

29 Ibid.

30 Reiman, *The Rich Get Richer*, pp. 129–130.

31 Skolnick, J. *Justice without Trial.* New York: John Wiley, 1967, p. 263.

[32] These studies are too numerous to summarize in their entirety here, so only a few representative samples are included. One of the earliest studies ever (regarded by many as a classic in the field of criminology) is Foote, C. (1956). "Vagrancy-Type Law and Its Administration." *University of Pennsylvania Law Review* 104 (March): 603–650; others include: Ares, C. E., A. Rankin, and H. Sturz (1963). "The Manhattan Bail Project: An Interim Report on the Use of Pre-Trial Parole," *New York University Law Review* 38 (January): 71–92; Suffet, F. (1966). "Bail Setting: A Study of Courtroom Interaction," *Crime and Delinquency* 12 (October): 318–331.

[33] Rankin, A. (1964). "The Effect of Pretrial Detention." *New York University Law Review* 39 (June): 641–655.

[34] Single, "The Unconstitutional Administration of Bail."

[35] Walker et al., *The Color of Justice*, pp. 130–131; Donziger, S. R. *The Real War on Crime*. New York: Harper/Collins, 1996, p. 111.

[36] Sabol, W. J. and T. D. Minton (June 2008). "Prison and Jail Inmates at Midyear 2007." Washington, DC: Department of Justice, Bureau of Justice Statistics, p. 5.

[37] Ibid.

[38] Miller, J. *Search and Destroy: African-American Males in the Criminal Justice System*. New York: Cambridge University Press, 1996; Mauer, M. *Race to Incarcerate* (2nd ed.). New York: The New Press, 2006.

[39] President's Commission on Law and Administration of Justice. *Task Force Report: Corrections*. Washington, DC: U.S. Government Printing Office, 1967; U.S. National Commission on Law Observance and Enforcement (Wickersham Commission). *Reports*. Washington, DC: U.S. Government Printing Office, 1931.

[40] Bromley Briefings Prison Factfile (June 2008). London. http://www.prisonreformtrust.org.uk/temp/FactfilespPROOFspJUNE08small.pdf; National Union of Public and General Employees. "Ontario Judge Opens Hearing into Inhuman Ottawa Jail." http://www.nupge.ca/news_2004/n04no04a.htm

[41] See http://www.usdoj.gov/crt/casebrief.php for special litigation involving institutionalized persons. You can search investigative findings, complaints, briefs, and settlements/consent decrees/judgments; see also ACLU (October 22, 2008). "Judge Calls Maricopa County Jail Conditions Unconstitutional." Maricopa County, Arizona. http://www.aclu.org/prison/conditions/37322prs20081022.html; and Roderick MacCarthur Justice Center (February 1, 2008). Judge to Investigate Cook County Jail Conditions. http://www.law.northwestern.edu/macarthur/treatment/overcrowding.html

[42] Scolforo, M. (December 20, 2005). "PA county prisons struggle to meet standards." Associated Press. http://realcostofprisons.org/blog/archives/2005/12/pa_68_county_ja.html

[43] Shelden et al., *Criminal Justice in American Society*, p. 251.

[44] Sabol and Minton, "Prison and Jail Inmates at Midyear 2007," p. 4.

[45] Bernstein, S. and M. Garvey (February 12, 2006). "Dorms Fuel Jail Unrest." *Los Angeles Times*. http://articles.latimes.com/2006/feb/12/local/me-jails12

[46] Shelden et al., *Criminal Justice in American Society*, pp. 250–252.

[47] Memorandum of Agreement between the United States and Los Angeles County, California Regarding Mental Health Services at the Los Angeles County Jail. http://www.usdoj.gov/crt/split/documents/lacountyjail_mh.htm; see also Domanick, J. (June 6, 2004). "After 12 Years, Handcuffs Stay on LAPD Reform; Blame a Resistant Culture and Bratton—And Don't Spare the City Council," *Los Angeles Times*.

[48] Guccione, J., S. Pfeifer, and R. Connell (February 5, 2006). "1 Killed, 50 Hurt in County Jail Race Riot." *Los Angeles Times*.

[49] Bernstein and Garvey, "Dorms Fuel Jail Unrest"; Pfeifer, S. and J. Garrison. (February 6, 2006). "Sheriff Blames Lack of Staff for Jail Riot." *Los Angeles Times*. http://articles.latimes.com/2006/feb/06/local/me-riot6

[50] Pierson, D. and M. Garvey (February 8, 2006). "Unrest Flares Up Again at L.A. County Jail." *Los Angeles Times*; Pfeifer, S. and J. Garrison (February 6, 2006). "L.A. County Jails Quiet after Flare-Up of Violence." *Los Angeles Times*.

[51] Mitford, J. *Kind and Usual Punishment.* New York: Vintage Books, 1974, pp. 29–30.

[52] Ibid., p. 30.

[53] Ibid., p. 31.

[54] Ibid., p. 30.

[55] James, D. L. and L. E. Glaze (September 2006). "Mental Health Problems of Prison and Jail Inmates." Washington, DC: Department of Justice, Bureau of Justice Statistics. http://www.ojp.usdoj.gov/bjs/pub/pdf/mhppji.pdf

[56] Goin, M. K. (July 8, 2007). "The Wrong Place to Treat Mental Illness." *Washington Post,* p. B7. http://www.washingtonpost.com/wp-dyn/content/article/2007/07/06/AR2007070601930.html

[57] Ibid.

[58] Fellner, J. (March 25, 2007). "Cruel and Sadly Usual." http://www.hrw.org/en/news/2007/03/25/cruel-and-sadly-usual

[59] Ranney, D. (April 10, 2006). "Mentally Ill Strain Resources at Jail." *Lawrence Journal-World.* http://www2.ljworld.com/news/2006/apr/10/mentally_ill_strain_resources_jail/?city_local

[60] Hammett, T., S. Kennedy, and S. Kuck (2007). National Survey of Infectious Diseases in Correctional Facilities: HIV and STDs, p. 4. http://www.ncjrs.gov/pdffiles1/nij/grants/217736.pdf

[61] The Bureau of Justice Statistics has not published information on HIV in jails since 2004 (data was for 2002).

[62] Maruschak, L. (April 2008). *HIV in Prison, 2006.* http://www.ojp.usdoj.gov/bjs/pub/html/hivp/2006/hivp06.htm

[63] Hammett et al., National Survey of Infectious Diseases, p. 4.

[64] Irwin, J. *The Jail: Managing the Underclass in American Society.* Berkeley: University of California Press, 1985, pp. 1–2.

[65] An interesting question (beyond the scope of this text) is: Which came first—few ties or unconventional values and beliefs?

[66] Irwin, *The Jail,* p. 2.

[67] Piven, F. F., and R. Cloward. *Regulating the Poor: The Functions of Social Welfare.* New York: Vintage Books, 1972.

[68] Irwin, *The Jail,* p. 17.

[69] Miller, *Search and Destroy.*

[70] Ibid., pp. 13–14.

[71] Wolfgang, R. E., R. Figlio, and P. Tracy (1981). "The Seriousness of Crime: The Results of a National Survey." *Final Report to the Bureau of Justice Statistics,* Washington, DC.

[72] Irwin, *The Jail,* pp. 20–22.

[73] Austin and Irwin, in their study of the prison system, discovered a similar distribution of offenders as Irwin did in his jail study. Austin, J. and J. Irwin. *It's About Time: America's Incarceration Binge* (3rd ed.). Belmont, CA: Wadsworth, 2001.

[74] Miller, *Search and Destroy,* p. 217.

[75] Federal Bureau of Investigation. *Crime in the United States, 2007.* Table 29. http://www.fbi.gov/ucr/cius2007/data/table_29.html

[76] Shelden, R. G. and W. B. Brown (1991). "Correlates of Jail Overcrowding: A Case Study of a County Detention Center." *Crime and Delinquency* 37 (July).

[77] Luscombe, R. (May 16, 2009) "Cash-Strapped Jails Begin Charging Inmates for Snacks—Even Room and Board." *The Christian Science Monitor.* http://www.csmonitor.com/2009/0515/p25s10-usgn.html

[78] Quoted in Ibid.

4

Slavery in the Third Millennium

The wide-ranging effects of the race to incarcerate on African American communities in particular is a phenomenon that is only beginning to be investigated. What does it mean to a community, for example, to know that three out of ten boys growing up will spend time in prison? What does it do to the fabric of the family and community to have such a substantial proportion of its young men enmeshed in the criminal justice system? What images and values are communicated to young people who see the prisoner as the most prominent pervasive role model in the community?[1]

A photo essay in a prominent sociology journal depicted Cummins Prison Farm in Arkansas. One photo showed about twenty convicts in a field picking cotton, while a white guard stood over them. Another photo showed a tractor pulling about eight carts filled with convicts returning from the fields, with four guards riding on horses along the left side. The black and white photos easily could have been taken 100 years ago at one of several "plantation prisons" in the south. They were among about 5,000 photographs taken by sociologist Bruce Jackson between 1971 and 1975.[2]

Plantation prisons, modeled after the slave plantation, emerged in the southern states shortly after the end of the Civil War. Black citizens were sent to these prisons "on the flimsiest pretexts and then put to hard labor in the fields of these prisons, often in chain gangs."[3] Prisons like Parchman in Mississippi and Cummins in Arkansas were little more than slave plantations which, along with convict leasing, extended the slave system long after emancipation.[4] The prisons were marked by notoriously brutal conditions, resulting in literally thousands of deaths. Tom Murton, a reform-minded warden at the Tucker Prison Farm, discovered numerous bodies of dead prisoners buried in the fields in the 1960s. The movie *Brubaker*, starring Robert Redford, was based in part on this scandal.[5]

Seeking Cheap Labor and Control of African Americans

Throughout history people in power have sought to control groups perceived to be a threat and/or to dominate groups for political or economic gain. The methods of control have varied from economic marginalization to thought control via propaganda to use of the legal system for total or partial segregation and, in the most extreme cases, total extermination (e.g., genocide).[6] In the United States such control has targeted Native Americans, African slaves, labor agitators, and many others.[7]

The use of inmates as a form of cheap labor has been part of the capitalist system from the beginning, as owners maximize profits by employing the cheapest form of labor—whether slaves, immigrants, or inmates. In the Roman Empire the term "slave" included prisoners of war, sailors captured and sold by pirates, or slaves bought outside Roman territory.[8] Taking advantage of the imprisoned (in various forms, including slavery) has been common among nations for centuries.[9]

The various forms of exploitation included enforced labor on ships until prisons became the prominent means of punishment in the early nineteenth century.[10] The practice of transporting pardoned prisoners on ships to North American plantations for a period of indentured servitude was developed by private merchant shippers in the seventeenth century. It was one of many methods of amassing large fortunes without the costs of paying prevailing wages. Most of the indentured servants were white and were separated from black slaves. The end of transportation as punishment coincided almost exactly with the increased use of slavery in Colonial America. Capitalists soon learned that there were even more benefits from the emerging African slave trade than from white indentured servants. One writer noted that among the many advantages of slaves was the fact that they "were held to perpetual instead of temporary servitude, they were cheaper to feed and clothe, they replaced themselves to some extent by natural breeding, and they endured the hot climate of the plantation much better than white men."[11]

In America, slaves were important to the colonial economy, providing cheap labor for a relatively small group of landowners. At the time the Declaration of Independence was written, the statement that "all men were created equal" applied to *white* men. Women were treated almost as if they were slaves, and slaves were classified as chattel—property. The white ruling class created an economic and political system, complete with a set of laws, that guaranteed slavery would remain intact.[12]

Standard history books report that the Civil War brought freedom to slaves. Well, not exactly. After the war, the South faced serious economic, political, and social problems. Economic recovery was among the first priorities. The economy of the South, previously based on a slave mode of production, was turning to a capitalist mode of production. Another crucial problem was what "to do with" the newly "freed" slaves. From the standpoint of the white power structure, this was a problem of social control. The solution to what eventually became known as the "Negro problem" was the systematic oppression of blacks and the maintenance of a system of *caste* rule.[13] *Sharecropping* replaced slavery as a method of controlling the labor of African Americans.[14] A system of agricultural (and eventually industrial) peonage emerged supported by vigilantism, intimidation, and Jim Crow laws.[15]

After the Civil War, white southerners used the law to segregate and discriminate against blacks. Individual states created separate versions of Black Codes in 1865, but almost all the states imposed the same types of restrictions limiting the freedom of ex-slaves. The codes regulated civil rights, such as marriage, freedom of movement, choice of occupation, and the right to hold and sell property. The Codes essentially compelled freedmen to work; if unemployed, blacks could be arrested and charged with vagrancy. Codes also dictated hours of labor and duties.[16] Many white Southerners believed blacks should work only as agricultural laborers and domestics. Working in any other occupation in South Carolina required a special license from a local judge. Some codes prevented blacks from raising their own crops. Restrictions on blacks renting or leasing land existed in parts of Mississippi. Many codes prohibited blacks from entering towns without permission. Federal officials suspended the Black Codes in 1866, but they were replaced with Jim Crow (a minstrel character who performed in blackface) laws.

An award-winning PBS series, *The Rise and Fall of Jim Crow*, explored segregation from the end of the civil war to the modern civil rights movement and described the brutal and repressive era as marked by: "Lynchings and beatings by night. Demeaning treatment by day. And a life of crushing subordination for Southern blacks that was maintained by white supremacist laws and customs known as 'Jim Crow.'"[17] The series points out that although the Jim Crow laws were passed in the South, the system had roots in the North as well and thrived because it was sanctioned by the national government.[18] In both the North and the South, blacks were "painfully and constantly aware that [they] lived in a society dedicated to the doctrine of white supremacy and Negro inferiority."[19]

The Supreme Court ruled in *Plessy* v. *Ferguson* in 1896 that separate facilities for whites and blacks were constitutional. The ruling encouraged passage of laws that regulated transportation (e.g., separate sections for blacks on buses and trains), public facilities (e.g., separate parks, segregated areas in restaurants and theaters, separate drinking fountains, separate hotels, separate hospitals), and schools, juvenile reform schools.[20] If the laws weren't sufficient to control the movements and behaviors of blacks, violence—especially lynching—was used. As several writers have documented, the use of force to keep African Americans in a subordinate position increased dramatically after the Civil War, one example being the rise of the Ku Klux Klan.[21]

Prisons and Convict Leasing Help Perpetuate Slavery

One popular method of controlling ex-slaves was *convict leasing*. "Free" blacks threatened white supremacy, and convict leasing as another form of chattel slavery counterbalanced the losses imposed by the war. It also provided an abundant source of cheap labor to help with the enormous task of rebuilding the war-torn South.[22]

Prison populations became predominately African American after the war. At the main prison in Nashville, Tennessee, for example, about one-third of the inmates were African Americans in October 1865. Two years later, the percentage had increased to 58% and then to 64% in 1869. Between 1877 and 1879, the percentage reached 67%.[23] Other Southern states had even greater disparity in the race of prisoners. In 1888 the prison at Baton Rouge, Louisiana, held 85 whites and 212 African Americans; in 1875 in North Carolina 569 African Americans and 78 whites were sentenced to prison.[24]

The actual increase in the populations within Southern prisons is staggering. In Georgia there was a tenfold increase in prison populations during a four-decade period (1868–1908); in North Carolina the prison population increased from 121 in 1870 to 1,302 in 1890; in Florida the population went from 125 in 1881 to 1,071 in 1904; in Mississippi the population quadrupled between 1871 and 1879; in Alabama it went from 374 in 1869 to 1,878 in 1903 and to 2,453 in 1919.[25]

Convict leasing involved private companies paying the state a fee for the labor of prisoners. The lessees, in particular, and the state profited financially, while the prisoners were exploited. After emancipation, Alabama had charged prisoners fees to cover the cost of prosecuting and detaining county arrestees.[26] Prisoners who could not pay for their trials were sentenced to serve additional time to pay the fees with their labor. When the state faced a budget crisis, it turned to leasing prisoners.

> Both leasing and slavery were systems of forced labor for profit that depended upon physical force and the absolute authority of either a white contractor or owner. Prisoners enjoyed none of the privileges of free labor. Like slaves, they had to do as they were told or suffer horrible punishment. Like slaves, their situation appears hopeless: the society at large had little interest in their plight other than to enforce the authority of those holding them in subordination. And both systems depended on the compliance of the state in enforcing the ultimate authority of either the contractor or the slave owner.[27]

In 1866 "the governor of Alabama leased the penitentiary to a contractor who was charged the sum of five dollars and given a sizable loan. The legislature granted him permission to work the prisoners outside the walls; they were soon found in the Ironton and New Castle mines."[28] Tennessee leased convicts to three separate railroad companies in1870. The railroad companies had suffered great losses during the war, and convicts essentially rebuilt the railroads. In 1871 coal mining companies began to use convict labor. By 1882 more than half of the convicts at the Nashville prison were leased out; in 1884 the Tennessee Coal, Iron and Railway Company leased the entire prison population.[29]

The conditions endured by a chain gang in Florida prompted a book titled *The American Siberia*.[30] This chain gang labored extracting turpentine in a semitropical jungle. "Prisoners worked in gangs, chained together in filthy bunkhouses, exposed to dysentery and scurvy."[31] The convict lease system was cruel and inhumane, to say the least. Sickness, suffering, and death were common. In a coal mine in Georgia convicts were routinely whipped if they did not produce the daily quota of coal.[32] In Georgia "it is morally certain that hundreds of innocent men are dragging out lives worse than that of slavery in the Georgia prisons and on convict farms, and that this system of reviving African servitude is growing extremely popular in the South."[33] A Louisiana newspaper reported that "it would be more humane to impose the death sentence upon anyone sentenced to a term with the lessee in excess of six years, because the average convict lived no longer than that." Indeed, the death rate in 1896 was 20%.[34] The mortality rate for inmates in the South was 41.3 per thousand convicts, compared to a rate of 14.9 in the North.[35]

The ideology of white supremacy dominated the entire leasing system. Lessees regarded black labor as a commodity, just as slaveholders had regarded slaves. The lease system fit well with the emerging industrial capitalist system. Indeed, convict labor "depended upon both the heritage of slavery and the allure of industrial capitalism."[36] The convict lease system was not merely a replacement for slavery but an extension of it, albeit in a new form and serving new interests. The control of the black labor force, writes Mark Colvin, "was a constant goal of the southern punishment system since the Civil War. This labor control function was enhanced with the rise of industrialism in the 'New South,' rather than eliminated."[37]

One additional fact needs to be underscored—especially as we consider arguments advanced today. Convict leasing received wide support in the South because of its alleged success in controlling the so-called "black crime problem."[38] Then, as now, proponents of imprisonment argued that the system effectively controlled crime. However, the alleged "black crime problem" after the Civil War was largely an invention. The vast majority of black prisoners had been convicted of rather petty crimes, such as "loitering," "vagrancy" and "trespassing."[39] Many were in fact just plain falsely accused.[40] Douglas Blackmon provides a detailed review of how such laws were used from just after the end of the Civil War until World War II in *Slavery by Another Name*. Literally thousands of blacks were arrested on charges of minor offenses like vagrancy or no offenses at all, other than being black.[41]

Although the convict lease system was eventually eliminated, other forms of convict labor continued (and still exist today). Blake McKelvey notes that the lease system "was not abandoned until profitable substitutes were perfected." [42] Substitutes included plantations, industrial prisons, and the chain gang. The chain gang actually developed alongside the convict lease system as one of the two major forms of convict labor. Robert Weiss graphically describes the chain gang: "Chained together in fetid bunkhouses, suffering malnutrition and exposed to rampant disease, these hapless charges suffered one of history's most degrading punishments."[43] The vast majority of people assigned to chain gangs were African Americans, often convicted for merely being black.

Slavery Revisited: The Return of the Chain Gang

If you think chain gangs are part of the distant past, think again. In Maricopa County, Arizona (the nation's largest sheriff's department), Joe Arpaio is the self-proclaimed "toughest sheriff in America."[44] In 1993 he began housing inmates in tents. Phoenix temperatures in the summer average well over 100 degrees. He instituted chain gangs (for men, women, and juveniles) to clean streets, paint over graffiti, and bury the indigent.[45] As he notes, the chain gangs contribute thousands of dollars of free labor to the community. Arpaio banned smoking, coffee, movies, and unrestricted TV. Inmates are fed only two meals a day, which saves costs of the meal and labor costs to deliver the meals. He stopped salt and pepper, claiming he saves tax payers $20,000 a year. Everything inmates wear—except for the black and white striped uniforms—is pink, as are sheets, towels, socks, and handcuffs. A Web site lists the 300 people booked and processed into the jail daily, which Arpaio describes as one of the most visible law enforcement sites on the World Wide Web.[46] The county Web site notes:

> No other detention facility in the country, state or county can boast of 2,000 convicts in tents; no other county or state facility can boast of a gleaning program that results in costs of under 15 cents per meal per inmate; few others can say they have women in tents or on chain gangs and no other sheriff's office in the United States today has a volunteer posse of 3,000 men and women, people from the community who spend their time and money to train to be volunteers helping to keep the county free from crime. [47]

Many of the 10,000 people confined in the Maricopa County Jail are awaiting trial simply because they could not afford bail. Others are serving short sentences. Arpaio says he serves the public, and he knows what the public wants. First elected in 1993, the seventy-six-year-old Arpaio was reelected to a fifth term by 55% of the voters in 2008.[48]

Chain gangs were reintroduced in Alabama in 1995 after a 30-year absence, although road gangs of unfettered prisoners had worked along state highways. The prison commissioner said many reasons contributed to his decision to reinstate chain gangs, but deterrence was a primary reason: "Every time a car passes and a child looks out on them, they will reinforce the idea that crime has consequences."[49] Some people approved of the practice: "I love seeing 'em in chains. They ought to make them pick cotton." [50] Critics, however, decried the return to chain gangs as punishment and the image projected of the criminal justice system. "A group of men, most of them black, chained to each other like animals, being marched along dusty country roads to perform meaningless but painful labor."[51] Tracey Meares concurs:

> The grim, racialized history of the chain gang cannot be separated from this entrepreneurial scheme. At the beginning of this century the chain gang was used to keep African Americans in servitude after Emancipation. Contract-enforcement laws—directed primarily at African American farm laborers—transformed contractual obligations into involuntary servitude by imposing criminal sanctions for a laborer's breach of an employment contract. These laborers had a choice: They could work out the contract or spend several months of forced, brutal labor on a chain gang, where death was not uncommon. The historical connection between chain gangs and slavery is well-entrenched in the minds of most Americans and probably all African Americans. For many, commercializing the chain gang is akin to commercializing slavery.[52]

The connection with slavery did not escape the notice of the Southern Christian Leadership Conference. In their lawsuit challenging the use of chain gangs as punishment, they noted that 60% of Alabama's inmates were black.[53] The practice was again discontinued in 1996.[54]

When Florida followed Alabama's lead and reintroduced the chain gang, Amnesty International was quick to point out the obvious: "Florida became the third state to use chain gangs in 1995, following the lead of Alabama and Arizona, where the authorities reintroduced chain gangs in May. Last used in the USA thirty years ago, chain gangs are being hailed by their supporters as an effective anticrime deterrent, but by opponents as a step backwards, evoking images of slavery."[55]

Most of the arguments by supporters of chain gangs echo the theme of deterrence expressed by the Alabama commissioner. After instituting chain gangs, the sheriff of Butler County, Ohio, said, "I want 'em to leave here with a bad feeling in their mouth."[56] Sheriff Arpaio says: "I use it for deterrence to fight crime. I put them right on the street where everyone can see them. If a kid asks his mother, she can tell them this is what happens to people who break the law." [57] When inmates complain he merely says, "If you don't like it, don't come back." However, a spokeswoman in his jail told a reporter that "60% of inmates did in fact come back for more than one term." Politicians play on public fears about crime and solicit votes by portraying themselves as protecting the public from predators. Because blacks are disproportionately represented in prison, the visibility of chain gangs reinforces stereotypes that began centuries ago. "Considering the fact that Whites kidnapped Africans and brought them to this country in chains, it would be a safe bet that White racism existed centuries before disproportionate rates of Black crime. For proof of this supposition, one need only review the slave codes and Black codes for blatant examples of White racism enshrined into early American criminal law."[58]

The Face of Crime

Jeffrey Reiman refers to the criminal justice system as a mirror.

> Whom and what we see in this mirror are functions of the decisions about who and what is criminal. Our poor, young, urban, black male, who is so well represented in arrest records and prison populations, appears not simply because of the threat he poses to the rest of society. As dangerous as he may be, he would not appear in the criminal justice mirror *if* it had not been decided that the acts he performs should be labeled "crimes," *if* it had not been decided that he should be arrested for those crimes, *if* he had had access to a lawyer who could persuade a jury to acquit him and a judge to expunge his arrest record, and *if* it had not been decided that he is the type of individual and his the type of crime that warrant imprisonment. *The shape of the reality we see in the criminal justice mirror is the outcome of all these decisions.*[59]

Katheryn Russell-Brown notes how crime and young black men have become synonymous in the American mind.[60] She discusses the role of the media in this stereotyped belief.

> Television's overpowering images of Black deviance—its regularity and frequency—are impossible to ignore. These negative images have been seared into our collective consciousness. It is no surprise that most Americans wrongly believe that Blacks are responsible for committing the majority of crime. No doubt, many of the suspects paraded across the nightly news are guilty criminals. The onslaught of criminal images of Black men, however, causes many of us to incorrectly conclude that most Black men are criminals. These images also make it hard for many people to believe that most crime is *intraracial*, involving an offender and

victim who are the same race. Regardless of race, the person most people fear is a young, Black man. This is what I refer to as the myth of the *criminalblackman*.[61]

The consequences of misconceptions and biases are evident in the statistics about who is imprisoned. Marc Mauer comments that reducing minority rates of confinement will be a complex process because current incarceration is based on multiple factors "including socioeconomic disadvantages, involvement in criminal behavior, resource allocation in the criminal justice system, sentencing policies, limited diversionary options, and biased decision making among practitioners."[62]

Uneven Justice

The scale of racial disparity within the criminal justice system is truly staggering. One of every nine black males between the ages of 20 and 34 is incarcerated in prison or jail, and one of every three black males born today can expect to do time in state or federal prison if current trends continue. For Hispanic males, the lifetime odds of imprisonment are one in six. . . . The effects of high rates of incarceration go beyond the experience of imprisonment itself, and have broad consequences for both the offender and the community. A prison term results in challenges in gaining employment, reduced lifetime earnings, and restrictions on access to various public benefits. Families of offenders themselves experience the shame and stigma of incarceration, as well as the loss of financial and emotional support with a loved one behind bars. And for the community at large, the challenges of reentry result in high rates of recidivism and the consequent costs of a burgeoning prison system.[63]

Chapter 1 introduced the disparity in the number of African Americans incarcerated for a drug offense; chapter 3 discussed the overrepresentation of African Americans in jail. When we consider all inmates (those held in state or federal prison and jails), the disparities remain. Table 4.1 shows the data for all male age groups in 2008 (chapter 6 discusses the punishment of women) by race. Note in table 4.2 that the incarceration rate for males at every age replicates the same order: black, Hispanic, white—bringing to mind the 1960s admonition: "If you're white, you're alright; if you're brown, stick around; if you're black, stay back."

The Bureau of Justice Statistics periodically estimates the lifetime chances of going to prison. Between 1974 and 2001, the lifetime chances of going to state or federal prison increased from 1.9% to 6.6%.[64] About 1 in 3 black males, 1 in 6 Hispanic males, and 1 in 17 white males are expected to go to prison during their lifetime. Table 4.3 shows the percentages by gender and race.

Table 4.1   Estimated Number of Male Inmates Held in State or Federal Prisons or in Local Jails, 2008

	Total[a]	White[b]	Black[b]	Hispanic
Total[c]	2,103,500	712,500	846,000	427,000
18–19	86,300	26,500	37,100	18,400
20–24	353,100	104,000	148,500	83,300
25–29	354,600	99,900	148,400	87,100
30–34	331,400	103,400	132,100	76,400
35–39	308,500	107,200	124,500	57,300
40–44	277,200	107,700	107,400	43,500
45–49	185,600	72,400	73,900	29,000
50–54	96,900	40,200	37,100	14,500
55–59	50,200	24,300	15,800	7,900
60–64	21,700	12,100	5,500	3,500
65 or older	17,500	9,900	4,800	2,200

Note: Based on the U.S. resident population estimates for July 1, 2008, by gender, race, Hispanic origin, and age. Detailed categories exclude persons who reported two or more races.
[a] Includes American Indians, Alaska Natives, Asians, Native Hawaiians, other Pacific Islanders, and persons identifying two or more races.
[b] Excludes persons of Hispanic or Latino origin.
[c] Includes persons under age 18.

Source: C. West, H. C. and W. J. Sabol (2009), "Prison Inmates at Midyear 2008—Statistical Tables." Table 17. Washington, DC: Bureau of Justice Statistics, March. NCJ 2255619. http://www.ojp.usdoj.gov/bjs/pub/pdf/pim08st.pdf

Table 4.2   Estimated Number of Male Inmates Held in State or Federal Prisons or in Local Jails per 100,000 U.S. Residents, 2008

	Total[a]	White[b]	Black[b]	Hispanic
Total[c]	1,403	727	4,777	1,760
18–19	1,934	976	5,543	2,376
20–24	3,256	1,564	9,776	4,281
25–29	3,241	1,550	10,408	3,792
30–34	3,328	1,793	11,137	3,446
35–39	2,919	1,643	10,120	2,868
40–44	2,580	1,529	8,622	2,510
45–49	1,641	912	5,854	2,011
50–54	920	520	3,330	1,320
55–59	556	356	1,790	976
60–64	299	213	899	607
65 or older	106	75	383	191

[a] Includes American Indians, Alaska Natives, Asians, Native Hawaiians, other Pacific Islanders, and persons identifying two or more races.
[b] Excludes persons of Hispanic or Latino origin.
[c] Includes persons under age 18.

Source: C. West, H. C. and W. J. Sabol (2009), "Prison Inmates at Midyear 2008—Statistical Tables." Table 19. Washington, DC: Bureau of Justice Statistics, March. NCJ 2255619. http://www.ojp.usdoj.gov/bjs/pub/pdf/pim08st.pdf

Table 4.3   Lifetime Chances of Going to State or Federal Prison for the First Time

Race	1974	1991	2001
White male	2.2%	4.4%	5.9%
White female	0.2%	0.5%	0.9%
Black male	13.4%	29.4%	32.2%
Black female	1.1%	3.6%	5.6%
Hispanic male	4.0%	16.3%	17.2%
Hispanic female	0.4%	1.5%	2.2%

Source: Bonczar, T. P. (2003). "Prevalence of Imprisonment in the U.S. Population, 1974–2001." Table 9, p. 8. Washington, DC: Bureau of Justice Statistics, August. http://www.ojp.usdoj.gov/bjs/pub/pdf/piusp01.pdf

Statistics are also kept on the percentage of the adult population "ever incarcerated" in prison. In 2001 the highest rate (16.6%) for ever having gone to prison was for black adult males. The rate was more than twice as high as for Hispanic males (7.7%) and more than six times as high as for white males (2.6%). Although female rates were significantly lower, they reflected similar racial disparity. Blacks (39%) and Hispanics (18%) combined constituted the majority of people who had ever served time in prison. The percentage of whites ever incarcerated dropped from 51% in 1974 to 39% in 2001.[65]

Funneling Minorities into Prison via the Drug War

Chapter 1 highlighted some of the effects of the war on drugs on the poor and racial minorities. Blacks are arrested on drug charges at more than three times the rates of whites; they are convicted of those charges and sent to state prisons at ten times the rate of whites. Although about six times as many whites use and sell drugs as blacks, almost half of state prisoners sentenced for drug violations are black.

> The "war on drugs" was not created to curb white drug use. It was born in the mid-1980s when crack hit the streets, was quickly demonized and it was widely thought (albeit erroneously) to be linked exclusively to blacks. While "drugs" and "tough on crime" were the words used by politicians wooing an anxious white electorate with draconian new drug laws, the real, although unspoken, subject was race.[66]

Drug laws have primarily been enforced against low-level dealers in minority neighborhoods. Police find this population of offenders because of *where they choose to look for them* (rather than, say, on college campuses or in the white suburbs).[67] Law professor Paul Butler believes racial profiling drives aggressive policing in black neighborhoods. Police, including black officers, selectively enforce the drug laws in black communities because of beliefs that blacks need more drug law enforcement.

> Police and prosecutors use the statistics about the number of African Americans who get arrested for drug use as a reason to look more closely at African Americans for that crime. And, of course, if you're especially looking among African Americans, then you'll find more African Americans. There's an important relationship between looking for something and finding it.[68]

The evidence of racial disproportionality in the drug war is overwhelming. For instance, arrest rates for minorities went from under 600 per 100,000 in 1980 to over 1500 in 1990, while for whites they essentially remained the same.[69] Data on court commitments to state prisons during the 1980s and early 1990s show that the increase in the number of blacks sentenced to prison for drug charges was almost three times greater than the increase in the number of white offenders. Between 1985 and 1995 the number of black prisoners who had been sentenced for drug crimes increased by 700%.[70] Arrests for drug possession have greatly exceeded arrests for drug sales every year since 1980, and the proportion of drug arrests for possession has been increasing, amounting to 80% or more annually since 1999.[71]

Blacks have been arrested on drug charges at higher rates than whites for nearly three decades, even though they engage in drug offenses at comparable rates. "Adult African Americans were arrested on drug charges at rates that were 2.8 to 5.5 times as high as those of white adults in every year from 1980 through 2007. . . . About one in three of the more than 25.4 million adult drug arrestees during that period was African American.[72] Jamie Fellner noted: "Jim Crow may be dead, but the drug war has never been color-blind. Although whites and blacks use and sell drugs, the heavy hand of the law is more likely to fall on black shoulders."[73]

Not only were more blacks sentenced for drug crimes, but the *severity* of their sentences also increased compared to whites. In 1992, in the federal system, the average sentence length for black drug offenders was about 107 months, compared to 74 months for white drug offenders. Contributing to the disparity are sentencing enhancements tied to particular drug offenses. As noted in chapter 1, there has been a 100 to 1 difference in the sentences for crack versus powder cocaine. In 1995, for instance, blacks constituted a phenomenal 88% of those sentenced for crack cocaine, compared to less than 30% of those sentenced for powder cocaine.[74] In 2006 81.8% of crack cocaine defendants were black. African Americans are sentenced to almost as much time in prison for a drug offense (58.7 months) as whites are sentenced for a violent offense (61.7 months)."[75]

Table 4.4 shows sentenced prisoners in state prisons by race and major offense in 2005. One-fourth of sentenced blacks are in prison for drugs, 23% of Latinos but only 13.5% of whites. Table 4.5 shows data by both race and specific drug. In 2004, the most serious charge for 44% of black felony defendants was a drug charge, compared to 27% for both whites and Hispanics.[76]

Table 4.4   Sentenced Prisoners by Race and Offense, 2005

Offense	Total 100%	White 100%	Black 100%	Hispanic 100%
Violent	53.0	50.1	54.6	54.7
Property	19.2	24.4	16.1	16.2
Drugs	19.5	15.4	22.5	21.3
Public order	7.6	9.4	6.3	7.3

Source: West, H. and Sabol, W. "Prisoners in 2007." Bureau of Justice Statistics, Bulletin. Washington, DC: U.S. Department of Justice, December 2008. Appendix Table 11. http://www.ojp.usdoj.gov/bjs/pub/pdf/p07.pdf

Table 4.5   Drug Offenders Sentenced in U.S. District Courts, 2008

Race	Total	Powder Cocaine	Crack	Heroin	Pot	Meth	Other
White	25.3%	16.6%	10.4%	16%	27.4%	52.4%	49.1%
Black	31.4	30.2	79.8	24.7	7.6	2.9	24.7
Hispanic	40.2	52.3	8.8	57.8	61.4	39.3	9.8
Other	3.1	1	1	1.5	3.6	5.3	16.5

Source: *Sourcebook on Criminal Justice Statistics,* http://www.albany.edu/sourcebook/pdf/t5392008.pdf

In a detailed study of the racial differences in incarceration in Chicago, Paul Street wrote that young blacks living in Chicago have a much different view of what "going downstate" means. For white youths it usually means a trip with mom and dad to one of the universities (e.g., University of Illinois at Urbana-Champaign or Southern Illinois University Carbondale) and for both races it may also mean a trip to the state basketball tournament. However, for black youths of Chicago it "more commonly means a trip under armed guard to take up residence at one of the state's numerous maximum or medium security prisons."[77] There were almost 20,000 more black males in the Illinois state prison system in 2001 than were enrolled in the state's public universities. In fact, the number of black males sentenced to correctional facilities on drug charges exceeded the number enrolled in undergraduate degree programs in state universities. In one primarily black district, police averaged 33 drug arrests per day—more than 12,000 total in one year in the mid–1990s. Blacks constituted 89% of all drug offenders in Illinois state prisons in 2001—the highest percentage of all states that year.

In 2006, blacks represented 80% of all drug arrests—the highest percentage in the nation, followed by 67% in Maryland and 66% in Georgia.[78] In every state, the rate of drug arrests per 100,000 black residents was considerably higher than the rate per 100,000 white residents, ranging from a low of 428 in Hawaii to a high of 4,210 in Illinois versus a range for whites of 169 in South Dakota to 1,029 in California. In nine states, blacks are arrested on drug charges at rates more than seven times the rate for whites.

> No doubt many Americans believe racial differences in imprisonment for drug offenses reflect racial differences in involvement with illegal drug activities—that blacks are sent to prison at higher rates on drug charges because they are more involved in drug offenses than whites. The heightened media and political attention to substance abuse and the drug trade in urban minority neighborhoods has promoted the public perception that illegal drugs are more prevalent in those neighborhoods than in more affluent white neighborhoods. The reality has long been the reverse. In absolute numbers, there are far more whites committing drug offenses than blacks. The disproportionate rates at which blacks are sent to prison for drug offenses compared to whites largely originate in racially disproportionate rates of arrest for drug offenses.[79]

Three federally sponsored surveys measure drug use. The majority of youths (grades 8, 10, and 12) using illicit drugs are white.

> Among the most dramatic and interesting subgroup differences are those found among the three largest racial/ethnic groups—Whites, African Americans, and Hispanics. Contrary to popular assumption, at all three grade levels African American students have substantially lower rates of use of most licit and illicit drugs than do Whites. These include any illicit drug use, most of the specific illicit drugs, alcohol, and cigarettes.[80]

The National Survey on Drug Use and Health found approximately the same percentages of whites and blacks using illicit drugs. This survey reports results in three categories for people aged 12 and older: use in a lifetime, use in the past year; and use in the past month (the category designated as current drug users). The percentages in the lifetime category were 50.3% white, 43.1% black, and 34.2% Hispanic. Because the white population in the United States is approximately six times larger than the black population, the number of white drug users is significantly higher than the number of black users. The number (lifetime) of white users of an illicit drug in 2007 was 85 million compared to 12.6 million blacks and 11.7 million Hispanics.[81] The numbers for users in the past month were 13.8 million whites, 2.8 million blacks, and 2.3 million Hispanics.

As noted above, drug arrests do not reflect the numbers reported in the surveys; rather, arrests are racially disproportionate to drug offending. A number of factors contribute to the disparity: blacks are more likely to live in urban areas; illicit drug use is higher in urban areas; law enforcement resources per capita are higher in urban areas, and there are more drug arrests in urban areas. "Drug law enforcement is not, however, evenly distributed within urban areas. Instead, it has focused on low-income, predominantly minority neighborhoods.[82] Drug transactions in such neighborhoods are more likely to be in public spaces, making arrests more likely. The disparities that start at the arrest level continue through conviction and sentencing.

> Prosecutorial discretion may play a role ... as prosecutors have essentially unchecked authority to choose what charges to bring and what pleas to accept. Blacks arrested on drug charges may also have higher prison admission rates because they are less likely to be able to afford private attorneys and must rely on public defenders overwhelmed with high case loads.[83]

The disparity in sentencing for crack cocaine contributes to the disproportionate numbers of blacks in prison for a drug offense.

> The choice of crack cocaine as an ongoing priority for law enforcement—instead of the far more prevalent powder cocaine—cannot be divorced from public association of crack with African Americans, even though the majority of crack users were white. In short, unconscious and conscious racial stereotypes have affected public perceptions of drugs, crime, disorder, and danger, and helped shape political and policy responses.[84]

More whites (5.8 million) have reported using crack in their lifetime than blacks (1.6 million).[85]

The physiological and psychotropic effects of crack and powder are the same.[86] The myth that crack cocaine is more often associated with violence than powder cocaine has been dispelled. The Sentencing Commission has been recommending since 1995 that the 100:1 disparity be removed, but Congress has not acted. In testimony before the Senate Judiciary Subcommittee on Crime and Drugs, Assistant Attorney General Lanny Breuer stated that the punishments are fundamentally unfair. However, the International Association of Chiefs of Police as well as the Fraternal Order of Police oppose reducing the penalties. Instead, they propose increasing the penalty for powder cocaine.[87]

Human Rights Watch acknowledges that the factors contributing to the disproportionate number of blacks imprisoned on drug charges are complex.

> It is impossible to determine whether and if so to what extent conscious racial hostility has influenced US drug control strategies. But even absent overt racial animus, race has mattered, influencing the development and persistence of antidrug strategies. The emphasis on penal sanctions, for example, cannot be divorced from widespread and deeply rooted public association of racial minorities with crime and drugs.

THE INTERNAL EXILE OF AFRICAN AMERICANS AND THE NEW AMERICAN APARTHEID

Chapter 3 introduced the concept of the modern penal system as a *ghetto or poorhouse*.[88] Some critics compare the criminal justice system to a form of *petit apartheid* (in contrast to *grand apartheid* that describes a societal policy of segregation and political and economic discrimination, such as was practiced in South Africa).[89] Those who are segregated from mainstream American society generally have reduced educational opportunities, resultant low incomes or no job prospects, and are vulnerable to the violence that sometimes results from the lack of legitimate means of goal attainment.[90]

An argument could be made that disadvantaged, uneducated blacks, especially males, are superfluous and expendable in American society—that is, they do not have the skills necessary to enhance corporate profits. Deindustrialization and corporate downsizing eliminated millions of jobs that formerly helped minorities escape poverty. The loss of opportunities created a large number of unemployed, and some form of social control was needed to insure that frustration did not spill over and jeopardize established relationships. The criminal justice system currently fills this need.[91]

While the "old" apartheid of residential segregation continues unabated,[92] the criminal justice system has created a "new" apartheid as well. Going to jail or prison, as noted in chapters 2 and 3, has become a common event in the lives of millions of racial minorities. Racial segregation characterizes many of the inner cities in the United States. Central cities house 80% of the urban nonwhite population, and one-third of the black urban population resides in the nation's ten largest central cities.[93] Attempts to reduce racial segregation have often been politicized or skewed to serve the interests of the elite—or the attempts have been grossly underfunded, insuring their failure.[94]

To illustrate, the Housing Acts of 1949, 1954, and 1965 provided federal funding to local authorities to acquire slum property and begin redevelopment. In order to qualify for federal funds, local governments had to insure that affordable living accommodations would be provided for displaced families living in the redevelopment zones. The process known as urban renewal (sometimes disparagingly referred to as "negro removal") invariably resulted in high-density public housing, commonly known as the "projects." Urban renewal often caused an overall reduction in living accommodations.[95] In a study of black youth gangs in Detroit, it was noted that for that city there was a net loss of 31,500 homes between 1980 and 1987. The "new apartheid" could also be described crassly as a "negro removal" program"—but the removal is away from inner cities to segregation in America's prison industry.[96]

Loic Wacquant offers a unique explanation of this phenomenon.[97] He argues that in the post-Civil Rights era the penal system has taken the place of previous methods of controlling the black population (slavery, Jim Crow laws, the urban ghetto). Wacquant explores the close union between the ghetto and the prison, both of which serve the purpose of segregating and controlling the poor. He argues that the penal system in the United States institutionalizes racism and reproduces the isolation of dispossessed groups. The ghetto and the prison are both instruments of closure and control, reinforcing societal views of the people confined there as "others"—different from mainstream society. Wacquant describes the ghetto as an "ethnoracial prison" that "encloses a stigmatized population which evolves within it its distinctive organizations and culture, while the prison functions as a 'judicial ghetto' relegating individuals disgraced by criminal conviction to a secluded space."[98]

Constantly increasing the imprisonment of blacks sustains caste divisions in society. The penal sector is upsized, while the social welfare sector is downsized. Wacquant argues that this trend represents a merging of the "invisible hand" of the market with an "iron fist" into a *carceral-assistential complex* that controls the targeted population.[99] The new "hyperghetto" no longer offers its residents a buffer from external forces. "At best," he argues, "the hyperghetto now serves the *negative economic function of storage of a surplus population* devoid of market utility, in which respect it also increasingly resembles the prison system."[100] Wacquant describes the hyperghetto as devolving "into a one-dimensional machinery for naked relegation, a human warehouse wherein are discarded those segments of urban society deemed disreputable, derelict, and dangerous."[101]

Wacquant discusses the extra-penological function of the criminal justice system as an instrument for the management of dispossessed and dishonored groups—a carceral continuum that entraps black men relegated to socioeconomic marginality. Even when released to the community, residents continue to be defined, confined, and controlled by probation or patrol officers. Public housing and homeless shelters often use methods of surveillance borrowed from the penal system. Public schools in the ghetto serve more to control than to educate.

The carceral atmosphere of schools and the constant presence of armed guards in uniform in the lobbies, corridors, cafeteria, and playground of their establishment habituate the children of the hyperghetto to the demeanor, tactics, and interactive style of the correctional officers many of them are bound to encounter shortly after their school days are over."[102]

Having a criminal record, especially a prison record, has always been a barrier to seeking reentry into society. In recent years it has become even worse as new laws deny public housing, welfare benefits, and grants for education to those convicted of a crime. Such laws impact many people; about 13 million Americans are either serving time for a felony conviction or have been convicted of a felony sometime in the past. Moreover, a total of about 47 million (one-fourth of the adult population) have some kind of criminal record on file with a federal or state criminal justice agency.[103]

Jeremy Travis likens this to a form of "internal exile," the domestic equivalent of convicts exiled to the American colonies or Australia during the seventeenth and eighteenth centuries. However, those exiles faced few barriers to participating in colonial life once they had served their sentence.[104] Today, however, a criminal record equates to "social exclusion," putting more distance between "them" and "us."

The principal new form of social exclusion has been to deny offenders the benefits of the welfare state. And the principal new player in this new drama has been the United States Congress. In an era of welfare reform, when Congress dismantled the six-decades-old entitlement to a safety net for the poor, the poor with criminal histories were thought less deserving than others. . . . There was little hesitation in using federal benefits to enhance punishments or federal funds to encourage new criminal sanctions by the states.[105]

What Travis doesn't say here (but says elsewhere) is that offenders that feel the heaviest brunt of this exclusion are racial minorities. Todd Clear has pointed out that in many urban, poverty-stricken neighborhoods as many as one-fourth of the adult male residents is either in prison or in jail at some time during the year.[106]

MORE EVIDENCE OF SLAVERY IN THE NEW MILLENNIUM: DISENFRANCHISEMENT

The disenfranchisement of felons is not a new phenomenon. In ancient Greece, criminals and convicts were pronounced "infamous" and stripped of their right to vote and suffered the loss of other rights as well.[107] The rationale behind current disenfranchisement laws are derived from this tradition as well as others. One of the primary rationales for disenfranchising felons is maintaining the "purity of the ballot box," colored by the belief that committing a crime makes ex-offenders impure and incapable of voting in the interest of the "common good." In 1978, the Fifth Circuit Court argued that "the state may exclude ex-offenders because they, like insane persons, have raised the questions about their ability to vote responsibly."[108]

Felon disenfranchisement is a growing problem in the United States because of the combination of rapidly rising numbers of convictions and the voting restrictions imposed by many states. Several other countries (including the United Kingdom and Russia) deny voting rights to prison inmates, but only the United States curtails the rights of nonincarcerated felons—three-quarters of the disenfranchised population. In many European countries, inmates can vote even while in prison. Other countries impose restrictions depending on the crime and length of sentence.[109]

Felon disenfranchisement laws have had the greatest impact on African Americans because they are disproportionately represented in the criminal justice system. As noted in chapter 2, all but two states deprive felons of the right to vote while serving a prison or jail sentence for a felony offense. One in 41 adults (5.3 million people) have lost the right to vote because of a felony conviction (mostly drug convictions). For blacks, however, 1 in 8 (1.4 million people) have been disenfranchised.[110] The disenfranchisement rate for African American males is nearly twice that of whites. In some states that disenfranchise felons indefinitely, up to 40% of African American men may permanently lose their right to vote.[111] Disenfranchisement has no deterrent effect and does little but make the ex-offender feel less like an average citizen and even more isolated.

Christopher Uggen and Jeff Manza noted that felons have somewhat lower levels of trust in government and political efficacy, which could reduce their levels of political participation. Their research indicates that disenfranchisement affects elections only in states with very strict laws and a close election.[112] While those outcomes are important, the researchers highlight other problems of disenfranchisement.

> Although we have specified the political consequences of felon disenfranchisement, we have only touched on the origins of these laws and the mass incarceration phenomenon that gives such force to them today. These questions are important for situating felon disenfranchisement within a broader model of social control of dispossessed groups. Proponents of the "new penology" argue that the focus of criminological interest has recently shifted from the rehabilitation of individual offenders to the social control of aggregate groups. The correctional population is subject to a number of exclusions: They are often ineligible for federal grants (such as Pell Grants), they have restricted access to social programs, they face sharp disadvantages in the labor market, and they must live with the social stigma associated with a felony conviction. Restricted

access to the ballot box is but a piece of a larger pattern of social exclusion for America's vast correctional population.[113]

It is important to emphasize here that the right to vote has been one of the central and most important features of democratic societies—as demonstrated in the struggles for women, blacks and others to gain this right. One method of controlling a given population is by excluding them from participation in this most fundamental aspect of civil society. For more than 100 years following the end of the Civil War, former slaves were prohibited from voting through various restrictions (e.g. an ex-slave could only vote if his grandfather was once a registered voter, reading tests, exams to test knowledge of the Constitution). Some of these methods have surfaced in recent years for ex-felons. Some states have instituted "character tests." In Florida, for example, ex-felons were asked if they drink alcohol, while in Kentucky an ex-felon has to provide letters of reference concerning his or her "good character" to be able to register.[114]

There have been some improvements in several states, and about 760,000 persons have regained the right to vote. Texas repealed the two-year waiting period, allowing 317,000 ex-offenders to vote. Florida simplified its clemency procedures, restoring the right to vote to 115,000 people. Iowa eliminated its lifetime disenfranchisement law. Despite these changes, 35 states still prohibit some combination of persons on probation, parole, and/or people who have completed their sentence from voting.[115]

Some Concluding Thoughts

The "war on crime" and the "war on drugs" disproportionately target racial minorities who find themselves in increasing numbers behind bars and exiled from mainstream American society.[116] The situation is not likely to improve, especially as long as federal, state, and local governments continue to increase expenditures on the crime control industry rather than on prevention. Increasing attention to our *reaction* to crime decreases attention to the ultimate *sources* of crime, exacerbating the problem further.[117] Going to prison has become a very common experience for racial minorities—a legacy of slavery and the creation of a new form of apartheid.

NOTES

[1] Marc Mauer quoted in Nellis, A., J. Greene, and M. Mauer. *Reducing Racial Disparity in the Criminal Justice System: A Manual for Practitioners and Policymakers* (2nd ed.). Washington, DC: The Sentencing Project, 2008, p. iii. http://www.sentencingproject.org/Admin/Documents/publications/rd_reducingracialdisparity.pdf

[2] Jackson, B. (2005). "Photo Essay: Seeing Wide." *Contexts* 4 (Winter): 48–55.

[3] Johnson, R. *Hard Time: Understanding and Reforming the Prison* (3rd ed.). Belmont, CA: Wadsworth, 2002, p. 43.

⁴ The thesis offered here has been thoroughly documented. See the following: Sellin, T. *Slavery and the Penal System*. New York: Elsevier, 1976; Oshinsky, D. M. *Worse than Slavery: Parchman Farm and the Ordeal of Jim Crow*. Detroit: Free Press, 1996; and Mancini, M. J. *One Man Dies, Get Another: Convict Leasing in the American South, 1866–1928*. Chapel Hill: University of North Carolina Press, 1996. The most up-to-date analysis is found in Hallett, M. *Private Prisons in America: A Critical Race Perspective*. Champaign: University of Illinois Press, 2005; and Blackmon, D. A. *Slavery by Another Name: The Re-Enslavement of Black Americans from the Civil War to World War II*. New York: Anchor, 2008.

⁵ Hyams, J. and T. Murton. *Accomplices to Crime: The Arkansas Prison Scandal*. New York: Grove Press, 1969.

⁶ On controlling the population see Chomsky, N. *Necessary Illusions: Thought Control in Democratic Societies*. Boston: South End Press, 1989; and Chomsky, N. *Year 501: The Conquest Continues*. Boston: South End Press, 1993.

⁷ Shelden, R. G. *Controlling the Dangerous Classes: A History of Criminal Justice in America* (2nd ed.). Boston: Allyn & Bacon, 2008.

⁸ Bradley, K. *Slaves and Masters in the Roman Empire: A Study in Social Control*. New York: Oxford University Press, 1987.

⁹ Sellin, *Slavery and the Penal System*.

¹⁰ Shelden, *Controlling the Dangerous Classes*.

¹¹ Smith, A. E. *Colonists in Bondage: White Servitude and Convict Labor in America, 1607–1776*. Chapel Hill: University of North Carolina Press, 1965, pp. 29–30.

¹² Volumes have been written about slavery, with several addressing the economics of this system. See, for example: Fogel, R. W. *Time on the Cross: The Economics of American Negro Slavery*. New York: W. W. Norton, 1995; Kolchin, P. and E. Foner. *American Slavery, 1619–1877*. New York: Hill and Wang, 1994; Elkins, S. M. *Slavery: A Problem in American Institutional and Intellectual Life*. Chicago: University of Chicago Press, 1976.

¹³ Shelden, R. G. (1980). "From Slave to Caste Society: Penal Changes in Tennessee, 1840–1915." *Tennessee Historical Quarterly* 38: 462–478.

¹⁴ Sharecropping was a system "which continued the workers in the routine of cotton cultivation under rigid supervision. Economic features of the system were gradually extended to poor white farmers. The cropper brought to the farm only his own and his family's labor. Most other requirements—land, animals, equipment, and seed—were provided by the landlord, who generally also advanced credit to meet the living expenses of the cropper family. Most croppers worked under the close direction of the landlord, and he marketed the crop and kept accounts. Normally in return for their work they received a share (usually half) of the money realized. From this share was deducted the debt to the landlord. High interest charges, emphasis on production of a single cash crop, and slipshod accounting" were some of the abuses of the system. *The Columbia Encyclopedia*. http://www.encyclopedia.com/doc/1E1-sharecro.html

¹⁵ Weiss, R. P. (1987). "Humanitarianism, Labour Exploitation, or Social Control? A Critical Survey of Theory and Research on the Origin and Development of Prisons." *Social History* 12: 331–350. See also the classic study by Woodward, C. V. *The Strange Career of Jim Crow*. New York: Oxford University Press, 1955.

¹⁶ McElreth, J. "The Black Codes of 1865." About.com. http://afroamhistory.about.com/od/blackcodes/a/blackcodes1865.htm

¹⁷ PBS, "About the Series." http://www.pbs.org/wnet/jimcrow/about.html

¹⁸ PBS, "A National Struggle." http://www.pbs.org/wnet/jimcrow/struggle.html

¹⁹ Woodward, *The Strange Career of Jim Crow*, p. 18.

²⁰ McElreth, J. "Jim Crow Laws." About.com. http://afroamhistory.about.com/cs/jimcrowlaws/a/jimcrowlaws.htm

²¹ Ample documentation can be found for these assertions. See the following: Cable, G. *The Silent South*. Montclair, NJ: Patterson Smith, 1962 (originally published 1888); Woodward, C. *Origins of the New South, 1877–1913*. Baton Rouge: Louisiana State Uni-

versity Press, 1971; and Woodward, *The Strange Career of Jim Crow*; Friedman, L. J. *The White Savage: Racial Fantasies in the Postbellum South*. Englewood Cliffs, NJ: Prentice-Hall, 1970; Johnson, C. S. *The Negro in American Civilization*. New York: Henry Holt, 1930; Meier, A. and E. Rudwick. *From Plantation to Ghetto*. New York: Hill & Wang, 1970.

[22] Weiss, "Humanitarianism, Labour Exploitation, or Social Control?", pp. 345–347; Sellin, *Slavery and the Penal System*, p. 145.

[23] Shelden, "From Slave to Caste Society," pp. 465–466.

[24] Sellin, *Slavery and the Penal System*, pp. 149–159.

[25] Mancini, M. J. (1978). "Race, Economics, and the Abandonment of Convict Leasing." *Journal of Negro History* 63: 343.

[26] Curtin, M. E. *Black Prisoners and Their World, Alabama, 1865–1900*. Charlottesville: University Press of Virginia, 2000, p. 62.

[27] Ibid., p. 102.

[28] Sellin, *Slavery and the Penal System*, pp. 146–150.

[29] Shelden, "From Slave to Caste Society," p. 467.

[30] Powell, J. C. *The American Siberia, or Fourteen Years Experience in a Southern Convict Camp*. Chicago: H. J. Smith, 1891.

[31] Barnes, H. E. and N. Teeters. *New Horizons in Criminology*. Englewood Cliffs, NJ: Prentice-Hall, 1959, p. 378.

[32] Mancini, "Race, Economics, and the Abandonment of Convict Leasing," p. 347.

[33] Curtin, *Black Prisoners and Their World*, p. 71.

[34] Sellin, *Slavery and the Penal System*, pp. 150–153.

[35] McKelvey, B. *American Prisons*. Montclair, NJ: Patterson Smith, 1968 (originally published 1936), p. 183.

[36] Lichtenstein, A. *Twice the Work of Free Labor: The Political Economy of Convict Labor in the New South*. New York: Verso, 1996, p. 21.

[37] Colvin, M. *Penitentiaries, Reformatories, and Chain Gangs: Social Theory and the History of Punishment in Nineteenth-Century America*. New York: St. Martin's Press, 1997, p. 265.

[38] Curtin, *Black Prisoners and Their World*, pp. 42–61; Hallett, *Private Prisons in America*.

[39] Ibid; see also Ayers, E. *Vengeance and Justice: Crime and Punishment in the 19th Century American South*. New York: Oxford University Press, 1984; Myers, M. *Race, Labor and Punishment in the New South*. Columbus: Ohio State University Press, 1998; Shelden, "From Slave to Caste Society"; Shelden, *Controlling the Dangerous Classes*.

[40] The famous "Scottsboro" case is one obvious example. This was where nine young black youth were accused of raping two white girls on a train. They were convicted and sentenced to prison despite the fact that one of the girls eventually recanted her testimony. For details see the following: Patterson, H. and E. Conrad. *Scottsboro Boy*. New York: Doubleday, 1950; Carter, D. *Scottsboro: A Tragedy of the American South*. Baton Rouge: Louisiana State University Press, 1979. There is an excellent movie on DVD based on this case called *Heavens Fall* starring Timothy Hutton and David Strathairn.

[41] Blackmon, *Slavery by Another Name*.

[42] McKelvey, *American Prisons*, p. 185.

[43] Weiss, "Humanitarianism, Labour Exploitation, or Social Control?", p. 345.

[44] http://www.mcso.org/index.php?a=GetModule&mn=sheriff_bio

[45] See a clip of the male and female chain gangs on YouTube: http://www.youtube.com/watch?v=_1tfIKUZ0fY

[46] The mug shot portion of the Maricopa Web site has the following notice: "Mugshots reflect bookings within the last 3 days. Individuals booked prior to that time will not be displayed. PRE-TRIAL INMATES ARE INNOCENT UNTIL PROVEN GUILTY!" It then lists the "crime of the week," provides a section to search by name, or viewers can click on a drop-down menu to select a crime "and see everyone." http://www.mcso.org/index.php?a=GetModule&mn=Mugshot

47 Maricopa County Web site: http://www.mcso.org/index.php?a=
GetModule&mn=About_Mcso

48 "Sheriff Joe Arpaio Re-Elected." (November 5, 2008). *East Valley Living.* http://
www.evliving.com/2008/11/05/1636/joe-arpaio-wins-fifth-term/

49 Bragg, R. (March 26, 1995). "Chain Gangs to Return to Roads of Alabama." *The New
York Times.* http://www.nytimes.com/1995/03/26/us/chain-gangs-to-return-to-roads-of-
alabama.html

50 Quoted in Meares, T. (February 1996). "For Many, Commercializing the Chain Gang Is
Akin to Commercializing Slavery." *The University of Chicago Magazine,* p. 1. http://
magazine.uchicago.edu/9602/9602Voices.html

51 Berger, P. (1995). "Chain Gangs." *First Things* 58 (December): 12–17.
http://www.leaderu.com/ftissues/ft9512/opinion/opinion.html

52 Meares, "For Many," 1996.

53 Cox, M. W. (June 14, 1995). "Chain Gangs Newest Wedge Issue." *Montgomery Adver-
tiser.* http://www.majorcox.com/columns/chain.htm

54 "Chain Gangs Are Halted in Alabama." (June 21, 1996). *New York Times.* http://
query.nytimes.com/gst/fullpage.html?res=9D02E0DE1539F932A15755C0A960958260&
n=Top/Reference/Times%20Topics/Subjects/P/Prisons%20and%20Prisoners

55 This report also noted several violations of International Human Rights provisions,
such as Article 33 of the United Nations Standard Minimum Rules for the Treatment of
Prisoners (SMR), which states: "Instruments of restraint, such as handcuffs, chains,
irons and strait jackets, shall never be applied as a punishment. Furthermore, chains or
irons shall not be used as restraints." Amnesty International (January 1996). "United
States of America: Florida Reintroduces Chain Gangs." http://web.amnesty.org/library/
Index/engAMR510021996

56 "U.S. Prisoners Go Back on the Chain Gang." http://www.mywire.com/a/AFP/
US-prisoners-go-back-chain/847081?&pbl=273. See also "Women Get Equal Rights in
Chain Gang." (July 5, 2005). http://www.mariononline.com/articles/news/articles/000007/
000726.htm

57 "Sheriff Runs Female Chain Gang." (October 29, 2003). CNN News. http://www.cnn.com/
2003/US/Southwest/10/29/chain.gang.reut/

58 Russell-Brown, K. *The Color of Crime* (2nd ed.). New York: NYU Press, 2009, pp. 146–147.

59 Reiman, J. *The Rich Get Richer and the Poor Get Prison* (8th ed.). Boston: Allyn &
Bacon, 2007, p. 65.

60 Russell-Brown, *The Color of Crime,* p. 101.

61 Ibid., p.14.

62 Mauer, M. (2009). "Racial Impact Statements: Changing Policies to Address Disparities,"
p. 1. http://www.sentencingproject.org/Admin/Documents/publications/rd_abaarticle.pdf

63 Ibid.

64 Bonczar, T. P. (August 2003). "Prevalence of Imprisonment in the U.S. Population, 1974–
2001." Washington, DC: Bureau of Justice Statistics, p. 1. http://www.ojp.usdoj.gov/bjs/
pub/pdf/piusp01.pdf

65 Ibid., p. 5. Until the 1990s Hispanics were included with whites, making comparisons
difficult. See Miller, J. G. *Search and Destroy: African American Males in the Criminal
Justice System.* Cambridge: Cambridge University Press, 1996. See also Hallett, M. *Private Prisons in America: A Critical Race Perspective.* Champaign: University of Illinois
Press, 2005.

66 Fellner, J. (March 5, 2009). "In Anti-Drug Policy, Race Remains." http://www.hrw.org/
en/news/2009/03/17/anti-drug-policy-race-remains

67 A Delaware prosecutor is quoted as follows: "Sure, it's true we prosecute a high percentage of minorities for drugs. The simple fact is, if you have a population, minority or
not, that is conducting most of their illegal business on the street, those cases are easy
pickings for the police." (Mauer, M. *Race to Incarcerate.* Washington, DC: The Sentencing Project, 1999, p. 142). An excellent history of the war on drugs is provided by

Baume, D. *Smoke and Mirrors: The War on Drugs and the Politics of Failure*. New York: Back Bay Books, 1997.

[68] Little, D. (July 22, 2007). "Drug War Enforcement Hits Minorities Hardest: Drug Arrests Reveal Racial Gap." *Chicago Tribune*, p. 1.

[69] Donziger, S. R. *The Real War on Crime: The Report of the National Criminal Justice Commission*. New York: Harper Perennial, 1996, p. 115; Tonry, M. *Malign Neglect: Race, Crime, and Punishment in America*. New York: Oxford University Press, 1995; Mauer, *Race to Incarcerate*; Cole, D. *No Equal Justice: Race and Class in the American Criminal Justice System*. New York: The New Press, 1999.

[70] Maguire, K. and A. L. Pastore, eds. *Sourcebook on Criminal Justice Statistics—1995*. Washington, DC: Department of Justice, Bureau of Justice Statistics, 1996, p. 550.

[71] Human Rights Watch (2009). "Decades of Disparity: Drug Arrests and Race in the United States," p. 1. http://www.hrw.org/en/reports/2009/03/02/decades-disparity-0

[72] Human Rights Watch (March 2, 2009). "U.S. Drug Arrests Skewed by Race: National Data on 1980–2007 Cases Show Huge Disparities." http://www.hrw.org/en/news/2009/03/02/us-drug-arrests-skewed-race

[73] Ibid.

[74] Maguire and Pastore, *Sourcebook on Criminal Justice Statistics—1995*, p. 492.

[75] The Sentencing Project (May 2009). "Federal Crack Cocaine Sentencing," p. 4. http://www.sentencingproject.org/Admin/Documents/publications/dp_crack_sentencing.pdf

[76] Kyckelhahn, T. and T. Cohen. *Felony Defendants in Large Urban Counties, 2004*. Washington, DC: Bureau of Justice Statistics, NCJ 221152, 2008, p. 2. http://ojp.usdoj.gov/bjs/pub/pdf/fdluc04.pdf

[77] Street, P. *The Vicious Circle: Race, Prisons, Jobs, and Community in Chicago, Illinois and the Nation*. Chicago: Chicago Urban League, 2002, p. 22.

[78] Human Rights Watch, "Decades of Disparity," pp. 8–11.

[79] Human Rights Watch. *Targeting Blacks: Drug Law Enforcement and Race in the United States*, 2008, p. 41. http://www.hrw.org/sites/default/files/reports/us0508_1.pdf

[80] Johnston, L. D., P. M. O'Malley, J. G. Bachman, and J. E. Schulenberg. *Monitoring the Future: National Results on Adolescent Drug Use. Overview of Key Findings 2008*. Bethesda, MD: National Institute on Drug Abuse (NIH Publication No. 09-7401), 2009, p. 45. http://www.drugabuse.gov/PDF/overview2008.pdf; see also Centers for Disease Control. *Health, United States 2008*, table 67, p. 302. http://www.cdc.gov/nchs/data/hus/hus08.pdf#067

[81] SAMHSA, Office of Applied Studies, *National Survey on Drug Use and Health, 2007*, table 1.19A. http://www.oas.samhsa.gov/NSDUH/2k7NSDUH/tabs/Sect1peTabs1to46.htm#Tab1.19A

[82] Human Rights Watch, *Targeting Blacks*, p. 46.

[83] Ibid., p. 48.

[84] Ibid., p. 4.

[85] SAMHSA, *National Survey on Drug Use and Health, 2007*, table 1.34A.

[86] Coyle, M. (2004). "Race and Class Penalties in Crack Cocaine Sentencing." Washington, DC: The Sentencing Project.

[87] Fields, G. (April 30, 2009). "Shorter Sentences Sought for Crack." *Wall Street Journal*, p. A3.

[88] Wagner, D. *The Poorhouse: America's Forgotten Institution*. New York: Rowman & Littlefield, 2005. For more detailed treatment of the notion of jails and prisons as "poorhouses" see Morris, N. and D. J. Rothman, eds. *The Oxford History of the Prison*. New York: Oxford University Press, 1995.

[89] As far as I can tell, the first scholar to use this term to describe the American criminal justice system was Daniel Georges-Abeyie in 1990: "The Myth of a Racist Criminal Justice System?" In Maclean, B. and D. Milovanovic, eds., *Racism, Empiricism, and Criminal Justice*. Vancouver: Collective Press. See his foreword to Milovanovic, D. and K. Russell, eds. *Petit Apartheid in the U.S. Criminal Justice System*. Durham, NC: Carolina

Academic Press, 2001; see also the following: Davis, C., R. Estes, and V. Schiraldi *"Three Strikes": The New Apartheid*. San Francisco: Center on Juvenile and Criminal Justice, 1996; Hewitt, C., K. Kubota, and V. Schiraldi. *Race and Incarceration in San Francisco: Localizing Apartheid*. San Francisco: Center on Juvenile and Criminal Justice, 1992; Shelden, R. G., W. B. Brown, and S. Listwan. "The New American Apartheid: The Incarceration of African-Americans." In S. L. Browning, R. R. Miller, and R. D. Coates, eds., *The Common Good: A Critical Examination of Law and Social Control*. Durham, NC: Carolina Academic Press, 2004.

[90] Fowles, R. and M. Merva (1996). "Wage Inequality and Criminal Activity: An Extreme Bounds Analysis for the United States." *Criminology* 34: 163–182.

[91] Parenti, C. *Lockdown America: Police and Prisons in the Age of Crisis*. New York: Verso, 1999.

[92] Massey, D. and N. Denton. *American Apartheid: Segregation and the Making of the Underclass*. Cambridge: Harvard University Press, 1993.

[93] Piven, F. F. and R. Cloward. *The Breaking of the American Social Compact*. New York: The New Press, 1997.

[94] Handler, J. F. and Y. Hasenfeld. *We the Poor People: Work, Poverty, and Welfare*. New Haven, CT: Yale University Press, 1997; Wilson, W. J. *The Truly Disadvantaged*. Chicago: University of Chicago Press, 1987; Massey and Denton, *American Apartheid*; for an historical look at the problem see two books by Michael Harrington: *The Other America*, New York: MacMillan, 1962; and *The New American Poverty*, New York: Penguin Books, 1984.

[95] Massey and Denton, *American Apartheid*.

[96] Brown, W. B. (1998). "The Fight for Survival: African-American Gang Members and Their Families in a Segregated Society." *Juvenile and Family Court Journal* 49 (2): 1–14.

[97] Wacquant, L. (2001). "Deadly Symbiosis: When Ghetto and Prison Meet and Mesh." *Punishment and Society* 3 (1): 95–134.

[98] Ibid., p. 103.

[99] Ibid., p. 97.

[100] Ibid, p. 105, emphasis in the original.

[101] Ibid., 107.

[102] Ibid., p. 108. The idea that schools are sort of "day prisons" has long been noted by critics. See Shelden, R. G. *Delinquency and Juvenile Justice in American Society*. Long Grove, IL: Waveland Press, 2006, chapter 10.

[103] Travis, J. "Invisible Punishment: An Instrument of Social Exclusion," p. 18. In M. Mauer and M. Chesney-Lind, eds., *Invisible Punishment: The Collateral Consequences of Mass Imprisonment*. New York: New Press, 2002, pp. 15–36.

[104] Ibid., p. 19.

[105] Ibid., p. 19.

[106] Clear, T. "The Problem with 'Addition by Subtraction': The Prison-Crime Relationship in Low-Income Communities." In Mauer and Chesney-Lind, eds., *Invisible Punishment*, pp. 181–193.

[107] "The Disenfranchisement of Ex-Felons: Citizenship, Criminality, and the Purity of the Ballot Box." (April 1989). *Harvard Law Review* 102.

[108] Ibid.

[109] Uggen, C. and J. Manza (2002). "Democratic Contraction? Political Consequences of Felon Disenfranchisement in the United States." *American Sociological Review* 67: 777–803. http://www.soc.umn.edu/~uggen/Uggen_Manza_ASR_02.pdf

[110] The Sentencing Project (September 2008). "Felony Disenfranchisement Laws in the United States." http://www.sentencingproject.org/Admin/Documents/publications/fd_bs_fdlawsinus.pdf

[111] Wheelock, D. (2005). "Collateral Consequences and Racial Inequality: Felon Status Restrictions as a System of Disadvantage." *Journal of Contemporary Criminal Justice* 21: 82–90.

[112] The "Felon Disenfranchisement Project": http://www.soc.umn.edu/%7Euggen/ FD_summary.htm. For the impact of the high disenfranchisement rate for African Americans during the 2000 election, see Palast, Greg. *The Best Democracy Money Can Buy*. New York: Penguin Books, 2002.

[113] Uggen and Manza, "Democratic Contraction?", p. 796. See also: Feeley, M. M. and J. Simon (1992). "The New Penology: Notes on the Emerging Strategy of Corrections and Its Implications." *Criminology* 30: 449–474; Wacquant, "Deadly Symbiosis"; Western, B. and K. Beckett (1999). "How Unregulated Is the U.S. Labor Market? The Penal System as a Labor Market." *American Journal of Sociology* 104: 1030–1060.

[114] Mauer, M. and T. Kansal. *Barred for Life: Voting Rights Restoration in Permanent Disenfranchisement States*. Washington, DC: The Sentencing Project, 2005. http://www.sentencingproject.org/pdfs/barredforlife.pdf

[115] King, R. S. *Expanding the Vote: State Felony Disenfranchisement Reform, 1997–2008*. Washington, DC: The Sentencing Project, 2008. http://sentencingproject.org/Admin/ Documents/publications/fd_statedisenfranchisement.pdf

[116] Travis, "Invisible Punishment."

[117] An even more alarming trend comes from another piece of legislation that clearly targets African Americans, namely the recent "Three Strikes" law in California. As reported by the Center on Juvenile and Criminal Justice, the results of this law are part of what they have called the "new apartheid." Their analysis of data on cases after the enactment of this law show that while African Americans make up only 7% of the California population, they constitute 23% of all felony arrests, but have so far constituted 43% of the state's "three strikes" prisoners (a rate that was 13 times that of whites). A detailed analysis of "three strikes" prosecutions in the counties of Los Angeles, San Diego, and Sacramento show that 90% of the cases were African Americans. The rate (per 100,000 population) for African Americans was 43.6, compared to only 2.6 for whites. Davis, Estes, and Schiraldi, *"Three Strikes"*; Hewitt, Kubota, and Schiraldi, *Race and Incarceration in San Francisco*; Schichor, D. and D. K. Sechrest, eds. *Three Strikes and You're Out: Vengeance as Public Policy*. Thousand Oaks, CA: Sage, 1996. For one of the most recent studies of "three strikes" see Elsner, A. *Gates of Injustice*. Upper Saddle River, NJ: Prentice-Hall, 2004.

5

Legalized Homicide
The Death Penalty in America

Throughout human history people have been put to death for a variety of crimes, ranging from the very petty (stealing bread) to the very serious (murder).[1] The penalty of death for certain crimes dates far back into history, at least to the eighteenth century BC. Every imaginable method of taking a human life has been used: stoning, drawing and quartering, beheading, burning at the stake, crucifixion, drowning, burying alive, breaking on a wheel, garroting, gibbeting, and disemboweling, to name some of the gruesome practices.[2] Most executions and other forms of punishment were conducted in public, often with large crowds watching. During the Medieval period, executions became ceremonial rituals, especially during the Inquisition. On many occasions the planned execution would be "announced thirty days in advance and would be scheduled to coincide with such momentous events as the coronation or marriage of a king or the birth of a royal child. . . . The pageantry would but thinly disguise the raw violence of the executions with which it culminated."[3] Often a grand procession would wend its way to the location of the execution.

After the Middle Ages public executions became relatively more tame, although often just as gruesome. Following a beheading, the head of the executed would be prominently displayed. Eventually public sensibilities changed for the better and put an end to most of these types of rituals, although not completely. In England many executions became "proper and dignified undertakings, marked by the ringing of church bells, special prayers for the condemned, and the final dropping of a handkerchief by the prisoner—if he was not overcome by fear—to signal his readiness to die."[4]

The Origins of the Death Penalty

The first established death penalty laws date as far back as the eighteenth century BC to the Code of King Hammurabi of Babylon, which prescribed the death penalty for 25 different crimes. The death penalty was also part of the fourteenth century BC's Hittite Code. The seventh century BC's Draconian Code of Athens made death the only punishment for all crimes. The fifth century BC's Twelve Tables of Roman law included death as punishment for singing a slanderous song or for a judge convicted of taking a bribe. Death sentences were carried out by such means as crucifixion, drowning, beating to death, burning alive, and impalement.

In the tenth century AD, hanging became the usual method of execution in Britain. In the following century, William the Conqueror would not allow persons to be hanged or otherwise executed for any crime, except in times of war. This enlightened approach ended. Under the reign of Henry VIII in the sixteenth century, estimates of the number of people executed reached 72,000. Some common methods of execution at that time were boiling, burning at the stake, hanging, beheading, and drawing and quartering. Executions were carried out for such capital offenses as marrying a Jew, not confessing to a crime, and treason.

The number of capital crimes in Britain continued to rise throughout the next two centuries. By the 1700s, 222 crimes were punishable by death, including stealing, cutting down a tree, and robbing a rabbit warren. Because of the severity of the death penalty, many juries would not convict defendants if the offense was not serious. This led to reforms of Britain's death penalty. From 1823 to 1837, the death penalty was eliminated for over 100 of the 222 crimes punishable by death.

In America during colonial times executions were also public, carried out on scaffolds located in the central part of town. The public executions were generally quite restrained. Although a few members of the nobility were put to death, the vast majority of those suffering capital punishment were outsiders—foreigners, minorities, or the poor. These were people "for whom spectators might feel the least sympathy."[5]

In 1612, Virginia passed the "Divine, Moral and Martial Laws," which applied the death penalty for such petty offenses as stealing grapes, killing chickens, and trading with Indians.[6] In Colonial America a large number of crimes mentioned as offenses in the Bible were theoretically punishable by death, including adultery, stubborn children, and cursing or smiting a parent. Rarely, however were offenders committing these acts executed.[7] In the Massachusetts Bay colony, statutory rape, rebellion, adultery, buggery, idolatry, witchcraft, bestiality, man-stealing, and blasphemy were all punishable by death, according to the law.[8] In practice, the death sentence was infrequently applied.

The Salem witchcraft trials from 1692 to 1693 were a notable exception. More than 200 people were accused of practicing witchcraft, and 20 people (mostly women) were executed. The trials have become synonymous with paranoia and injustice.[9]

The first execution in the colonies occurred in 1608. Captain George Kendall was executed in Virginia for being a spy for Spain.[10] From that time until 1972, there were 14,489 executions (see table 5.1). The Supreme Court invalidated all death penalty laws in 1972 in *Furman v. Georgia* because of the arbitrariness with which the laws were applied.[11] Although many believed the decision would end capital punishment in the United States, *Furman* resulted only in a four-year hiatus. In *Gregg v. Georgia*, the Supreme Court ruled that Georgia's new bifurcated proceedings (one trial to determine guilt and another trial to determine the sentence) sufficiently addressed the capricious imposition of death sentences.[12] Since *Gregg* in 1976 through June 11, 2009, there have been 1,168 executions.

Table 5.1   Executions in America, 1608–2004

	Espy File 1608–1972	DPIC 1976–2009*
White	41% (5,902)	57% (653)
Black	49% (7,084)	34% (405)
Native American	2% (353)	1% (15)
Hispanic	2% (295)	7% (85)
Other (includes Asian Pacific and unknown)	6% (855)	1%(9)
Total Executions	14,489	1,167

*executions as of 6/3/09

Source: Death Penalty Information Center. Executions 1608–1976 & 1976 to Present
http://deathpenaltyinfo.org/executions-united-states-1608-1976-state and Executions in 2009
http://deathpenaltyinfo.org/executions-united-states-2009

The movement to abolish the death penalty has a long history that can be traced to the writings of classical European writers such Montesquieu, Voltaire, and Bentham and to English prison reformer John Howard. Perhaps the strongest anti-death penalty statement comes from Cesare Beccaria in *On Crimes and Punishment*. He argued that the death penalty was "an act of war on the part of society" and it "is not useful because of the example of savagery it gives to men."[13] In America the first attempt to reform the death penalty was Thomas Jefferson's bill to revise Virginia's death penalty. The bill proposed that the death penalty be applied for just two crimes: murder and treason. It was defeated by only one vote. Benjamin Rush, one of the signers of the Declaration of Independence (also a founder of the Pennsylvania

Prison Society), was probably the first to challenge the belief that the death penalty is a deterrent and may have been the first American to discuss the brutalization effect, suggesting that the death penalty actually causes an increase in homicides. Largely through the efforts of Rush, along with Benjamin Franklin and William Bradford, Pennsylvania repealed the death penalty in 1794 for all offenses except first degree murder.[14]

Michigan became the first state to abolish the death penalty for all crimes except treason (in 1846). Later in the century Rhode Island and Wisconsin abolished the death penalty for all crimes. The abolitionist movement picked up steam through the Progressive Era (1900–1920); six states eliminated the death penalty, and three limited it to treason and first degree murder of a law enforcement officer. However, this reform was short-lived. The U.S. entry into World War I and the Bolshe-

Figure 5.1   Executions by State and Region

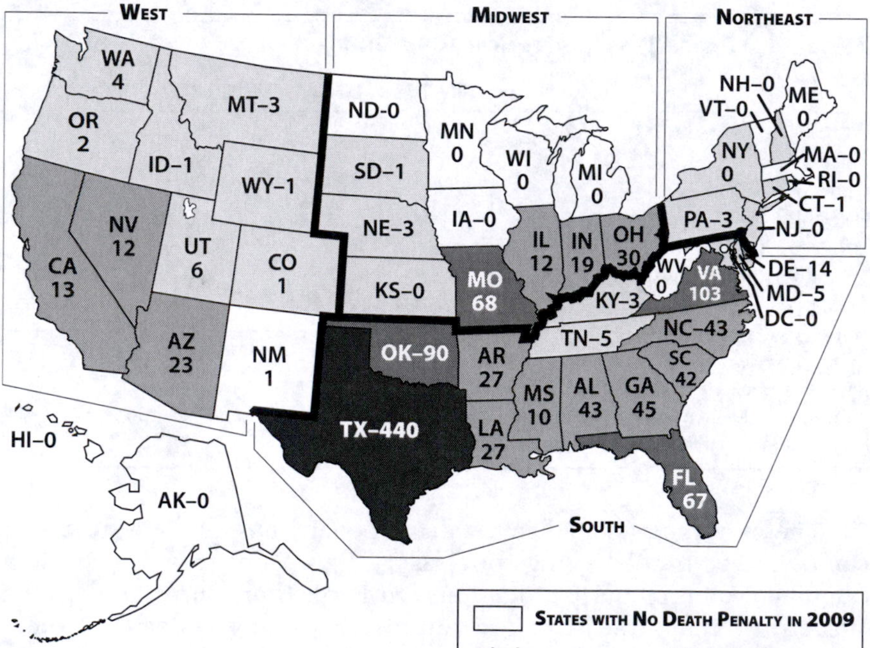

EXECUTIONS BY REGION
Northeast—4
Midwest—133
West—67
South—964

STATES WITH NO DEATH PENALTY IN 2009
Alaska, Hawaii, Iowa, Maine, Massachusetts, Michigan, Minnesota, New Mexico, North Dakota, Rhode Island, Vermont, West Virginia, Wisconsin, District of Columbia

Source: Death Penalty Information Center. "Executions by State." http://www.deathpenaltyinfo.org/executionmap2006.gif

vik Revolution prompted public fear, and five of the six abolitionist states reinstated the death penalty. The use of the death penalty increased during the Depression years, averaging 167 per year.

By the 1950s the abolitionist movement again gathered momentum, supported by a growing change in public opinion. Many nations around the world abolished the death penalty. Executions in the United States dropped from 1,296 in the 1940s to 724 in the 1950s and to 192 from 1960 to 1967 (there were no executions after June 2, 1967 until January 17, 1977).[15]

Lynching: Forerunner to the Death Chamber

A common form of punishment in frontier justice or *vigilantism* was lynching. The term originated during the American Revolution and was named after Virginian Charles Lynch. With his militia officers, he would capture Tory sympathizers and administer extralegal justice. In the early years of westward expansion, there was an absence of legitimate authority in the form of law enforcement or courts, and lynching was a common method of social control for cattle rustlers, gamblers, horse thieves, and others.[16]

It was not merely the absence of law but also the fact that, unlike Europe, there was never a reverence for the law in the United States and the corresponding respect for the tradition and ancient customs behind the law. In the West and the South, most people rarely came into contact with representatives of the law and hence felt that they were a "law unto themselves." In the representative form of government that emerged in the United States, people make the laws.

> Since they say what a judge can do, they entertain the idea that they may do this thing themselves. To execute a criminal deserving of death is to act merely in their sovereign capacity. . . . The tendency toward public disorder has existed in this country from its earliest settlement, and as the line of the frontier has slowly moved westward there has always been a region on the border where the forces of law were unorganized. There has thus been a constant opportunity for a plea of necessity in certain cases for resorting to the popular execution of justice.[17]

The readiness of citizens to take the law into their own hands is unmatched in other countries. This is one reason why lynching was a practice peculiar to the United States.

Shortly after the end of the Civil War, however, lynching took on racial and ethnic overtones. The targets of violence were primarily former slaves, ethnic immigrants (Jews, Asians, and European immigrants), and Native Americans.[18] The emancipation of slaves resulted in an increase in the fear of blacks. Having lost the tighter social control that existed on plantations, some white Southerners feared losing their status in relation to former slaves.

The plantation had been a self-contained world that encouraged owners to see themselves so much in control that they did not need the law or courts. Lynching flourished in this culture.[19] Lynching was most common in areas

> likely to have few towns, weak law enforcement, poor communication with the outside, and high levels of transiency among both races. . . . Lynching served as a method of law enforcement in sparsely populated places where white people felt especially insecure. . . . The sporadic violence of lynching was a way for white people to reconcile weak governments with a demand for an impossibly high level of racial mastery, a way to terrorize blacks into acquiescence by brutally killing those who intentionally or accidentally stepped over some invisible and shifting line of permissible behavior.[20]

Fear became a driving force behind lynching—fear of blacks getting "uppity," fear of blacks associating with white women, and worse still, fear of blacks "taking over."[21]

> In the nineteenth century most white people believed that lynching was an appropriate and constitutional approach to crime control, when courts proved too corrupt or incompetent to handle the problem. Since many whites believed blacks too animalistic for the courts to control, they always viewed lynching as an appropriate response to alleged or real black criminality. Since the Constitution protected the right of local government to control crime without any outside scrutiny or supervision, it also protected the custom of lynching.[22]

Accurate figures on the number of lynchings are impossible to come by since so many went unreported, but the best estimates available suggest that 4,740 people were lynched in the years from 1882 to1964. As shown in table 5.2, blacks constituted almost three-fourths of those lynched. Lynching of black people (mostly men) began to outnumber whites after 1886. In many years over 90% of those lynched were blacks. Again, these numbers reflect only the *reported* cases. Several researchers have argued that there were a large number of unreported cases of lynching in the South, especially between 1865 and 1875. The bodies of victims were either buried or burned. It is not unreasonable to assume that there are a number of unknown, unreported lynchings.[23]

Lynching became one of the most gruesome methods of vigilantism in American history. One historian describes it this way:

> By the 1890s lynchers increasingly employed burning, torture, and dismemberment to prolong suffering and excite a "festive atmosphere" among the killers and onlookers. White families brought small children to watch, newspapers sometimes carried advance

Table 5.2   Lynchings in the United States, by Race: 1882–1964

Year	White	Black (Percent of Total)	Total
1882–1886	475	301 (39%)	776
1887–1891	276	431 (61%)	707
1892–1896	272	604 (69%)	876
1897–1901	109	520 (83%)	629
1902–1906	37	364 (91%)	401
1907–1911	40	343 (90%)	383
1912–1916	24	270 (92%)	294
1917–1921	26	284 (92%)	310
1922–1926	17	136 (89%)	153
1927–1932	8	71 (90%)	79
1933–1937	4	73 (95%)	77
1938–1964	7	48 (87%)	55
Total	1,295	3,445 (73%)	4,740

Source: Tuskegee Institute Archives.
http://www.law.umkc.edu/faculty/projects/ftrials/shipp/lynchingyear.html

notices, railroad agents sold excursion tickets to announced lynching sites, and mobs cut off black victims' fingers, toes, ears, or genitalia as souvenirs. Nor was it necessarily the handiwork of a local rabble; not infrequently, the mob was encouraged or led by people prominent in the area's political and business circles. Lynching had become a ritual of interracial social control and recreation rather than simply a punishment for crime.[24]

Those involved in lynchings were rarely ever indicted by a grand jury (all white of course). In the rare instances where a trial took place, the court participants—the judge, prosecutor, jurors, and witnesses—were all white, from the same community, and sympathetic to the lynchers. If any were sentenced (a rarity), they were usually pardoned. A 1930s study of one hundred lynchings found that in at least half of the cases local police officers participated, and in virtually all of the rest the officers condoned the mob action.[25]

Black people could be lynched for a variety of reasons, and often for no reason at all. According to research by the Tuskegee Institute, between 1882 and 1951 41% were lynched for alleged felonious assault and 25% for alleged rape or attempted rape. More than one-fifth (22.7%) were lynched for miscellaneous offenses or no offense at all. The remaining 11% were for various trivial "offenses" such as "disputing with a white man," attempting to register to vote, "unpopularity," self-defense, testifying against a white man, "asking a white woman in marriage," and "peeping in a window."[26]

The lynching of black men accused of raping white women was notorious throughout this period—the "usual crime," in the words of

Mark Costanzo.[27] Even legal executions for rape were common, and almost all those executed were black men accused of raping white women. One study found that out of 361 rape convictions between 1945 and 1965 resulting in the death sentence, 89% of those sentenced to death were black men. After controlling for a number of variables, the best predictor of receiving the death sentence was the race of the victim—black men accused of raping white women were the most likely candidates to receive the death penalty.[28] One study looked at Georgia and North Carolina between 1882 and 1930, comparing blacks who were executed and those who were lynched. The study found that rape constituted 41% of those lynched in Georgia, compared to 34% in murder cases. In North Carolina the proportions were about equal (39% each).[29]

Lynching gave "dramatic warning to all black inhabitants that the ironclad system of white supremacy was not to be challenged by deed, word or even thought."[30] Lynching served as an extreme reminder of the power whites had over blacks. Indeed, as Ralph Ellison noted, "The ultimate goal of lynchers is that of achieving ritual purification through destroying the lynchers' identification with the basic humanity of their victims."[31] Lynchers were seemingly deaf to the screams of pain from victims and the sight and stench of burning flesh.

As mentioned above, most lynchings took place in small towns in isolated rural communities of the South. Of the documented lynchings, the largest numbers took place in Mississippi (581), Georgia (531), Texas (493), Louisiana (391), and Alabama (347). Most of the people responsible for the violence were poor and illiterate; their economic status was not very different from the blacks whose lives they took. Black men were often seen as economic competitors, and many whites resented any progress made by blacks. Raising a mob was "a quick and simple process, and racial antagonism made the killing of Negroes a type of local amusement which broke the monotony of rural life."[32] Lynchings imprinted a terrifying message on the hearts and minds of Southern blacks. The constant threat of violence from the KKK and lynchings enabled the white south to maintain a caste society, not unlike slavery, for decades.[33]

Shortly after the end of the Civil War, various organizations attempted to stop the practice of lynching. The antilynching campaigns lasted well into the twentieth century. Participants included the National Association of Colored Women (NACW), the National Association for the Advancement of Colored People (NAACP), the Council for Interracial Cooperation (CIC), and the Association of Southern Women for the Prevention of Lynching (ASWPL).[34] By the 1930s the campaigns were beginning to have an effect; the number of lynchings began to drop significantly. In the early 1930s, the Costigan-Wagner Act called for federal trials "for any law enforcement officers who failed to exercise their responsibilities during a lynching incident." Despite overwhelming public support, the bill did not pass. A national poll taken in 1937 found that "65 per cent of all southerners supported legislation that would have made lynching a federal crime."[35]

There is considerable evidence that the decline in lynchings was matched by an increase in legal executions. Terance Miethe and Hong Lu found an almost perfect correlation (see figure 5.2). In the 1890s the number of lynchings exceeded legal executions by a ratio of about 1.5: 1. By the second decade of the twentieth century, the numbers were about the same; by the 1930s legal executions far exceeded lynchings.[36] Throughout the history of the death penalty in America, blacks have been proportionately far more likely to receive the death penalty. It has become, in short, a form of *legalized lynching*.

Figure 5.2   Lynchings and State-Based Execution

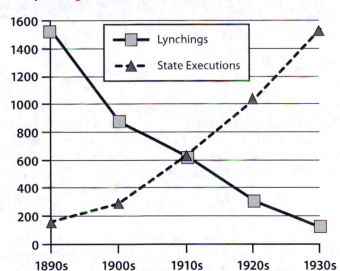

Source: Miethe, T. and H. Lu (2005). *Punishment: A Comparative Historical Perspective*. New York: Cambridge University Press, p. 98.

The Death Penalty Today

On January 1, 2009, there were 3,297 people on death row.[37] From 1993 to 1999, the number of death sentences per year averaged more than 300. By 2008, the number of death sentences declined by 60%[38] California leads the way with 678 on death row, followed by Florida (402), Texas (358), Pennsylvania (226), Alabama (207) and Ohio (181).[39] Of the inmates on death row, 45% are white, 42% black, and 11% Hispanic.

Figure 5.3   Size of Death Row by Year

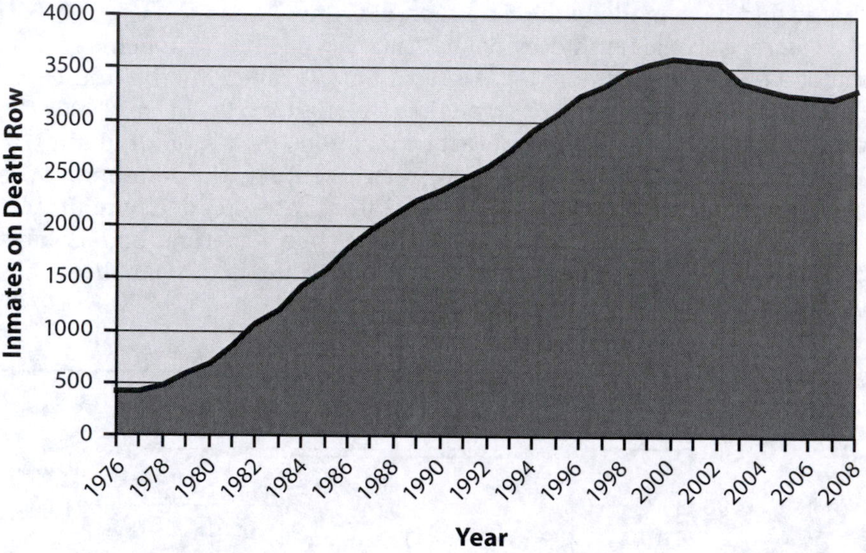

Earlier we mentioned the two landmark Supreme Court decisions in the 1970s: *Furman v. Georgia* and *Gregg v. Georgia*. There were nine separate opinions, one from each of the justices, in *Furman*. Overall, the Court ruled that the death penalty *as it was administered* constituted cruel and unusual punishment, in violation of the Eighth and Fourteenth amendments of the Constitution. The Court did not rule that the death penalty *in and of itself* constituted cruel and unusual punishment. The response by the states was almost immediate. Appeals began flowing into the court system, and within four years of *Furman* the Supreme Court made a significant ruling on capital punishment

In *Gregg v. Georgia*, the Court upheld the Georgia statute calling for the death penalty for murder. The Court ruled: "A punishment must not be excessive, but this does not mean that the states must seek the minimal standards available. The imposition of the death penalty for the crime of murder does not violate the Constitution." In two other decisions the Court ruled similarly (*Proffit v. Florida*, 1976 and *Jurek v. Texas*, 1976). However, in *Coker v. Georgia* (1977) the Court ruled that the death penalty for rape constituted cruel and unusual punishment.

Gary Gilmore was the first person executed after *Gregg* ended the *de facto* abolition of the death penalty of *Furman*. He was executed in 1977 by a firing squad in Utah (the state was the only one that allowed the prisoner a choice between the firing squad or hanging). In June 2009, 35 states plus the federal government had the death penalty (including New Hampshire and Kansas that have had no executions since the *Gregg* decision).[40] Fifteen states plus Washington DC do not have the death penalty (including New Mexico that eliminated the death penalty in 2009; two people remain on death row because the law was not retroactive). In 2009, ten states and Congress were considering proposals to eliminate the death penalty.[41]

THE RACE FACTOR

Race figures prominently in the imposition of the death penalty. Of the 1,168 people executed since 1976, 56% (654) were white, 35% (405) were black, 7% (85) were Hispanic, and 2% (24) were other races. Nationally, 50% of murder victims are white, but 80% of the victims in cases involving a death sentence were white.[42] Several studies have noted that there are vast discrepancies in the application of the death penalty according to the race of the victim and the race of the offender.

In North Carolina, the odds of receiving a death sentence increased 3.5 times if the victims were white.[43] In California, people who killed whites were more than three times as likely to be sentenced to death as those who killed blacks and four times more likely as those who killed Latinos.[44] A Maryland study by criminologists Raymond Paternoster and Robert Brame found that the state's death penalty system was "tainted with racial bias" at every stage of the process, including whether or not the prosecutor sought the death penalty in a murder case.[45] Analysis of 1,936 indictments from October 1981 through 2002 in Ohio found that offenders "facing a death penalty charge for killing a white person were twice as likely to go to death row than if they had killed a black victim. Death sentences were handed down in 18% of cases where the victims were white compared with 8.5% of cases where victims were black."[46] Studies in Indiana, Virginia, North Carolina, New Jersey and the federal system also found strong evidence of racial bias in the death penalty process.[47]

Research documenting racial bias in the death penalty has a long history. Some studies date back more than seventy years.

- Guy B. Johnson studied homicide cases in Richmond, Virginia, and in five counties in North Carolina during the 1930s. He found that the death penalty was most often applied when the victim was white and the offender was black and least likely when both the offender and the victim were black.[48]

- Wolfgang, Kelly, and Nolde studied 439 cases of men sentenced to death in Pennsylvania for murder between 1914 and 1958. They found that 20% of whites had their sentences commuted to life imprisonment versus 11% of blacks.[49]

- Of the more than 15,000 executions between 1608 and 1986, a mere 30 cases were found (about 0.2%) in which a white person was executed for killing a black.[50]

- Elmer Johnson, in a study of rape cases resulting in the imposition of the death penalty in North Carolina between 1909 and 1954, found that blacks were more likely than whites to be executed. A study of Florida cases found that blacks who raped whites were much more likely to receive the death penalty than whites who raped blacks.[51]

Bias begins with the charging process; blacks are more likely than whites to be charged with capital crimes and more likely to be sentenced to death if so charged.[52] There is evidence that juries are often prejudiced against minorities, so that in capital cases they are more likely to convict minorities than whites.[53]

McCleskey v. Kemp

Perhaps the most famous of the studies about racial bias was an investigation of almost 2,500 capital cases in Georgia from 1973 through 1979. In their extensive, two-part study David Baldus, George Woodworth, and Charles Pulaski found that the race of the victim played a key role in prosecutorial decisions to seek the death penalty and decisions by juries to impose it. Even after controlling for 230 nonracial variables, race remained the most significant variable.[54] The NAACP Legal Defense Fund (LDF) presented evidence from the study in *McCleskey v. Kemp*, another landmark case that originated in Georgia, as did *Furman* and *Gregg*.

A black defendant, Warren McCleskey, claimed that his death sentence for the murder of a white police officer was unconstitutional because it was imposed on the basis of his race and the race of the victim in violation of the Fourteenth Amendment's equal-protection clause. He also argued that discriminatory application of the death penalty was arbitrary and capricious and violated the Eighth Amendment prohibition of unreasonable punishment.[55] The Supreme Court ruled in 1987 that statistical proof of systemic racial disparities did not demonstrate a constitutionally significant risk of racial bias.

> Our assumption that the Baldus study is statistically valid does not include the assumption that the study shows that racial considerations actually enter into any sentencing decisions in Georgia. Even a sophisticated multiple regression analysis such as the Baldus study can only demonstrate a *risk* that the factor of race entered into some capital sentencing decisions and a necessarily lesser risk that race entered into any particular sentencing decision.[56]

The Court addressed McCleskey's contention that the Baldus study proved that the state of Georgia acted with a discriminatory purpose in allowing the capital punishment statue to remain in force despite discriminatory application of the sentence. The Court ruled that discriminatory purpose implies more than intent as volition or intent as awareness of consequences. It implies that the decisionmaker, in this case a state legislature, selected or reaffirmed a particular course of action at least in part "because of," not merely "in spite of," its adverse effects upon an identifiable group.[57]

The Court also cautioned that McCleskey's statistical evidence must be viewed in the context that he was challenging decisions "at the heart of the State's criminal justice system." The decision mentioned that society achieves one of its most basic tasks—protecting the lives of its citizens—through criminal laws against murder, which "necessarily requires discretionary judgments."

> Because discretion is essential to the criminal justice process, we would demand exceptionally clear proof before we would infer that the discretion has been abused. The unique nature of the decisions at issue in this case also counsels against adopting such an inference from the disparities indicated by the Baldus study. Accordingly, we hold that the Baldus study is clearly insufficient to support an inference that any of the decisionmakers in McCleskey's case acted with discriminatory purpose.[58]

The ruling stated that the exercise of discretion means that people can reach different conclusions when looking at exactly the same situations. It rejected what it characterized as the Baldus approach of attributing different results in cases with similar circumstances to racial bias. It said the approach ignores realities.

> There are, in fact, no exact duplicates in capital crimes and capital defendants. The type of research submitted here tends to show which of the directed factors were effective, but is of restricted use in showing what undirected factors control the exercise of constitutionally required discretion.[59]

This phrase appears twice within the ruling—once near the beginning and once near the end: "At most, the Baldus study indicates a discrepancy that appears to correlate with race."[60] The first occurrence reads:

> At most, the Baldus study indicates a discrepancy that appears to correlate with race, but this discrepancy does not constitute a major systemic defect. Any mode for determining guilt or punishment has its weaknesses and the potential for misuse. Despite such imperfections, constitutional guarantees are met when the mode for determining guilt or punishment has been surrounded with safeguards to make it as fair as possible.

Randall Kennedy noted sarcastically that the qualifier "at most" is like saying that "at most" the many studies on lung cancer "indicate a discrepancy that appears to correlate with smoking."[61]

What is perhaps most interesting about this ruling is that the Court appeared to be afraid of what the logical conclusions of such evidence might be. Justice Powell, writing for the majority, noted that such evidence "throws into serious question the principles that underlie our entire criminal justice system . . . if we accepted McCleskey's claim that racial bias impermissibly tainted the capital sentencing decision, we would soon be faced with similar claims as to other types of penalty."[62]

The four dissenting justices leveled the first attacks on the ruling. In his dissent, Justice Brennan (with Blackmun, Marshall, and Stevens concurring) remarked on the Court's unwillingness to accept McCleskey's evidence based on the Baldus study because of the fear that such acceptance would bring into question all aspects of criminal sentencing:

> Taken on its face, such a statement seems to suggest a fear of too much justice. Yet surely the majority would acknowledge that if striking evidence indicated that other minority groups, or women, or even persons with blond hair, were disproportionately sentenced to death, such a state of affairs would be repugnant to deeply rooted conceptions of fairness.[63]

Most of the critics voiced the opinion that this ruling sent a message that racial bias is perfectly constitutional. *McCleskey v. Kemp* "nearly eliminated the incentive of federal and state courts and legislatures to address meaningfully the issue of racial discrimination in the administration of the death penalty and has provided them with a political and legal framework for denying and avoiding the issue."[64] McCleskey was eventually executed in the electric chair on September 26, 1991. Justice Thurgood Marshall, who joined two other justices in a dissent for a stay of execution, stated that it appears that "the court values expediency over human life."[65]

David Cole has argued that it would be nearly impossible to prove that a prosecutor and a jury have imposed the death penalty in a particular case because of the defendant's race. He notes that there are "longstanding rules" that prohibit defendants from obtaining discovery from the prosecution and therefore "unless the prosecutor admits to acting for racially biased reasons, it will be difficult to pin discrimination on the prosecutor." Defendants encounter the same problem in proving discrimination by jurors. In short, says Cole, "defendants are precluded from discovering evidence of intent from the two actors whose discriminatory intent the *McCleskey* Court required them to establish."[66]

Although *McCleskey* ostensibly allowed claimants in federal courts to present evidence of bias based on the race of victims, the procedural victory was undermined by the two substantive rulings that violations of the Fourteenth Amendment require direct evidence of intentional discrimination by the prosecutor or jury (an almost impossible burden of proof) and that the provisions of the Eighth Amendment cannot be based solely on evidence of a significant risk of racial bias.[67] Essentially the Court insulated laws and policies from challenges based on disparate treatment.

Within a decade of McCleskey, the number of minorities in prison
exceeded the total number of persons incarcerated in the U.S. in the
year preceding the decision. Today, race plays a critical role in every
aspect of the criminal justice process with African Americans and
other minorities ticketed, searched, arrested, convicted and sentenced at significantly disproportionate rates.[68]

Subsequent cases on this issue had almost identical results. In
Dobbs v. Zant (a 1989 case—once again involving Georgia), the Court
rejected the appeal even though several jurors referred to African
Americans as "coloreds" and two jurors admitted using "nigger" in
their conversations. Even the defense attorney (a court-appointed attorney) admitted using "nigger" and believed that African Americans
make good basketball players, but not teachers.[69]

Some members of Congress responded to the *McCleskey* decision
by adding a "Racial Justice Act" to the Omnibus Crime Bill of 1994. By a
slim majority, the House voted for this provision, which would have
allowed those on death row to challenge their sentence based on statistical evidence of race discrimination in capital cases, as had McCleskey.
But it was defeated in the Senate and dropped from the 1994 bill. Sena-
tor Orin Hatch stated that the "so-called Racial Justice Act has nothing
to do with racial justice and everything to do with abolishing the death
penalty. . . . It would convert every death penalty case into a massive
sideshow of statistical squabbles and quota quarrels."[70] In 1998, the
Kentucky legislature passed its Racial Justice Act, which allows a capital defendant to use statistical evidence to show that race influenced
the decision to seek the death penalty in her or his case. North Carolina
was considering a similar statute in 2009.

Defendants in capital cases have fared somewhat better when seeking a new trial by challenging peremptory strikes in the selection of
juries. *Batson v. Kentucky* (a noncapital case decided in 1986) created a
new standard for determining whether a prosecutor's use of peremptory
strikes against African Americans in the jury selection process was
influenced by racial discrimination.[71] The previous standard had been
decided in *Swain v. Alabama* in 1965. In that decision, the Supreme
Court declared that a prosecutor's strikes would be presumed legitimate
unless the defendant could show a long-standing pattern of discrimination in the jury selection process by the prosecutor. Proving continuous
discrimination over a long period was essentially impossible. *Batson*
removed that standard, which the Court characterized as "crippling."

Miller-El v. Dretke challenged the jury selection based on *Batson*.[72]
He had been sentenced to death for murder. The Dallas County prosecutors used peremptory strikes to prevent 10 of the 11 qualified black
jurors from serving on the jury hearing his case. The Supreme Court
ruled Miller-El had met the *Batson* standard and noted:

> It is well known that prejudices often exist against particular classes in the community, which sway the judgment of jurors, and which, therefore, operate in some cases to deny to persons of those classes the full enjoyment of that protection which others enjoy. Defendants are harmed, of course, when racial discrimination in jury selection compromises the right of trial by impartial jury, but racial minorities are harmed more generally, for prosecutors drawing racial lines in picking juries establish state-sponsored group stereotypes rooted in, and reflective of, historical prejudice.[73]

Miller-El was granted a new trial. He accepted a plea for a 20-year sentence on the same day that the Supreme Court ruled similarly in *Snyder v. Louisiana*.[74] Allen Snyder, an African American, was sentenced to death by an all-white jury in Louisiana. The prosecutor had used peremptory strikes to exclude all black prospective jurors from the jury.

WRONGFUL CONVICTIONS

The question of innocent people being convicted in capital cases is a critical issue, which has received increasing attention in the last two decades. Some of the factors contributing to wrongful convictions include: inadequate legal representation, racial prejudice, police and prosecutorial misconduct, suppression and/or misinterpretation of mitigating evidence, perjured or mistaken eyewitness testimony. jailhouse "snitch" testimony, and community/political pressure to solve a case.[75]

Baze v. Rees was not a challenge to capital punishment itself (the question considered was whether lethal injection constituted cruel and unusual punishment because improper administration could result in needless suffering), but two justices mentioned the topic of wrongful convictions. Justice Stephen Breyer noted:

> The death penalty itself, of course, brings with it serious risks, for example, risks of executing the wrong person, risks that unwarranted animus (in respect, e.g., to the race of victims) may play a role, risks that those convicted will find themselves on death row for many years, perhaps decades, to come. These risks in part explain why that penalty is so controversial.[76]

Justice John Paul Stevens stated: "The risk of executing innocent defendants can be entirely eliminated by treating any penalty more severe than life imprisonment without the possibility of parole as constitutionally excessive."[77]

One detailed study found evidence of 400 defendants from 1900 through 1991 who were sentenced to death but were innocent; an estimated two dozen were executed—and many more spent years in prison. A disproportionate number were African Americans.[78] A Columbia University study of 4,578 capital appeals between 1973 and 1995 found serious "reversible errors" in almost 70% of the cases.[79]

Death sentences were overturned in two-thirds of the appeals, and 95 death row prisoners were completely exonerated.

The Death Penalty Information Center maintains a list of defendants sentenced to death whose convictions were overturned (charges were dropped or they were acquitted in a second trial) or they were pardoned based on evidence of innocence. From 1973 to June 2009, 133 people have been released from death row, including one woman. The average number of years between sentencing and exoneration is 9.8 years (years of incarceration served total 1,303). Of the 133 exonerated, 67 were black, 52 white, 12 Latino, and 2 other races. Twenty-two of the exonerations were in Florida, 19 in Illinois, and 9 in Texas; the remaining 83 exonerations occurred in 23 other states. From 1973 through 1999, exonerations averaged 3.1 per year. Since 2000, there have been an average of 5 exonerations per year.[80]

There are a number of reasons for the increased attention to innocence. Programs providing pro bono assistance to determine the innocence of wrongfully convicted inmates were established in journalism and law schools throughout the country. The efforts of the Center on Wrongful Convictions and the Medill Innocence Project at Northwestern University convinced the governor of Illinois to institute a moratorium on executions. The number of media stories on exonerations is 10 times greater than before 1991.[81] Scientific technologies, such as DNA testing, also play a major role.

The Innocence Project is affiliated with the Benjamin N. Cardozo School of Law at Yeshiva University. It was founded in 1992 and is dedicated to exonerating wrongfully convicted people through DNA testing and reforming the criminal justice system to prevent future injustice. To date, 240 people nationwide have been exonerated through DNA testing. Kirk Bloodsworth was the first death row inmate to be released on the basis of DNA evidence in 1993; since that time, DNA evidence has helped exonerate 16 others.[82]

The Innocence Project took the case of William Osborne, who sought DNA testing to prove his innocence in a 1993 rape. The Supreme Court's 5–4 decision in 2009 found that Osborne's constitutional rights were not violated.[83] The decision left it to state legislatures and state courts to determine how and when people who have been convicted of crimes can get access to DNA testing. Although the Innocence Project characterized the decision as flawed and disappointing, it believes the ruling will have a limited impact. Congress and 47 states have passed legislation granting DNA testing in at least some cases. Peter Neufeld, who argued the case, said: "Today's decision recognized the unique power of DNA testing to prove guilt or innocence and noted the progress we've made in state legislatures. We are more determined than ever to pass laws granting DNA testing in Alaska, Massachusetts and Oklahoma."[84]

INTERNATIONAL COMPARISONS

In 1977, only 16 countries had abolished the death penalty for all crimes; by 2009, the number had grown to 94. Ten countries allow the death penalty only for exceptional crimes, and 35 countries are abolitionist in practice (no executions in the last ten years). In the past decade, an average of over three countries a year have abolished the death penalty.[85] Of the 58 retentionist countries, only 25 carried out executions in 2008.[86] In 2008, at least at least 8,864 people (7,003 in China) were sentenced to death in 52 countries around the world; 2,390 people (76% in Asia; 21% in the Middle East and North Africa) were known to have been executed. The following countries carried out executions in 2008: China (at least 1,718), Iran (at least 346), Saudi Arabia (at least 102), the United States (37), Pakistan (at least 36), and Iraq (at least 34).[87]

DETERRENCE

Americans generally agree that the death penalty is not a deterrent and 38% believe it is imposed unfairly.[88] Previous Gallup research has shown that they widely acknowledge that some innocent people have been executed. In October 2008, 64% favored the death penalty as punishment for murder. In the 1980s and 1990s, support averaged 75%, with the peak at 80% in 1994. Support for capital punishment was substantially lower from the late 1950s through the early 1970s; 41% opposed the penalty in 1972.

Michael Radelet and Traci Lacock surveyed leading criminologists, asking them to answer questions about capital punishment based on their understandings of the empirical research. Eighty-eight percent do not believe the death penalty acts as a deterrent to homicide and expressed the view that abolition of the death penalty would not have any significant effect on murder rates.

> Our survey indicates that the vast majority of the world's top criminologists believe that the empirical research has revealed the deterrence hypothesis for a myth. . . . The consensus among criminologists is that the death penalty does not add any significant deterrent effect above that of long-term imprisonment.[89]

Juveniles and the Death Penalty

Critics of the death penalty have consistently charged that the most severe punishment is an inappropriate penalty for individuals who have not attained full physical or emotional maturity at the time of their actions. In 2005, the U.S. Supreme Court arrived at the same conclusion. In a 5–4 decision the Court ruled in *Roper v. Simmons* that applying the death penalty against juveniles who commit their crimes when under the age of 18 violated the Eighth Amendment to the Constitution. Writing for the majority, Justice Anthony Kennedy wrote: "The age of 18 is the point where society draws the line for many purposes between childhood and adulthood. It is, we conclude, the age at which the line for death eligibility ought to rest."[90]

The Supreme Court, which had abolished executions for the mentally retarded in 2002, decided to take a closer look at the death penalty for crimes committed as juveniles. Four members of the Supreme Court had already gone on record as being against the practice, with Justice John Paul Stevens noting that "The practice of executing such offenders is a relic of the past and is inconsistent with evolving standards of decency in a civilized society." His opinion was shared by Justices David H. Souter, Ruth Bader Ginsburg, and Stephen Breyer. These views echoed the court's *Atkins v. Virginia* ruling in 2002 that it is unconstitutional to execute the mentally retarded.[91] In both cases, a primary issue was the defendants' ability to understand their situation, plus their level of culpability.[92]

At the time of *Roper v. Simmons*, 38 states and the federal government had statutes authorizing the death penalty for certain forms of homicide. Of these 38 states, four had chosen the age of 17 and 20 states used age 16 as the minimum age a person must be in order to receive the death penalty. At the time, about one in every 50 individuals on death row was a juvenile offender. Almost 3% of all new court commitments to death row were youths who had committed their crimes while a juvenile.[93] Imposing sentences of "life without parole" on waived (tried as adults) juveniles for crimes committed at 13 or 14 years of age and executing them for crimes committed at 16 or 17 challenged the social construction of adolescence and the idea that juveniles are less criminally responsible than adults.[94] One study found that executions for crimes committed by youths under 18 accounted for 1.8% (357) of all confirmed legal executions carried out between 1642 and the present. As of March 2004, there were 73 persons (28 in Texas) on death row who were juvenile offenders when they committed their crime. Between 1976 and March 2004, 22 juvenile offender executions have been carried out in the U.S.[95]

Internationally, the U.S. had accounted for the majority of known juvenile offender executions, and it had more juveniles on death row compared to any other country. More than 72 countries that retain the death penalty in law have abolished it for juvenile offenders. The United States—the only Western democratic nation—was one of six countries (the others were Iran, Pakistan, Saudi Arabia, Yemen, and Nigeria) to execute juveniles in the 1990s.

The legality of capital punishment for juveniles had previously been decided by individual jurisdictions. In the case of *Thompson v. Oklahoma* (487 U.S. 815, 1988), the Supreme Court ruled that executing youths under the age of 16 was unconstitutional and "the chrono-logical age of the minor is itself a relevant mitigating factor."[96]

Media coverage of high-profile juvenile homicides had prompted public calls for the death penalty for juvenile offenders. Several politi-cians appeared to be in a contest for who could appear to be the tough-est. In 1996 the governor of New Mexico (Gary Johnson) publicly stated that he favored the death penalty for juveniles as young as 13.[97] In 1997 the governor of California (Pete Wilson) supported the death penalty against 14-year-olds, and the speaker of the California assem-bly stated that he would support the death penalty for "hardened crimi-nals" as young as 13. A Texas state representative contemplated introducing legislation under which 11-year-olds who commit murder could be sentenced to death.

THE CASE OF *ROPER V. SIMMONS*

Roper v. Simmons marked the first use of medical science to deter-mine policy on the sentencing of juveniles. Research on the develop-ment of the adolescent brain contributed to the decision.

It is well recognized and documented that the adolescent years are marked by trials and tribulations—storm and stress, as it is often called. A friend once gave this definition of adolescence: "adults with less sense." The term "juvenile delinquent" and the existence of a "juvenile" court reflect the popular recognition that kids are still growing up. The term "juvenile" means "young, immature, redeemable, subject to change." As a society, we have long recognized this, which is why we impose age requirements for certain behaviors—voting, serving on a jury, entering into contracts, getting married, consuming alcohol and tobacco, and many more. We even limit what kinds of movies juveniles can see without an adult present.

Before *Roper v. Simmons*, however, the United States was one of a small number of nations (Congo, Nigeria, Saudi Arabia, and Iran) to treat juveniles as adults for serious crimes.[98] Christopher Simmons was 17 when he was arrested for the murder of Shirley Crook in Missouri in 1993. In 2003, the Missouri Supreme Court reviewed his case. The court determined that juvenile executions violated the Eighth Amend-ment's provision against cruel and unusual punishment under the "evolving standards of decency" test. Simmons' death sentence was vacated, and he was sentenced to life without parole. The case was appealed by the State of Missouri in July 2004.[99]

In their decision to overturn the death penalty, the Missouri Supreme Court cited the case of *Atkins v. Virginia*. The U.S. Supreme Court in that case reasoned that mentally retarded people "have dimin-ished capacities to understand and process information, to communi-cate, to abstract from mistakes and learn from experience, to engage in logical reasoning, to control impulses, and to understand others' reactions. Their deficiencies do not warrant an exemption from criminal sanctions, but diminish their personal culpability."[100]

In *Roper v. Simmons*, defense lawyers cited recent research on brain development during adolescence. Briefs filed jointly by eight medical and mental health associations cited numerous studies in the developmental biology and behavioral literature to support the argument that the brains of adolescents that relate to criminal responsibility do not develop until after the age of 18.

> Adolescents as a group, even at the age of 16 or 17, are more impulsive than adults. They underestimate risks and overvalue short-term benefits. They are more susceptible to stress, more emotionally volatile, and less capable of controlling their emotions than adults. In short, the average adolescent cannot be expected to act with the same control or foresight as a mature adult. . . . Cutting-edge brain imaging technology reveals that regions of the adolescent brain do not reach a fully mature state until after the age if 18. These regions are precisely those associated with impulse control, regulation of emotions, risk assessment, and moral reasoning. Critical developmental changes in these regions occur only after late adolescence.[101]

Juveniles need time for their brains to link new cells and to solidify the millions of connections that allow them to think and behave like adults. The cascade of adolescent hormones during and after puberty causes the amygdala, which governs emotional responses, to override other areas of the brain. The result is that teens look at things differently than adults, which affects the legal responsibility of adolescents. The neuroscience of intentional behavior helps to determine responsibility. Research found that adults use both the advanced prefrontal cortex and the more basic amygdala to evaluate what they see. Younger teens relied entirely on the amygdala, and older teens progressively shifted toward using the frontal area of the brain. "Just because teens are physically mature, they may not appreciate the consequences or weigh information the same way as adults do. Good judgment is learned, but you can't learn it if you don't have the necessary hardware."[102] Many teenagers have not developed the capacity to anticipate the consequences of actions, which can lead to increased risk-taking. They have difficulty generating hypotheses of what might happen, partially because they don't have as many experiences that adults do.[103]

Certainly the lack of brain development does not mean that every youth will go out and kill someone. What factors are present in such tragic cases? The background characteristics of those on death row who committed their crimes when under the age of 18 are revealing. One study found that about three-fourths of the individuals experienced various kinds of family dysfunction, 60% were victims of abuse and/or neglect, 43% had a diagnosed psychiatric disorder, 38% were addicted to drugs, and 38% lived in poverty. This same study also noted that 30% had experienced six or more "distinct areas of childhood trauma with an overall average of four such experiences per offender." Few children and adolescents experience even one of these kinds of trauma, yet these distinguishing factors have been presented to less than half of the juries in the trials of juveniles.[104]

Scientists who engage in research on human behavior, especially criminal behavior, are often accused of "excusing" the behavior, when in fact they are merely trying to *explain* the behavior. An attorney in Miami who has represented juveniles facing capital punishment noted that science is quite often ahead of the law. For instance, the courts did not immediately support the use of DNA evidence. As he observes, "If you just focus on how horrible the crime was, a lot of people do not care how old the offender was. But the brain research begins to demonstrate that adolescents are less culpable than adults."[105]

The Court began applying the evolving standards of decency when it eliminated the death penalty for mentally retarded offenders and then applied the same logic to juveniles.

> The Eighth and Fourteenth Amendments against "cruel and unusual punishments" must be interpreted according to its text, by considering history, tradition, and precedent, and with due regard for its purpose and function in the constitutional design. To implement this framework this Court has established the propriety and affirmed the necessity of referring to "the evolving standards of decency that mark the progress of a maturing society" to determine which punishments are so disproportionate as to be "cruel and unusual.[106]

Some Concluding Thoughts

While the number of executions and death sentences have decreased in recent years, many issues surrounding capital punishment recede and then resurface. For example in 2009, the Supreme Court ruled unanimously in *Bobby v. Bies* that prosecutors in Ohio should have an opportunity to prove that a conviction mitigated by a finding of mental retardation was inaccurate and that the inmate should be eligible for execution.[107] Michael Bies was convicted in 1992 of kidnapping and murdering a 10-year-old boy. During the sentencing hearing, a psychiatrist testified that Bies was mildly to borderline mentally retarded. The jury recommended a death sentence without indicating what role the evidence about retardation had played in its decision, and the trial judge accepted that recommendation. A federal appeals court ordered Bies to be resentenced to a sentence other than death. Ohio appealed to the Supreme Court. Lawyers for Bies argued that requiring a new hearing on the question of retardation would subject their client to a form of double jeopardy. The Court said double-jeopardy protection was unavailable because Bies had not prevailed at his trial and because the lower federal courts should have allowed the state court to go forward with a hearing on whether Bies was indeed retarded. The ruling stated that the Court envisioned "remitting to the states responsibility for implementing the *Atkins* decision."

Some Court rulings eliminated Constitutional violations, while others like *McCleskey* opened the door for individual jurisdictions to continue discriminatory practices. Baldus and his associates have reached the conclusion that individual states cannot solve the problems presented by capital punishment. Theoretically, the forums with the greatest potential for reform are state supreme courts, but more than a dozen such courts have considered allegations of bias in the administration of the death penalty and all but one (New Jersey) have rejected them.

> The New Jersey record indicates that the race-of-victim disparities in capital charging persisted in spite of the system's enhanced selectivity and draws into question the capacity of any state court to address this issue meaningfully. . . . Heretofore, we have argued that courts have the capacity to purge race effects from their death penalty systems. However, the record of denial and avoidance in the United States Congress, and in our state legislatures and state courts over the last twenty years, now convinces us that in jurisdictions with clear evidence of systemic racial disparities in the administration of the death penalty, abolition of the death penalty or a drastic legislative narrowing of the breadth of death eligibility to the most highly aggravated cases coupled with close scrutiny by the state supreme court is the only way to solve the problem.[108]

NOTES

[1] Portions of this chapter are from Shelden, R., W. Brown, K. Miller, and R. Fritzler. *Criminal Justice in American Society*. Long Grove, IL: Waveland Press, 2008, chapter 10, with permission of the publisher.

[2] Newman, G. *The Punishment Response* (2nd ed.). Albany, NY: Harrow and Heston, 1985, chapter 3.

[3] Johnson, R. *Death Work: A Study of the Modern Execution Process*. Belmont, CA: Wadsworth, 1998, p. 15.

[4] Ibid., p. 17.

[5] Masur, L. P. *Rites of Execution: Capital Punishment and the Transformation of American Culture, 1776–1865*. New York: Oxford University Press, 1989, p. 39.

[6] Death Penalty Information Center. "Introduction to the Death Penalty." http://www.deathpenaltyinfo.org/article.php?scid=15&did=410#1823

[7] Friedman, L. M. *Crime and Punishment in American History*. New York: Basic Books, 1993, pp. 41–42.

[8] Costanzo, M. *Just Revenge: Costs and Consequences of the Death Penalty*. Belmont, CA: Wadsworth, 1997, p. 8.

[9] Blumberg, J. (2007). "A Brief History of the Salem Witch Trials." *Smithsonian Magazine*. http://www.smithsonianmag.com/history-archaeology/brief-salem.html

[10] Costanzo, *Just Revenge*, p. 7.

[11] 408 U.S. 238, 1972. http://supreme.justia.com/us/408/238/case.html

[12] 428 U.S. 153, 1976. http://supreme.justia.com/us/428/153/case.html

[13] Quoted in Ishay, M. R., ed., *The Human Rights Reader.* New York: Routledge, 1997, pp. 125–126.

[14] Death Penalty Information Center, "Introduction to the Death Penalty."

[15] The ESPY File: Executions by Date, pp. 324–382. http://www.deathpenaltyinfo.org/ESPYyear.pdf

[16] Miethe, T. and H. Lu. *Punishment: A Comparative Historical Perspective.* New York: Cambridge University Press, 2005, pp. 97–98.

[17] Quotation from James Elbert Cutler. Excerpts from his 1905 book found in Waldrep, C. *Lynching in America: A History in Documents.* New York: New York University Press, 2006, p. 12. Cutler's book was one of the first scholarly treatments of lynching. Cutler, J. E. *Lynch Law: An Investigation into the History of Lynching in the United States.* New York: Longman, Green, 1905. Ida B. Wells was apparently the first to compile statistics on the number of lynchings in *A Red Record: Tabulated Statistics and Alleged Causes of Lynchings in the United States, 1892–1893–1894.* Chicago: Donohue and Henneberry, 1895. Noted in Waldrep, *Lynching in America*, pp. 5–6.

[18] Zangrando, R. L. "About Lynching." In Foner, E. and J. A. Garraty, eds., *The Reader's Companion to American History.* New York: Houghton Mifflin, 1991, pp. 684–686. http://www.english.illinois.edu/Maps/poets/g_l/lynching/lynching.htm

[19] Waldrep, *Lynching in America*, p. 18.

[20] Edward Ayers in Ibid., p. 19.

[21] Ibid., pp. 13–19.

[22] Waldrep, C. *African Americans Confront Lynching: Strategies of Resistance from the Civil War to the Civil Rights.* Lanham, MD: Rowman & Littlefield, 2009, p. xvi.

[23] Bowers, W. *Legal Homicide: Death as Punishment in America, 1864–1982.* Boston: Northeastern University Press, 1984; Wright, G. C. (1997). "By the Book: The Legal Execution of Kentucky Blacks." In W. F. Brundage, ed., *Under Sentence of Death: Lynchings in the South.* Chapel Hill: University of North Carolina Press. Cited in Miethe and Lu, *Punishment*, p. 112.

[24] Zangrando, "About Lynching."

[25] Raper, A. A. *The Tragedy of Lynching.* Chapel Hill: University of North Carolina Press, 1933, pp. 13–14.

[26] Gibson, R. A. (1979). "The Negro Holocaust: Lynching and Race Riots in the United States, 1880–1950." Yale-New Haven Teachers Institute. http://www.yale.edu/ynhti/curriculum/units/1979/2/79.02.04.x.html#b

[27] Costanzo, *Just Revenge*, p. 80.

[28] Wolfgang, M., and M. Riedel (1973). "Race, Judicial Discretion, and the Death Penalty." *The Annals of the American Academy of Political and Social Science* 407 (1): 119–133.

[29] Beck, E. M., J. L. Massey, and S. E. Tolnay (1989). "The Gallows, the Mob, and the Vote: Lethal Sanctioning of Blacks in North Carolina and Georgia, 1882–1930." *Law and Society Review* 23: 317–329.

[30] Friedman, L. J. *The White Savage: Racial Fantasies in the Postbellum South.* Englewood Cliffs, NJ: Prentice-Hall, 1970, p. 191.

[31] Ellison, R. (1986). *Going to the Territory.* Quoted in "Lynching" by J. Callahan (1997) from *The Oxford Companion to African American Literature.* New York: Oxford University Press.

[32] Gibson, "The Negro Holocaust."

[33] Shelden, R. G. (1980). "From Slave to Caste Society: Penal Changes in Tennessee, 1840–1915." *Tennessee Historical Quarterly* 38: 462–478.

[34] Zangrando, R. L. (1965). "The NAACP and a Federal Anti-Lynching Bill, 1934–1940." *Journal of Negro History* 50: 106–117; Rable, G. C. (1985). "The South and the Politics of Anti-Lynching Legislation, 1920–1940." *Journal of Southern History* 51: 201–220; Reed, J. S. (1968). "An Evaluation of an Anti-Lynching Organization." *Social Problems* 16: 172–182.

[35] Tolnay, S. E. and E. M. Beck. *Festival of Violence.* Chicago: University of Illinois Press, 1995, p. 202.

[36] Miethe and Lu, *Punishment*, p. 98. Miethe and Lu cite a study that finds an exception to the general rule of an inverse relationship between legal executions and lynchings. See Massey, J. and M. Myers (1989). "Patterns of Repressive Social Control in Post-Reconstruction Georgia, 1882–1935." *Social Forces* 68: 458–488.

[37] NAACP Legal Defense and Educational Fund (Winter 2009). Death Row U.S.A. http://www.naacpldf.org/content/pdf/pubs/drusa/DRUSA_Winter_2009.pdf

[38] Death Penalty Information Center (2009). "Facts about the Death Penalty." http://www.deathpenaltyinfo.org/documents/FactSheet.pdf

[39] NAACP, Death Row U.S.A.

[40] Death Penalty Information Center. Facts about the Death Penalty; States with and without the Death Penalty. http://www.deathpenaltyinfo.org/states-and-without-death-penalty

[41] Death Penalty Information Center. Recent Legislative Activity. http://www.deathpenaltyinfo.org/recent-legislative-activity#2009

[42] Death Penalty Information Center. Facts about the Death Penalty.

[43] Boger, J. and I. Unah (2001). "Race and the Death Penalty in North Carolina: An Empirical Analysis 1993–1997." http://www.deathpenaltyinfo.org/race-and-death-penalty-north-carolina

[44] Pierce, G. and M. Radelet (2005). "The Impact of Legally Inappropriate Factors on Death Sentencing for California Homicides, 1990–1999." *Santa Clara Law Revue.* http://www.ccfaj.org/documents/reports/dp/expert/Radelet.pdf

[45] Paternoster, R. and R. Brame (2003). An Empirical Analysis of Maryland's Death Sentencing System with Respect to the Influence of Race and Legal Jurisdiction. http://www.newsdesk.umd.edu/pdf/finalrep.pdf

[46] Associated Press (May 7, 2005). "AP: Race, Pleas Affect Ohio Death Penalty." *New York Times.*

[47] Death Penalty Information Center, "Race and the Death Penalty." http://www.deathpenaltyinfo.org/race-and-death-penalty#rpts

[48] Johnson, G. B. (1941). "The Negro and Crime." *The Annals* 217: 93–104; see also Garfinkel, H. (1949). "Research Note on Inter- and Intra-Racial Homicides." *Social Forces* 27: 369–381.

[49] Wolfgang, M. E., A. Kelly, and H. C. Nolde (1962). "Comparisons of the Executed and the Commuted among Admissions to Death Row." *Journal of Criminal Law and Criminology* 58: 301–310.

[50] Radelet, M. L. (1989). "Executions of Whites for Crimes against Blacks: Exceptions to the Rule?" *The Sociological Quarterly* 30: 529–544.

[51] Johnson, E. H. (1957). "Selective Factors in Capital Punishment." *Social Forces* 36: 165–169.

[52] Harries, K. and D. Cheatwood. *The Geography of Execution: The Capital Punishment Quagmire in America.* Lanham, MD: Rowman & Littlefield, 1997; International Commission of Jurists (1997). "Administration of the Death Penalty in the United States." *Human Rights Quarterly* 19: 165–213.

[53] Barkan, S. B. and S. F. Cohen (1994). "Racial Prejudice and Support for the Death Penalty by Whites." *Journal of Research in Crime and Delinquency* 31: 202–209.

[54] Baldus, D. C., G. Woodworth, and C. A. Pulaski. *Equal Justice and the Death Penalty: A Legal and Empirical Analysis.* Boston: Northeastern University Press, 1990; Gross, S. R. and R. Mauro. *Death and Discrimination: Racial Disparities in Capital Sentencing.* Boston: Northeastern University Press, 1989.

[55] Baldus, Woodworth, and Pulaski, *Equal Justice and the Death Penalty*, p. 311.

[56] *McCleskey v. Kemp*, 481 U.S. 279 (1987), footnote 7. http://caselaw.lp.findlaw.com/scripts/getcase.pl?court=US&vol=481&invol=279

[57] Ibid., II B.

[58] Ibid., II A.

[59] Ibid., I.

[60] Ibid., 3.(c) and IV C.

[61] Kennedy, R. *Race, Crime and the Law.* New York: Vintage, 1997, p. 336.

[62] *McCleskey v. Kemp*, V.

[63] Ibid., Brennan dissent, IV.

[64] Baldus, D., G. Woodworth, and C. Grosso (February 2008). "Race and Proportionality Since *McCleskey v. Kemp* (1987): Different Actors with Mixed Strategies of Denial and Avoidance," p. 144. *Columbia Human Rights Law Review* 39: 143–177. http://www3.law.columbia.edu/hrlr/hrlr_journal/39.1/g.%20Baldus-F.pdfp

[65] Walker, S., C. Spohn, and M. DeLone. *The Color of Justice: Race, Ethnicity, and Crime in America* (4th ed.). Belmont, CA: Wadsworth, 2007, p. 252.

[66] Cole, D. *No Equal Justice: Race and Class in the American Criminal Justice System.* New York: The New Press, 1999, p. 135.

[67] Baldus, Woodworth, and Grosso, "Race and Proportionality Since *McCleskey v. Kemp*."

[68] Columbia Law School (2007). "Pursuing Racial Fairness in Criminal Justice: Twenty Years after *McCleskey v. Kemp*." http://www.naacpldf.org/issues.aspx?subcontext=81

[69] Cole, *No Equal Justice.*

[70] Quoted in Kennedy, *Race, Crime and the Law*, p. 346.

[71] *Batson v. Kentucky* 476 U.S. 79 (1986). http://supreme.justia.com/us/476/79/case.html. Batson was granted a new trial but accepted a plea bargain.

[72] *Miller-El v. Dretke*. No. 03-9659. Decided June 13, 2005. http://supreme.justia.com/us/545/03-9659/case.html

[73] Ibid., IIA.

[74] *Snyder v. Louisiana*. No. 06-10119. Decided March 19, 2008. http://www.wilmerhale.com/files/upload/snyder_amicus2.pdf

[75] Amnesty International U.S.A. "Death Penalty and Innocence." http://www.amnestyusa.org/death-penalty/death-penalty-facts/death-penalty-and-innocence/page.do?id=1101086

[76] *Baze v. Rees* 553 U.S. Decided April 16, 2008. Breyer, J. concurring, p. 7. http://www.scotusblog.com/wp/wp-content/uploads/2008/04/07-5439.pdf. Because lethal injection is used in almost every capital punishment state, executions were halted until the Court ruled. After it decided that the method was not cruel and unusual, executions resumed.

[77] Stevens, J. concurring, in *Baze v. Rees*, p. 17.

[78] Radelet, M. L., H. A. Bedau, and C. E. Putnam. *In Spite of Innocence.* Boston: Northeastern University Press, 1992.

[79] Liebman, J. S., J. Fagan, S. Rifkind, and V. West (June 2000). "A Broken System: Error Rates in Capital Cases, 1973–1995." *The Justice Project.* New York: Columbia University. http://www2.law.columbia.edu/instructionalservices/liebman/liebman2.pdf

[80] Death Penalty Information Center. The Innocence List. http://www.deathpenaltyinfo.org/innocence-list-those-freed-death-row

[81] Baumgartner, F., S. De Boef, and A. Boydstun. *The Decline of the Death Penalty and the Discovery of Innocence.* New York: Cambridge University Press, 2008, p. 52.

[82] Death Penalty Information Center, Innocence List.

[83] *District Attorney's Office for the Third Judicial District, et al., Petitioners v. William G. Osborne* 557 U.S.#08-6. Decided June 18, 2009. http://www.supremecourtus.gov/opinions/08pdf/08-6.pdf

[84] "U.S. Supreme Court Decision on DNA Testing Is Disappointing but Will Have Limited Impact, Innocence Project Says." (June 18, 2009). http://www.innocenceproject.org/Content/2042.php

[85] Amnesty International. "Abolitionist and Retentionist Countries." http://www.amnesty.org/en/death-penalty/abolitionist-and-retentionist-countries

[86] Amnesty International. "Figures on the Death Penalty." http://www.amnesty.org/en/death-penalty/numbers

[87] Amnesty International. (March 2009). "Death Sentences and Executions in 2008," pp. 8, 13, 24. http://www.amnesty.org/en/library/asset/ACT50/003/2009/en/0b789cb1-baa8-4c1b-bc35-58b606309836/act500032009en.pdf

[88] Saad, L. (November 17, 2008). Americans Hold Firm to Support for Death Penalty. http://www.gallup.com/poll/111931/americans-hold-firm-support-death-penalty.aspx

[89] Radelet, M. and T. Lacock (2009). "Do Executions Lower Homicide Rates? The Views of Leading Criminologists." *The Journal of Criminal Law & Criminology* 99 (2): 504. http://www.deathpenaltyinfo.org/files/DeterrenceStudy2009.pdf

[90] Yen, H. (March 1, 2005). "Supreme Court Strikes Down Death Penalty for Juveniles." *Associated Press*. For complete Supreme Court ruling see http://www.law.cornell.edu/supct/html/03-633.ZS.html

[91] *Atkins v. Virginia* 536 U.S. 304, 318, 122 S. Ct. 2242, 2250 (2002). http://caselaw.lp.findlaw.com/scripts/getcase.pl?court=US&vol=000&invol=00-8452

[92] Associated Press (January 26, 2004). "Supreme Court to Consider Banning Execution of Teens." *New York Times*.

[93] Strieb, V. L. (1999). "The Juvenile Death Penalty Today: Death Sentences and Executions for Juvenile Crimes, January, 1973–June, 1999." http://www.internationaljusticeproject.org/pdfs/JuvDeathApril2004.pdf

[94] Feld, B. *Bad Kids: Race and the Transformation of the Juvenile Court*. New York: Oxford University Press, 1999, p. 236.

[95] Strieb, "The Juvenile Death Penalty Today"; American Bar Association, Juvenile Justice Center (2004). "Cruel and Unusual Punishment." Washington, DC: American Bar Association. http://www.abanet.org/crimjust/juvjus/EvolvingStandards.pdf

[96] *Eddings v. Oklahoma* 455 U.S. 104, 1982.

[97] Verhovek, S. H. (April 18, 1998). "Statehouse Journal; Texas Legislator Proposes the Death Penalty for Murderers as Young as 11." http://www.nytimes.com/1998/04/18/us/statehouse-journal-texas-legislator-proposes-death-penalty-for-murderers-young.html

[98] American Bar Association, Juvenile Justice Center (March 16, 2004). "Cruel and Unusual Punishment: The Juvenile Death Penalty." Washington, DC: American Bar Association.

[99] The Death Penalty Information Center provides complete coverage of this case. See the following Web site: http://www.deathpenaltyinfo.org/article.php?scid=38&did=885

[100] *Atkins v. Virginia*.

[101] Writ of Certiorari to the Supreme Court of Missouri, amici curiae in support of respondent, filed with the U.S Supreme Court in *Roper v. Simmons*. http://www.abanet.org/crimjust/juvjus/simmons/ama.pdf

[102] Bowman, L. (May 11, 2004). "New Research Shows Stark Differences in Teen Brains." *Scripps Howard News Service*.

[103] Beckman, M. (July 30, 2004). "Crime, Culpability and the Adolescent Brain." *Science Magazine*. http://www.deathpenaltyinfo.org/node/1225

[104] Mallett, C. (2003). "Socio-Historical Analysis of Juvenile Offenders on Death Row." *Juvenile Corrections Mental Health Report* 65, cited in American Bar Association, Juvenile Justice Center, "Cruel and Unusual Punishment."

[105] Quoted in Davies, P. (May 26, 2004). "Psychiatrists Question Death for Teen Killers." *The Wall Street Journal*, p. B1.

[106] *Roper v. Simmons*.

[107] Liptak, A. (June 1, 2009). "Court to Hear Case on Inmate's Retardation." *New York Times*. http://www.nytimes.com/2009/06/02/us/02scotus.html?_r=1

[108] Baldus, Woodworth, and Grosso, "Race and Proportionality Since *McCleskey v. Kemp*," pp. 176–177.

6

Punishing Women

Women offenders have been subjected to differential forms of punishment reflecting their subservient position throughout world history. In the Middle Ages, a pregnant woman might receive lenient punishment if she were to "plead her belly," yet could be burned at the stake for the "crime" of adultery or for murdering her spouse (the latter of which still receives harsher punishment than men murdering their wives). Prior to the rise of imprisonment in the nineteenth century, daughters and wives who were unwanted were often forced into convents and similar institutions, along with political prisoners, the mentally defective, and other outcast persons.[1]

Much of Roman law was eventually incorporated into the English common law that was then copied (with few significant changes) in America. For several years the only law book used was Blackstone's *Commentaries on the Laws in England*, originally published in 1765. American family law incorporated Blackstone's dictum that the husband and wife are as one and that one is the husband.[2]

Throughout colonial America women had no identity, other than their relationships with their father or later with their husband. The husband had rights over his wife that resembled in many ways the rights of masters over their slaves. Even if a man killed his wife, he would be treated under the law with far more leniency than if his wife had killed him. In fact, a man killing his wife was treated almost the same as if he had killed an animal or a servant. Colonial law was often very specific about women; some crimes were, in effect, "women's crimes" and were severely punished. For instance, the crime of being a "common scold" was applied "to a woman who berated her husband or was too vocal in public settings."[3] The most appropriate punishment for scolding was the "ducking stool" and "branks." The former was placing the female offender in a chair and ducking her in a pool of water several times, for the purpose of drowning her. The latter was a type of metal headgear placed over the head of a woman who was accused of scolding. If the woman tried to move her tongue to speak, sharp spikes would dig into her.

In colonial America several women were singled out for committing various religiously based "crimes." Anne Hutchinson was persecuted for expressing alternative religious views and eventually was banished from Massachusetts in the 1630s. Perhaps the most famous case was that of Mary Dyer, who sympathized with the emerging Quaker movement (a religion strongly resisted by the puritans). She visited several Quakers who were in jail in Boston. She also visited Anne Hutchinson when she was jailed. Dyer was convicted and banished in 1659. A few months later she defiantly returned to Boston. For this "crime" she was hanged in June of that year.[4] Two centuries later the state of Massachusetts constructed a statue of her that stands in front of the state capitol of Boston. It is directly across the street from Boston Common, the starting point of the Freedom Trail. The inscription on her statue reads "Witness for Religious Freedom."

The witch hunts, both in Europe and in the American colonies, are classic examples of the use of the legal system to punish women who dared challenge the male power structure. In New England during the 1600s at least 36 women were executed for the crime of being a "witch." The crime of witchcraft was one of many laws on the books during colonial times based on religion. Women who were "unattached"—as wives, sisters, and daughters of men—received the most severe treatment. Most of the women accused of witchcraft were those who were outspoken in their views or had a great deal of informal power either as healers or as community leaders.[5] Witchcraft was stricken from the list of capital crimes in the 1770s.

More women were punished for witchcraft and adultery than for all other crimes combined. Most were poor and isolated. In reflecting on the history of the punishment of women, Christina Rathbone noted:

> There has to be some explanation for the fact that men are still punished mostly for crimes against property and people—theft, assault, and murder—while the majority of women continue to be punished for transgressions against conventional morality. . . . Adulterers and "consorters with malevolent spirits" in the eighteenth century, drunks and prostitutes in the nineteenth, drug-addicted single mothers in the twentieth.[6]

The unequal treatment of women by the law is clearly evident in their processing through the criminal justice system and the use of imprisonment as a method of control. The historical development of women's prisons discussed in the next section illustrates the brutal treatment of women as a group as well as the class and racial dimensions of imprisoning women.

A Brief History of Women's Prisons

In colonial America few women (or any) offenders were subjected to long-term imprisonment, which was not yet the favored type of punishment. Serious crimes were punished by execution; lesser crimes by very visible, public punishment. After arrest, offenders were held in local jails for trial. The usual punishment was a public reprimand, such as whipping or the stocks and pillory.[7]

The situation was different for African American women, the majority of whom were slaves or sometimes indentured servants.[8] Most violations of laws were handled informally within the plantation, but occasionally the slave owners had to rely on the local criminal justice system. In such cases they often used what were called "Negro Courts" set up specifically for violations applicable only to slaves. For example, "striking the master three times" was punishable by death, although neither death nor incarceration was usually inflicted because of the unprofitability of losing a worker. After the Civil War, African Americans appeared in penal institutions in large numbers, largely as a result of the Black Codes and Jim Crow laws (see chapter 4). After incarceration, many were subjected to the convict lease system.[9]

As noted in chapter 3, early American jails were often mere extensions of the earlier "workhouses" and "almshouses." Deplorable conditions marked the confinement of men, women, children, and the mentally ill—whether petty or serious offenders. In 1797, Newgate Prison opened in New York. It was the first institution for felons only, and women offenders were housed in an area separate from men.

Treatment of prisoners changed dramatically in 1819 with the opening of Auburn State Prison. New York authorities believed prisoners should be compelled to work. The fortress prison was essentially a silent (prisoners were not allowed to speak to one another) factory and involuntary labor pool.[10] New York officials believed a steady, unrelenting routine of hard work would transform the idle and corrupt into virtuous laborers. "Prisoners were not in a state of grace with society, and their condition was made as graceless as possible, lest they forget their corrupt condition."

While only a small number of women were imprisoned in the early nineteenth century, they were considered a nuisance, at best. Men at Auburn were confined in small, single cells. Women were housed together in whatever space was available. At one time, there were 70 women inmates in a one-room attic. The segregation often led to neglect.[11] The prison chaplain remarked that conditions were bad enough for male prisoners, "but to be a female convict, for any protracted period, would be worse than death."[12]

It was widely believed that women offenders should be treated more harshly than their male counterparts. Women were regarded as being born pure. As a result, their straying from acceptable behavior was viewed as falling further from grace than a man who strayed. "As woman falls from a higher point of perfection, so she sinks to a profounder depth of misery than man."[13] The fallen woman was considered beyond hope.

> The condemnation of women criminals derived in part from the pressures placed on women to maintain a morality superior to men's. . . . Men's crime was more "rational" than women's, for men were made for an "agitated life." Because she had denied her own pure nature, the female criminal was more depraved than her male counterpart. . . . [She] was more likely to reach the depths of sinfulness and commit the most heinous crimes. . . . Most men expressed outright hostility to the fallen woman and blamed her for men's crimes as well. Her defiance of the law, they reasoned, had more serious social consequences than a man's, for by removing her influence as a virtuous wife and mother she undoubtedly encouraged male criminality.[14]

The conditions of the confinement of women were horrible—filthy, overcrowded, and at risk of sexual abuse from male guards. Rachel Welch became pregnant at Auburn while serving a punishment in a solitary cell; she died after childbirth as the result of a flogging by a prison official earlier in her pregnancy.[15] Her death prompted New York officials to build the Mount Pleasant Prison Annex for women on the grounds of Sing Sing in Mount Pleasant, New York in 1839.[16] The governor of New York had recommended separate facilities in 1828, but the legislature did not approve the measure because the washing, ironing, and sewing performed by the women saved the Auburn prison system money.[17] A corrupt administration at the Indiana State Prison used the forced labor of female inmates to provide a prostitution service for male guards.[18]

After the Civil War, the imprisonment of women began to increase (as it did for men). The increase in imprisonment rates was particularly noteworthy for African American women and men in the South. The rate of convictions for women increased enough to justify the building of more prisons.[19] Separate facilities for women gradually began to emerge following the 1870 meeting of the National Congress on Penitentiary and Reformatory Discipline in Cincinnati. One of the resolutions of this conference was that the goal of prisons should be *rehabilitation* rather than punishment. In 1873 the first prison for women was opened, the Indiana Women's Prison.[20] Several other women's prisons were opened over the next 40 years, including the Massachusetts Prison at Framington (1877), the New York Reformatory for Women at Westfield Farm (1901), the District of Columbia Reformatory for Women (1910), and the New Jersey Reformatory for Women at Clinton (1913).

The large number of deaths during the Civil War created a class of poor women who began to be arrested on mostly "public order" offenses and offenses against morality.[21] Several reformers placed the blame of the rise of female criminality on the attitudes and sexist practices of men. One noted reformer, Josephine Shaw Lowell, complained that many women "from early girlhood have been tossed from poorhouse to jail, and from jail to poorhouse, until the last trace of womanhood in them has been destroyed."[22] She condemned law officers who "wantonly assaulted and degraded numerous young women prisoners."[23] Many specifically blamed the "double standard" whereby men condemned female sexual activity while condoning their own and, moreover, arrested and imprisoned prostitutes but not the men who enjoyed their services.[24] Finally, reformers complained of male guards in prisons where women were confined. Investigations found that women "may be forced to minister to the lust of the officials or if they refused, submit to the inflection of the lash until they do."[25]

The majority of nineteenth- and early twentieth-century prison reformers were women of the middle and upper class.[26] Elizabeth Fry, a Quaker reformer (1780–1845), along with such notables as Dorothea Dix (1802–1887), Clara Barton (1821–1912), and Josephine Shaw Lowell (1843–1905), began to advocate for separate facilities for women and other reforms. One of the first results of reform activities was the hiring of female matrons. Reformers argued that women prisoners would be treated more fairly and would stand a better chance of being reformed if they were confined in separate institutions controlled by women. Reformers countered male resistance by arguing that "the shield of a pure woman's presence" would enable them "to govern the depraved and desperate of her own sex."[27]

Custody versus Reform

Two major types of prisons emerged during the nineteenth century: the *custodial prison*, which was the most common, and the *reformatory*. Custodial prisons, as the name implies, emphasized custody and security as the main goals. The custodial prison resembled the classic penitentiary for male prisoners, and the purpose was to warehouse (or, in modern vernacular, to incapacitate) prisoners. There were three main types of custodial prisons for women: (1) those that were either within or attached to male prisons; (2) prison farms in the South; and (3) totally independent prisons. By the late nineteenth century, almost every state operated a custodial unit for women. The goal of reformatories was to provide treatment for reform.[28]

In the late 1860s, middle-class women who had been abolitionists during the Civil War turned their attention to improving conditions for incarcerated women. They believed the traditional prison was unsuitable for women's more passive nature and that women needed fewer restraints than men. Walled fortresses were not necessary. They developed the cottage plan where groups of twenty women would live with a matron in a familial setting in rural areas away from the corrupting influence of the city. The reformatory movement began in 1870. By 1900, there were only four reformatories. Over the next thirty-five years, seventeen states began operating reformatories.[29]

The reformers hoped to rescue women, whom they believed needed protection. They were concerned about vagrants, unwed mothers, and prostitutes who had not yet been subject to state punishment in custodial prisons. The women sentenced to reformatories would previously have been liable only for brief terms in local jails. As Nicole Rafter notes, "In the course of saving fallen women, then, the founders of women's reformatories institutionalized a double standard, one that made it possible to incarcerate women for minor offenses for which men were not subject to lengthy punishment by the state."[30]

The first reformatories relied on teaching domestic routines; after release, women were placed in "suitable" private homes as housekeepers. While the women reformers often claimed to be staunch feminists, the organization of prison life they created was perfectly suited to keeping women in traditional roles. In fact, the design won the approval of many skeptical men, one of whom commented that: "Girls and women should be trained to adorn homes with the virtues which make their lives noble and ennobling. *It is only in this province, that they may most fittingly fill their mission.*"[31] The end result, of course, would perpetuate women's traditional roles of dependency as housewives and maids.

Estelle Freedman suggests that although reformers "claimed that their goal for each inmate, as for each prison, was female self-sufficiency, they trained women inmates for dependency in domestic employment and in other ways treated them as juveniles, referring even to elderly prisoners as 'girls' and setting up cottage households with the inmates in the role of children."[32] Even a cursory look at women's prisons today reveals that little has changed, especially the treatment of women as children and training them to continue their domestic roles. The reformatory movement ended in 1935. During the Great Depression, states were unwilling to maintain expensive institutions to rehabilitate petty offenders.

The federal prison system for women developed much later than the state prison system. Women convicted of federal crimes generally had been sentenced to state prisons. The first federal prison for women only opened in 1927 in Alderson, West Virginia. It housed 50 women in a total of 14 cottages. By 1929 there were more than 250 inmates, most of whom had violated drug laws (the Harrison Act of 1914 outlawed several kinds of drugs) or the Volstead Act of 1919 (prohibition of alcohol).[33] Today there are six federal facilities that house only female inmates—Alderson, Bryan, and Carswell in Texas, Danbury in Connecticut, Dublin in California, and Tallahassee in Florida (Dublin and Tallahassee each have a small male detention unit). Twenty-one federal facilities have mixed populations.[34]

DIFFERENTIAL TREATMENT OF BLACK WOMEN

Most of the women in custodial institutions were black, while most of the women in reformatories were white. For black women prisoners, the custodial prisons were a continuation of their slave status prior to the Emancipation Proclamation. This was especially the case in the South, where penal servitude replaced the enforced labor of slave plantations. Black women prisoners were often, like their male counterparts, leased out to local businesses such as farms, mines, and railroads to work on various kinds of "chain gangs."[35]

The proportion of black women prisoners was even higher than their male counterparts in some states. In New York, for instance, 44% of the women inmates were black, compared to 20% of the male inmates. In Tennessee, in 1868, *every female inmate was black*, compared to around 60% of the male prisoners.[36]

The overrepresentation of blacks varied widely by region. In 1880, the percentage of women prisoners who were black ranged from 7% in the Northeast to 29% in the Midwest to 85.8% in the South. By 1904, the percentages increased in every region, reaching 90% in the South, 48% in the Midwest, and 18% in the Northeast. By 1923 percentages in the South declined to 79.6 and to 15.4 in the Northeast. In 1923 almost two-thirds (64.5%) of the women inmates in custodial prisons were black, compared to only 11.9% in reformatory institutions. Ranges by specific institutions were marked. Between 1860 and 1934, fully four-fifths of the inmates at the Tennessee Penitentiary for Women were black, in contrast to only 3% at the Albion State Prison in New York.[37]

The proportion of women in prison who are black has continued to increase over the years. By 1978 black women constituted half of the total female prison population.[38] As will be noted later in the chapter, in all sections of the country black women continue to be imprisoned in numbers vastly disproportionate to their percentage in the general population. Percentages declined somewhat by the end of the 1980s and early 1990s because of an increase in the incarceration of Hispanic women and increasing numbers of white women being sentenced on drug charges.

Women in Today's Prisons

The numbers of incarcerated women are increasing faster than those of any other group. Driven largely by the drug war and mandatory sentencing, the total number of women offenders in state or federal prisons increased from 12,331 in 1980 to 115,779 in 2008. The rate increased from 11 women per 100,000 population to 69 (see table 6.1). The 527% increase was more than double the increase in the rate for men (from 275 to 957).[39] The numbers continue the historical pattern for specific regions. The imprisonment rate for women in the South was 80, 67 in the West, 52 in the Midwest, and 29 in the Northeast. Including women held in local jails, the number of incarcerated women rises to 207,700.[40]

> Increases in institutionalization cannot be explained by increases in female crime patterns; women and girls still typically commit nonviolent and less serious crimes than men and boys. Female offenders tend to show violence only to themselves. In spite of this fact, it seems unlikely that public opinion, stoked by the media, will change the lock-'em-up approach to crime.[41]

There were 2,587,284 arrests of women in 2007—24.2% of all arrests.[42] The number of males arrested decreased 6.1% from the number arrested in 1998, while the number of females arrested increased 6.6%.[43] Arrest data reveal that women are more likely to be arrested for minor property crimes or drug offenses. Larceny-theft accounted for 13.9% of all arrests of women (versus 6.6% of male arrests) followed by drug abuse violations at 10.1% (13.9% for men—the most frequent

Table 6.1   Incarceration Rates of Men and Women, State and Federal Institutions, 1925–2008

Year	Total	Male	Female	Ratio
1925	79	149	6	24.8:1
1935	113	217	8	27.1:1
1945	98	193	9	21.4:1
1955	112	217	8	27.1:1
1965	108	213	8	26.6:1
1975	111	220	8	27.5:1
1985	202	397	17	23.4:1
1995	411	789	47	16.8:1
2005	491	929	65	14.3:1
2008	509	957	69	13.9:1
% increase				
(1975–85)	82	81	113	
(1985–06)	148	138	300	
(1975–06)	351	329	750	

Source: *Sourcebook on Criminal Justice Statistics,* table 6.28. http://www.albany.edu/sourcebook/pdf/t6282007.pdf.; West, H. C. and W. J. Sabol (2009). "Prison Inmates at Midyear 2008,"Table 10. http://www.ojp.usdoj.gov/bjs/pub/pdf/pim08st.pdf

cause of arrest).[44] In 2008, there were 99,175 women in local jails. Approximately 38% had been convicted of a crime; 41.9% were white; 41.3% were black; 15.2% were Hispanic.[45]

As mentioned above, much of the increase in the incarceration of women comes from the impact of mandatory sentencing laws, passed during the 1980s crackdown on crime. Under many of these laws, mitigating circumstances (e.g., having children, few or no prior offenses, nonviolent offenses) are rarely allowed. One survey found that just over half (51%) of women in state prisons had none or only one prior offense, compared to 39% of the male prisoners.[46]

The number of incarcerated mothers increased from 29,500 in 1991 to 65,600 in 2007—a 122% increase compared to an increase of 76% for incarcerated fathers.[47] Half of all incarcerated men and women are parents. The number of minor children with a parent in prison increased 82% since 1991 to 1.7 million. One in 43 American children has a parent in prison. Two-thirds of the incarcerated parent population is non-white, resulting in 1 in 15 black children with a parent in prison and 1 in 42 Latino children versus 1 in 111 white children. The majority of parents (84% in federal prison and 62% in state prisons) are incarcerated more than 100 miles away from their place of arrest, making visits with children very difficult.[48]

One woman's story highlights a number of social, legal, and policy problems. Regina Kelly was a mother at age 13. In 2000, she was a 24-year-old single mother living in a housing project with her four young daughters in rural East Texas (Hearne). She worked as a waitress and needed government assistance to feed and house her family. During a drug sweep, more than 28 residents of the housing project (primarily black) were arrested and charged with selling cocaine. Kelly was handcuffed, arrested, and jailed on a felony charge carrying a potential sentence of 20 years. She had no record of drug arrests, and no drugs were found near her when she was taken into custody, but Texas law at the time deemed uncorroborated testimony from a single informant sufficient to press charges. She refused to accept a plea bargain for a crime she did not commit, even though her court-appointed attorney suggested the felony plea and 10 years probation was a gift.

Bill Haney was listening to National Public Radio and heard about Kelly's choice to plead guilty and become a convicted felon (and ineligible for the government welfare and housing) but go home to her children or stay in jail (she could not afford the bail set) to challenge the powerful prosecutor and risk 20 years in prison. "I found the story so emotional. I was kind of overcome by the idea of our government leaning on a young mother in this way on one hand and by her heroism in deciding to stand up for what she believed in on the other."[49] Haney called Kelly's lawyers and flew to Texas, where he went over the legal documents of her case and other similar cases. "I wanted to discover if what was happening to her was unique or whether it was a national trend. To my dismay, I discovered these kinds of circumstances were happening by the hundreds of thousands across America every year." He originally intended to make a documentary but decided the story might reach a wider audience as a feature film. It took him four years to write the script for *American Violet.*

The American Civil Liberty Union's Drug Law Reform Project filed a class-action lawsuit on behalf of 15 of the arrestees, accusing the local district attorney and the South Central Texas Narcotics Task Force with conducting racially motivated drug sweeps for more than 15 years.[50] The charges against all the ACLU's clients, including Kelly, were dropped due to insufficient evidence and the tainted testimony of an unreliable police informant. The lawyer for the Hearne plaintiffs, Graham Boyd, discussed the role of Byrne grants (legislation originally passed in 1988 to help states and local jurisdictions fight drugs and the violent crime associated with drug trafficking) in raids such as the one conducted in Hearne.

> Byrne grants are consistently used to target very low-level drug dealers for arrest and long-term incarceration. You have a drug task force whose goal is to arrest as many people as they can, their funding stream is based on that, so they rely on confidential informants, and their racial profiling is staggering."[51]

The beneficial outcome of the case was that Texas became the first state in the country to require corroboration of informant information to make a drug arrest. It also stopped taking Byrne money for drug cases and made them the responsibility of the state police (the Texas Rangers). Officers are no longer graded on how many arrests they make; rather the identification of drug trafficking organizations is the measurement. Drug arrests in Texas dropped by 40% in 2008, and drug seizures doubled. The bad news was that Hearne reelected the district attorney to another term.

THE SOCIAL CONTEXT

Women's crime cannot be separated from the overall social context within which it occurs. In recent years the plight of women has not improved a great deal. About 46.4% of the workforce are women. However, their employment is still found largely in traditional "female" occupations, especially in retail trade and service occupations. Women still constitute over 90% of all nurses, 97% of all pre-school and kindergarten teachers and 82% of all elementary and middle school teachers, almost 80% of all secretarial and administrative support positions (e.g., clerical work or cashiers) and about 78% of all the hairdressers and other "personal service occupations."[52] Furthermore, while gains have been made, women still earn less than men.[53] Also, a greater proportion of women are working part-time (24.7%) compared to men (10.5%).[54]

While women's occupations remain relatively the same, increasing numbers of households are headed by a woman with children. While in 1960 only 6% of all families with one or more children were headed by a woman, by 2008 the number was 22.8%.[55] In 2008, 51.1% of all black families were headed by a woman compared to only 17.5% of white families.[56] In 1980, 80% of all American children lived with two parents.[57] In 2008, the percentage decreased to 70%, with the following breakdown: white children 76%, Hispanic children 70%, and black children 37.5%.[58] The vast majority of children living with one parent live with their mother, who is far more likely to be living in poverty (28.3% all races; 36% Hispanic, and 36.6% black).[59] Women who head households have a median income of $28,829 compared with $58,407 for all American households.[60] More than a quarter of such households earn less than $15,000 annually, and 43.5% earn less than $25,000.

Kathleen Daly conducted a detailed study of 40 women offenders in a court system in New Haven, Connecticut. Twenty-four (60%) were African American, five (12%) were Puerto Rican, and the remainder (28%) were white. Half of the women were raised in single-parent families, and only two of the women were described as growing up in "middle class households." In about two-thirds of the cases, the biological fathers were absent, contributing to precarious economic circumstances. Only one-third completed high school or the equivalent GED (General Education Diploma). Over 80% were unemployed at the time of their most recent arrest, and two-thirds had either sporadic or no history of employment.[61] Although almost 30 years have elapsed since Daly conducted her study, the circumstances of most women in prison remain remarkably the same. As Jennifer Schwartz and Darrell Steffensmeier explain:

> Patriarchal power relationships shape gender differences in crime, pushing women into crime through victimization, role entrapment, economic marginality, and survival needs. . . . It is female inequality and economic vulnerability that are more likely to shape female offending patterns. . . . Adverse economic pressures on women have been aggravated by heightened rates of divorce, illegitimacy, and female-headed households, coupled with greater responsibility for children.[62]

Ruth Zaplin summarizes the social context: "The life of the female offender is embedded in complex social reality encompassing her relationships, personal history, and the many contextual, sociological forces inducing her criminality. The prospects for her rehabilitation and reintegration into society cannot validly be disentangled from this context."[63]

THE GROWING INCARCERATION OF BLACK WOMEN

The interrelationship between class and race is integral to any analysis of women, crime, and criminal justice. The vast majority of female offenders come from the lower class and/or racial minorities.[64] About one-half of the women in state or federal prison or local jails are black or Hispanic. The rate of incarceration for black women (349) is almost 4 times greater than for white women (93). The rate for Hispanic women (147) is 1.5 times the rate for white women.[65] In contrast, around two-thirds of the women on probation are white.[66]

A frequent explanation for why fewer women are imprisoned than men is that the criminal justice system practices "chivalry." If that assessment is accurate, the chivalry practiced is largely racist and classist. Lenient treatment is typically reserved for white women from the higher social classes. Moreover, any "lenient" treatment granted to women is due largely to the fact that their crimes are so minor compared to men and the criminal careers are not nearly as lengthy as men, two variables that are highly predictive of receiving treatment in the criminal justice system.[67]

The most dramatic illustrations of the lack of chivalry toward black and other minority women comes from examining who gets sentenced to prison. And this has been, in recent years, a direct result of the "war on drugs." As already noted, there is little relationship between race and illicit drug use, yet blacks and Latinos are far more likely to be arrested and sent to prison. For women, the poor in general and blacks in particular have been singled out, as incarceration rates illustrate.

Table 6.2   Rate of Sentenced Prisoners in State and Federal Prisons, by Race and Gender, 1980–2007

Gender and Race	Incarceration Rate				
	1980	1990	2000	2007	% increase 1980–2007
Males					
White	168	339	410	481	186%
Black	1,111	2,376	3,188	3,138	182%
Females					
White	6	19	33	50	733%
Black	45	125	175	150	233%
Black/White ratio					
Males	6.6:1	7.0:1	7.8:1	6.5:1	
Female	7.5:1	6.6:1	5.3:1	3:1	

Source: Beck, A. J. and D. K. Gillard (1995). "Prisoners in 1994." Washington, DC: Bureau of Justice Statistics, August. West, H. C. and W. J. Sabol, (December 2008). "Prisoners in 2007," table 6. NCJ 224280 http://www.ojp.usdoj.gov/bjs/pub/pdf/p07.pdf

The War on Drugs and Women

As noted in previous chapters, there is no way we can separate the phenomenal growth in prison populations from the war on drugs. According to one report, during the 1990s "drug offenders accounted for the largest source of the total growth among female inmates (36%) compared to male inmates (18%)."[68] Almost 29% of all women prisoners in state prison in 2005 were convicted of drug offenses.[69] In contrast only 10% of women in state prison in 1979 were drug offenders.[70] From 1986 to 1996, the rate at which women used drugs declined substantially, but the number of women incarcerated in state facilities for drug offenses increased by 888% compared to a rise of 129% for non-drug offenses.[71]

> The growing rate of women's incarceration calls for a critical evaluation of the social impact of our nation's increasing reliance on correctional facilities to deal with women's involvement in crime. Increasing arrests for property and public order offenses are partly responsible for women's incarceration rate outpacing that of men. The "war on drugs," however, has been most influential in the nationwide expansion of the prison population, having a particularly devastating impact on women over the past 25 years. Women are now more likely than men to serve time for drug offenses and are subject to increasingly punitive law enforcement and sentencing practices, despite the fact that women are less likely than men to play a central role in the drug trade.[72]

DRACONIAN DRUG LAWS

Data from states where the drug law penalties are especially high reveal an even more dramatic change. In New York, for instance, the Rockefeller drug laws were enacted in 1973 and became a model for harsh sentencing for drug sentences around the nation. The laws resulted in a rapid increase in drug convictions. From 1973 to 2008, the number of women in New York prisons increased by almost 580%.[73] Critics argued that the laws criminalized a public health problem, incarcerated nonviolent felons, increased recidivism rates, and eliminated judicial discretion in sentencing. Drug offenders peaked at 35% of New York's prison population in 1994. In 1990, 61.2% of all female prisoners were committed for a drug offense, compared to 32.2% of men. Between January 1987 and December 1989 drug commitments for females rose 211% versus 82% for males. African American women accounted for 46.1% of those convicted, Latina women 36.3%, and whites 17.5%.[74] In 2009, 30% of the women were incarcerated for a drug offense; 77% of the women in custody for a drug offense were women of color.[75] In 2009, the governor of New York stated: "I can't think of a criminal justice strategy that has been more unsuccessful than the Rockefeller Drug Laws."[76]

In California, 12% of women admitted to prison in 1980 were drug offenders; by 1990 the percentage grew to 47%, and by 1999 it reached 50.1%. Over a 40-year period there had been a 210% increase in women drug offenders, compared to 187% for men.[77] One of the first major reforms of draconian drug laws, Proposition 36, was passed by California voters in 2000, Adults convicted of nonviolent drug offenses are now sentenced to probation with drug treatment.[78]

The history of women incarcerated for drug charges underscores their secondary status in the world of illegal drug dealing. The war on drugs has been marked by punitive policing, prosecutorial, and sentencing policies. Street-level sweeps catch women selling small amounts of drugs to support a habit or, perhaps, women who live with someone engaged in selling drugs. As relatively minor players in the drug trade, women are unlikely to have information about larger drug market operations to use as bargaining chips. As the *American Violet* example demonstrates, many women feel trapped into accepting plea bargains. Mandatory minimum sentencing laws restrict judges from exercising discretion to consider mitigating circumstances such as family situations or the need for substance abuse treatment.

> Barbara Bloom maintains that the intersection of race, class and gender puts low-income women of color, especially African American women, in "triple jeopardy" and contributes to their disproportionate incarceration. Cultural stereotypes limit their access to programs and services that could help them improve their economic circumstances, strengthen their family units, and avoid criminal involvement. Natalie Sokoloff contends that since African American women—who comprise 12 percent of the female population in the U.S.—now comprise more than 50 percent of women in prison, the "war on drugs" has become a "war on poor black women."[79]

Women are usually very small cogs in the illegal drug market. Many get involved because they are unemployed and need income or to supplement low-wage and/or uncertain employment. The lack of affordable housing and cuts to social programs such as child care, social assistance, and health care can also be contributing factors. Their role might be limited to answering telephones or living in a home used for drug-related activities. An ACLU report provided the example of one young woman's circumstances.

> Chrissy Taylor was incarcerated at the age of 19 based on her marginal involvement in her boyfriend's scheme to manufacture methamphetamine. Her boyfriend asked her to go to a store in Mobile, Alabama to pick up a shipment of chemicals. Based on his assurance that the mere purchase and possession of the chemicals was legal, she went to the store and bought them. As it happened, agents from the Drug Enforcement Administration (DEA) were working with the chemical store in a reverse-sting operation. The agents sold

Chrissy the chemicals and then arrested both her and her boyfriend, not for possession or purchase of the chemicals—neither of which is in and of itself illegal—but for possession with intent to manufacture methamphetamines.[80]

The ACLU report cites a review of 60,000 federal drug cases by the *Minneapolis Star Tribune*, which found that "men were more likely than women to offer evidence to prosecutors in exchange for shorter sentences, even if the information placed others, including the women in their lives, in jeopardy."[81] The study found that women were less willing to divulge information—if, indeed, they had such knowledge—because of a reluctance to implicate a partner or family member.

Peripherally involved women and other low-level participants tend to bear the brunt of enforcement efforts and punitive approaches ostensibly aimed at more significant players. In many cases, they face charges and sentences of the same severity as their male counterparts, despite lesser involvement in the underlying offense. Indeed, the marginal roles women play in drug-dealing operations actually make them more vulnerable to long prison terms for drug crimes. Because their peripheral roles afford little access to information, they are often unable to give prosecutors evidence about others' crimes and contacts—women have less currency with which to bargain their way out of harsh sentences.[82]

An Outrageous Example: The "Pregnancy Police"[83]

Perhaps the most outrageous form of judicial sexism was the attempt to criminalize pregnant women addicted to drugs, especially crack cocaine. The intense media frenzy over the alleged crack epidemic helped create an environment that had zero tolerance for mothers who used drugs during pregnancy. The frenzy peaked in 1986. Six of the nation's most prestigious newspapers and newsmagazines had run more than one thousand stories about crack. *Time* and *Newsweek* each ran 74 stories in 6 months; more than 15 million Americans watched a prime-time special, *48 Hours on Crack Street*, on CBS. Politicians and the media warned that an entire generation—primarily black urban youth—would be born addicted and diseased.[84]

Nationally broadcast news footage of premature infants hooked up to tubes in nurseries sickened viewers. "Here were the fruits of indulgence, the horrifying issue of women whose moral compasses were so screwed up they had essentially abandoned their babies in the womb."[85] Experts weighed in with frightening predictions that hundreds of thousands of babies exposed to crack cocaine would never lead normal lives.

When the expected tidal wave of brain-damaged, unteachable monsters failed to materialize, a handful of thoughtful people started looking into some of the original assumptions. They discovered that

> the crack-baby epidemic . . . was a total fabrication—a blend of dis-
> torted data and sloppy journalism. The tiny infants trembling in
> their incubators were real enough—no question about that—but
> they were usually the victims of an older, more established ailment.
> What the cameras were capturing were the well-documented effects
> of malnutrition and poverty.[86]

The media were far less diligent about publishing the actual facts than
they had been about sensationalizing the plight of infants born to
addicted mothers.

The panic created conditions under which 200 pregnant women in
20 states would be prosecuted.[87] Most of the women arrested were low-
income women of color with untreated drug addictions. Although no
state legislature at the time had passed a statute specific to drug use
during pregnancy, local prosecutors expanded the reach of criminal
laws to criminalize the taking of drugs while pregnant as drug delivery,
assault with a deadly weapon, manslaughter, and homicide.

In the fall of 1988, staff members at the Charleston public hospital
operated by the Medical University of South Carolina (MUSC) were
concerned about an increase in the use of cocaine by patients receiving
prenatal treatment. When cocaine use by pregnant patients continued
despite referrals for counseling and treatment, a MUSC nurse
approached a prosecutor in Charleston, offering to cooperate in prosecuting mothers whose children tested positive for drugs at birth. A task
force made up of MUSC personnel, police, and local officials developed
the Interagency Policy on Cocaine Abuse in Pregnancy (IPCAP) in
1989, which described procedures for nonconsensual drug testing of
pregnant patients suspected of drug use and reporting the results to
law enforcement. Women who tested positive for cocaine before giving
birth were arrested and sent to jail, brought to MUSC every week for
checkups, and some were chained to hospital beds during labor and
delivery. Women who tested positive after giving birth were arrested
and jailed immediately.

In June 1991, Crystal Ferguson was tested, without her consent,
during a routine prenatal checkup. When told she had tested positive,
she agreed to attend substance abuse counseling. When she delivered
her child in August, she again was tested without her consent. Because
traces of cocaine were found, she was told to enter a two-week residential treatment program or face arrest and prosecution. Unable to find
childcare for her two older children, she requested a referral to an out-
patient treatment program. After her request was rejected, she was
arrested on August 7, 1991, for failing to comply with an order to
receive drug treatment.[88]

Ferguson was one of 42 women (all of whom were black except 1)
arrested under IPCAP. An initial lawsuit was filed on behalf of Ferguson
and one other woman; eventually the challenge included ten patients

arrested at MUSC. In October 2000, the U.S. Supreme Court heard arguments in *Ferguson v. City of Charleston* about whether the state had violated the Fourth Amendment protections against unwarranted searches.[89] The Court ruled 6–3 in favor of the plaintiffs on March 21, 2001.

> A state hospital's performance of a diagnostic test to obtain evidence of a patient's criminal conduct for law enforcement purposes is an unreasonable search if the patient has not consented to the procedure. The interest in using the threat of criminal sanctions to deter pregnant women from using cocaine cannot justify a departure from the general rule that an official nonconsensual search is unconstitutional if not authorized by a valid warrant.[90]

The defeat in *Ferguson v. City of Charleston* did little to deter South Carolina. Regina McKnight, a black woman, is serving a 12-year sentence for murder. She gave birth to a stillborn child, and she took cocaine while pregnant. While no research evidence links cocaine use and stillbirth, prosecutors charged her with murder. South Carolina was the only state with a child abuse law that could be applied to viable fetuses (upheld by the South Carolina Supreme Court in 1997). McKnight became the first woman in the nation to be convicted of murder for using cocaine while pregnant. Lynn Paltrow, an attorney and the executive director of National Advocates for Pregnant Women, warned: "What South Carolina has done, in effect, is made pregnancy a crime waiting to happen." Paltrow was one of the attorneys who appealed McKnight's case to the U.S. Supreme Court, which decided not to review it. The appeal was joined by 27 medical and drug policy groups (e.g., American Public Health Association, American Nurses Association, and the American Society of Addictions), who wrote that the prosecution of this case "contradicts the clear weight of available medical evidence, violates fundamental notions of public health, and undermines the physician-patient relationship."[91]

South Carolina was one of the earliest and most aggressive states (more than 70 prosecutions since 1989) in charging drug-abusing mothers, but Texas, New York, Arizona, Hawaii, Utah, and California have also prosecuted women who use drugs during pregnancy. In 1989, Illinois became the first state to charge a woman with manslaughter after her baby was stillborn. A grand jury refused to indict, and prosecutors have since been reluctant to bring such charges. In contrast, Riverside County, California (sometimes referred to as the nation's methamphetamine capital), declared such prosecutions a top priority. In 2003, prosecutors nationwide were pressing criminal charges against women who abused drugs or alcohol while pregnant. Stacey Gilligan in New York was accused of drinking so much vodka during her eighth month of pregnancy that her baby was born drunk. Tayshea Aiwohi in Hawaii was charged with consuming so much crystal meth while she was pregnant that her son died of methamphetamine poisoning two days after his birth.[92] Charges ranged from misdemeanor counts of endangering the welfare of a child to criminal homicide. At least two women were sentenced to life in prison.

Since 2000, rural Covington County, Alabama, has had the highest number of arrests for drug abuse in the state. Over an eighteen-month period (through March 2008), eight women—young, white, and working-class—were prosecuted for testing positive for drugs after giving birth or for using drugs while pregnant. Across the nation doctors and advocacy groups maintain that the effects of drug use during pregnancy on fetuses are not fully known, but those arguments have not been made in Alabama. Women have accepted plea bargains rather than risk trial. Doctors, lawyers, and community members rarely discuss the cases—indicating a "powerful, unspoken community sanction against the combination of drugs and pregnant women."[93]

Greg Gambril, the district attorney, does not distinguish between fetus and child, saying his duty is to protect both. However, the Alabama law he employs was passed to protect children from exposure to methamphetamine when parents use their homes to produce the drug and makes no reference to unborn children. Gambril argues that taking drugs during pregnancy endangers the child and "is what I call a continuing crime."[94] He asserts that the statute was intended to insure "a safe environment, a drug-free environment."

Tiffany Hitson (22) and her baby daughter tested positive for cocaine after the baby was born. "Like most other women arrested on the child endangerment charge, Hitson was too poor to hire her own attorney and was represented by a court-appointed lawyer. And like most others, she faced other nonviolent charges—in her case, credit card fraud."[95] The judge set bond at $200,000. She pleaded guilty to child endangerment and was sentenced to prison for a year and one year in a drug rehabilitation center. Rachel Barfoot, a mother of four, had been charged with beating her niece. She told her probation officer she was three months pregnant. After testing positive for cocaine, she was arrested and spent five weeks in jail. Police affirm that local doctors are cooperating in investigations of drug use during pregnancy. Convicted women are sentenced to county jails, state prisons, or drug rehabilitation clinics. They "often emerge bitter at the collaboration of police, prosecutors, judges, doctors and social workers" who seem intent on punishment rather than help.[96]

Shekelia Ward, a 29-year-old single mother, and her baby tested positive for cocaine after the girl was born in January 2008, healthy despite being five weeks premature. She is challenging the use of the child endangerment law. The Covington County circuit judge rejected Ward's motion to dismiss the charges, and the case went to the Alabama Court of Criminal Appeals.[97] Appellate courts in Maryland, New

Mexico, Kentucky, Nevada, and Ohio have struck down cases in which prosecutors used child endangerment or abuse laws to prosecute drug use during pregnancy.[98] As the ACLU notes, state policies aimed at policing pregnant women essentially reduce the rights of women, making them wards of the state and regarding them as different from other competent adults—requiring them to forfeit their constitutional rights because they are pregnant.

> It is hard to imagine subjecting fathers or soon-to-be fathers to the same level of state interference in their private lives as we do pregnant women. We do not strip fathers of their constitutional rights, even when their behavior may have deleterious effects on their offspring. We do not, for example, arrest fathers and remove them from their families if they smoke two packs of cigarettes a day around their children and their pregnant wives, though there is ample evidence that exposure—even prenatal exposure—to secondhand smoke can have serious long-term health effects.[99]

Paltrow lists other significant problems with such prosecutions: (1) criminal charges do not address addiction, the root of the problem; (2) the collateral damage is that drug-addicted pregnant women will not seek treatment or prenatal care if they believe they will be prosecuted; and (3) minorities and the poor are the most frequent targets. Richard Wexler, director of the National Coalition for Child Protection Reform, states: "This has become a general assault on poor people, and disproportionately on minorities."[100]

Scapegoating low-income women of color who take drugs provides political cover for larger social issues. The public has little sympathy for a politically disempowered group that appears to have little regard for the welfare of their children. Arrests target people for whom the public has expressed little support.

> Poor women of color have overwhelmingly been the ones targeted and arrested for using drugs while pregnant. There are many factors contributing to these discrepancies, with race and class prejudices playing a major role in all of them. Because poor women of color are far more likely to give birth at public institutions and have more contact with state agencies, their drug use is far more likely than that of middle-class white women to be detected and reported.[101]

The Alabama prosecutions highlight what can happen when prosecutors decide to target drug use. The net extended to white women, although still low income. However, any pregnant woman is vulnerable to state control and punishment under the same extensions of the law if prosecutorial power remains unchecked.[102]

Characteristics of Women in Prison

The wars on crime and drugs have effectively been wars on women and minorities. As are male prisoners, most women in prison are poor and uneducated.

- 35% of women incarcerated in state prisons had committed no prior offense.
- 29% of women offenders were using alcohol at the time of the offense (versus 38% of men).
- 23% of women in state prisons and 17% in jails were receiving medication for an emotional disorder.
- Almost 6 in 10 women in state prisons had experienced physical or sexual abuse; more than one-third had been abused by an intimate, and just under a quarter reported prior abuse by a family member.
- Most women in prison are unmarried.[103]

The majority of women on probation (62%) are white.[104] Of the 207,700 women in jail or state or federal prison in 2008, 94,500 (45.5%) were white, 67,800 (32.6%) black. and 33,400 (16%) Hispanic. Most of the incarcerated women were between the ages of 20 and 44.[105] Forty-four percent of women in state prisons have not graduated from high school or earned a GED.[106] Sixty percent of the women on probation have completed high school.[107]

The economic circumstances for most of the women were more difficult than for their male counterparts. Only about 40% had been employed full time prior to their arrest (compared to 60% of male prisoners). About 37% of the women (compared to 28% of the men) had incomes of less than $600 per month, well below the poverty level. Almost 30% of these women had been receiving public assistance.[108]

Alcohol and substance abuse were common among these women. About half of the women in state prisons had been using alcohol and/or drugs at the time of committing the offense for which they were incarcerated. About 40% of the women (compared to 32% of male inmates) were under the influence of drugs when the crime occurred. Around one-third of the women said they committed the offense in order to buy drugs.

While more women than men had no prior convictions (35% versus 23%), they were more likely to have had a correctional status at the time of the offense for which they were imprisoned. About one in three women inmates had been on probation compared to one in 5 male inmates. Nineteen percent of female inmates had a juvenile history, compared to 38% of male inmates. Twenty percent of women inmates (versus 8% of males) were serving their first sentence for a nonviolent crime.[109] As the statistics show, the majority of women in prison have not been "career criminals." The war on drugs has, in effect, criminalized those who in previous years would have been placed on probation (if arrested at all) rather than being sent to prison.[110]

A California survey revealed stark contrasts between men and women prisoners, and family circumstances, in particular, differed greatly. For instance, 57% of the women compared to 16% of the men had been either physically or sexually abused prior to being sent to

Table 6.3   Characteristics of Women in the Correctional System

Characteristic	Probation	Local Jails	State Prisons	Federal Prisons
Major Offense				
Violent	9%	12%	28%	7%
Property	44	34	27	12
Drugs	19	30	34	72
Public Order	27	24	11	8
Race				
White	62%	36%	33%	29%
Black	27	44	48	35
Hispanic	10	15	15	32
Other	1	5	4	4
Age				
Under 25	20%	21%	12%	9%
25–34	39	46	43	35
35–44	30	27	34	32
45–54	10	5	9	18
55+	1	1	2	6
Marital Status				
Married	26%	15%	17%	29%
Widowed	2	4	6	6
Separated	10	13	10	21
Divorced	20	20	20	10
Never Married	42	48	47	34
Education				
8th grade or less	5%	12%	7%	8%
Some high school	35	33	37	19
High school grad or GED	39	39	39	44
Some college or more	21	16	17	29
History of Abuse				
Ever	41%	48%	57%	NA
Before 18	16	21	12	
After 18	13	11	20	
Both	**13**	**16**	**25**	

Source: Greenfeld, L. A. and T. L. Snell (1999). "Women Offenders." Washington, DC: Bureau of Justice Statistics December.

prison, and 27% of the women (versus 12% of the men) were in therapy for mental health concerns. Only 40% of the women, compared to 60% of the men, were employed at the time of their arrest.[111] The survey identified significant gender differences in the offenses committed. Violent crimes were committed by a much smaller percentage of women (13% versus 28% for men). Almost half (47%) of the women were convicted of a property crime, compared to 31% of the men. Drug charges were more similar, but a greater percentage of women (34%) were serving time for drug charges than men (29%). Significantly, 42% of the women were classified as "low-level" offenders, compared to 15% of the men.[112]

Another study confirmed that the family backgrounds of women who were incarcerated had been quite dysfunctional.[113] The majority of women reported having only one parent in the household (normally the mother), while about half had at least one family member who had been incarcerated (compared to 37% of the men in prison). Drugs and alcohol abuse were prevalent within their families, and sexual and physical abuse were far more common than for women in the general population. Most of the women witnessed violence in their families. The percentages of women who have experienced abuse vary depending on the state; studies in California, New York, Nevada, and North Carolina have reported high percentages.[114]

The physical health of incarcerated women is much worse than that of people in the general population or that of male prisoners. They are about three times more likely than men to go to sick call every day (20–35% versus 7–10%). About 5% of the women are pregnant when they enter prison. Sexually transmitted diseases are also a much greater problem for women than for men. Women are 50% more likely to be HIV positive; since 1991 the number of women with HIV went up by 69%, compared to a 22% rise among men.[115]

Mental health issues are more common among women than men. Around one-fourth have been diagnosed with a mental illness (primarily depression, post-traumatic stress disorder [PTSD], and substance abuse). PTSD is strongly related to sexual abuse and other kinds of trauma, and most of the disorders are strongly correlated with experiences of abuse. Just over one-fifth of women in jail have been diagnosed with PTSD. Around one-fourth of women in prison are getting medication for various psychological disorders. The failure to monitor indicators of potential problems can lead to tragedies. Carina Montes, 29, was jailed for shoplifting thirty lipsticks. When she arrived at Riker's Island in September 2002, her medical file included the following notations: a childhood of sexual abuse, diagnosis of manic depression, suicide attempt at age 13.[116] She was never seen by a psychiatrist. Her file was sometimes misplaced, and she was passed from one staff member to another. She was eventually placed on suicide watch in

December. In February the guard on duty was not aware of the suicide watch. She was found hanging from bedsheets five months after being jailed. Carina was one of six suicides in six months (not since 1985 had there been so many suicides in that amount of time). None of the people who committed suicide had been convicted of the charges that put them in jail. Prison Health Services (see chapter 2) had a contract to provide medical services for the New York jails. Investigators found that patients' charts were missing, alerts about despondent inmates were lost or unheeded, and neither medical personnel nor correction officers were properly trained in preventing suicide—the leading cause of death in American jails.

THE PATHWAYS PERSPECTIVE

Women's pathways into the criminal justice system differ from those of men. Research indicates that gender matters significantly in shaping criminality. For women, "the most common pathways to crime are based on survival (of abuse and poverty) and substance abuse."[117] Women are at greater risk of experiencing sexual abuse, sexual assault, and domestic violence. Women frequently become involved in criminal behavior through relationships with family members and significant others. The economic and social marginality of women impact their responsibilities for children and other dependent family members. The intersecting issues of trauma, mental health, substance abuse, and economic marginality all contribute to how women enter the correctional system. Once there, most policies and procedures were designed for male offenders; "the overwhelming number of male offenders often overshadows the issues relevant to women offenders."[118] The realities of women's lives in the community prior to committing an offense, differences in women's pathways to crime, and the behavior of women under supervision offer clues to more effective correctional practices for women.

THE "CONCRETE WOMB"

Both males and females who go to prison suffer a number of "pains of imprisonment."[119] For women, however, there are some important qualitative differences. Kathryn Watterson notes that a process referred to as "reception" introduces a female inmate to the "concrete womb," and she quotes a sheriff about reception procedures at the Los Angeles County jail.

> For a new booking the officer types up a booking slip while another officer has the inmate in custody. She gives her a number and then goes through her purse to search for contraband. After everything is complete, the inmate is sent through number three gate and delivered to a female deputy, still in full view of the control center and hall leading to the administrative offices. At that time the deputy

gives her a pat search. She removes her wig, rings, shoes and socks. Anything such as a leather belt, drugs or medication is taken. She can keep up to ten dollars—but no more than two dollars in change. More than two dollars in change is not allowed because it could be put into a sock and used as a weapon.

This is where I am generally assigned. The pat search means I also look in your ears, your nose and mouth. I search your bra and around your waist and look up your pants leg. If they have dentures I ask them to remove the dentures and look at this for contraband possibly being concealed under it. Then we put them into one of the *two* holding blocks.[120]

From the moment the inmate enters a custodial institution, there is no privacy. Every action is monitored, and every activity routinized. The institutionalization process in women's prisons is "synonymous with forced dependency." You learn to take orders. The custodial regime erodes self-determination, independence, and a sense of responsibility.[121]

Men in prison form a number of informal groups, gangs, and cliques. These relationships are often short-lived, and close attachments are rare. In contrast, relationships are a central, organizing feature in women's development.[122] Women need connections. In fact; they often find themselves involved in criminal activities because of unhealthy relationships or because they have experienced a damaging disconnection in a relationship.[123] Effective custodial policies would allow women to experience relationships that "do not reenact their histories of loss, neglect, and abuse. . . . Disconnection and violation have characterized most of the adult relationships of women in the system."[124] Unfortunately, correctional settings often recreate disconnected relationships on a systemic level. The criminal justice system is based on rank, power, and control—imitating the dominant/subordinate model of patriarchal society. Correctional employees who work with women offenders often earn less than those who work with men.

Stephanie Covington describes the custodial experience of women offenders as "condemned isolation."[125] Having been removed from families and children, women often try to create "pseudo-families" within the institution.[126] Even if the families on the outside were highly dysfunctional and abusive, women have been socialized to seek relationships and they try to adapt to the prison world using the model they learned outside the prison walls.[127] Some women play the role of "husband" and wear their hair short, wear slacks, walk and talk in a masculine way, while others play the role of "wife," "grandmother," and even "sons" and "daughters." Watterson writes: "In the context of prison society, it is not shocking to meet someone's institutional wife or grandfather. On several occasions while visiting prisons, I met a woman's entire prison 'family' and saw the interweaving of wife, grandmother, son, wife-in-law, daughter." Most of these "families" evolve in a natural way as an inevitable adaptation to the deprivations of prison life.[128]

For women in prison, in contrast to men in prison, the close bonds of a "family" help to alleviate the pains of imprisonment. Such relationships, although not without problems of their own, help to create the kind of ideal family many of them never had on the outside. Because of this, many women never want to leave. Some, upon release, do things that will automatically bring them hack to prison. As one female prisoner stated: "It's that security. It's that instant gratification . . . coming back and having everybody holler and say, 'Look, Pat's back,' all happy to see you."[129]

The "concrete womb" is reinforced every day within women's prisons, sometimes subtly and sometimes not so subtly. While many modern women's prisons offer some college courses and some training with computers, the bulk of the programming reinforces traditional female roles—sewing, food services, secretarial training, and cosmetology.[130] In her research, Joanne Belknap found that women in prison have less access than men to vocational, educational, and recreational programs and inadequate access to health care.[131] Vocational programs in jails were both too few in number and inadequate in quality to prepare women for career-oriented training.[132] Prisons offer a narrow range of job-training programs for stereotypical occupations, such as cosmetology and low-level clerical work.[133] Women in prison receive fewer institutional work assignments and lower rates of pay than male inmates, and men have greater access to work-release programs. Less than one in three women is enrolled in a vocational program while in prison.[134] One in five women take high school or GED classes in prison. Only 1 in 8 women in federal prisons and 1 in 5 in state prisons with a history of substance abuse receive treatment. Fewer than 25% of women in jails receive mental health services.

In addition to the pains of imprisonment, many women in prison are mothers and face an additional, permanent deprivation—the termination of their parental rights.

> Enactment of harsh drug laws, mandatory minimums, and repeat offender statutes has resulted in more women being incarcerated for longer sentences. The majority of incarcerated women are mothers, and many of these mothers are raising their children alone. Single mothers who are incarcerated are more likely to have their parental rights terminated than male prisoners who are fathers because the children of male inmates overwhelmingly reside with their natural mothers.[135]

Some Concluding Thoughts

Women offenders frequently lived on the socioeconomic fringes of society before incarceration, and they are disproportionately minorities.

Today (and in the past) most women offenders are poor and unskilled. Many experienced dysfunctional home environments where they were often victims of physical or sexual abuse. They frequently use drugs. Their crimes are usually nonviolent, and they often do not have a history of criminal behavior. Two-thirds of the women in prison lived with young children before going to prison. The shift in thinking about the basic purpose of the criminal justice system from a means to rehabilitate people to rejoin society to the necessity to incapacitate and punish those who break the law has been especially detrimental to women.

Joanne Belknap and Kristi Holsinger provide a synopsis of the history of punishment of women and the unintended consequences of some of the efforts.

> Reformers in any movement usually have the best intentions, but it is important to recognize that some implemented policies that initially appear as important achievements to feminists and others who advocate for women and girls have often backfired. Specifically, many policies implemented originally to help women and girls have often been applied in sexist manners. Examples of this include penal reform movements to separate women from men in prison that resulted in sexist treatment and punishment for women, movements to make changes in sentencing for males and females that resulted in exceptionally long sentences for females, and the mandatory arrest policy in domestic violence that has resulted in numerous women victims being arrested for resisting their batterers' abuse.[136]

The vicious cycle of high incarceration rates have devastating collateral effects on communities. Former inmates are far less likely to be employed. The declining economic opportunities can lead to reoffending, further straining families and communities.

> High rates of incarceration invite closer and more punitive police enforcement and parole surveillance, contributing to the growing number of repeat admissions and the resilience of incarceration even as crime rates fall. Incarceration begets more incarceration, and incarceration also begets more crime, which in turn invites more aggressive enforcement, which then re-supplies incarceration.[137]

Unless the United States alters its current emphasis on punishment and embarks on a more innovative approach, women will continue to be at risk—along with everyone else caught in the imprisonment net.

NOTES

[1] Dobash, R. E., R. Dobash, and S. Gutteridge. *The Imprisonment of Women*. New York: Basil and Blackwell, 1986; Lorde, A. "Age, Race, Class, and Sex: Women Redefining Difference." In P. S. Rothenberg, ed., *Race, Class, and Gender in the United States: An Integrated Study* (4th ed.). New York: St. Martin's Press, 1998, pp. 533–540.

[2] Eisenstein, Z. R. *The Female Body and the Law*. Berkeley: University of California Press, 1998, pp. 58–59.

[3] Shelden, R. G. *Controlling the Dangerous Classes: A History of Criminal Justice in America* (2nd ed.). Boston: Allyn & Bacon, 2008, p. 235.

[4] Knappman, E. W. *Great American Trials: From Salem Witchcraft to Rodney King*. Detroit, MI: Visible Ink Press, 1994; Semmes, R. *Crime and Punishment in Early Maryland*. Montclair, NJ: Patterson Smith, 1970; Tolles, F. B. "Mary Dyer." In E. T. James, J. W. James, and P. S. Boyer, eds., *Notable American Women, 1906–1950*. Cambridge, MA: Belknap Press of Harvard University Press, 1971.

[5] Pollock, J. M. "Gender, Justice, and Social Control: A Historical Perspective." In A. V. Merlo and J. M. Pollock, eds., *Women, Law, and Social Control* (2nd ed.). New York: Allyn & Bacon, 2006, pp. 3–31.

[6] Rathbone, C. *A World Apart: Women, Prison, and Life Behind Bars*. New York: Random House, 2006, p. 27.

[7] Collins, C. F. *The Imprisonment of African-American Women*. Jefferson, NC: McFarland, 1997, p. 5.

[8] Sellin, T. *Slavery and the Penal System*. New York: Elsevier, 1976.

[9] Shelden, R. G. (1980). "From Slave to Caste Society: Penal Changes in Tennessee, 1840–1915." *Tennessee Historical Quarterly* 38: 462–478.

[10] The Evolution of the New York Prison System. Part I. http://www.correctionhistory.org/html/chronicl/state/html/nyprisons.html

[11] Rafter, N. *Partial Justice: Women, Prisons, and Social Control* (2nd ed.). New Brunswick, NJ: Transaction Books, 1990, p. 7.

[12] Freedman, E. B. *Their Sisters' Keepers: Women's Prison Reform in America, 1830–1930*. Ann Arbor: University of Michigan Press, 1981, p. 16.

[13] Ibid., p. 18.

[14] Ibid., pp. 17–18.

[15] Rafter, *Partial Justice*, p. 6; Freedman, *Their Sisters' Keepers*, p. 15.

[16] Watterson, K. *Women in Prison: Inside the Concrete Womb*. Boston: Northeastern University Press, 1996, p. 196; Rafter, *Partial Justice*, p. 6.

[17] Freedman, *Their Sisters' Keepers*, p. 17.

[18] Rafter, *Partial Justice*, p. 16.

[19] Shelden, "From Slave to Caste Society."

[20] Watterson, *Women in Prison*, p. 198.

[21] Freedman, *Their Sisters' Keepers*, p. 14.

[22] Ibid., p. 49.

[23] Ibid., p. 59.

[24] Ibid., pp. 42–43.

[25] Ibid., p. 60.

[26] Rafter, *Partial Justice*, p. 24. See also Platt, A. *The Child Savers* (rev. ed.). Chicago: University of Chicago Press, 1977.

[27] Ibid., p. 61.

[28] Rafter, *Partial Justice*, p. 83.

[29] Ibid., p. xxvii.

[30] Ibid., p. xxviii.

[31] Freedman, *Their Sisters' Keepers*, p. 62, emphasis added by Freedman.

[32] Ibid., p. 61.

[33] Collins, *The Imprisonment of African-American Women*, p. 21.

[34] Bureau of Prisons. http://www.bop.gov/locations/female_facilities.jsp

[35] According to the 1880 census, in Alabama, Louisiana, Mississippi, North Carolina, Tennessee, and Texas, more than one-third of the 220 black female prisoners were leased out, compared to only one white woman prisoner out of a total population of 40. Rafter, *Partial Justice*, p. 150.

[36] Ibid., p. 141.

[37] Ibid., pp. 142–146.

[38] Ibid., p. 142.

[39] Sourcebook of Criminal Justice Statistics, table 6.28. http://www.albany.edu/sourcebook/pdf/t6282007.pdf; West, H. C. and W. J. Sabol (March 2009). "Prison Inmates at Midyear 2008—Statistical Tables." NCJ 225619, tables 1 and 10. http://www.ojp.usdoj.gov/bjs/pub/pdf/pim08st.pdf

[40] Ibid., table 16.

[41] Zaplin, R. T. "Female Offenders: A Systems Perspective," p. 82. In R. Zaplin, ed., *Female Offenders: Critical Perspectives and Effective Interventions* (2nd ed.). Sudbury, MA: Jones and Bartlett, 2008, pp. 77–98.

[42] Federal Bureau of Investigation (2008). *Crime in the United States, 2007*, table 42. http://www.fbi.gov/ucr/cius2007/data/table_42.htmlhttp://www.fbi.gov/ucr/cius2007/data/table_42.html

[43] Ibid., table 33.

[44] Ibid., table 42.

[45] Minton, T. D. and W. J. Sabol (March 2009). "Jail Inmates at Midyear 2008—Statistical Tables." NCJ 225709, tables 6 and 7. http://www.ojp.usdoj.gov/bjs/pub/pdf/jim08st.pdf

[46] Donziger, S. *The Real War on Crime.* New York: Harper/Collins, 1996, p. 152.

[47] Schirmer, S., A. Nellis, and M. Mauer. *Incarcerated Parents and Their Children: Trends 1991–2007.* Washington, DC: The Sentencing Project, 2009, p. 2. http://sentencingproject.org/Admin%5CDocuments%5Cpublications%5Cinc_incarceratedparents.pdf. The population of incarcerated parents follows the trend for all incarcerated individuals. While the prison population almost doubled during those years, the largest increase occurred between 1991 and 1997; the rate of increase has been slower in the last decade.

[48] Ibid., p. 8.

[49] Tremblay, B. (April 30, 2009). "Haney's *American Violet* Shines Light on Drug Policy, Criminal Justice System." GateHouse News Service. http://www.norwichbulletin.com/entertainment/x342374951/Haneys-American-Violet-shines-light-on-drug-policy-criminal-justice-system; movie trailer on You-tube. http://www.youtube.com/watch?v=Qv8Jq09qU1Q

[50] Beale, L. (April 17, 2009). Taking Drug Task Forces to Task. http://www.miller-mccune.com/legal_affairs/taking-drug-task-forces-to-task-1074.print

[51] Ibid.

[52] U.S. Department of Labor, Bureau of Labor Statistics (2008). "Women in the Labor Force: A Databook," table 13. http://www.bls.gov/cps/wlf-databook2008.htm

[53] Ibid., table 17.

[54] Ibid., table 20.

[55] Statistical Abstracts of the U.S. (2009). Table C9. Children/1 by Presence and Type of Parent(s), Race, and Hispanic Origin/2: 2008. http://www.census.gov/population/www/socdemo/hh-fam/cps2008.html

[56] Ibid.

[57] Statistical Abstracts of the U.S. (2004). Table 56. http://www.census.gov/prod/2004pubs/04statab/pop.pdf

[58] Statistical Abstracts of the U.S. (2009). Table C9.

[59] Ibid., table 694. http://www.census.gov/compendia/statab/tables/09s0694.xls

[60] Ibid., table 676. http://www.census.gov/compendia/statab/tables/09s0676.xls

[61] Daly, K. (1992). "Women's Pathways to Felony Court: Feminist Theories of Lawbreaking and Problems of Representation," pp. 23–24. *Southern California Review of Law and Women's Studies* 2: 11–52.

[62] Schwartz, J. and D. Steffensmeier. "The Nature of Female Offending: Patterns and Explanation," p. 49. In R. Zaplin, ed., *Female Offenders*, pp. 43–76.

[63] Zaplin, "Female Offenders," p. 84.

[64] Daly, "Women's Pathways to Felony Court"; Miller, E. *Street Woman.* Philadelphia: Temple University Press, 1986; Chesney-Lind, M. and L. Pasko. *The Female Offender: Girls, Women, and Crime* (2nd ed.). Thousand Oaks, CA: Sage, 2004.

[65] West and Sabol, table 18.

[66] Chesney-Lind and Pasko, *The Female Offender.*

[67] Chesney-Lind and Pasko, *The Female Offender.*

[68] Austin, J., M. Bruce, L. Carroll, P. McCall, and S. C. Richards (2000). "The Use of Incarceration in the United States." *The American Society of Criminology* November: 8. http://www.ssc.wisc.edu/~oliver/RACIAL/Reports/ascincarcerationdraft.pdf

[69] West, H. C. and W. J. Sabol (December 2008). *Prisoners in 2007,* table 10. NCJ 224280 http://www.ojp.usdoj.gov/bjs/pub/pdf/p07.pdf

[70] Donziger, S. *The Real War on Crime: The Report of the National Criminal Justice Commission.* New York: HarperCollins, 1996; U.S. Department of Justice (March 1994). "Women in Prison, Survey of State Prison Inmates, 1991."

[71] The Sentencing Project (May 2007). Women in the Criminal Justice System: Briefing Sheets. http://www.sentencingproject.org/Admin/Documents/publications/womenincj_total.pdf

[72] Ibid.

[73] Women in Prison Project. "Women in Prison Fact Sheet 2009." Correctional Association of New York. http://www.correctionalassociation.org/publications/download/wipp/factsheets/Wome_in_Prison_Fact_Sheet_2009_FINAL.pdf

[74] Wilson, A. Rockefeller Drug Laws Information Sheet. Partnership for Responsible Drug Information. http://www.prdi.org/rocklawfact.html

[75] Women in Prison Project, "Women in Prison Fact Sheet 2009."

[76] Gray, M. (April 2, 2009). "A Brief History of New York's Rockefeller Drug Laws." http://www.time.com/time/nation/article/0,8599,1888864,00.html As noted in chapter 1, the New York legislature passed the Drug Law Reform Act in 2004, which changed the sentencing guidelines. In 2009, the legislature was considering legislation to reduce penalties further.

[77] Prisoner Action Coalition (2000). "Women in California Prisons." Berkeley, CA. http://www.boalt.org/PAC/stats/women-prison-fact-sheet.html

[78] New York Civil Liberties Union (2009). "The Rockefeller Drug Laws: Unjust, Irrational, Ineffective." http://www.nyclu.org/rockefeller-report

[79] Greene, J. and K. Pranis. *Hard Hit: The Growth in the Imprisonment of Women, 1977–2004.* "Part I: Growth Trends and Recent Research," 2006, p. 24. http://www.wpaonline.org/institute/hardhit/part1.htm

[80] American Civil Liberties Union. *Caught in the Net: The Impact of Drug Policies on Women and Families.* New York: American Civil Liberties Union, 2005, p. 11. http://www.aclu.org/images/asset_upload_file431_23513.pdf

[81] Ibid., p. 10.

[82] Ibid., pp. 11–12.

[83] The phrase comes from: Siegel, L. "The Pregnancy Police Fight the War on Drugs." In C. Reinarman and H. G. Levine, eds., *Crack in America: Demon Drugs and Social Justice.* Berkeley: University of California Press, 1997, pp. 249–259.

[84] Gagan, B. (November 2000). "*Ferguson v. City of Charleston, South Carolina:* 'Fetal Abuse,' Drug Testing, and the Fourth Amendment." *Stanford Law Review.* http://caselaw.lp.findlaw.com/scripts/getcase.pl?court=US&vol=000&invol=99–936 http://www.accessmylibrary.com/coms2/summary_0286-28751147_ITM

[85] Gray, M. *Drug Crazy: How We Got into this Mess and How We Can Get Out.* New York: Routledge, 1998, p. 108.

[86] Ibid., p. 109.

[87] Paltrow, L. (1999). "Pregnant Drug Users, Fetal Persons, and the Threat to *Roe V. Wade.*" *Albany Law Review* 62:Alb.L.Rev.999. http://www.publicpolicy.umd.edu/puaf650–Fullinwider/materials-Responsibility-Paltrow.htm

[88] Ibid.

[89] American Civil Liberties Union (November 1, 2000). Policing Pregnancy: *Ferguson v. City of Charleston.* http://www.aclu.org/reproductiverights/lowincome/12511res20001101.html

[90] *Ferguson et al. v. City of Charleston et al.* No. 99–936. http://caselaw.lp.findlaw.com/scripts/getcase.pl?court=US&vol=000&invol=99-936

[91] Talvi, S. (December 3, 2003). "Criminalizing Motherhood." *The Nation.* http://www.thenation.com/doc/20031215/talvi

[92] Scharnberg, K. (November 23, 2003). "Prosecutors Targeting Pregnant Drug Users: Some Fear Women Will Shun Treatment." *Chicago Tribune.* http://advocatesforpregnantwomen.org/main/publications/articles_and_reports/prosecutors_targeting_pregnant_drug_users_some_fear_women_will_shun_treatment.php

[93] Nossiter, A. (March 15, 2008). "In Alabama, a Crackdown on Pregnant Drug Users." http://www.nytimes.com/2008/03/15/us/15mothers.html

[94] Ibid.

[95] Rawls, P. (August 1, 2008). "National Ire over Ala. Prosecuting Pregnant Moms." http://www.sfgate.com/cgi-bin/article.cgi?f=/n/a/2008/08/01/national/a090134D94.DTLProsecutors Targeting

[96] Nossiter, "In Alabama, a Crackdown on Pregnant Drug Users."

[97] Rawls, "National Ire over Ala. Prosecuting Pregnant Moms." Case undecided at time book went to press.

[98] Ibid.; Nossiter, "In Alabama, a Crackdown on Pregnant Drug Users."

[99] American Civil Liberties Union, Policing Pregnancy.

[100] Scharnberg, "Prosecutors Targeting Pregnant Drug Users."

[101] American Civil Liberties Union, Policing Pregnancy.

[102] Paltrow, "Pregnant Drug Users."

[103] Greenfeld, L. A. and T. L. Snell (1999). "Women Offenders." Washington, DC: Bureau of Justice Statistics Special Report, pp. 1, 7–9. http://www.ojp.usdoj.gov/bjs/pub/pdf/wo.pdf

[104] Ibid., p. 7.

[105] West and Sabol, Prison Inmates at Midyear 2008, table 17.

[106] Sentencing Project, Women in the Criminal Justice System.

[107] Greenfeld and Snell, "Women Offenders," p. 7.

[108] Ibid., p. 8.

[109] Ibid., p. 9.

[110] Chesney-Lind and Pasko, *The Female Offender;* see also Owen, B. *"In the Mix": Struggle and Survival in a Women's Prison.* Albany, NY: SUNY Press, 1998.

[111] Little Hoover Commission. *Breaking the Barriers for Women on Parole.* Sacramento, CA: Little Hoover Commission, 2004.

[112] Surveys in other states reveal the same patterns. See the following: Marcus-Mendoza, S. and R. Briody (n.d.). Female Inmates in Oklahoma: An Updated Profile and Programming Assessment. http://www.doc.state.ok.us/offenders/ocjrc/96/Female%20Inmates%20in%20Oklahoma.pdf

[113] Bloom, B., B. Owen, and S. Covington. *Gender-Responsive Strategies: Research, Practice, and Guiding Principles for Women Offenders.* Washington, DC: National Institute of Corrections, 2003. http://www.nicic.org/pubs/2003/018017.pdf

[114] Owen, B. and B. Bloom (1995). "Profiling Women Prisoners: Findings from National Survey and California Sample." *The Prison Journal* 5: 165–185; Jordan, B. K., W. E. Schlenger, J. A. Fairbank, and J. M. Cadell (1996). "Prevalence of Psychiatric Disorders among Incarcerated Women." *Archives of General Psychiatry* 53: 513–519; Browne, A., B. Miller, and E. Marguin (1999). "Prevalence and Severity of Lifetime Physical and Sexual Victimization among Incarcerated Women." *International Journal of Law and Psychiatry* 153: 369–375; Jordan, M. (2005). "Abuse Histories among Female Inmates." Master's Thesis, Department of Criminal Justice, University of Nevada-Las Vegas.

[115] Bloom et al., *Gender-Responsive Strategies.*

[116] von Zielbauer, P. (February 28, 2005). "In City's Jails, Missed Signals Open Way to Season of Suicides." *New York Times.* http://www.nytimes.com/2005/02/28/nyregion/28jail.html

117 Bloom et al., *Gender-Responsive Strategies*, p. 52.

118 Ibid., p. vi.

119 The phrase "pains of imprisonment" was first used by sociologist Gresham Sykes more than 50 years ago. Sykes, G. *Society of Captives*. Princeton, NJ: Princeton University Press, 1958.

120 Watterson, *Women in Prison*, p. 66.

121 Ibid., pp. 77–79.

122 Covington, S. "The Relational Theory of Women's Psychological Development: Implications for the Criminal Justice System." In R. Zaplin, ed., *Female Offenders*, pp. 135–164.

123 Ibid., p. 144.

124 Ibid., p. 148.

125 Ibid.

126 Giallombardo, R. *Society of Women: A Study of Women's Prisons*. New York: Wiley, 1966; Giallombardo, R. *The Social Order of Imprisoned Girls*. New York: John Wiley, 1974; Ward, D. H., and K. S. Kassebaum. *Women's Prisons*. Chicago: Aldine, 1965; Heffernan, E. *Making It in Prison: The Square, the Cool and the Life*. New York: John Wiley, 1972; and Heffernan, E. "Making It in a Woman's Prison: The Square, the Cool and the Life." In R. M. Carter, D. Glaser, and L. T. Wilkins, eds., *Correctional Institutions* (2nd ed.). Philadelphia: Lippincott, 1977; Owen, *In the Mix*.

127 Watterson, *Women in Prison*, pp. 285–308.

128 Ibid., p. 288.

129 Ibid., p. 63.

130 Pollock-Byrne, J. M. *Women, Prison, and Crime*. Belmont, CA: Wadsworth, 1990, p. 93.

131 Cited in Greene and Pranis, *Hard Hit*, pp. 25–26.

132 Bloom et al., *Gender-Responsive Strategies*, p. 26.

133 Ibid., p. 23.

134 Sentencing Project, Women in the Criminal Justice System.

135 Bloom et al., *Gender-Responsive Strategies*, p. 128.

136 Belknap, J. and K. Holsinger. "An Overview of Delinquent Girls: How Theory and Practice Have Failed and the Need for Innovative Changes," p. 30. In R. Zaplin, ed., *Female Offenders*, pp. 1–42.

137 Fagan, J., V. West, and J. Holland (March 31, 2003). "Reciprocal Effects of Crime and Incarceration in New York City Neighborhoods." *Fordham Urban Law Journal*: 3. http://papers.ssrn.com/sol3/papers.cfm?abstract_id=392120

7

Punishing Kids

Imprisonment has been a dominant form of punishment in the United States for about 200 years.[1] The effects, on both the guarded and the guards, have continued to be the same, while failing to put a significant dent in crime. Abuses within the walls of "total institutions" have been well documented. The Stanford Prison Experiment conducted more than 30 years ago is a notable example.

The experiment consisted of setting up a mock prison in the basement of a psychology department building at Stanford University.[2] Two groups of university students were selected. One group was assigned the role of guards, while the other group played the roles of prisoners. The experiment was originally designed to last two weeks, but it was halted after just six days. Ordinary people role-playing prison guards became extremely abusive. Some of the prisoners rebelled, and one escape was barely averted. As the lead author of the study, Philip Zimbardo, stated:

> We had created an overwhelmingly powerful situation—a situation in which prisoners were withdrawing and behaving in pathological ways, and in which some of the guards were behaving sadistically. Even the "good" guards felt helpless to intervene, and none of the guards quit while the study was in progress.[3]

At an encounter session after the experiment ended, all of the "prisoners" were happy it was over, but most of the "guards" were disappointed.

Punishing young offenders with imprisonment began in the 1820s in New York. While the stated goals differed, the institutions borrowed heavily from those imprisoning adults.

Houses of Refuge

Although entirely separate systems to monitor and control the behavior of young people began to appear during the early part of the nineteenth century, differential treatment based on age did not come about

163

overnight. The roots of the juvenile justice system can be traced to much earlier legal and social perspectives on childhood and youth. One of the most important of these was a legal doctrine known as *parens patriae*.

Parens patriae originated in medieval England's chancery courts. At that point it had more to do with property law than concern for children; it was, essentially, a means for the crown to administer landed orphans' estates.[4] *Parens patriae* established that the king, in his presumed role as the "father" of his country, had the legal authority to take care of his people, especially those who were unable (for various reasons including age) to take care of themselves. By the nineteenth century this legal doctrine had evolved into the practice of the state's assuming wardship over a minor child and, in effect, playing the role of parent if the child had no parents or their parents had been declared unfit.

In the American colonies, for example, officials could "bind out" as apprentices "children of parents who were poor, not providing good breeding, neglecting their formal education, not teaching a trade, or were idle, dissolute, unchristian or incapable."[5] Later, during the nineteenth century, *parens patriae* supplied (as it still does to some extent), the legal basis for court intervention into the relationship between children and their families.[6] Another legal legacy of the colonial era that relates to the state's involvement in the lives of youth is the *stubborn child law*. Passed in Massachusetts in 1646, it established a clear legal relationship between children and parents and made it a capital offense for a child to disobey his or her parents.

In the United States, interest in the state regulation of youth was directly tied to explosive immigration and population growth. Between 1750 and 1850 the population of the United States went from 1.25 million to 23 million. The population of some states, like Massachusetts, doubled. New York's population increased fivefold between 1790 and 1830.[7] Many of those coming into the United States during the middle of the nineteenth century were of Irish or German background; the fourfold increase in immigrants between 1830 and 1840 was in large part a product of the economic hardships faced by the Irish during the potato famine.[8] The social controls in small communities were simply overwhelmed by the influx of newcomers, many of whom were either foreign born or of foreign parentage.

The transition to capitalism (specifically the factory system in the New England area) during the late eighteenth and early nineteenth centuries brought more changes. Poor, homeless young people flocked to the cities of the Northeast, particularly New York, looking for work. With this increase came a growing concern among prominent citizens about the "perishing and dangerous classes," as they would be called throughout the nineteenth century.

Prominent citizens in the cities of the East began to notice the poor, especially the children of the poor. The parents were declared unfit because their children wandered the streets unsupervised, committing various crimes to survive. Many believed uncontrolled youths were the source of social problems that, unchecked, would result in even greater problems in the future. Poor and immigrant (in this era, the Irish) children, their lifestyles, and social positions would soon be associated with crime and juvenile delinquency.

A number of philanthropic associations emerged in eastern cities to deal with these problems. One of the most notable was the *Society for the Reformation of Juvenile Delinquents* (SRJD), founded in the 1820s.[9] The SRJD, composed primarily of wealthy businessmen and professional people, convinced the New York legislature to pass a bill in 1824 that established the *New York House of Refuge*, the first correctional institution for young offenders in the United States. The bill created the first statutory definition of juvenile delinquency and authorized the managers of the refuge "to receive and take into the house of refuge . . . all children as shall be convicted of criminal offenses . . . or committed as vagrants if the court deems that they are 'proper' objects."[10]

The general aims of the house of refuge, including a definition of "delinquents," are reflected in the following extract from the SRJD:

> The design of the proposed institution is, to furnish, in the first place, an asylum, in which boys under a certain age, who become subject to the notice of our police, either as vagrants, or homeless, or charged with petty crimes, may be received, judiciously classed according to their degree of depravity or innocence, put to work at such employments as will tend to encourage industry and ingenuity, taught reading, writing, and arithmetic, and most carefully instructed in the nature of their moral and religious obligations, while at the same time, they are subjected to a course of treatment, that will afford a prompt and energetic corrective of their vicious propensities, and hold out every possible inducement to reformation and good conduct.[11]

The statute contained vague descriptions of behaviors and lifestyles which were synonymous with the characteristics of the urban poor. Being homeless, begging, vagrancy, and coming from an "unfit" home (as defined from a middle-class viewpoint) are examples. The legislation that was passed also established specific procedures for identifying the type of youths requiring intervention and the means for the legal handling of cases. According to law, the state, or a representative agency or individual, could intervene in the life of a child if it was determined that he or she needed "care and treatment," the definition of which was left entirely in the hands of the agency or individual who intervened.

Immigrants received the brunt of enforcement of these laws, especially children of Irish parents. At the time, Irish immigrants were viewed as corrupt and unsuitable as parents. Robert Pickett notes that one superintendent accounted for a boy's delinquency because "the lad's parents are Irish and intemperate and that tells the whole story."[12] Stereotyped beliefs were evident in the percentage of children of Irish heritage committed to the refuge between 1825 and 1855, which reached 63%.[13]

Children confined in the houses of refuge were subjected to strict discipline and control. A former army colonel working in the New York House of Refuge said: "He [the delinquent] is taught that prompt unquestioning obedience is a fundamental military principle."[14] It was strongly believed that rigid discipline would add to a youth's training in self-control (specifically to avoid the temptations of evil surroundings) and respect for authority (which was a basic requirement of a disciplined labor force). Corporal punishments (including hanging children from their thumbs, the use of the "ducking stool" for girls, and severe beatings), solitary confinement, handcuffs, the "ball and chain," uniform dress, the "silent system," and other practices were commonly used in houses of refuge.[15]

Following the lead of New York, other cities soon constructed houses of refuge. Within a few years, there were refuges in Boston, Philadelphia, and Baltimore. It soon became evident, however, that the original plans of the founders were not being fulfilled, for crime and delinquency remained a problem in the cities. In the refuges, protests, riots, escape attempts, and other disturbances were almost daily occurrences.[16] While at first limited to housing first-time youthful offenders and pre-delinquents, the refuges eventually confined more hardened offenders (most of whom had been hardened by the experiences of confinement); overcrowding became a problem. The cycle would repeat itself in institutions of confinement throughout the nineteenth and twentieth centuries and continues today.

The rhetoric of the founders and managers of houses of refuge about the best interests of the child fell far short of the reality experienced by the youths held in these facilities. The origins of the juvenile justice system were rooted in court challenges to the refuge movement.

Court Decisions and Effects

Ex Parte Crouse

Argued in 1838, *Ex Parte Crouse* arose from a petition of *habeas corpus* filed by the father of Mary Ann Crouse. Without her father's knowledge, Crouse had been committed to the Philadelphia House of Refuge by her mother on the grounds that she was "incorrigible." Her father argued that the incarceration was illegal because she had not been given a jury trial. The Pennsylvania Supreme Court noted that Mary had been committed on the following complaint:

said infant by reason of vicious conduct, has rendered her control beyond the power of the said complainant [her mother], and made it manifestly requisite that from regard to the moral and future welfare of the said infant she should be placed under the guardianship of the managers of the House of Refuge.[17]

The court rejected the appeal, saying that the Bill of Rights did not apply to juveniles. Based on the *parens patriae* doctrine, the court asked, "May not the natural parents, when unequal to the task of education, or unworthy of it, be superseded by the *parens patriae* or common guardian of the community?"[18] Note that the court ignored the fact that Crouse's father had filed the suit, clearly an indication that he felt "equal to the task." Further, the court observed that: "The infant has been snatched from a course which must have ended in confirmed depravity."[19] Barry Krisberg notes: "It is important to recognize the significance of both social class and hostility toward Irish immigrants in the legal determination of the Crouse case."[20] The court predicted future behavior based on vague criteria—a practice that became quite common and continues today.

The ruling assumed that the Philadelphia House of Refuge (and presumably all other houses of refuge) had a beneficial effect on residents. It "is not a prison, but a school," the court said, and because of this, not subject to procedural constraints. Further, the aims of such an institution were to reform youngsters by training them "to industry; by imbuing their minds with the principles of morality and religion; by furnishing them with means to earn a living; and above all, by separating them from the corrupting influences of improper associates."[21]

What evidence did the justices consult to support their conclusion that the Philadelphia House of Refuge was not a prison but a school? They solicited testimony only from those who managed the institution. The justices of the court came from the same general class background as those who supported the houses of refuge and believed the rhetoric of these supporters. In short, they believed the promises rather than the actions of the reformers. A more objective review of the treatment of youths housed in these places, however, might have led the justices to a very different conclusion.

Subsequent investigations found that there was an enormous amount of abuse within these institutions. The strict military regimen, the use of corporal punishment, solitary confinement, and the silent system were examples of punishment with deleterious rather than beneficial effects. Work training was practically nonexistent, and outside companies contracted for cheap labor. Religious instruction was often little more than Protestant indoctrination (many of the youngsters were Catholic). Education, in the conventional meaning of the word, was almost nonexistent.

THE O'CONNELL CASE

People v. Turner provided an intriguing addendum to the history of the houses of refuge (and to the *Crouse* case) in 1870. Daniel O'Connell was incarcerated in the Chicago House of Refuge—not because he had committed a criminal offense but because he was "in danger of growing up to become a pauper." His parents, like Mary Crouse's father, filed a writ of *habeas corpus*, charging that his incarceration was illegal. Although the facts were almost identical to the *Crouse* case, the outcome was the exact opposite.

The case went to the Illinois Supreme Court, which reached three conclusions. First, Daniel was being *punished*—not treated or helped by incarceration in the house of refuge. (Recall that the court had concluded that Mary Crouse was being *helped;* gender could have contributed to the disparate findings.[22]) Second, the Illinois court based its ruling on the *realities* or *actual practices* of the institution, rather than merely on "good intentions" as happened in the *Crouse* case. Third, the Illinois court rejected the *parens patriae* doctrine. They reasoned that the outcome for Daniel was the same as imprisonment and subject to *due process* safeguards in the criminal law. In short, while the Pennsylvania court viewed the house of refuge uncritically in the *Crouse* case, the Illinois court viewed it in a much more negative light in the O'Connell case, addressing its cruelty and harshness of treatment.[23] After the O'Connell case, only children who had committed felonies could be sent to reform schools.

The O'Connell decision played a major role in the movement to establish the juvenile court in Chicago in 1899. The founders of the juvenile court, in part, were attempting to get around the argument in the O'Connell case. In the 1905 case of Frank Fisher (ironically another Pennsylvania case), the court returned to the logic used in the *Crouse* case. In this case, the Pennsylvania Supreme Court ruled:

> To save a child from becoming a criminal, or continuing in a career of crime, to end in maturer [sic] years in public punishment and disgrace, the legislatures surely may provide for the salvation of such a child, if its parents or guardians be unwilling or unable to do so, by bringing it into one of the courts of the state without any process at all, for the purpose of subjecting it to the state's guardianship and protection.[24]

This case would not be overturned until 1967.

GAULT AND KENT: CHALLENGES TO THE PUNITIVE NATURE OF JUVENILE JUSTICE

Despite the obvious failures of the houses of refuge, reformers continued to respond to juvenile offenders by building institutions. The "edifice complex" endorses building large edifices like "reform schools," "training schools," and most recently "youth correctional centers." The problems found within the houses of refuge continued unabated throughout the twentieth century and into the twenty-first. While there were occasional "voices in the wilderness" calling attention to abuses within institutions, they mostly fell on deaf ears until the 1960s. At that time, the U.S. Supreme Court began to hear cases challenging the underlying foundation of the juvenile justice system, the *parens patriae* doctrine.

The two most significant cases were *Kent v. United States* and *In re Gault*. In the *Kent* case, the Court addressed the *certification* of a juvenile offender as an adult. The Court ruled that when a case is transferred from the juvenile court to an adult court, the court must provide a written statement giving the reasons for the waiver, the juvenile must be given a hearing, is entitled to counsel, and the defense counsel must be given access to all records and reports used in reaching the decision to waive. Justice Abe Fortas issued a strong indictment of the juvenile court: "There is evidence, in fact, that there may be grounds for concern that the child receives the worst of both worlds; that he gets neither the protection accorded to adults nor the solicitous care and regenerative treatment postulated for children."[25]

The circumstances of the *Gault* case involved an overly punitive response to a crank call to a neighbor; a 15-year-old was sentenced to a six-year term in a state training school in Arizona. The Court ruled that at the adjudicatory hearing stage, juvenile court procedures must include adequate written notice of charges, the right to counsel, privilege against self-incrimination, and the right to cross-examine accusers. Fortas once again provided the concise critique, stating that "the condition of being a boy does not justify a kangaroo court."[26]

Most observers thought that such a critique was long overdue and anticipated significant improvements within the juvenile justice system. Some of the most glaring injustices were eliminated. Access to lawyers helped safeguard the legal rights of juveniles, although the scandal in Pennsylvania in 2009 discussed below poignantly illustrates that *Gault* did not eliminate abuses. Most status offenders were no longer imprisoned, but the system continued to rely on incarceration in local detention centers and in state and county custodial institutions.[27]

UNREASONABLE SEARCHES AND SEIZURES

The Supreme Court first addressed the application of the Fourth Amendment's protection against unreasonable searches to students in 1985. In 1980, a teacher at Piscataway High School in New Jersey found two girls smoking in a restroom, a violation of school rules. One girl admitted smoking after meeting with the assistant vice principal. The other, age 14, denied the allegation, and the vice principal searched her purse. He found cigarettes, cigarette rolling papers, some marihuana and paraphernalia, a list of students who owed money to the girl, and two letters implicating her in dealing marijuana. He turned the evidence over to the police, and the girl later confessed.

The state brought delinquency charges in the Juvenile Court. The girl moved to suppress the evidence found in her purse under the Fourth Amendment protection against unreasonable searches, but the court ruled the search reasonable, found her delinquent, and sentenced her to a year's probation. The New Jersey Appellate Division affirmed the trial court's finding on the search. The New Jersey Supreme Court reversed and ordered the suppression of the evidence found in respondent's purse, holding that the search of the purse was unreasonable. The Supreme Court ruled in *New Jersey v. T.L.O.* in 1985 that the search was reasonable but emphasized that students have legitimate expectations of privacy and the school's interest in enforcing rules to protect all students should be balanced by the privacy rights of individual students.

> The Fourth Amendment's prohibition on unreasonable searches and seizures applies to searches conducted by public school officials, and is not limited to searches carried out by law enforcement officers. Nor are school officials exempt from the Amendment's dictates by virtue of the special nature of their authority over schoolchildren. In carrying out searches and other functions pursuant to disciplinary policies mandated by state statutes, school officials act as representatives of the State, not merely as surrogates for the parents of students, and they cannot claim the parents' immunity from the Fourth Amendment's strictures.[28]
>
> Schoolchildren have legitimate expectations of privacy.... But striking the balance between schoolchildren's legitimate expectations of privacy and the school's equally legitimate need to maintain an environment in which learning can take place requires some easing of the restrictions to which searches by public authorities are ordinarily subject. Thus, school officials need not obtain a warrant before searching a student who is under their authority. Moreover, school officials need not be held subject to the requirement that searches be based on probable cause to believe that the subject of the search has violated or is violating the law. Rather, the legality of a search of a student should depend simply on the reasonableness, under all the circumstances, of the search. Determining the reasonableness of any search involves a determination of whether the search was justified at its inception and whether, as conducted, it was reasonably related in scope to the circumstances that justified the interference in the first place. Under ordinary circumstances, the search of a student by a school official will be justified at its inception where there are reasonable grounds for suspecting that the search will turn up evidence that the student has violated or is violating either the law or the rules of the school. And such a search will be permissible in its scope when the measures adopted are reasonably related to the objectives of the search, and not excessively intrusive.[29]

The desire to deter student drug use influenced Supreme Court rulings in 1995 (*Vernonia School District v. Acton*) and 2002 (*Board of Education of Independent School District No. 92 v. Earls*). In both cases, the Supreme Court upheld a specific type of search—drug testing of urine—for students involved in athletics and other extracurricular activities. In *Vernonia*, a divided Court upheld an Oregon school district policy that required students participating in interscholastic athletics to consent to random drug testing. Balancing expectations of privacy against the government's interest in drug-free schools, the Court held that the drug policy did not violate the Fourth Amendment. They cited the relatively low expectation of privacy for athletes—communal undress and preseason physical exams. They also noted that athletes were leaders in the school's drug culture, which was "in a state of rebellion" and that drug use increases the risk of sports related injury.[30]

In the 2002 case, the Court held 5 to 4 that an Oklahoma school policy of randomly drug testing students who participate in competitive, nonathletic extracurricular activities was constitutional. The decision reversed a federal court ruling. The majority opinion found the school's policy "a reasonably effective means of addressing the school district's legitimate concerns in preventing, deterring and detecting drug use." Justice Ginsberg dissented: "The particular testing program upheld . . . is not reasonable, it is capricious, even perverse."[31] One commentator said the decision would make high school more like prison, saying the court's decision allows "public schools to treat their students—future citizens—as though they're likely to commit a drug crime."[32]

The intersection of policies about preventing drug abuse and the rights of students from unreasonable searches were starkly at issue in *Safford United School District v. April Redding*. Safford Middle School is located in a small, eastern Arizona mining town, about 100 miles from Tucson. In 2003, a student facing punishment after being caught with prescription strength Ibuprofen (the school has a zero-tolerance policy for all prescription and over-the-counter medication without prior written permission) said 13-year-old Savana Redding had brought the medication to school. She denied the accusation. The vice-principal searched her backpack but found no drugs. Despite being an honor-roll student and having no history of disciplinary problems, she was ordered to the school nurse's office and told to strip to her undergarments in front of the nurse and the vice-principal's female assistant. She was then required to pull open the underwear so that two female officials could determine if she had hidden pills. No pills were found.

When Savana's mother arrived at the school, a student called out, "What are you going to do about them strip-searching Savana?" Angered and upset, April Redding went to both the principal's and the superintendent's office. Both denied knowledge of the strip search. Of the experience, April states: "It was wrong. I didn't think anything like that could happen to my daughter at school."[33] At a second meeting with the principal, April was told she "should be happy we didn't find anything." When no one apologized, April Redding, with the help of the American Civil Liberties Union, sued the school district for damages.

A federal magistrate in Tucson held that the search was reasonable because the vice principal was relying on the tip from another student. In a 2–1 decision, the U.S. 9th Circuit Court of Appeals agreed. The full 9th Circuit Court heard the case in 2008 and ruled 6 to 5 for the Reddings. "Common sense informs us that directing a 13-year-old girl to remove her clothes, partially revealing her breasts and pelvic area, for allegedly possessing ibuprofen . . . was excessively intrusive. . . . The overzealousness of school administrators in efforts to protect students has the tragic impact of traumatizing those they claim to serve."[34] The appeals court ruled that the search was unreasonable and unconstitutional and that school officials who had ordered the search were liable for damages.[35] Judge Kim McLane Wardlaw said the vice principal's action defied common sense as well the Constitution; rather than protecting Savana he subjected her to a traumatic search over ibuprofen. She stated: "A school is not a prison. The students are not inmates"—and that juvenile prisoners have more rights than were given to Savana.[36]

The school, characterizing itself as "on the front lines of a decades-long war against drug abuse among students," defended the search as necessary because increasingly younger students are abusing prescription and over-the-counter drugs.[37] They appealed to the Supreme Court to preserve the flexibility of administrators to deal with problems to protect campus safety, arguing that requiring probable cause to conduct student searches would cast a "roadblock to the kind of swift and effective response that is too often needed to protect the very safety of students, particularly from the threats posed by drugs and weapons."[38]

The Supreme Court would decide whether a school setting gives administrators greater discretion to control students suspected of illegal activity than police are allowed in cases involving adults in public spaces.[39] The hearing took place one day after the ten-year anniversary of the Columbine school shootings, which had tipped the balance away from student freedom toward discipline and zero-tolerance policies that imposed harsh punishments for violations.[40] Kris Krane, executive director of Students for Sensible Drug Policy, argues that intrusive searches are counterproductive. "Zero-tolerance policies don't foster trust. The intentions may be well and good, but they are dangerous policies."[41]

The Juvenile Law Center filed an amicus brief citing children's unique vulnerability and urging that the application of constitutional rules should protect rather than harm children. "Strip searches are demeaning, dehumanizing, undignified, humiliating, terrifying, unpleasant, embarrassing, repulsive, signifying degradation and submission. Strip searches have a more serious impact on children than on adults; in fact, a child may well experience a strip search as a form of sexual abuse."[42] After the strip search, Savana never returned to Safford Middle School. She transferred to other schools but never obtained her high school degree.

In an 8–1 (Thomas dissenting) decision, the Court ruled the search unreasonable and unconstitutional, saying that a strip search at school is categorically distinct from other inspections for drugs. The Court also rejected the suit against the school employees because the law had not been clear. They sent the case back to Arizona to consider whether the district should face liability. Justice Stevens wrote: "It does not require a constitutional scholar to conclude that a nude search of a 13-year-old child is an invasion of constitutional rights of some magnitude."[43]

Punishing Youths: Abuses and Scandals Today

Americans avoid discussing how young offenders are punished. In Orwellian fashion, we obfuscate the reality through the use of euphemistic terminology.[44] The plain and simple truth is that juvenile "correctional institutions" are prisons. The juvenile court process that determines if the juvenile committed the act with which he or she is charged is called adjudication. "Adjudicated" is the equivalent of "convicted" in adult court and "disposed" is the equivalent of "sentenced." Juveniles are sometimes confined in a facility as part of a *diversion* agreement without going through adjudication. *Detained* indicates the status of being held in custody until the adjudication hearing in juvenile court or awaiting placement after the disposition. Juveniles are also detained before being transferred to adult criminal court. *Committed* describes the status of juveniles placed in a facility by the court-ordered disposition. Committed juveniles include those convicted and sentenced in criminal court.[45]

A commitment to a juvenile prison often represents the "end of the line" for some youthful offenders; they may never recover from the pains of their imprisonment. Conditions in many of these institutions have improved very little since the houses of refuge. Any treatment programs are the exception rather than the rule; punishment is the hallmark of these institutions.

There are several different prisons to which a youth can be committed. Some are public (i.e., run by state or local governments), and others are privately funded. Prisons for young offenders can be further subdivided into short-term (usually ranging from a few days to a couple of months) and long-term confinement (ranging from three or four months to one or two years). Each of these examples has had its share of scandals associated with abuse.

Of the 92,854 juveniles in custody in 2006, 13,758 were 14 or younger and 13,115 were 18 or older. In comparison, there were 105,055 youths in custody in 1997; 18,404 were under the age of 14 and 12,649 were 18 or older.[46] Committed youths in 2006 numbered 64,558, detained 26,344, and youths in diversion 1,865.[47] While most of those committed in (94%) had been adjudicated delinquent, 5.6% were committed for a status offense (the percentages for detained youths were 97% delinquent and 3% status offenses). Of those committed, 86.2% were male and 13.8% female; 36.7% were white, 39% black, and 19.8% Hispanic. Detentions were 82% male and 18% female, with 31% white, 42% black, and 23.7% Hispanic.

RECEPTION AND DIAGNOSTIC CENTERS

Offenders, prior to starting their long-term sentence, are evaluated by a psychologist or social worker to determine what sort of treatment will be required. The stay in the reception center, usually attached to a juvenile prison, is no more than a month. Various tests are given to assess the youth's level of intelligence, attitudes, degree of maturity, emotional problems, academic problems and the like. While in theory such assessments should be useful indicators, in practice the value depends on the competence of the evaluator.

"Diagnostic" can be a lucrative tool for those more interested in enriching themselves than helping children. On his first day in custody, Charlie Balasavage met with a psychologist who diagnosed him as having an antisocial disorder, anxiety, depression, and other maladies. His parents had wanted him to see a doctor covered by their medical insurance, but the county said no. The psychologist who diagnosed him was the brother-in-law of one of the corrupt Pennsylvania judges who devised a kickback scheme in Pennsylvania (discussed below). The Balasavages were charged $250 for the evaluation, and the state of Pennsylvania eventually paid the psychologist $836,636 for such exams.[48]

Some of these facilities also do not fit the image suggested by "reception and diagnostic center." On the contrary, some resemble large institutions. The state of Oklahoma, for instance, has a "Reception and Orientation Center" (ROC). On their Web site, this center is described as a place where "residents" (as they are called, rather than "prisoners" or "inmates") are first admitted to the Southwest Oklahoma Juvenile Center. It states that the staff's initial responsibility is to gain control of the resident's behavior.

> While residents are on the ROC unit, they first learn to memorize eighteen rules of appropriate behavior and how they apply to the crimes they've committed on the "outside." While on the ROC unit, their behavior is strictly and closely monitored. These residents learn compliance. For instance, a resident is only allowed to speak by raising his/her hand, being acknowledged by staff and given permission. All new residents begin their stay at the Southwest Okla-

homa Juvenile Center on the ROC unit. This allows staff to gain control of the residents' behavior at the beginning of his/her treatment, which results in a smoother cognitive behavioral pattern after he/she leaves this unit. On ROC, residents not only ask permission to speak, but also to enter and exit certain areas. They have no television or radios on this unit, have school on the unit, eat on the unit, and get off the unit only one hour a day for outside recreation.[49]

The military model of discipline is readily apparent. Given the high rates of recidivism of juveniles who have been confined in such institutions, there is no evidence that the military model is effective.

DETENTION CENTERS

Detention centers are holding facilities that function similarly to an adult jail. The likelihood of detention varies by the offense category. The most recent report indicates that person offense cases were the most likely to involve detainment (25%), followed by public order offense cases (24%), drug offense cases (18%), and property offense cases (16%). Between 1985 and 2005, the number of delinquency cases increased 46%. Although the delinquency caseload declined after 1997, the number of cases in which the juvenile was detained increased 2%.[50] Despite the reforms of the past half century, the conditions within many of the nation's detention centers remain horrible. This is especially true for the growing numbers of youth with serious mental health problems.

Two-thirds of juvenile detention facilities hold youths who are waiting for mental health treatment (about 7% of all youths held). Thousands of mentally ill youths are held in 698 juvenile detention centers. In 33 states, mentally ill youths being held had not been charged with a crime. Youths waiting for mental health average 23.4 days in detention, compared with an average of 17.2 days for all detainees. Detention places such youths at high risk of suicide or aggressive behavior. One detention facility reported holding a 7-year-old child who was awaiting mental health treatment; 117 facilities were holding children 10 years old and younger.[51] An 11-year-old boy charged with molesting a 4-year-old has been detained almost one year in a juvenile hall in Santa Clara County, California. He is so small that counselors worry about breaking his arms when they restrain him to control his tantrums. Attempts to place him in a more suitable environment have failed.[52]

Overcrowding invariably leads to abuses, as indicated in the following example about Colorado's juvenile detention centers.

> Holding cells for youngsters waiting for court appearances in the City and County building are so overcrowded that handcuffed children have been detained for several hours on the buses the sheriff uses to transport them. A Denver newspaper photo showed several juveniles handcuffed to their seats when the outside temperature was more than eighty degrees. The buses are not air-conditioned.

Fights are frequent, and many assaults go unreported. Children sleep on floors, crammed two, three and even four at a time into rooms designed for one. . . . The committed children repeatedly described the staff as indifferent, verbally abusive and sometimes physically abusive. The Colorado Director of Youth Corrections Programs, Betty Marler, said that the staff is frustrated by the overcrowded conditions. "The system brutalizes everyone," she told us. "It leads to burnout and negative attitudes."[53]

JUVENILES IN CUSTODY

The ghosts of houses of refuge remain today. Child advocates nationwide have deplored the conditions of confinement for young offenders. The U.S. Justice Department filed lawsuits against facilities in 11 states for supervision that is either abusive or negligently harmful. The Civil Rights of Institutionalized Persons Act (CRIPA) passed in 1997 authorizes the attorney general of the United States to conduct investigations and litigation relating to conditions of confinement in state or locally operated institutions (the statute does not cover private facilities). The Special Litigation Section of the Civil Rights Division of the U.S. Department of Justice investigates facilities to determine whether there is a pattern or practice of violations of federal rights.

Robert Boyd, Jr., an assistant attorney general for the United States, submitted the report of a CRIPA investigation of the Oakley Training School (also known as the Mississippi Youth Correctional Complex) in Raymond, Mississippi, and the Columbia Training School in Columbia, Mississippi, to the governor of the state.

We find that conditions at Oakley and Columbia violate the constitutional and statutory rights of juveniles. Youth confined at Oakley and Columbia suffer harm or the risk of harm from deficiencies in the facilities' provision of mental health and medical care, protection of juveniles from harm, and juvenile justice management. There are also sanitation deficiencies at Oakley. In addition, both facilities fail to provide required general education services as well as education to eligible youth as required by the Individuals with Disabilities Education Act.[54]

In the section on findings, the report stated:

Oakley and Columbia do not have any system of positive incentives to manage youth, but instead rely on discipline and force. This leads to unconstitutionally abusive disciplinary practices such as hogtying, pole-shackling, improper use and overuse of restraints and isolation, staff assaulting youth, and OC spray abuse. . . .

Girls in the SIU [Special Intervention Unit] at Columbia are punished for acting out or for being suicidal by being placed in a cell called the "dark room." The "dark room" is a locked, windowless isolation cell with lighting controlled by staff. When the lights are turned out, as the girls reported they are when the room is in use,

the room is completely dark. The room is stripped of everything but
a drain in the floor which serves as a toilet.[55]

In 2007, the Associated Press contacted each state agency that over-
sees juvenile correction centers and asked about the number of deaths
in confinement and the number of allegations and confirmed cases of
physical, sexual, and emotional abuse by staff members since Jan. 1,
2004. The survey found more than 13,000 claims of abuse—an astounding number since the total population of detainees at the time was
about 46,000. Ten percent of the claims were confirmed by authorities.
"Experts say only a fraction of the allegations are ever confirmed."[56]

Although Mississippi settled the CRIPA suit in 2005, abuses continue at the Columbia Training School. Eight of the 37 girls confined
there filed a lawsuit alleging physical and sexual abuse. Some of the
detainees said they were shackled for 12 hours a day.[57]

The Juvenile Justice Project of Louisiana filed a lawsuit on behalf of
juvenile offenders awaiting trial at the New Orleans detention center. The
facility has rats and mold, lacks adequate educational services and trained
staff, and keeps youths in their cells 20 hours a day or longer. The inhumane conditions have continued despite mediation to avoid litigation.[58]

The Southern Poverty Law Center filed a federal lawsuit against the
Harrison County Juvenile Detention Center in Biloxi, Mississippi.
Youths were locked in filthy, insect-infested cells for 23 hours a day.
Many slept on the floor in the overcrowded facility.[59] Toilets and walls
were covered with mold, rust, and excrement. The squalid conditions
caused widespread contraction of scabies and staph infections.[60]
Youths were punished by being shackled. Most of the youths were in
detention awaiting court hearings; they had not been found guilty.
Some were there for minor offenses or status offenses like truancy. A
private corporation, the Mississippi Security Police, has operated the
facility for more than nine years at an annual cost of $1.6 million. The
lawsuit was filed on behalf of a youth who attempted suicide his first
week in detention. A staff member stopped him, but he was given no
access to mental health treatment. Rather, staff members taunted him
that his mother didn't care about him. The suit alleged: "Staff frequently resort to physical violence and respond to youths' request for
help or assistance with taunts, profanity, and indifference."

In 2007, the Texas juvenile-justice system underwent radical change
after it was discovered that juveniles were being held years beyond
their original sentence and that many were sexually abused. Detentions
increased 44% from 1985 to 2002. In addition, approximately 200,000
youths annually are tried, sentenced, or incarcerated as adults.[61]

Litigation against the California Youth Authority (CYA) propelled
reform to remove youths from state CYA facilities.[62] Unfortunately,
conditions in many county juvenile halls were equally appalling. In

2006, California juvenile halls were plagued by severe overcrowding, no educational opportunities, lack of mental health care or rehabilitative programs, months of twenty-three hours a day of isolation, and use of excessive force by authorities.[63] Attorney Richard Ulmar states, "California law expressly requires that a juvenile hall not be regarded as a penal institution, but rather be a safe and supportive homelike environment. But many juvenile halls in the state are more like penitentiaries than homes."[64]

The Justice Department filed a lawsuit against Arizona after three youngsters committed suicide. Arizona invested $8 million to $10 million to improve facilities and raised the starting salary of youth correctional officers to more than $30,000. Nancy Molever, an Arizona Juvenile Department of Corrections spokeswoman, said it would have been difficult to meet recommendations made by the federal government without a willingness to change the culture of the agency that oversees juvenile facilities. Weeding out employees slow to conform to the new rules helps improve the culture, but employee turnover—a nationwide problem—also has downsides.[65]

In 2004, the U.S. Justice Department uncovered 2,821 allegations of sexual abuse by juvenile correction staffers. Incidents are probably considerably more frequent than reported—whether because of fear of retaliation, the belief by juveniles that no one will believe them, or differences in perception. Some youths regard sexual relationships with staff members as consensual rather than as adults in positions of authority abusing their power. An investigator for the Youth Law Center in San Francisco interviewed males at a juvenile facility in Florida about encounters with the female staff. "One of the boys I interviewed said he didn't think it was fair that his roommate had a relationship with one of the staffers and he didn't." A 50-year-old male guard at the Hawaii Youth Correctional Facility was convicted of sexual assault in 2005 for squeezing and twisting a boy's testicles. He was sentenced to five years probation and 90 days in jail to be served on weekends.

Some physical confrontations end in death. At least five juveniles died after being forcibly placed in restraints in facilities run by state agencies or private facilities with government contracts since Jan. 1, 2004. Martin Lee Anderson, age 14, died at a Florida boot camp after several guards hit him while he was restrained. Even though the incident was videotaped, six guards and a nurse were acquitted of manslaughter charges. Their attorneys successfully argued that the guards used acceptable tactics. Isaiah Simmons, 17, lost consciousness and died after he was held face down on the floor at a privately owned facility in Maryland. The staff waited 41 minutes after he was unresponsive to call for help. Three other boys (ages 13, 15, and 17) died in facilities in Georgia, New York, and Tennessee. There have been 24 deaths in juvenile correction centers since 2004.

The list of abuses of youths detained in state or county institutions is endless. A scandal uncovered in Pennsylvania in 2009 encapsulated the helplessness of juveniles against authorities who use the system with utter disregard for the people confined within it. Luzerne County is located in the heart of Pennsylvania's struggling coal country. Pennsylvania has the second highest number of private detention facilities after Florida, accounting for about 11% of the private facilities in the United States.[66] "For years, the juvenile court system in Wilkes-Barre operated like a conveyor belt: Youngsters were brought before judges without a lawyer, given hearings that lasted only a minute or two, and then sent off to juvenile prison for months for minor offenses."[67]

The scheming of two Luzerne County judges starkly demonstrates what can go wrong with for-profit prisons and detention centers.[68] Critics have long argued that private prisons create perverse incentives to incarcerate nonviolent offenders even though community-based alternative programs would offer better treatment at reduced cost. Michael Conahan oversaw the budget for the court in Luzerne County, and Mark Ciavarella oversaw the juvenile courts. The two judges instituted a kickback scheme in December 2002. Conahan shut down the county-run juvenile detention center and helped secure contracts worth tens of millions of dollars for two private detention centers.[69] Ciavarella sentenced thousands of youths to the facilities. Many of the offenses were minor, and he routinely ignored requests for leniency. A lawyer with the Juvenile Law Center in Philadelphia noted, "There was a culture of intimidation surrounding this judge and no one was willing to speak up about the sentences he was handing down."[70]

In re Gault guaranteed the right to counsel to juveniles. However, only Illinois, New Mexico, and North Carolina require that juveniles have representation when they appear before judges. About half of the states allow waivers to be signed for juveniles to appear before a judge without an attorney. Under Pennsylvania law, juveniles may not waive their right to an attorney unless the decision is made "knowingly, intelligently, and voluntarily."[71] The judge must formally question defendants to make sure they understand their rights. Ciavarella ignored the law. Many of the juveniles said they did not realize they were admitting to crimes.[72] Ciavarella sent about half of the children who waived counsel to confinement—compared to 8.4% of juveniles elsewhere in Pennsylvania sentenced to placement.[73]

Phillip Swartley, 14, was arrested for stealing change from unlocked cars to purchase chips and soft drinks. His mother, single and raising two boys, thought there was no need for an attorney, expecting her eighth-grade son to be fined or sentenced to perform community service. Instead, he was handcuffed and shackled in the courtroom and sentenced to a youth detention center for nine months.[74] Jamie Quinn, 14, was detained for nine months for slapping a friend. Charlie Balasavage, 16, was accused of buying a stolen scooter. He had no criminal history but was sentenced, shackled, and sent to the detention center without being allowed to explain that he bought the scooter from a relative and did not know it was stolen. According to state guidelines, the recommended sentence for an adult convicted of the same offense would have been probation to one month in jail.[75] Hillary Transue, 15, was an excellent student who had never been in trouble. When she appeared before Judge Ciavarella in 2007 for a My Space page that mocked the assistant principal at her high school, she expected to receive a stern lecture. Her mother had been persuaded to waive the girl's right to a lawyer. In a hearing that lasted less than two minutes, she was found guilty of harassment and sentenced to three months at a juvenile detention. Her parents were stunned as they watched her be handcuffed and taken away.[76] After the Juvenile Law Center took her case to the Pennsylvania Supreme Court, the FBI began an investigation.

The judges tried to conceal the kickbacks as payments to a company they control in Florida. They pleaded guilty to taking $2.6 million in payments from the former owner of the detention centers and agreed to spend 87 months in prison. Two other officials have been charged, including a Luzerne County probation official. Experts express the view that while the actions of these two judges were particularly egregious, the situation results from a "juvenile-justice system racked with abuses yet subject to far less scrutiny than the adult system it increasingly mirrors."[77]

The Juvenile Law Center filed suit in the Federal District Court in Scranton, seeking to have all profits that the detention centers earned from the scandal placed in a fund that would compensate juveniles for their emotional distress. "In a wave of unprecedented lawlessness, the judges failed to advise Charlie and other youths of their right to counsel, accepted their guilty pleas without explaining what they had been charged with, and garnisheed the wages of their parents to pay the costs of detention."[78] Two others suits were filed by private lawyers. The Pennsylvania Supreme Court gave a judge the discretion to overturn the cases of as many as 1,200 first-time juvenile offenders convicted of minor crimes who appeared without counsel before Ciavarella between 2003 and 2008. An investigation uncovered "routine deprivation of children's constitutional rights to appear before an impartial tribunal and have an opportunity to be heard."[79] Ciavarella ruled on approximately 2,500 cases during those years; the disposition of the remaining 1,300 cases await review. Whether the records are expunged or not, the impressions of the juveniles whose lives were rocked by the greed of two judges will remain. The mother of the boy sentenced for taking change from unlocked cars asked: "What do these kids see of the legal system and of authority figures? These kids see people who abuse their power. Now, we have a whole county and generation of children who have lost trust in the system."[80]

SOME EFFECTS OF INCARCERATION:
THE INMATE SOCIAL SYSTEM AND VICTIMIZATION

There are a number of reasons why large custodial institutions fail. We can begin by taking a look at what life in custody is like for confined youths. Sadly, there has not been much improvement over the years.[81] The pattern established with the New York House of Refuge continues.

Let's begin with a survey of 42 juvenile prisons conducted in the 1970s by the National Assessment of Juvenile Corrections. The study focused on the effects on youths of being institutionalized. It distinguished between newcomers (those who had been at the facility two months or less) and veterans (those who had been incarcerated nine months or more). The survey found significant differences between programs having large proportions of veterans and those having relatively few veterans.[82] Veterans were significantly more likely than newcomers to: (1) commit more offenses and have friends who had committed offenses while incarcerated; (2) learn more ways to break the law while incarcerated (46% of the veterans, compared to 20% of the newcomers); and (3) become more hardened over time ("hardened" was measured in several ways, such as being critical of the staff, previous encounters with institutions, and number and seriousness of offenses while incarcerated).

It was also found that the longer a youth remained in the institution, the more likely the youth would: (1) fight with other youths, (2) use drugs, (3) steal something, (4) run away, and (5) hit a staff member. These problems become the most acute when, as the authors put it, there is a "critical mass" of veterans within a program. John Irwin's study of adult felons found that a significant number were what he termed *state-raised youth*.[83] These offenders more or less grew up in various institutions (juvenile detention centers or other institutions such as foster care or group homes), rarely spending any significant amounts of time in free society. Irwin describes the worldview of state-raised youths as distorted, stunted, and incoherent. Living in custody has become their only meaningful world.

Numerous studies, some dating back to the 1950s, have found that the strong prey on the weak in institutions. In addition, a potent inmate subculture, similar to the one in adult prisons, has existed since the first of these institutions was established in the nineteenth century.[84] In most of the larger institutions, the peer subculture includes a strongly defined hierarchy.

Youths entering the institution quickly earn reputations, either as strong boys or weak ones.

> Once boys were in the intake cottage, the other boys immediately subjected them to tests designed to ascertain whether they could be exploited for food, clothes, cigarettes, and sex. . . . If the new boy

looked and acted tough, exploitation was minimized; if any weak-
nesses were shown, he was immediately misused by the others.[85]

Three criminologists studied an institution in Columbus, Ohio, in
the 1970s. They focused on the extent of victimization within these
institutions and described a brutal social system. Within the "jungle"
(the term the inmates themselves used), the powerful prey on the weak.
The overwhelming majority engaged in some form of exploitation.[86]
The researchers observed a number of social roles in the institution.
Some youths were classified as "aggressive," while others were "manip-
ulative" and still others were "passive."

The authors of the study returned 15 years later for a follow-up.
What they found was not encouraging. They discovered that the youth
culture still existed and continued to victimize the weak, although less
for sex than for food, clothing, and toiletries. Violent offenders were in
the minority; most of the juveniles were minor drug dealers, addicts,
and users of drugs. Gangs did not dominate the institution, as was popu-
larly believed. While some of those factors were mildly encouraging, the
most discouraging fact was that treatment had "all but disappeared,"
with the lone exception of a drug abuse program. The authors quoted
one social worker: "We don't do anything in here for kids." Another
member of the staff added: "This place is a warehouse for children."[87]

HIGH RECIDIVISM RATES PLAGUE JUVENILE PRISONS

A standard measure of the success of any program dealing with
offenders is *recidivism*. Recidivism can be operationally defined in several ways. In juvenile cases, it can be measured as an arrest, a referral
to juvenile court, a petition filed, or a recommitment to an institution.[88].

A very comprehensive study found that among a cohort of more
than 3,000 juvenile offenders, about half of those released from Oregon
youth prisons at age 17 or 18 ended up in the adult prison system;
about 40% of those released at age 16 ended up in adult prison.[89] The
total recidivism rate was 42%. The study also found that females had a
significantly lower rate of recidivism (21%) than males (45%). Note
here that the definition of "recidivism" was an arrest as an adult. Consistent with other longitudinal studies, the earlier the age of first contact with the juvenile court, the higher the proportion of those who
ended up in the adult system (e.g., 57% of those age 12 ended up in the
adult system versus 43% of those whose first referral was at age 17).[90]
Another interesting finding, also consistent with prior research, was
that the longer a youth spent at a juvenile institution, the higher was
the recidivism rate.[91]

A research project examined 805 cases of youths released from the
Hawaii Youth Correctional Facility (HYCF) between 1995 and 1999.
The study found that 82% of those released were rearrested within two

years; 57% were reconvicted; 32% were reconfined at either HYCF or an adult facility. Recidivism rates were significantly higher for those with the greatest number of commitments, the greatest number of parole returns, the most escapes, and the highest number of misconduct reports. The number of runaways, the age of first use of drugs, and the number of suicide risk indicators were also related to recidivism. The report also noted that the recidivism rates for the period studied were greater than in a prior study completed in 1984.[92]

The recidivism rates in California were among the highest anywhere. The *San Jose Mercury News* used a computerized review of police records of more than 28,000 youths who were released between 1988 and 2000 and found that 74% were arrested within three years of their release. Property offenders had a higher recidivism rate than violent offenders (80% vs. 70%). The recidivism rate was lower for females (52%) than males (75%). The youngest (under 17) and the oldest (over 21) youths released had a recidivism rate of 60%; youths between 17 and 21 years of age had a rate of 76%.[93]

Recidivism rates are significantly lower among youths who receive dispositions other than youth prisons. Holding constant other variables, those who are given probation and provided with a variety of intensive services (e.g., drug treatment, tutoring, mental health counseling, and/or family counseling) have much lower recidivism rates.[94] The need for such services is demonstrated by the many barriers facing youths who are released from an institution. The study by the Center on Juvenile and Criminal Justice found the following barriers to successful reentry:[95]

- lack of housing options;
- limited skills and education;
- institutional identity; "state-raised youth" are poorly prepared for independent life after release[96];
- drug problems;
- mental health problems;
- lack of community support and role models; most youths released return to the same impoverished conditions they confronted before confinement (family dysfunctions, drug problems, violence, and gangs); and
- legislative barriers that limit access to education, cash assistance, housing, and employment.

Promising Alternatives to Punishing Children

Building a system that works for troubled youths and for the public requires informed participants. The public is largely unaware of the realities of youth prisons, and reforms are all too frequently cosmetic changes—a political solution to allay public fears based on inadequate information. Many current systems are proven failures that should be abandoned and replaced. For more than a century, the juvenile justice system was marked primarily by despair. Punishing children by incarcerating them has failed.

Shay Bilchik, director of Georgetown University's Center for Juvenile Justice Reform, says, "We cannot incarcerate our way out of this problem of juvenile crime.[97] What's wrong with incarcerating young offenders in large institutions?

> Large, congregate-care juvenile facilities, such as training schools, camps, and ranches, have not been effective at rehabilitating juvenile offenders. . . . Small, community-based facilities providing intensive treatment services and special programming in a secure environment offer the best hope for successful treatment of juveniles who require a structured setting. These services include individual and group counseling, educational and training programs, medical services, and intensive staff supervision. Proximity to the community permits direct, regular family involvement with the treatment process, independent living, and a phased reentry into the community.
>
> Since closing its traditional training schools in 1972, Massachusetts has relied on a sophisticated network of small, secure programs for violent youth coupled with a broad range of highly structured, community-based programs for most committed youth. Secure facilities are reserved for the most serious offenders. A study of the State's community-based juvenile system revealed recidivism rates equal to or lower than those of other jurisdictions. In addition, Massachusetts has saved an estimated $11 million a year by relying on community-based sanctions.[98]

Florida, Illinois, and Louisiana have focused on improving conditions at state facilities to keep young offenders from returning. Some states have worked at the county level to avoid confinement altogether, keeping youths in their communities while they receive rehabilitative services, which advocates say is a cheaper alternative to residential care.[99] Texas and California (the two largest state systems) reduced long-term youth confinement by requiring counties to house low-level offenders in detention halls. Within two years, Texas reduced its population to 2,500—half the previous numbers. California's reduction was even more dramatic—from 10,000 in 1997 to 2,500.[100] As noted above, city and county detention programs are not an automatic improvement, and states often do not provide sufficient monitoring and oversight. However, there have been some promising results with alternatives to institutional incarceration.

Missouri is phasing out its large juvenile-detention institutions in favor of smaller facilities and now has a highly regarded juvenile correction system that offers services such as education, mental-health care, and drug counseling. It has one of the lowest recidivism rates in the country—10%, compared with a national rate of 40% to 50%.[101]

On his fourteenth birthday, VonErrick Williams stole a car after beating the driver. He had a long record of truancy, assault, and breaking and entering. He was sent to the Missouri Hills group home, where his two older brothers had previously been sent. One brother plans to attend college; the other has a job and no reoffenses for four years. All three say they benefited from what is known as the Missouri Model of juvenile justice, which emphasizes rehabilitation in small groups, constant therapeutic interventions, and minimal force.[102]

There is no barbed wire around facilities like Missouri Hills, where a maximum of 10 youths live with 2 adult facilitators in cottage-style dormitories in a wooded setting. There are male health and wellness classes, group counseling and game rooms—far different from institutions that resemble penitentiaries, dismal county lockups or overcrowded community programs in other states. If a group member becomes aggressive, the other youths are trained to de-escalate the conflict. A spokesperson for the Missouri Department of Social Services notes: "It's just a different approach that we take. It's a treatment approach. In other states, they take a more punitive approach, more like corrections."[103]

The Anne E. Casey Foundation of Baltimore launched the Juvenile Detention Alternatives Initiative (JDAI) in 1992 believing that youths are often inappropriately detained at great expense, with long-lasting negative consequences for both public safety and youth development.[104] JDAI promotes changes in juvenile detention policies and practices to:

- reduce reliance on secure confinement;
- improve public safety;
- reduce racial disparities and bias;
- save taxpayers' dollars; and
- stimulate overall juvenile justice reforms.

There are approximately 100 JDAI sites in 24 states and the District of Columbia. By following the recommendations of JDAI, Santa Cruz County in California reduced the number of detainees by 40%.[105]

Five counties in New Jersey began participating in JDAI in 2003. They have reduced the number of juveniles locked up by more than 2,600 (41%).[106] Only juveniles who pose the greatest risk to public safety are confined; low-risk offenders are placed in community programs. New Jersey's child advocate is urging the counties to invest the money saved into youth programs for prevention and treatment programs.

Founded in 1995 to keep disturbed children ages 5 to 18 out of correctional facilities and other costly institutions, Wraparound Milwaukee blends all juveniles—whether they enter as foster youths, juvenile offenders, or mental patients—into one program. There are 100 sex offenders among the 400 juveniles n the program; 80% are placed at home with support services or in homelike settings. Director Bruce Kamradt said the program succeeds by treating each case individually and offering a variety of treatment options. "We put a real strong emphasis on what's keeping that boy in that institution—and how can we get him back in the community. Our judges won't let us keep these kids in the hall; they expect us to get them out in 24 to 48 hours."[107]

The New Horizons program in Humboldt County, California, treats mentally ill juvenile offenders in an intensive six-month program at a secure facility. They employ family therapy, individual counseling, and a six-month aftercare program; 76% of the juveniles return to their families after completing the six months. The reoffense rate is 20%, contrasted with rates of 50 to 80% for young offenders nationwide.[108]

In 2005, Vincent Schiraldi was appointed director of the Department of Youth Rehabilitation Services in Washington DC. The department was on the brink of federal takeover. "Schiraldi has been praised nationally for trying to reduce the racial disparity in criminal prosecution of black youths and for trying to steer his department, and its workers, away from punishment and toward rehabilitation."[109]

It is illegal to make information about a juvenile's criminal record public, but information can be shared with police and community groups that offer services to released offenders. Schiraldi's department agreed to compile a list of the 60 most serious juvenile offenders in detention. They will provide information on the backgrounds of the offenders to police and some community groups. The criteria for putting a youth on the most-serious list include: previous convictions, behavior in confinement, and attempts to escape.[110] Schiraldi said the program emphasizes the safety of the juvenile offenders and their communities. The city is expanding a program that currently includes 15 to 35 youths. Every Thursday, case managers meet with school, recreation, mental health officials, and police to discuss progress. Three groups committed to fighting violence (Peaceoholics, the Alliance for Concerned Men, and the East of the River Clergy-Police-Community Partnership) are critical components in the program. Schiraldi's agency has made $6.2 million available so community agencies can design reentry programs for young offenders.

Some Concluding Thoughts

Although it has been quoted hundreds of times, the statement by the philosopher George Santayana (1863–1952) is appropriate here: "Those who cannot remember the past are condemned to repeat it."[111] A common definition of "insanity" is repeating the same behavior after repeated failures and thinking that the outcome will be different. This is the legacy of almost 200 years of juvenile imprisonment. The reduction in the numbers of juveniles in the system in the twenty-first century and some efforts to change centuries-old methods of punishment offer hope that we will heed Santayana's warning and avoid repeating the failures of the past.

Notes

[1] Portions of this chapter are from Shelden, R. G. and D. Macallair, eds., *Juvenile Justice in America: Problems and Prospects*. Long Grove, IL: Waveland Press, 2008, chapter 1, with permission of the publisher.

[2] See the following Web site for details about this famous experiment: http://www.prisonexp.org/

[3] Ibid.

[4] Sutton, J. R. *Stubborn Children: Controlling Delinquency in the United States*. Berkeley: University of California Press, 1988.

[5] Rendleman, D. "*Parens Patriae:* From Chancery to Juvenile Court," p. 63. In F. Faust and P. Brantingham, eds., *Juvenile Justice Philosophy* (2nd ed.). St. Paul, MN: West, 1979.

[6] Teitelbaum, L. E. and L. J. Harris. "Some Historical Perspectives on Governmental Regulation of Children and Parents." In L. E. Teitelbaum and A. R. Gough, eds., *Beyond Control: Status Offenders in the Juvenile Court*. Cambridge, MA: Ballinger, 1977.

[7] Empey, L. T., ed. *The Future of Childhood and Juvenile Justice*. Charlottesville: University Press of Virginia, 1979, p. 59.

[8] Brenzel, B. *Daughters of the State*. Cambridge: MIT Press, 1983, p. 11.

[9] This group was formerly called the Society for the Prevention of *Pauperism* (another word for poverty). For a discussion of this group and a detailed description of its upper-class backgrounds see: Pickett, R. *House of Refuge*. Syracuse: Syracuse University Press, 1969, pp. 21–49.

[10] Ibid., p. 33.

[11] Abbott, G. *The Child and the State*. Chicago: University of Chicago Press, 1938, p. 348.

[12] Pickett, *House of Refuge*, p. 15.

[13] Ibid., p. 6.

[14] Mennel, R. *Thorns and Thistles: Juvenile Delinquents in the U.S., 1820–1940*. Hanover, NH: University Press of New England, 1973, p. 103.

[15] Pisciotta, A. (1982). "Saving the Children: The Promise and Practice of *Parens Patriae*, 1838–98." *Crime and Delinquency* 28: 410–425.

[16] Ibid.; Hawes, J. *Children in Urban Society*. New York: Oxford University Press, 1971, pp. 47–48; Bremner, R. H., ed. *Children and Youth in America*. Cambridge: Harvard University Press, 1970, pp. 689–691.

[17] The wording is taken *verbatim* from the law passed in Pennsylvania in 1826, which authorized the House of Refuge, "at their discretion, to receive into their care and guardianship, infants, *males under the age of twenty-one years, and females under the age of eighteen years*, committed to their custody" (emphasis added). Note the obvious distinction based on gender. This exact same statute was reproduced in numerous state laws throughout the nineteenth century. I found an example in my own study of Memphis, Tennessee (Shelden, R. G. [1976]. "Rescued from Evil: Origins of the Juvenile Justice System in Memphis, Tennessee, 1900–1917." Ph.D. dissertation, Southern Illinois University, Carbondale; Shelden, R. G. and L. T. Osborne. [1989]. "'For Their Own Good': Class Interests and the Child Saving Movement in Memphis, Tennessee, 1900–1917." *Criminology* 27: 801–821).

[18] *Ex Parte Crouse*, 4 Wharton (Pa.) 9 (1938).

[19] *Ex Parte Crouse*; for the significance for girls see Shelden, R. G. (1998). "Confronting the Ghost of Mary Ann Crouse: Gender Bias in the Juvenile Justice System." *Juvenile and Family Court Journal* 49: 11–26.

[20] Krisberg, B. *Juvenile Justice: Redeeming Our Children.* Thousand Oaks, CA: Sage, 2005, p. 29.

[21] *Ex Parte Crouse.*

[22] For further discussion of this issue see Chesney-Lind, M. and R. G. Shelden. *Girls, Delinquency and Juvenile Justice* (3rd ed.). Belmont, CA: Wadsworth, 2004.

[23] Bernard, T. J. *The Cycle of Juvenile Justice.* Oxford: Oxford University Press, 1992, pp. 70–72.

[24] *Commonwealth v. Fisher*, 213 Pa. 48 (1905).

[25] *Kent v. United States*, 383 U.S. 541 (1966). http://caselaw.lp.findlaw.com/cgi-bin/getcase.pl?court=US&vol=383&invol=541

[26] *In re Gault*, 387 U.S. 1 (1967). http://caselaw.lp.findlaw.com/scripts/getcase.pl?court=US&vol=387&invol=1

[27] Miller, J. *Last One Over the Wall* (2nd ed.). Columbus: Ohio State University Press, 1998.

[28] *New Jersey v. T.L.O.*, 469 U.S. 325 (1985). Argued March 28, 1984; reargued October 2, 1984; decided January 15, 1985, pp. 333–337. http://supreme.justia.com/us/469/325/case.html

[29] Ibid.

[30] *Vernonia School District 47J v. Acton* (94-590), 515 U.S. 646 (1995). http://www.law.cornell.edu/supct/html/94-590.ZS.html

[31] ACLU (October 2002). "Student Drug Testing: Relevant Case Law." http://www.aclu.org/drugpolicy/testing/10840res20021021.html

[32] Lithwick, D. (July 3, 2002). Urinalysis: The Supreme Court's Torturous Justification of High-School Urine Tests. http://www.slate.com/id/2067710/

[33] Savage, D. (April 19, 2009). "Strip-Searches at Schools Go to Supreme Court." *Los Angeles Times.* http://www.latimes.com/news/nationworld/nation/la-na-stripsearch19-2009apr19,0,2354915.story

[34] Mears, B. (April 16, 2009). "Court to Hear Case of Teen Strip-Searched for Ibuprofen." http://www.cnn.com/2009/CRIME/01/16/teen.strip.search/index.html

[35] Savage, D. (April 21, 2009). "Strip Searching Students Illegal? Supreme Court Not So Sure." *Los Angeles Times.* http://articles.latimes.com/2009/apr/22/nation/na-scotus-stripsearch22

[36] Ibid.

[37] Biskupic, J. (April 16, 2009). "Strip Search Review Tests Limits of School Drug Policy." *USA Today.* http://www.usatoday.com/news/washington/judicial/2009-04-15-stripsearch_N.htm?csp=34

[38] Mears.

[39] Ibid.

[40] Biskupic, "Court to Hear Case."

[41] Ibid.

[42] Juvenile Law Center (June 26, 2009). "Juvenile Law Center Commends U.S. Supreme Court Ruling: Strip Search of 13 Year-Old Unconstitutional." http://www.jlc.org/news/29/scsearch/

[44] Savage, D. (June 26, 2009). "Strip Search Unconstitutional." *Chicago Tribune*, p. 19.

[44] In the Vietnam War we did the same thing, such as calling the unnecessary killing of innocent civilians "collateral damage."

[45] Sickmund, M., T. Sladky, and W. Kang. (2008) "Census of Juveniles in Residential Placement Databook." Glossary. http://ojjdp.ncjrs.org/ojstatbb/Cjrp/asp/glossary.asp

[46] Ibid., Age on Census Date by Sex for United States, 2006 and 1997. http://ojjdp.ncjrs.org/ojstatbb/Cjrp/asp/Age_Sex.asp

[47] Ibid., Detailed Offense Profile by Placement Status for United States, 2006. http://ojjdp.ncjrs.org/ojstatbb/Cjrp/asp/Offense_Adj.asp

48 Sullivan, J. (March 8, 2009). "A Corrupt Judge, a Damaged Life." *Philadelphia Inquirer.* http://www.philly.com/philly/hp/news_update/40912957.html

49 Oklahoma Department of Corrections. http://www.state.ok.us/~oja/roc.htm

50 Sickmund, M. (June 2009). "Delinquency Cases in Juvenile Court," p. 3. http://www.ncjrs.gov/pdffiles1/ojjdp/224538.pdf

51 Werner, E. (July 7, 2004). "Thousands of Mentally Ill Youths 'Warehoused' in U.S." http://www.redorbit.com/news/science/70436/thousands_of_mentally_ill_youths_warehoused_in_us/

52 de Sa, K. (June 4, 2009). "Boy, 11, Has Spent Nearly a Year in Santa Clara County Juvenile Hall." *Mercury News.* http://www.mercurynews.com/topstories/ci_12523488

53 Human Rights Watch (1997). "High Country Lockup: Children in Confinement in Colorado." http://www.hrw.org/reports/1997/usacol/

54 Ibid., p. 1.

55 Ibid., pp. 5, 7.

56 Ibid.

57 Mohr, H. (March 2, 2008). "13K Claims of Abuse in Juvenile Detention Since '04." http://www.usatoday.com/news/nation/2008-03-02-juveniledetention_N.htm

58 Associated Press (February 4, 2009). "New Orleans Juvenile Detention Center's Lawsuit Receives Class Action Status." http://www.nola.com/news/index.ssf/2009/02/new_orleans_juvenile_detention.html

59 Southern Poverty Law Center (June 30, 2009). Preliminary Agreement Reached in Miss. Juvenile Detention Center Case. http://www.splcenter.org/news/item.jsp?aid=382

60 Broughton, A. (April 20,2009). "Suit Claims Abuse, Filth at Juvenile Detention Center." http://www.cnn.com/2009/CRIME/04/20/juvenile.detention.suit/index.html

61 Stier, K. (March 24, 2009). "Getting the Juvenile-Justice System to Grow Up." *Time.* http://www.time.com/time/nation/article/0,8599,1887182,00.html

62 For a detailed discussion of the history of the CYA, see Shelden and Macallair, *Juvenile Justice in America*, pp. 16–23.

63 Mohr, "13K Claims of Abuse."

64 Richard Ulmar (2006). "California Juvenile Justice System in Crisis; Lawsuits to End Abuses Against Children." PR Newswire, April 19.

65 Mohr, "13K Claims of Abuse."

66 Chen, S. (February 23, 2009). "Pennsylvania Rocked by 'Jailing Kids for Cash' Scandal." CNN. http://www.cnn.com/2009/CRIME/02/23/pennsylvania.corrupt.judges/index.html

67 *USA Today* (February 11, 2009). "Pennsylvania Judges Accused of Jailing Kids for Cash." http://www.usatoday.com/news/nation/2009-02-11-judge-juveniles_N.htm

68 Page, C. (March 1, 2009). "When Prisons Jail Kids for Cash." *Chicago Tribune,* p. 27.

69 Chen, "Pennsylvania Rocked."

70 Urbina, I. and S. Hamill (February 12, 2009). "Judges Plead Guilty in Scheme to Jail Youths for Profit." *New York Times.* http://www.nytimes.com/2009/02/13/us/13judge.html?ref=us

71 Rubinkam, M. (March 27, 2009). "High Court Voids Hundreds of Juvenile Convictions." http://www.mcall.com/news/nationworld/state/all-a7_kickbacks.6833785mar27,0,1811014.story

72 Sullivan, J. (March 27, 2009). "Judge May Overturn Hundreds of Cases in Luzerne Scandal." http://www.philly.com/inquirer/home_top_stories/20090327_Judge_may_overturn_hundreds_of_cases_in_Luzerne_scandal.html

73 Chen, "Pennsylvania Rocked."

74 Ibid.

75 Sullivan, "A Corrupt Judge, a Damaged Life."

76 Urbina and Hamill, "Judges Plead Guilty."

77 Stier, "Getting the Juvenile-Justice System to Grow Up."

78 Sullivan, "A Corrupt Judge, a Damaged Life."

79 Sullivan, "Judge May Overturn Hundreds of Cases in Luzerne Scandal."

80 Chen, "Pennsylvania Rocked."

[81] For a particularly gruesome account of actions within one of these "correctional" institutions, see the movie *Sleepers* (staring Brad Pitt, Robert DeNiro, and Dustin Hoffman).

[82] Vinter, R. D. et al., eds. *Time Out: A National Study of Juvenile Correctional Programs*. Ann Arbor: National Assessment of Juvenile Corrections, The University of Michigan, 1976.

[83] Irwin, J. *The Felon*. Englewood Cliffs, NJ: Prentice-Hall, 1970, p. 74. These types still can be found in many prisons today. See Austin, J. and J. Irwin. *It's About Time: America's Incarceration Binge* (3rd ed.). Belmont, CA: Wadsworth, 2001.

[84] Barker, G. E. and W. T. Adams. (1959). "The Social Structure of a Correctional Institution." *Journal of Criminal Law, Criminology and Police Science* 49: 417–499; Polsky, H. *Cottage Six*. New York: Russell Sage Foundation, 1962; Jesness, C. F. *The Fricot Ranch Study*. Sacramento: State of California, Department of the Youth Authority, 1965; Street, D., R. D. Vinter, and C. Perrow. *Organization for Treatment*. New York: Free Press, 1966.

[85] Bowker, L. *Prisoner Subcultures*. Lexington, MA: Heath, 1977, p. 100.

[86] Bartollas, C., S. H. Miller, and S. Dinitz. *Juvenile Victimization: The Institutional Paradox*. Beverly Hills: Sage, 1976.

[87] Miller, S. H., C. Bartollas, and S. Dinitz. *Juvenile Victimization Revisited: A Study of TICO Fifteen Years Later* (unpublished manuscript), cited in Bartollas et al., *Juvenile Victimization*, pp. 265–266.

[88] See Shelden, R. G. (September 1999). "Detention Diversion Advocacy: An Evaluation." *OJJDP Juvenile Justice Bulletin*. Here I used several different measurements of recidivism.

[89] State of Oregon, Oregon Youth Authority (May 23, 2003). "Previously Incarcerated Juveniles in Oregon's Adult Corrections System." Salem: State of Oregon, Office of Economic Analysis. http://www.oregon.gov/DAS/OEA/docs/oya/oya-to-corrections.pdf

[90] For a good review of "age of onset" see Dryfoos, J. G. *Adolescents at Risk: Prevalence and Prevention*. New York: Oxford University Press, 1990.

[91] Vinter et al., *Time Out*; Beck, J. L. and P. B. Hoffman (1976). "Time Served and Release Performance: A Research Note." *Journal of Research in Crime and Delinquency* 13: 127–132; Orsagh, T. and J. R. Chen (1988). "The Effect of Time Served on Recidivism: An Interdisciplinary Theory." *Journal of Quantitative Criminology* 4: 155–171; Makkai, T., J. Ratcliffe, K. Veraar, and L. Collins (2004). "ACT Recidivist Offenders." Canberra: Australian Institute of Criminology. http://www.aic.gov.au/publications/rpp/54/09_appendix1.html.

[92] Department of the Attorney General, State of Hawaii (February 2001). "Incarcerated Juveniles and Recidivism in Hawaii." Honolulu: State of Hawaii.

[93] Bailey, B. and G. Palmer (October 17, 2004). "High Rearrest Rate: Three-Fourths of Wards Released over 13 Years Held on New Charges." *San Jose Mercury News*.

[94] See, for example, Dryfoos, *Adolescents at Risk*.

[95] Byrnes, M., D. Macallair, and A. Shorter. "Aftercare as Afterthought." In R. Shelden and D. Macallair, eds., *Juvenile Justice in America: Problems and Prospects*. Long Grove, IL: Waveland Press, 2008, pp. 83–114.

[96] An interesting concept is what some researchers have called the *Post-Incarceration Syndrome*, which has been defined as "set of symptoms that are present in many currently incarcerated and recently released prisoners caused by prolonged incarceration in environments of punishment with few opportunities for education, job training, or rehabilitation. The severity of symptoms is related to the level of coping skills prior to incarceration, the length of incarceration, the restrictiveness of the incarceration environment, the number and severity of institutional episodes of abuse, the number and duration of episodes of solitary confinement, and the degree of involvement in educational, vocational, and rehabilitation programs." "News from the Worlds of Research and Clinical Practice." (2001). *Addiction Exchange* 3 (4); Gorski, T. T. (March 1, 2001). "Post Incarceration Syndrome." http://www.tgorski.com/criminal_justice/cjs_ pics_&_ relapse.htm

[97] Stier, "Getting the Juvenile-Justice System to Grow Up."

[98] *Combating Violence: The National Juvenile Justice Action Plan* (1996). Objective 1. Washington, DC: Office of Juvenile Justice and Delinquency Prevention. http://ojjdp.ncjrs.org/action/sec1.htm

[99] Moore, S. (March 26, 2009). "Missouri System Treats Juvenile Offenders with Lighter Hand." *New York Times*. http://www.nytimes.com/2009/03/27/us/27juvenile.html

[100] Ibid.

[101] Stier, "Getting the Juvenile-Justice System to Grow Up."

[102] Moore, "Missouri System."

[103] Mohr, "13K Claims of Abuse."

[104] http://www.aecf.org/MajorInitiatives/JuvenileDetentionAlternativesInitiative.aspx

[105] Moore, "Missouri System."

[106] "NJ Child Advocate Pushes Detention Alternatives." (March 18, 2009). *Chicago Tribune*. http://www.chicagotribune.com/topic/ny-bc-nj--juveniledetention0318mar18,0,6820643.story?obref=outbrain

[107] de Sa, K. (June 15, 2009). "California's Locked-Up Children Languish without Mental Health Services." http://www.mercurynews.com/crime/ci_12582936

[108] Ibid.

[109] Pierre, R. (March 11, 2009). "D.C. to Share Data about Top Youth Offenders." *The Washington Post*, p. B01. http://www.washingtonpost.com/wp-dyn/content/article/2009/03/10/AR2009031003439.html

[110] Ibid.

[111] Seldes, G. *The Great Thoughts*. New York: Ballantine Books, 1985, p. 404.

8

Parole
Punishment without Walls

The most recent figures available show an estimated 824,365 people on parole in 2007.[1] Individuals released from prison face a number of problems. Perhaps the most critical is that they will continue to be punished in a variety of ways because of the assortment of barriers to their success. Those barriers increase the possibility of getting into trouble again.

> The past few decades have witnessed a significant increase in the number of ex-prisoners returning to communities nationwide. These trends are important for a number of reasons, not the least of which is that this population presents multiple needs for services, including employment, housing, and social services. Often overlooked are the physical and social-behavioral health concerns of this population and, consequently, the role that health care plays in influencing the success of reintegration. Examining the demographic and health profiles of the prison population shows that it is disproportionately sicker on average than the U.S. population in general, with substantially higher rates of infectious diseases (such as HIV/AIDS, tuberculosis, and hepatitis B and C), serious mental illness, and substance abuse disorders.[2]

Origins of Parole

Parole is the release of an offender from prison prior to the expiration of the original sentence. It was originally intended to mitigate the severity of punishment. It can be argued that parole was originally established as a "politically expedient method of controlling inmate resentment over disparate sentences."[3]

Prior to the mid-nineteenth century offenders were sentenced to determinate sentences. In 1840 the superintendent of the Norfolk Island penal colony off the coast of Australia, Alexander Maconochie,

193

developed a system where prisoners could progress through five stages of increasing responsibility: (1) strict imprisonment; (2) labor on chain gangs; (3) freedom within a limited area; (4) ticket of leave on parole with conditional pardon; (5) full restoration of liberty. Maconochie's "mark system" rewarded good conduct, labor, and study. He was the first to employ positive conditioning. Typically, harsh punishment was used to coerce inmates to obey. Maconochie believed criminals would not be rehabilitated through brutality but rather through education and training.[4]

After his appointment as the superintendent of Elmira Reformatory for youthful offenders in New York in 1876, Zebulon Brockway instituted similar reforms. Brockway believed that inmates should be able to earn their way out of prison. He also believed that sentencing should be indeterminate so that behavior in prison would determine the length of the sentence. Indeterminate sentencing provided an incentive for offenders to adjust their behavior to earn early release. In addition to helping with rehabilitation, the incentives were useful for managing prison populations.[5] Youths at Elmira were graded on their conduct, achievement, and education. Good behavior earned parole. In French, "parole" means *word*—the inmate promises to behave according to certain rules in exchange for release. After release, parolees reported to guardians (volunteer supervisors) each month. The guardians submitted written reports about the behavior of parolees in the community.

In the late 1890s Charles Cooley observed that social and economic circumstances had as much influence on criminal behavior as biological traits. "The criminal class is largely the result of society's bad workmanship upon fairly good material."[6] Reformers pushed for a change to indeterminate sentences and parole based on a medical model that viewed delinquency and crime as a product of behavior amenable to treatment. Reformers believed the fixed sentence was retributive, crude, and unfair—the result of an impulse to retaliate with evil for evil and to exact vengeance. They believed it was impossible to measure the guilt of individuals because environmental influences, state of mind, and/or heredity all affect behavior.[7] They argued that determinate sentences were an attempt to "cure crime by a system childishly futile. As well might we sentence the lunatic to three months in the asylum, or the victim of smallpox to thirty days in the hospital, at the end of these periods to turn them loose, whether mad or sane, cured or still diseased."[8]

Reformers believed offenders should be dealt with as individuals rather than a class. They also believed indeterminate sentences gave inmates the responsibility for deciding how long they would remain in prison. David Rothman notes:

> Reformers saw no reason to circumscribe narrowly the discretion of
> the state because there was no opposition between its power to help

and its power to police. By attempting to adjust the offender to society, the state was providing the offender with the optimal circumstances for realizing his own well-being. From these principles Progressives moved logically and consistently to design and promote probation, parole, and the indeterminate sentence. Each innovation endowed the state with the discretion to accomplish the individualization of criminal justice, to bring a new spirit of humanitarianism and a new capacity for rehabilitation to every stage of the post-conviction process.[9]

While they had decried the lack of a scientific basis for determinate sentences, reformers ignored the critical fact that parole boards had the power to grant or deny release. In the early twentieth century, the seriousness of the crime was believed to be the primary determinant in the parole board's decision. However, there was no consensus on what defined a serious crime; therefore, personal preferences determined who was paroled. Those preferences often resulted in racial and gender bias and disparities in the time served.[10] There were no controls against abuse of discretion or the discriminatory exercise of power.

In 1907 New York became the first state to institute a parole system, which established indeterminate sentences, a system for granting release, postrelease supervision, and specific criteria for parole revocation. By 1927, only Florida, Mississippi, and Virginia did not have a parole system. Every state and the federal government had systems in place by 1942. The percentage of prisoners released on discretionary parole rose from 44% in 1940 to 72% in 1977.[11]

> The use of parole release grew, and instead of using it as a special privilege to be extended to exceptional prisoners, it began to be used as a standard mode of release from prison, routinely considered upon completion of a minimum term of confinement. What had started as a practical alternative to executive clemency and then come to be used as a mechanism for controlling prison growth gradually developed a distinctively rehabilitative rationale, incorporating the promise of help, assistance, and surveillance. By the mid-1950s, indeterminate sentencing coupled with parole release was well entrenched in the United States, such that it was the dominant sentencing structure in every state.[12]

As noted in the introduction to this book, belief in the rehabilitative ideal declined rapidly in the 1970s. Fear of crime ignited the trend toward more punitive sanctions. States began abolishing discretionary parole boards. "The pillars of the American corrections systems—indeterminate sentencing coupled with parole release, for the purposes of offender rehabilitation—came under severe attack and basically collapsed during the late 1970s and early 1980s."[13] Proponents argued that abolishing parole would reduce disparities in prison time served. Some argued that there was little scientific evidence that parole release and supervision reduced recidivism. Prisoners argued that not knowing when they would be released was one more painful aspect of imprisonment. Others argued that the unsupervised discretion of parole boards resulted in inconsistent and discriminatory decisions.

Maine was the first state to eliminate parole followed by California and Indiana.[14] In 1977, California passed its determinate sentencing law and amended its penal code to state that the goal of imprisonment was punishment not rehabilitation. By 2002 16 states abolished discretionary release; 5 additional states abolished discretionary parole for violent offenses or felonies. The federal government and all 50 states have mandatory minimum-sentencing policies; 24 states have 3-strikes laws; 27 states and Washington DC have truth-in-sentencing where prisoners must serve 85% of the sentence.[15]

Granting Parole

In most states, parole is decided by a board or commission appointed by the governor; it is thus the responsibility of the executive branch of government.[16] Parole is defined as a contractual release of offenders from a correctional institution after they have served a portion of a court-imposed sentence to incarceration, under the continued custody of the state, and under conditions that permit reincarceration if the terms of parole are violated (the violation would not necessarily be a criminal offense if committed by someone not under the obligations of parole). The state retains legal control of parolees until they fulfill the conditions of the parole contract and are formally dismissed from parole—usually a period of 1–3 years.

Approximately 1,600 people are released each day from state and federal prisons in the United States. About 20% leave prison having served their full sentence (maxed out); they leave with no post-prison supervision requirement. Those who are paroled (i.e., leave prison before the end of their sentence) can be released by two methods. The most common method (about 50% of the cases) is *mandatory release*. The prisoner has served his or her entire sentence, minus "good time." *Discretionary release* is determined by a parole board. About 30% of prisoners receive discretionary releases prior to the expiration of their sentences. Parolees will serve the remainder of their sentences in the community under the supervision of state parole authorities. Both mandatory and discretionary releases are conditional. All states except Maine and Virginia have mandatory or discretionary parole supervision.[17]

Most parole boards are autonomous units—that is, they are not situated within a department of corrections, and they have no direct institutional ties. Nevertheless, parole boards work very closely with institutional officials in making their decisions. They rely very heavily on the information and recommendations of prison staff, and they place a heavy emphasis on an inmate's performance while in prison. The decision to grant parole is made during a parole hearing. At the hearing are the offender, the parole board, and sometimes prison officials and interested citizens. (Most state laws stipulate that any citizen may attend a parole hearing. Some boards require an inmate to have either a specific job awaiting him or her following release or other resources (such as family or friends) that would keep him or her financially viable until a job is found.

What factors weigh most heavily in the decision to parole? The prisoner's behavior *prior* to going to prison plays a significant role— meaning that the behavior continues to be judged after conviction and sentencing. The most important factor is the offense itself, followed closely by "history of prior violence" and "prior felony convictions." Other factors, in order of importance, are: possession of a firearm at the time of the offense, previous incarceration, prior parole adjustment, prison disciplinary record, psychological reports, and victim input.[18] In short, rehabilitation is not a contributing factor.

The number of parolees increased from 220,400 in 1980 to 799,000 at year end 2007—a 263% increase and a rate of 360 parolees per 100,000 population. In 2007 an estimated 555,900 prisoners were released to the supervision of state parole systems. Most (88%) were male; 42% were white, 37% were black, and 19% were Hispanic. The most frequent offense was drugs at 37%; 24% had been imprisoned for a property offense, 26% for a violent offense, and 6% for a public order offense.[19] The average time served was 29 months.[20] The average parolee was in his or her mid-30s. Eventually, 93% of all U.S. prisoners will be released.

As discussed in chapter 2, the impulse to punish by imprisonment continues unabated. Incarceration rates began climbing in the 1970s, reaching the unprecedented point where more than one in one hundred adults is incarcerated. The corollary of those numbers is that record numbers of prisoners are released each year. Recidivism rates have changed very little in the last 30 years, and the frequent revocation of parole has contributed significantly to the rise in incarceration rates. Two-thirds of those released from prison—whether supervised or not— are rearrested within three years; more than half are reincarcerated. Any reductions in recidivism would help ameliorate the $65 billion annual corrections costs in the United States.[21]

James Austin and John Irwin conducted a thorough investigation of the prison and parole system and observed the increasing numbers of parolees returned to prison.

> This trend is attributable in large part to dramatic changes in the nature of parole supervision and the imposition of increasingly more severe conditions of supervision on parolees. Instead of a system designed to help prisoners readjust to a rapidly changing and more competitive economic system, the current parole system has

been designed to catch and punish inmates for petty and nuisance-type behaviors that do not in themselves draw a prison term.[22]

Parole supervision relies heavily on surveillance, despite the fact that research repeatedly shows surveillance alone has little impact on recidivism. Supervision programs without a focus on treatment do not reduce recidivism rates. The Crime and Justice Institute states: "The conventional approach to supervision in this country emphasizes individual accountability from offenders and their supervising officers."

Until 1972, the courts had taken a hands-off position concerning parole. It was believed that parole boards performed administrative functions and that intervention would damage their role as *parens patriae* (substitute guardian or parent) and interfere with rehabilitative efforts. It was commonly held that parole was a privilege rather than a right. As mentioned above, parole was a contract between the parolee and the parole board; violating a parole condition constituted a violation of the contract. Parole was still a form of custody, albeit outside prison walls. Revocation was not thought to be part of normal "criminal" prosecution and hence due process rights were not applicable.

In *Morrissey v. Brewer,* the Supreme Court opened the door to granting due process rights to parolees.

> We see, therefore, that the liberty of a parolee, although indeterminate, includes many of the core values of unqualified liberty and its termination inflicts a "grievous loss" on the parolee and often on others. It is hardly useful any longer to try to deal with this problem in terms of whether the parolee's liberty is a "right" or a "privilege." By whatever name, the liberty is valuable and must be seen as within the protection of the Fourteenth Amendment. Its termination calls for some orderly process, however informal.[23]

The Court specifically stated that it was the responsibility of each state to write a code of procedure. It did, however, list minimum requirements of due process: written notice of the claimed violations of parole; disclosure to the parolee of evidence against him or her; opportunity to be heard in person and to present witnesses and documentary evidence; (d) the right to confront and cross-examine adverse witnesses unless the hearing officer specifically finds good cause for not allowing confrontation; a "neutral and detached" hearing body such as a parole board; a written statement by the fact finders as to the evidence relied on and reasons for revoking parole. The Court also emphasized that parole revocation hearings were a narrow inquiry and did not equate to a criminal prosecution nor did the court rule on whether a parolee is entitled to the assistance of counsel.

Supervision remains the strongest component in the duties of parole agents, and parole boards retain a great deal of power over the liberty of parolees.

Most agents have the legal authority to carry and use firearms and to search places, persons, and property without a warrant and without probable cause (otherwise required by the Fourth Amendment to the U.S. Constitution). The search power applies to the household where a parolee is living and the business place where a parolee is working. The ability to arrest, confine, and, in some cases re-imprison a parolee for violating the conditions of the parole agreement gives parole agents a great deal of discretionary authority. Standard parole conditions include not committing crimes, not carrying a weapon, seeking and maintaining employment, reporting changes of address, reporting to one's parole agent, drug testing, and paying required victim and court restitution costs.[24]

Criminologists have coined the term "back-end sentencing" to describe the parole revocation process. As noted above, parole board members are appointed. When parole is revoked, the back-end sentence is levied by political appointees instead of judges. In addition, the standard of evidence is much lower than that required in a court of law.[25]

Being on Parole

Austin and Irwin note that parolees must immediately struggle to achieve some degree of financial support, affordable housing, and clothes before they can begin trying to find a job. They receive little in the form of financial assistance. In Nevada, for instance, they receive only $21 when they leave prison. Some have help from their families and friends, many of whom struggle to help since they are also poor.

The Urban Institute conducted a longitudinal study in Illinois, Ohio, and Texas about the challenges prisoners face when returning to their communities (Chicago, Cleveland, and Houston). Interviews with prisoners before and after release revealed the most challenging problems.[26] The majority of prisoners in the three states studied exited prison through mandatory release (94% in Illinois, 71% in Ohio, and 62% in Texas). The determinate sentences in the three states include postrelease supervision.

The average age of the released prisoners in the three states was 36; about one-third were under age 30. Fifteen percent were white. Sixty-eight percent had been incarcerated previously, and more than two-thirds had been on parole or probation at least once before their most recent incarceration. Almost one-third of the released prisoners had been serving a sentence because of a violation of parole conditions (66% for a new crime and 34% for a technical violation).[27] The prisoners subject to postrelease supervision had the following expectations. Almost one-third expected to find a job without assistance, and 16% already had a job lined up. Only 9% hoped the agent would be able to help them find a place to live; 19% were going to look for a place to live, and 69% knew where they would be living. More than three quarters of those who had not been supervised before believed it would be easy to avoid a violation after release, as did 69% of those who had been supervised previously.

Parolees listed an average of 10 supervision conditions. The most common were: notification of a change in residence; reporting an arrest; maintaining face-to-face contact; random drug testing; avoiding places where illegal substances are used; not associating with others on parole; consenting to search of one's person, residence, or property; and not associating with gang members. Eight months after release, 24% reported that they had violated a condition. When asked to identify the areas in which supervision agents had been most helpful, 26% said providing encouragement; 21% identified the agent's communication and understanding; 13% listed help with job search; 3% replied help finding a drug treatment program; 2% responded help with their living situation.[28]

The biggest challenges for most of the released prisoners were finding employment and staying out of trouble. Before release 50% had anticipated they would ask their parole agent for help finding a job, but only 19% asked for help, and less than 1% actually found their current job through their parole agent; 56% were unemployed. Of the 42% employed, most (85%) reported wages between $5 and $15 per hour. Fifteen percent were receiving drug treatment. One out of five (21%) returned to prison in the 12 months after release—14% for supervision violations and 7% for new crimes.[29]

One in five of the 70,000 people released annually from state prisons in Texas return to metropolitan Houston. Local officials, service providers, and residents in the neighborhoods with the greatest concentration of returning prisoners told researchers that housing and employment were paramount for the successful reentry of former prisoners, along with educational opportunities, vocational training, and substance abuse treatment during and after incarceration."[30] Returning prisoners face multiple challenges—reuniting with family, finding housing, securing employment, locating substance abuse treatment, and reintegrating into the community. The numbers of returning prisoners keep increasing, and most return to a small percentage of communities, compounding the impact of reentry on both individuals and the communities to which they return. Todd Clear notes the irony of justifying prisons to protect the safety of those who live in high-crime communities. "Yet cycling a large number of young men from a particular place through imprisonment, and then returning them to that place, is not healthy for the people who live in that place. There are sound theoretical reasons to expect high incarceration rates to make many of these places worse, not better."[31]

> Communities that provide large numbers of prisoners to the state
> and federal prison system struggle in a variety of ways. They have
> limited human and social capital. Incarceration, because it further

damages the men who go to prison, eats away at the meager human capital that exists and erodes the social networks that provide the small doses of social capital on which people can call. Because it removes supports on which those who do *not* go to prison rely for quality of life, it makes their lives less capable of producing the benefits they seek. Prison is a constant and virtually omnipresent factor in poor communities.[32]

The challenges faced by returning prisoners in Texas provide more details about life on parole. Most (75%) exiting male prisoners were African American or Latino (15%). The average age at the time of release was 37. Many (61%) reported frequent illegal drug use in the months before they were imprisoned, and 25% reported heavy drug use. Large numbers (41%) had used drugs for nine years or more. Most (79%) had been convicted of at least one criminal offense prior to their most recent incarceration. The average age of first arrest was 18. The median time served was 37 months. More than a third of the men reported wanting to participate in programs while incarcerated, but were unable to do so because the programs were full, not offered, or open only to eligible prisoners. Job training was the first choice for participation, followed by life skills, employment readiness, parenting, and GED classes.[33]

Most releasees are in debt when they exit prison. The average amount owed was about $650, which increased to $900 after eight to ten months. The two most common forms of debt were supervision fees and child support. Others included fines, restitution, and court costs.[34] When released, most (73%) men had only one set of street clothing. Only 37% had photo identification.

The first challenge is transportation. Half of the men had no one to meet them. Some were given a bus ticket, voucher, or money for transportation; 28% left the facility by bus. The next challenge is where to sleep. One in four had a home to which he returned; 60% stayed with a family member. Having a criminal record interfered with finding and keeping housing for 19% of the men. Of those who found housing, 39% reported moving at least once eight to ten months after incarceration. Family members often provide housing, transportation, cash, food, and emotional support. Prior to release, prisoners reported that employment and housing would be the determining factors in keeping them out of prison. Eight to ten months later, 38% listed family support as the most important factor.[35]

Without photo identification and professional attire, finding employment is very difficult; 68% reported having a criminal record as a barrier. Despite the challenges, 75% were employed eight to ten months after release. The most common jobs were construction or manual labor (29%), delivery services (12%), the food service industry (10%), or warehouse and shipping (6%). More than half the men reported a chronic physical (43% high blood pressure; 26% Hepatitis B or C) or mental health condition (21% depression).[36]

During the first few weeks on parole the parolee becomes aware that there is an important distinction between the formal expectations of the parole system itself and the informal expectations of the parole officer to whom the parolee is assigned. The parolee soon learns that the parole officer has a great deal of discretion. Furthermore, the parolee learns that some of the conditions of parole are so vague and comprehensive that it is almost impossible not to violate some of them. Indeed, in order to meet certain conditions of everyday living, some rules must be broken. For instance, in some jurisdictions one condition is that the parolee must obtain permission in order to drive a car and must also have a driver's license. To register a car, one must have insurance (which is not stated in the conditions). But before the parolee can afford insurance (and thus drive), the parolee must find a job and often must drive to where he or she works.

Another rule specifies that the parolee must not associate with ex-inmates and with people with "bad reputations." For most parolees, this is virtually impossible. Many of the people in the neighborhoods to which most parolees return often have arrest records (if for nothing else than being arrested on "suspicion"). Also, the parolee must not drink alcoholic beverages "in excess." These two restrictions, especially the latter, reveal that the parole officer has a great deal of discretion in deciding what constitutes a violation.

Is the Parole System Set up to Fail?

The preceding discussion may lead the reader to believe that the entire parole system is set up and operated in such a way that failure is almost guaranteed for most ex-cons. A study in Kentucky, provocatively titled "Kentucky's Perpetual Prisoner Machine: It's About Money," provides some evidence of built-in failure.[37]

Detailed interviews with a sample of paroled men who had been returned to prison revealed several key reasons for their failure. One was the lack of programs within the prison itself that could help prepare them for coping following their release. Massive cutbacks have resulted in virtually no college courses being offered (this has been a national trend, as various kinds of grants used in prior years have been eliminated, such as Pell Grants). Although some vocational courses were offered, there was often a two- to three-year wait because of a shortage of space and available instructors.

The Kentucky prisoners faced the same problem as the Texas prisoners—very little money when released. "The only interviewees who had money when they left the prison were those who had money sent to them. The prisons do not provide 'gate money,' street clothes, or even a bus ticket home. Upon release, prisoners not picked up by family or friends at the front gate are forced to literally walk home."[38]

Perhaps the most significant problem was finding work. The available jobs paid minimum wage. Since most of the prisoners had families to support, the earnings were insufficient to provide for the household. Many parolees needed more than one job.

The Kentucky parolees frequently distrusted parole officers, who seemed to perceive their jobs as law enforcement rather than social work—catching violators rather than trying to help the paroled prisoners adjust to life in the community. Indeed, one parole officer remarked: "We ride them until they drop."[39] The equestrian metaphor referred to the use of drug testing, surveillance, and investigation to monitor the behavior of parolees. The relationship with the parole officer is strained further because parolees must pay for the supervision and for mandatory drug testing.

> The result is the parolees are unable to confide in or share their problems with the parole officers. Instead, they go through the monthly "report day" ceremony paying their fees (for supervision, drug tests, restitution, crime victims, programs) and pretending to "make it." They play a game of hide and seek, cops and robbers, or cops and dopers, and when they lose they are returned to prison.[40]

As noted in the previous section, the conditions of parole are often so taxing that most people find it impossible to avoid behavior that while noncriminal is still considered a violation. One woman who was interviewed was returned to prison three times. The first time she violated curfew and failed the urine test. The second time she violated curfew and absconded. (Recall that absconding includes failure to report to a parole officer.) The third time the violation was possession and use of alcohol.

The concept of "time" is, understandably, of critical importance to prisoners. Many reported that they did not get credit for the time served while in parole custody (awaiting a parole revocation hearing and/or waiting to be transferred back to prison). In many cases, they served more time than their original sentence—painful to prisoners and increased cost to taxpayers.

Perhaps the greatest obstacle to success is economic status. Most prisoners lived in poverty before their sentence, and most returned to the same (or worse) conditions. Lack of education and job skills limit economic resources, which can lead to parolees committing crimes to survive.

> The prison system is perpetuating growth on its own institutional failure to properly prepare prisoners for release. The parole system compounds the problem with the law enforcement style of supervision. The result is a revolving door that shuffles prisoners from one level of

custody to another, from prison to parole, and from parole back to prison. The Kentucky state prison population will continue to grow because it is "recycling" the same individuals through the system.[41]

After listening to a presentation of the Kentucky study in a criminal justice class, a student asked: "What are we supposed to do, feel sorry for them? They knew the rules and they broke them." This perspective on punishment dismisses the social context of the lives of offenders and contributes to our "perpetual prisoner machine," which consumes enormous sums of money and creates more problems when prisoners are released without any preparation for reentry. Punishment without options for breaking the cycle dooms prisoners and their communities to repeated failures.[42]

The Cost of Failure

As noted in previous chapters, the United States incarcerates more than one out of every 100 adult Americans—more than 2.3 million people. Prison populations have increased steadily over the last 15 years, far exceeding the numbers and percentages in all other industrialized countries. The expansion has been expensive. As budgets are overdrawn, the cost to incarcerate consumes tax dollars that could be spent on education or health care. Policy makers are beginning to question whether imprisonment is the most effective means of achieving public safety. When prisons divert funds from social services, some of which help prevent crime, the problems multiply.

Most prison systems are overcrowded, and the communities to which prisoners return with little preparation for life outside prison walls suffer negative consequences. As noted above, Todd Clear argues that incarceration can destabilize the community rather than protecting public safety. Incarceration threatens the economic infrastructure of already struggling neighborhoods; it disrupts families; it disenfranchises prisoners, further diminishing the voting power of the disadvantaged community. He refers to the cumulative negative effects of incarceration as "death by a thousand little cuts."

> Each effect, no matter how small, cannot be considered in isolation from the others. It is not just a single effect, like reduced rates of marriage, that is important, but rather the sum of reduced marriage rates, more teenage motherhood, diminished parental supervision, and so on in those communities where incarceration is so concentrated . . . building a sense that incarceration slices its way into almost every aspect of community life.[43]

While all states are affected by the costs of imprisonment, California is in the most precarious position. One in 7 state prisoners in the United States is incarcerated in California. While the prison population quadrupled nationally from 1980 to 2007, the prison population in California increased by a factor of 7.[44] The National Institute of Justice funded a 3-year study of the causes and consequences of parole violations and revocations in California. The study tracked every adult on parole at any time during 2003 and 2004 (almost 255,000 individuals).

In the mid-1990s, California adopted a "zero tolerance" policy for parolees who had been convicted of a serious offense. Parole agents must report any violation of parole by such offenders to the Board of Parole Hearings (BPH). The individuals in the study committed 151,750 parole violations that reached the court (felony hearings) or board (technical and/or felony review) hearing level.[45] The politically appointed body returned most (90%) parolees who appeared before it to prison.[46]

Parole and parole revocation greatly affect the number of prisoners in California. Six in 10 admissions to state prisons each day are returning parolees; 66% of parolees return to prison in California versus 40% nationally. The determinate sentencing law passed in 1977 required prisoners to serve the original sentence less any good time credit (up to a 50% reduction). Release is automatic; there is no appearance before a parole board. Only prisoners serving a life term (19% in 2007) are subject to discretionary release. California is the only state that combines determinate sentencing and post-release supervision of all released prisoners.[47] Prior to the 1977 law, released prisoners were subject to one year of supervision; after the law, most prisoners received a post-incarceration sentence to three years of supervision. Almost all parolees are subject to drug testing, and approximately 66% have substance abuse problems. Few received treatment while in prison. Half of all exiting California prisoners did not participate in any rehabilitation or work program. Parole revocations in the last 20 years are six times higher nationally—in California, they are thirty times higher.

As mentioned above, a politically appointed official decides whether parole has been violated. The maximum term for a parole violation in California is one year (increased from 6 months prior to 1977), and 20% are sentenced to less than one month.

> This system of "catch and release" makes little sense from the standpoints of deterrence, incapacitation, treatment, or cost. Parolees quickly learn that being revoked from parole doesn't carry serious consequences, and the State will have wasted the resources of the police, the parole board, and parole officers, who have to reprocess the same individuals over and over again. This constant churning of parolees also disrupts community-based treatment, since parolees who are enrolled in community treatment programs are constantly having that treatment disrupted for what, in the treatment providers' views, are predictable and minor rule violations (e.g., testing positive for drug use). . . . There is the high opportu-

nity cost of occupying a limited number of prison beds that, in some cases, could be used for offenders who pose a greater risk to the public safety.

Parolees were predominantly male (90%), minority (70%), and young (52% younger than 30). Almost half had been paroled previously; 10% had been paroled six or more times. The most recent prison term was for a drug conviction (35%), a property crime (29%), or a violent crime (20%).[48] There were almost 297,000 violations by the 255,000 individuals in the study. Noncriminal (technical) violations accounted for 35%. Two-thirds of the technical violations were for missing an appointment (labeled absconding, which also includes parolees that cannot be located). More than a third of all violations were related to drugs. The risk of violations was highest during the first 180 days after release from prison.

California faced additional challenges in August 2009. A federal judicial panel ordered California to reduce its prison population by more than 40,000 inmates within two years. It was the largest state prison reduction ever imposed by a federal court over the objection of state officials. The three judges said that reducing prison crowding was the only way to correct an unconstitutional prison health care system responsible for one unnecessary death a week. The panel described a chaotic system where prisoners were stacked in triple bunk beds in gymnasiums, hallways and day rooms and inmates died for lack of treatment. "In these overcrowded conditions, inmate-on-inmate violence is almost impossible to prevent, infectious diseases spread more easily, and lockdowns are sometimes the only means by which to maintain control. In short, California's prisons are bursting at the seams and are impossible to manage." The judges recommended imprisoning fewer nonviolent criminals and reducing the number of technical parole violators.[49]

The panel established a cap of 110,000 state prisoners—137% of the capacity of the 33 prisons, which were designed to hold 85,000 inmates.[50] The state was appealing the decision, but the corrections department began planning for carrying out the order. They were considering allowing low-level offenders to serve the final year of their sentences under house arrest; reducing sentences of inmates who complete prison rehabilitation programs; and changing sentencing guidelines so that drug possession would be prosecuted as a misdemeanor rather than a felony.

Almost a third (30%) of California's prison population is from Los Angeles County. Cash-strapped local governments will need to meet the challenge of an influx of released inmates at a time of underfunded social-services programs. A study completed by Los Angeles County found that 20% of released prisoners would require mental-health treatment, and 70% would need alcohol and drug treatment—while budget cuts restrict programs to help offenders reenter the community.[51]

Barriers to Parole Success

Jeremy Travis clearly explains the challenges of reentry. "We have reached an important moment in our nation's history. With record high incarceration rates, unprecedented extension of state supervision over individuals leaving prison, and a complex maze of legal barriers to reintegration, more people than ever before are returning home after serving time in prison, and are facing daunting barriers to successful reintegration."[52] Congress passed the Second Chance Act in 2008, which authorizes federal grants to government agencies and nonprofit organizations to provide employment assistance, substance abuse treatment, housing, family programming, mentoring, victims support, and other services to reduce recidivism. In 2009, an appropriations bill provided funding of $25 million. As Travis noted, the funding was a welcome start, but if federal funds were evenly distributed across individuals leaving prisons, the funds would amount to $100 per state prisoner. The administration requested $212 million for prisoner reentry programs in 2010.[53] The Second Chance Act may help address the numerous barriers to successful parole.

Being convicted of a crime has always had serious consequences. In recent years, however, the consequences have become more and more negative. Some scholars have argued that the overreliance of imprisonment as a form of social control has had "collateral consequences" (a term appropriately borrowed from terminology associated with war, since America has in recent years undertaken a "war on crime" and more specifically a "war on drugs").[54]

Travis distinguishes between "visible" and "invisible" punishments. Prisons and bars are visible reminders of the punishment for breaking society's laws.[55] We can count the number of people in prison; calculate the costs of incarceration; and record the length of sentences served for a particular crime. However, there are many less obvious punishments. As Travis notes, these punishments are "accomplished through the diminution of the rights and privileges of citizenship and legal residency in the United States."[56] The inclination to punish does not end with the sentence for a crime and the time served in prison. Laws that affect where an ex-prisoner lives, what employment is available, access to loans for education, or the right to vote are invisible punishments. Travis also observes that laws curtailing the rights of former prisoners are not defined as punishments, rather they are characterized as a civil response to criminal convictions—the collateral consequences of breaking society's laws. Indeed, much of the legislation bypasses the committee process and is attached as a rider to other legislation—unlikely to spur public debate. They are not codified as criminal sanctions; they are sometimes called "civil disabilities."[57]

Travis traces the inclination to deny the benefits of citizenship to convicted offenders back to the Greeks and Romans. The Greeks imposed the penalty of "infamy," which denied offenders the rights to hold office, make speeches, or serve in the army. The Romans assessed the penalty of "outlawry," under which a wife was considered a widow and children orphans; possessions and rights were forfeited. During the medieval period, "civil death" denied the offender the right to vote, to inherit property, and to enter into contracts.[58]

Today's version of civil death includes the denial of public housing,[59] welfare benefits, certain parental rights, and access to education loans. Such a civil death impacts a large proportion of the population—an estimated 47 million people have criminal records, while about 13 million are either serving time or have been convicted of a felony in the past. Travis focuses on the impact of invisible punishments on the social fabric. The "disabilities" permanently diminish the social status of convicted offenders, excluding them from full participation as citizens.[60] Restrictions vary by state and can include: revocation or suspension of drivers' licenses of people convicted of drug felonies; prohibitions from employment in certain professions such as teaching or child care; restrictions on the right to vote; termination of parental rights; felony convictions as a grounds for divorce; restrictions on the right to hold public office; and restrictions on owning firearms. Every state requires sex offenders to register with the police. The duration of the registration requirements range from ten years to life.[61]

THE IMPACT OF COERCIVE MOBILITY ON CONTROLS

Dina Rose and Todd Clear contend that an overreliance on incarceration as punishment undermines a community's attempts to use informal methods of control.[62] This in turn leads to more, rather than less, social disorganization. This idea runs counter to commonsense beliefs that removing "bad elements" from a community makes things safer. As noted above, high incarceration rates contribute to such problems as inequality, family deterioration, and poverty. "Coercive mobility" (the dual process of incarceration and reentry) undermines the building blocks of social order. High levels of incarceration in areas that already struggle for assets are "a kind of double whammy. First, they suffer the disruptions that occur when large numbers of residents are coercively removed and imprisoned. Then, they struggle with the pressures that occur when large numbers of former convicts return to community life."[63]

Clear refers to the assumption that incarceration increases public safety as "addition by subtraction"—the belief that removing offenders from communities subtracts only problems and improves conditions for those who remain.[64] The belief dovetails with public perception that criminals are automatically defined as people who make no contribution to society. Subtracting them from the community can only be an improvement. In many poor neighborhoods, up to 25% of the adult males are behind bars on any given day. This results in the removal of both *human capital* (the innate and acquired talents an individual brings to social life) and *social capital* (capacity to achieve personal goals through connections to others) from these communities.[65]

Incarceration affects three major disorganizing factors originally identified by Shaw and McKay.[66] First, incarceration results in an alteration of both the labor market and the marriage market.[67] Second, there is an increase in transience in that there is a constant movement in and out of prison: as one person enters prison, someone else is released. This in turn leads to the third factor: as new people move in, the neighborhoods become increasingly heterogeneous as far as cultural norms and values are concerned. Part of this is caused by the impact of the prison subculture on individuals; often they bring prison norms and values to the community after release.

DENIAL OF PUBLIC HOUSING

Housing is a key ingredient for everyone, ex-offender or not. Twelve percent of United States prisoners are homeless when released from prison.[68] Most offenders have no resources, and many lack the skills necessary to acquire employment that will provide sufficient income for adequate housing—even without the stigma of being an ex-offender. Federally subsidized housing was designed to provide affordable housing for low-income people and families. Most released offenders fall in this category, but implementation of the "one-strike" policy eliminates this option for some individuals. The housing authority has the right to deny housing to:

1. Those who have been evicted from public housing because of drug-related criminal activity for a period of three years following eviction.

2. Those who have in the past engaged in a pattern of disruptive alcohol consumption or illegal drug use, regardless of how long ago such conduct occurred.

3. The catch-all category of those who have engaged in any drug-related criminal activity, any violent activity, or any other criminal activity if the public housing authority deems them a safety risk.[69]

Eviction procedures were written into law in the Anti-Drug Abuse Act of 1988. The Act was amended in 1994 so that leases for public housing agencies should "provide that any criminal activity that threatens the health, safety, or right to peaceful enjoyment of the premises by other tenants or any drug-related criminal activity on or off such premises, engaged in by a public housing tenant, any member of the tenant's household, or any guest or other person under the tenant's control, shall be cause for termination of tenancy."[70] Public housing authorities had not been enforcing these lease terms because of concern over possible legal actions based on the constitutionality of eviction. In 1996, the Department of Housing and Urban Development (HUD) introduced guidelines to help public housing administrators screen and evict tenants involved in drug or other criminal activity. The "One Strike and You're Out" policy established procedures for evictions. HUD announced that enforcement of the policy would be considered in their evaluation and grading of public housing systems. Systems that followed the guidelines would be eligible for more funding and less oversight from the federal government.[71] In introducing the guidelines, then President Bill Clinton said hard-working, law-abiding people who live in public housing should not live in fear. "I know that for some, one strike and you're out sounds like hard ball. Well, it is. It is because it's morally wrong for criminals to use up homes that could make a big difference in the lives of decent families."[72]

On March 26, 2002, the U.S. Supreme Court unanimously upheld the "one-strike" rule in *Department of Housing and Urban Development v. Rucker*. The petitioners claimed that the terms of the lease did not apply if the tenant did not know of the illegal activity. HUD claimed that the terms held regardless of whether the tenant knew or had reason to know. The Court agreed with HUD. "Congress' decision not to impose any qualification in the statute, combined with its use of the term 'any' to modify 'drug-related criminal activity,' precludes any knowledge requirement."[73]

There is no system of checks and balances when it comes to the housing authority and their decision-making practices, which allows most local housing authority agencies to be as stringent as they choose. The harshness of this policy has severe consequences for offenders, especially those convicted of a drug offense. Being denied public housing and being denied the right to reside with family members who live in public housing without putting the entire family at risk for eviction leaves ex-offenders with few options. A study of a cohort of prisoners released from New York State prisons found that 11.4% ended up in a homeless shelter; of this group, one-third were sent back to prison within a two-year period.[74] "Recidivism becomes a self fulfilling prophecy when offenders are released from incarceration with scant survival options."[75] With no income and no place to live, many are forced to go back to committing the crimes for which they were originally imprisoned.

DENIAL OF OTHER FEDERAL BENEFITS

Congress passed the Personal Responsibility and Work Opportunity Reconciliation Act (PRWOR) in 1996. The Act eliminated a number of welfare programs and replaced them with block grants known as Temporary Assistance for Needy Families (TANF). Welfare recipients must work in order to receive benefits and may only receive benefits for a five-year period. PRWOR "requires that states permanently bar individuals with drug-related felony convictions from receiving federally funded public assistance and food stamps during their lifetime" (states can choose to adjust the length of the ban). The Act also states that eligibility for TANF, food stamps, Social Security benefits, and public housing can be suspended for those who violate probation or parole conditions.[76] Ironically, murderers and other violent felons may be eligible for some of these benefits, but not drug offenders. Ex-offenders have little or no money; public aid is a tool that is necessary for successful reentry. Without such benefits, recidivism is highly likely to occur.[77]

Denying ex-offenders public housing, food stamps, and other benefits affects not only the ex-offender but the entire household and the community. The denial increases the chance of re-offending, which in turn diverts taxpayer dollars into the criminal justice system.

Programs for Successful Reentry

Despite the many barriers to reentry, there are some programs with proven track records and many new programs that have promise.

DELANCEY STREET FOUNDATION

From its beginnings in 1971 in San Francisco, Delancey Street Foundation has expanded to five locations (Los Angeles, New Mexico, New York, North Carolina, and San Francisco). The slogan on the Foundation's Web site reads: "Enter with a history, leave with a future."[78] More than 14,000 people have benefited from the education at Delancey.

> We said we were going to take ex-convicts and ex-addicts and teach them to be teachers, general contractors, and truck drivers. They said it couldn't be done. We said we were going to take 250 people who had never worked and had no skills and teach them to build a 400,000 square foot complex as our new home on the waterfront. They said it couldn't be done. We said we were going to partner with colleges and get people who started out functionally illiterate to achieve bachelor of arts degrees. They said it couldn't be done. We said we were going to run successful restaurants, moving companies, furniture making, and cafés and bookstores without any professional help. They said it couldn't be done. . . . For over 35 years we've been developing a model of social entrepreneurship, of education, of rehabilitation and change that is exciting and full of hope.

The minimum stay is 2 years, and the average is 4 years. "The average resident has been a hard-core drug and alcohol abuser, has been in prison, is unskilled, functionally illiterate, and has a personal history of violence and generations of poverty."[79] Mimi Silbert, one of the founders, believes "It does not matter how many mistakes you make, it only matters that you fix them."[80] Delancey Street residents earn a high school equivalency degree (GED), marketable skills, and social skills that allow them to live successfully in mainstream society. Graduates have included the first ex-felon to be admitted to the bar in California, the first real-estate license for an ex-felon, and the first deputy sheriff.[81]

> This is testimony to what can be accomplished when the disadvantaged of society are afforded opportunity. . . . Delancey Street is self-supporting, running more than a dozen various training schools for its residents. These training schools provide vocational skills and the opportunities to put them to use, generating income and pooling the monies earned. Each resident plays an integral role. The foundation evolved and now runs a moving company, a popular gourmet restaurant and catering service, an event planning company, limousine and paratransit driving services, a special events decorating company, a bookstore, a café and art gallery, an automotive service center, a printing company, and a Christmas tree sales lot.[82]

Delancey Street follows six tenets:

1. First and foremost, we believe people can change. When we make a mistake we need to admit it and then not run from it, but stay and work to fix the mistake. And though no one can undo the past, we can balance the scales by doing good deeds and earning back our own self-respect, decency, and a legitimate place in mainstream society.

2. We believe that people can learn to live drug free, crime free lives of purpose and integrity. Rather than following a medical model or a therapeutic model, we've developed an educational model to solve social problems. We teach people to find and develop their strengths rather than only focusing on their problems.

3. Rather than solving one issue at a time (e.g., drugs or job skills) we believe that all aspects of a person's life interact, and all people must interact legitimately and successfully with others to make their lives work. Delancey Street is therefore a total learning center in which residents learn (and teach) academics, vocational skills, and personal, interpersonal, practical and social survival skills. We believe the best way to learn is to teach; and that helping others is an important way to earn self-reliance. Person A helps person B and person A gets better.

4. Delancey Street functions as an extended family, a community in which every member helps the others with no staff of experts, no "program approach." Everyone is both a giver and a receiver in an "each-one-teach-one" process.

5. Economic development and entrepreneurial boldness are central to our model's financial self-sufficiency and to teaching residents self-reliance and life skills.

6. Delancey Street is value-based in a strong traditional family value system stressing the work ethic, mutual restitution, personal and social accountability and responsibility, decency, integrity and caring for others in a pro bono public approach.[83]

AMERICA WORKS, INC.—CRIMINAL JUSTICE PROGRAM

Lee Bowes, a sociologist, and Peter Cove, an anti-poverty activist, started America Works in New York in 1984 to help welfare recipients obtain employment. In 2001 they added a criminal justice component that has focused on helping ex-cons through job readiness training, job placement, and job retention services.

During its first year of operations, it placed 77.6% of the approximately 500 people who completed a one-day orientation. Of those placed, 44.5% kept their job for at least 90 days, and 90 held their jobs for more than six months. The evaluators concluded that

> Even if America Works could not improve on the first year performance rate, the public saves $184,000 annually at the six-month final payment date. For every month those 90 ex-offenders continue to work, up to another $225,000 is saved, or an additional $2.7 million a year. The cost-benefit ratio for this program to date is excellent. If employment can be sustained and retention rates improved, the savings to the taxpayer become enormous.[84]

Most of the people placed by America Works qualify for the Work Opportunity Tax Credit Program. The federal government offers employers a tax incentive of $2,400 to hire parolees. Some municipalities do the same. After its prison population reached an all-time high of 9,250 in 2008, Philadelphia offered employers a $10,000 tax incentive for every ex-offender they hired. The deputy mayor noted: "These people are trying to turn their lives around and stay crime free. The best anti-crime package includes giving people a good job."[85]

PROJECT RIO

The Re-Integration of Offenders program began in 1985 in the state of Texas. Its stated goals are to reintegrate ex-offenders into the labor force, "thereby promoting public safety, reducing recidivism, and meeting the needs of Texas employers."[86] It helps ex-offenders acquire the knowledge and skills to enter the workforce and to contribute to society through a market-driven approach to job training and placement. The Texas Workforce Commission (TWC) administers the program in close collaboration with the Texas Department of Criminal Justice (TDCJ) and the Texas Youth Commission (TYC). Texas releases 70,000 offenders from TDCJ facilities each year (10% of the offenders released in the United States).

Services for adult offenders are based on projected release dates. In state prisons, offenders begin participation 24 months before release;

offenders in state jails begin 18 months prior to release; for youths, the date is six months before release. While in TDCJ or TYC facilities, the emphasis is on vocational, academic, and life skills preparation. Participants receive career counseling, help developing resumes and completing job applications, as well as help in securing driver's licenses and social security cards. Project RIO helps offenders develop reentry plans. After release, services continue for up to a year. There are 262 TWC offices across the state offering post-release. The goal is to help ex-offenders obtain employment as quickly as possible through referral services. In 2007, 44% of the 72,000 offenders released in Texas participated in Project RIO while incarcerated; 72% (21,807) of participants exiting post-release services found employment.[87]

An independent evaluation of the program found that almost 70% of RIO participants found employment compared to 36% of a matched group of nonparticipants. Also, within one year after release, only 23% of RIO participants were returned to prison within one year of release compared to 38% of a control group. The evaluation also found that the project saved more than $15 million in re-incarceration costs.[88]

PIONEER HUMAN SERVICES

This social enterprise program began in Seattle, Washington, in 1962 and is one of the longest running programs in the country. The front page of its Web site includes the phrase, "people finding new pathways," and describes the organization as improving "the lives of people on the margins of society through an integrated array of services, including housing; employment/training; treatment; counseling; and corrections."[89] It has helped more than 100,000 people, with the philosophy that "every individual has untapped potential and, given the chance for change, can become a contributing member of our community."[90] It is a nonprofit organization; 99% of its income is through the sale of its products or services. Enterprises include retail cafes, institutional food, sheet-metal fabrication, aerospace precision machining, wholesale food distribution, packaging, and fulfillment.[91] Pioneer operates the majority of the Washington Department of Corrections work-release programs.[92] A University of Washington study found that participants had a recidivism rate of about 6% after two years and that they had higher earnings than a control group.[93]

THE SAFER FOUNDATION

Established in 1972, the Foundation recognized that individuals leaving prison desperately needed jobs if they were to support their families and turn their lives around. The mission is "to reduce recidivism by supporting, through a full spectrum of services, the efforts of people with criminal records to become employed, law-abiding members of the community."[94] As the president states: "If America is to succeed in addressing this complex and expensive issue [of prisoner reentry], it must be a cooperative effort. And that includes you and every other concerned citizen and taxpayer."[95] The Safer Foundation now has nine locations in Illinois and Iowa. It operates two secured work-release facilities for the Illinois Department of Corrections, the only nonprofit, private facility to do so.[96] An evaluation of the program found that 59% of the clients placed in jobs remained in the job for 30 days and that these clients "were also more likely to remain employed and crime free up to a year after release."[97]

Some Concluding Thoughts

This chapter highlighted the challenges faced by individuals on parole and the communities to which they return. The final section discussed promising programs that have facilitated reentry. Perhaps a fitting conclusion would be a brief reflection on society's attitudes about punishment. Is there agreement that incarceration is payment for a debt to society? Do fears about safety justify ongoing punishment for breaking society's laws?

Two very different examples shed some light on society's reactions to ex-offenders. Michael Vick, a professional quarterback for the Atlanta Falcons, pleaded guilty in 2007 to felony charges of operating an interstate dog-fighting ring. He was sentenced to 23 months in prison and was suspended from the National Football League. The owner of the team said Vick would not be a Falcon again even if reinstated by the NFL. Vick lost two years of his professional career; eight years of his 10-year, $130 million contract with the Falcons; and an estimated $25–30 million in endorsements. He filed for bankruptcy in 2008, losing his $1.39 million home.[98] After serving 18 months of his sentence, he was paroled. He was conditionally reinstated by the NFL and signed with the Philadelphia Eagles. Animal rights activists protested his hiring, and the public remains divided about whether he deserves a second chance.

Sex offenders face the most virulent opposition when they return. Thirty states have residency restrictions, as do many municipalities. There is an exponential effect as first one city enacts a measure, followed by another, and then another—sometimes leaving offenders with no place to live. Jacob Wetterling's abduction and disappearance led to the creation of the first sex-offender registry in 1994. His mother, Patty, notes: "If an offender ends up with no residence, that shouldn't make any of us feel safer. What they need is stability, support, counseling, and treatment."[99]

In Florida, Ron Book worked tirelessly to help 60 cities and counties throughout Florida pass restrictions barring sex offenders from living within 2,500 feed of schools, parks, and playgrounds. Book's daughter, Lauren, had been abused by her nanny. The impact on offenders was severe. In Miami, a three-year-old settlement of 70 sex offenders spend the hours from 10 PM to 6 AM under a six-lane bridge that spans Biscayne Bay. There is no running water or sewage system. Shopping bags are used for toilets and then tossed on a refuse pile that is burned periodically. Lauren Book viewed conditions at the Julia Tuttle Causeway as a public-policy calamity.[100] She convinced her father, who now admits he was wrong and has vowed to work to help solve the consequences of the residency restrictions. As he notes, the problem is that no public official wants to back a measure (such as shrinking restrictions from 2,500 feet to 1,750 feet) that could be labeled propredator. He has also worked to find alternative housing but knows that if he settles too many offenders in a particular politician's district, he will face opposition.

These two examples span a large continuum of people facing challenges. Highlighting the barriers faced by people returning to their communities after serving punishment by incarceration can increase public awareness and invite innovation to develop solutions.

NOTES

[1] Glaze, L. E. and T. P. Bonczar (December 2008). "Probation and Parole in the United States, 2007, Statistical Tables." Washington, DC: Bureau of Justice Statistics. http://www.ojp.usdoj.gov/bjs/pub/pdf/ppus07st.pdf

[2] Davis, L., N. Nicosia, A. Overton, L. Miyashiro, K. Derose, T. Fain, S. Turner, P. Steinberg, and E. Williams III (2009). "Understanding the Health Implications of Prisoner Reentry in California." Summary. The RAND Corporation. http://www.rand.org/pubs/technical_reports/2009/RAND_TR687.sum.pdf; see also RAND Corporation (June 24, 2003). "Prisoner Reentry: What Are the Public Health Challenges?" Santa Monica: RAND Corporation. http://www.rand.org/pubs/research_briefs/RB6013/index1.html

[3] Simon, J. *Poor Discipline: Parole and the Social Control of the Underclass, 1890–1990.* Chicago: University of Chicago Press, 1993, p. 34.

[4] Petersilia, J. *When Prisoners Come Home: Parole and Prisoner Reentry.* New York: Oxford University Press, 2003, pp. 55–56.

[5] Ibid., p. 58.

[6] Cited in Caplan, J. (2006). "Parole System Anomie: Conflicting Models of Casework and Surveillance." *Federal Probation* 70 (3). http://www.uscourts.gov/fedprob/December_2006/parolesystem.html

[7] Rothman, D. *Conscience and Convenience, Revised Edition.* Piscataway, NJ: Aldine Transaction, 2002, p. 68.

[8] Ibid., p. 69.

[9] Ibid., p. 61.

[10] Petersilia, *When Prisoners Come Home,* p. 62.

[11] Ibid., p. 58.

[12] Ibid., p. 62.

[13] Ibid., p. 63.

[14] Ibid., p. 65.

[15] Ibid., p. 68.

[16] National Research Council. *Parole, Desistance from Crime, and Community Integration.* Washington, DC, 2007, p. 9. http://www.nap.edu/catalog.php?record_id=11988

[17] Ibid., p. 8.

[18] Runda, J., E. Rhine, and R. Wetter. *The Practice of Parole Boards*. Lexington, KY: Association of Paroling Authorities, 1994.

[19] Glaze and Bonczar, "Probation and Parole," tables 3, 5.

[20] National Research Council, *Parole*, p. 8.

[21] Solomon, A., J. Osborne, L. Winterfield, B. Elderbroom, P. Burke, R. Stroker, E. Rhine, and W. Burrell (December 2008). "Putting Public Safety First: 13 Parole Supervision Strategies to Enhance Reentry Outcomes." Washington, DC: The Urban Institute, p. 1. http://www.urban.org/url.cfm?ID=411791

[22] Austin, J. and J. Irwin. *It's About Time* (3rd ed.). Belmont, CA: Cengage Learning, 2001, p. 144. The figures on parole failures are also from this source.

[23] *Morrissey v. Brewer* 408 U.S. 471 (1972). http://caselaw.lp.findlaw.com/cgi-bin/getcase.pl?court=us&vol=408&invol=471

[24] National Research Council, *Parole*, p. 9.

[25] Grattet, R., J. Petersilia, and J. Lin (October 13, 2008). "Parole Violations and Revocations in California." http://www.ncjrs.gov/pdffiles1/nij/grants/224521.pdf

[26] Yahner, J., C. Visher, and A. Solomon (July 2009). "Returning Home on Parole: Former Prisoners' Experiences in Illinois, Ohio, and Texas." Washington, DC: Urban Institute, p. 1. http://www.urban.org/UploadedPDF/411744_returning_home.pdf

[27] Ibid., p. 2.

[28] Ibid., p. 3.

[29] Ibid., pp. 3–5.

[30] Cronen, E. (June 22, 2009). "Experiences of Ex-prisoners in Houston Analyzed in New Reports." Urban Institute. http://www.urban.org/publications/901266.html

[31] Ibid., p. 93.

[32] Clear, T. *Imprisoning Communities: How Mass Incarceration Makes Disadvantaged Communities Worse*. New York: Oxford University Press, 2007, pp. 117, 120.

[33] La Vigne, N., T. Shollenberger, and S. Debus (June 2009). "One Year Out: Tracking the Experiences of Male Prisoners Returning to Houston, Texas." Washington, DC: The Urban Institute, pp. 3–4. http://www.urban.org/UploadedPDF/411911_male_prisoners_houston.pdf

[34] Ibid., p. 11.

[35] Ibid., pp. 7–8.

[36] Ibid., p. 11.

[37] Richards, S., J. Austin, and R. S. Jones (2004). "Kentucky's Perpetual Prisoner Machine: It's About Money." *Review of Policy Research* 21 (1): 93–106.

[38] Ibid., p. 99.

[39] Ibid., p. 100.

[40] Ibid.

[41] Ibid., p. 102.

[42] Dyer, J. *The Perpetual Prisoner Machine: How America Profits from Crime*. Boulder, CO: Westview Press, 2000; Austin, J. and P. L. Hardyman (2004). "The Risks and Needs of the Returning Prisoner Population." *Review of Policy Research* 21: 13–29; Petersilia, *When Prisoners Come Home*.

[43] Clear, *Imprisoning Communities*, p. 94.

[44] Grattet, Petersilia, and Lin, "Parole Violations," p. 4.

[45] Ibid., p. 8.

[46] Ibid., p. 10.

[47] Ibid., p. 5.

[48] Ibid., p. 10.

[49] Moore, S. (August 4, 2009). "California Prisons Must Cut Inmate Population." *New York Times*. http://www.nytimes.com/2009/08/05/us/05calif.html?_r=1

[50] White, B. and R. Knutson (August 7, 2009). "California Scrambles to Prepare for Inmate Release." *The Wall Street Journal*, p. A4.

[51] Ibid.

[52] Travis, J. (March 12, 2009). Statement at a Hearing on "What Works" for Successful Prisoner Reentry before the House of Representatives Appropriations Subcommittee on Commerce, Justice, Science and Related Agencies.

[53] Reentry Policy Council, Second Chance Act. http://reentrypolicy.org/government_affairs/second_chance_act

[54] Mauer, M. and M. Chesney-Lind, eds. *Invisible Punishment: The Collateral Consequences of Mass Imprisonment.* New York: New Press, 2002.

[55] Indeed, prisons occupy a clearly demarcated "space" within both the urban and rural landscape. While some are tucked away in very remote areas, most are clearly visible "edifices" that seem to rise up from out of nowhere. The very structure of modern prisons seem to serve as imposing messages to the general population that herein are found the nation's "outlaws" while providing a harsh reminder that "crime does not pay." The physical reminder of "general deterrence" as a social policy is hard to miss. Yet it is also a physical reminder of the failure of deterrence, given the high recidivism rates.

[56] Travis, J. "Invisible Punishment: An Instrument of Social Exclusion," pp. 15–16. In Mauer and Chesney-Lind, eds., *Invisible Punishment*, pp. 15–36.

[57] Ibid., p. 16.

[58] Ibid., p. 17.

[59] Fernandez, M. (October 1, 2007). "Barred from Public Housing, Even to See Family." *New York Times.* http://www.nytimes.com/2007/10/01/nyregion/01banned.html?ex=1191902400&en=5c40a1aff9589b6f&ei=5070&emc=eta1

[60] Ibid., pp. 18–19.

[61] Ibid., p. 22.

[62] Rose, D. and T. Clear (December 2001). "Incarceration, Reentry, and Social Capital: Social Networks in the Balance." http://aspe.hhs.gov/HSP/prison2home02/Rose.htm

[63] Clear, T. "The Problem with 'Addition by Subtraction': The Prison-Crime Relationship in Low-Income Communities," p. 183. In Mauer and Chesney-Lind, eds., *Invisible Punishment*, pp. 181–193.

[64] Ibid., p. 181.

[65] Ibid., pp. 184–185.

[66] Shaw, C. and H. McKay. *Juvenile Delinquency and Urban Areas.* Chicago: University of Chicago Press, 1972 (originally published 1942).

[67] William Julius Wilson discusses at length the decline in the "marriage market" for black women largely as a result of severe unemployment within the inner cities. Wilson, W. J. *The Truly Disadvantaged.* Chicago: University of Chicago Press, 1987.

[68] Petersilia, *When Prisoners Come Home.*

[69] Human Rights Watch (November 2004). "No Second Chance. People with Criminal Records Denied Access to Public Housing." http://hrw.org/english/docs/2004/11/18/usdom9695_txt.htm

[70] *Department of Housing and Urban Development v. Rucker* (00-1770) 535 U.S. 125 (2002).

[71] National Drug Strategy Network (May 1996). HUD Announces "One Strike" Rules for Public Housing Tenants. http://www.ndsn.org/may96/onestrik.html

[72] Quoted in Ibid.

[73] *Department of Housing and Urban Development v. Rucker.*

[74] Metraux, S. and D. P. Culhane (March, 2004). "Homeless Shelter Use and Reincarceration Following Prison Release." *Criminology and Public Policy* 3: 139–160. It appears that the growth in homelessness has paralleled the growth in prison populations. See Burt, M. R., L. Y. Aron, E. Lee, and J. Valente. *Helping America's Homeless: Emergency Shelter or Affordable Housing.* Washington, DC: Urban Institute, 2001; Gowan, T. (2003). "The Nexus: Homelessness and Incarceration in Two American Cities." *Ethnography* 3: 500–534.

[75] Human Rights Watch, "No Second Chance."

[76] Travis, "Invisible Punishment," p. 23.

77 Rubenstein, G. and D. Mukamal. "Welfare and Housing Denial of Benefits to Drug Offenders," p. 49. In Mauer and Chesney-Lind, eds., *Invisible Punishment*, pp. 37–49.

78 Delancey Street Foundation. "Welcome to the Delancey Street Foundation Web site." http://www.delanceystreetfoundation.org/

79 Delancey Street Foundation, "Who We Are." http://www.delanceystreetfoundation.org/wwa.php

80 Metzler, B. R. *Passionaries: Turning Compassion into Action*. West Conshohocken, PA: Templeton Foundation Press, 2006, p. 20.

81 Ibid., p. 19.

82 Ibid., p. 18.

83 Delancey Street Foundation, "What We Believe." http://www.delanceystreetfoundation.org/wwb.php

84 The Web site for this program is: http://www.americaworks.com/; for the Manhattan Institute study see Eimicke, W. B. and S. Cohen (March, 2004). "'America Works' Criminal Justice Program: Providing Second Chances through Work." http://www.manhattan-institute.org/html/cb_29.htm#07

85 Tahmincioglu, E. (May 5, 2008). "Getting Out of Prison and into a Job: Federal, Local Governments Offering Tax Incentives to Hire Parolees." MSNBC. http://www.americaworks.com/state-and-local/welfare-to-work-programs/PageId/17/News.html

86 Project RIO Strategic Plan Fiscal Years 2008–2009, p. 1. http://www.twc.state.tx.us/svcs/rio_plan_08.pdf

87 Ibid., p. 42.

88 Finn, P. (1998). "Texas' Project RIO." Washington, DC: National Institute of Corrections. http://www.ncjrs.gov/pdffiles/168637.pdf

89 Pioneer Human Services. http://www.pioneerhumanservices.org/

90 Ibid., "About Us." http://www.pioneerhumanservices.org/aboutus.html

91 Ibid., "Products with a Mission." http://www.pioneerhumanservices.org/products.html

92 Ibid., "The Power of Partnerships: Annual Report 2008," p. 6. http://www.pioneerhumanservices.org/annual_report/08_annual_report.pdf

93 Sommers, P., B. Mauldin, and S. Levin (2000). "Pioneer Human Services: A Case Study." Seattle, WA: Northwest Policy Center, Institute for Public Policy and Management, Daniel J. Evans School of Public Affairs, University of Washington. http://depts.washington.edu/npc/npcpdfs/phsrep.pdf

94 The Safer Foundation, "Mission." http://www.saferfoundation.org/viewpage.asp?id=270

95 "Letter from the President." http://www.saferfoundation.org/viewpage.asp?id=269

96 The Safer Foundation, "A Consistent Advocate." http://www.saferfoundation.org/viewpage.asp?id=271

97 Finn, P. (1998). "Chicago's Safer Foundation: A Road Back for Ex-Offenders." Washington, DC: National Institute of Justice, U.S. Department of Justice, NCJ 167575. http://www.ncjrs.org/pdffiles/167575.pdf

98 Barra, A. (August 18, 2009). "He's Done His Time, Passed His Prime." *Wall Street Journal*, p. D7.

99 Campo-Flores, A. (August 3, 2009). "A Bridge Too Far." *Newsweek*, p. 48.

100 Ibid., p. 50.

Is There a Better Way?

There is no trickle down, only a siphoning up from the toiling many to the moneyed few.

Michael Parenti[1]

This chapter contains recommendations for rethinking punishment that I think should be among our top priorities. While not exhaustive, the suggestions address issues raised in the previous chapters, especially those centering on inequalities of class, race, and gender.

I would like to begin by noting that we cannot have equal justice in an unequal society. This fact is rarely discussed in books and articles written about crime and criminal justice. Although there are many different causes of crime, one of the most important is social inequality. It stares us in the face no matter where we look—that is, if we are looking. Therefore, before any meaningful reforms can be attempted, before there is any serious attempt to reduce crime, and before we can make the criminal justice system more effective at reducing crime, we must address the existence of social inequality in our society.

Addressing the Problem of Social Inequality

Research spanning more than a century has consistently demonstrated a close connection between crime and social inequality. Adolphe Quetelet (a Belgian astronomer and mathematician) and Michel Guerry (a French lawyer and statistician) in the mid-nineteenth century were the first to use statistical measures to document the correlation between crime and socioeconomic factors. They examined the residences of offenders, matching them with various socioeconomic variables, such as poverty, infant mortality, unemployment, and other social indicators. There was a strong correlation between poverty and unemployment and crime. University of Chicago researchers pursued a similar line of investigation in the late nineteenth and early twentieth centuries; their findings were similar. More than 100 years later researchers continue to show the correlation between various components of social inequality and crime.[2]

Social inequality in the United States has reached its highest point since the start of the Great Depression. Technological changes, the emergence of a global economy, the flight of capital, and the shift from manufacturing to services have all contributed to economic disparity. During the past 40 years the wealth of the country has become increasingly concentrated in the hands of a few.[3]

The Gini index measures the extent to which the distribution of income deviates from perfectly equal (0) to perfect inequality (100). From 1947 to 1973 income inequality declined slightly; since 1974 it has grown. The Gini index was 39.4 in 1970; it grew to 46.9 in 2005 before declining to 45.0 in 2007.[4] High levels of social inequality adversely affect the social health of a nation. Elizabeth Hutchison notes:

> A culture of inequality develops in countries with high rates of inequality. The interests of the rich begin to diverge from the interests of the average family. There is good cross-national evidence that societies with high levels of inequality make smaller investments in public education and other social supports. These societies also have higher levels of violence, less trust and more hostility, and lower levels of involvement in community life.[5]

The wealth of the richest 1% of U.S. households in 1962 was about 125 times greater than that of the average household, compared to 190 times greater in 2004.[6] The top 1% of households (the upper class) owned 34.3% of all privately held wealth. Combining that wealth with the 50.3% held by the next 19% of households (the managerial, professional, and small business stratum), we find that 20% of households own 85% of the wealth—leaving only 15% for the bottom 80% of households (wage and salary workers).[7] The top 1% owns about 36.7% of all corporate stock. Inflation-adjusted net worth of the Forbes 400 went from $470 billion in 1995 to $1.25 trillion in 2006.[8] Savings among Americans went from about 11% in 1982 to minus 1% in 2006. The average wage of workers has changed little in constant dollars during the past 30 years, while more people live in poverty than 30 years ago.

Most commentary about economic downturns focuses almost exclusively on the middle class—ignoring the poor and especially the growing marginality of the urban underclass. One important function of the punishment business is processing this underclass into the prison system. As Bruce Western explains, there is a "pipeline" from the inner-city black underclass to the prison system.[9] The prison system is too frequently a dumping ground for this class of people.

To break this "pipeline" we might very well need something like what Paul Krugman has called a "New, New Deal."[10] He suggests starting with universal health care and creating jobs plus other reform measures, as FDR did with the original "New Deal." Perhaps a public works program like the WPA in the 1930s would be required.[11] Some have suggested instituting a Marshall Plan for the inner cities.[12]

The unemployment rate was 4.9% in December 2007; it reached 9.4% (14.5 million people unemployed) in July 2009.[13] A total of 4.8 million jobs have been lost since December 2007, the most since 1945. It should be noted that the current economic crisis has had the most devastating impact on racial minorities. A phrase (mentioned in chapter 4) popular in the 1960s retains its currency: "If you're white, you're alright; if you're brown, stick around; if you're black, stay back." The unemployment rate for whites was 8.6% in July 2009, 12.3% for Hispanics, and 14.5% for blacks. Almost 30% of blacks have zero net worth.[14] Clearly, racial inequality continues and needs to be addressed.

Ending the War on Drugs

As noted in previous chapters, the negative consequences of drug policies have been far-reaching: the exploding prison population, the targeting of racial minorities (and their disenfranchisement), and the enormous costs to taxpayers with little or no impact on drug use. I recommend a "cease-fire" in the war on drugs until other options are studied and tried.

In chapter 4 we introduced Jeffrey Reiman's concept of the criminal justice mirror presenting a distorted image of crime—namely, that the poor are primarily responsible for the crimes that threaten society. Reiman notes that this viewpoint deflects the potential discontent of the middle class away from people in positions of power and toward the lower classes. His Pyrrhic defeat theory argues that the failure of the system to reduce crime yields sufficient benefits to those in positions of power that it amounts to success.[15] "Nothing succeeds like failure" is the subtitle of his chapter on crime control in America.[16] The drug war is one among many examples. Rather than seeking solutions that would, at a minimum, reduce the criminalization of otherwise law-abiding citizens, policies continue to rely on interdiction, drug-law enforcement, and incarceration.

Mike Gray, author of an insightful book on the drug war, writes:

> Not only has America nothing to show for this monumental effort, but the failed effort has clearly made everything worse. After blowing hundreds of billions of dollars and tens of thousands of lives, the drugs on the street today are stronger, cheaper, more pure, and more widely available than at any time in history. . . . You can buy it [drugs] in the school yard, in the alley, and you can buy it in small Indiana farm towns that just a few years ago had never even heard of the stuff.[17]

Yet the drug war failures have been very beneficial to some groups, including law enforcement agencies that have received enormous sums of money to fight the "war."[18]

If there is a demand for a commodity, someone will risk engaging in the act of supply. When the commodity is illegal and the criminal justice system attempts to limit access to it, the price increases. The demand does not disappear, but the rewards for risking supply increase. When we have attempted to use the law to reduce either the supply or the demand of something that is desired—whether prostitution, gambling, alcohol during prohibition, or drugs—we have always failed miserably. If the general public strongly desires a commodity society makes illegal, the stage is set for suppliers to make large profits, which often entails payoffs to ignore illegal activity or bribes to stop prosecution.

Opportunities aren't limited to those willing to engage in illegal activities and corruption. There is also a great deal of money to be earned legitimately. Indeed, largely as a result of fighting the drug war, the "criminal justice industrial complex" (of which the prison is one part) has become a booming business. There have been lucrative contracts to build prisons to house those convicted of drug possession; budgets for police agencies have expanded for more tools and technology to enforce the laws; companies providing drug testing kits have profited—to name just a few of those who have benefited from drug-war policies. In 2008, the cost to taxpayers for the drug war was $50 billion.[19]

If society's goal is to reduce substance abuse, evidence indicates that tax dollars are better spent on education than on prohibition.[20] Decriminalizing drug use would reduce the numbers of people in prisons and jails. What are the options for decriminalization? Do we legalize all drugs? Do we legalize them with some regulations and restrictions (e.g., minors prohibited from using)? Do we legalize only some drugs (e.g., marijuana)? Do we "decriminalize" some or all drugs by limiting the penalties or some other options? Do we involve the criminal justice system in only indirect ways, such as having drug courts or drug treatment sentences instead of jail or prison?

Mexico and Argentina decriminalized small amounts of drugs in 2009—joining a Latin American trend toward easing sanctions on consumers while shifting the enforcement focus to trafficking networks.[21] Mexico exempted "personal use" amounts (5 grams of marijuana, one-half gram of cocaine, 50 milligrams of heroin, 40 milligrams of methamphetamine, and 0.015 milligrams LSD) from criminal prosecution. The attorney general's office stated: "This is not legalization, this is regulating the issue and giving citizens greater legal certainty."[22] Prosecutors said the new law would prevent corrupt police from shaking down casual users. People caught with drug amounts under the new limits will be encouraged to seek treatment; if caught a third time, treatment is mandatory. A cabinet chief in Argentina said that the Supreme Court decision in that country in August 2009 ended the repressive policies instituted by the military government that ruled Argentina in the 1970s and early 1980s. That government followed the U.S. lead in establishing punitive policies that have not "reduced a single hectare of crops in any place in the world."[23] While legalizing all drugs in the United States could be the ultimate solution, it is not politically feasible, at least not for the foreseeable future. I would recommend three actions as a beginning.

First, legalize marijuana, with age restrictions (as there are for alcohol). During the past 35 years about 16.5 million people have been arrested for marijuana (80% for possession)—at a cost to taxpayers of $20 billion.[24] Despite the expenditures and lives interrupted by incarceration, use of pot has changed little—about 94 million Americans have used the drug.[25]

The usual argument against legalizing marijuana is that such a policy equates to condoning the use of marijuana. I am tempted to reply, so what? We condone the use of alcohol and, until recently, we condoned the use of tobacco (now taxed severely and prohibited in many public places but still legal). We can *discourage* use of marijuana—and other drugs as well—by using the methods that were so successful in reducing the demand for tobacco. Further, because there is no evidence that marijuana use leads to any serious problems (with some exceptions, to be sure)—and no one dies from it—why criminalize it?[26]

Second, a persistent problem is the large number of probationers (and parolees) whose liberty is revoked for failing their urine tests. A national survey found that 27% of the motions to revoke probation were for failing a drug test.[27] Eliminating the tests would help end the "catch and release" revolving door.

Finally, for those addicted to drugs, treatment options would be a more effective alternative than incarceration. Treatment would help the individual overcome addiction and allow him or her to contribute to society rather than spending tax dollars on jails or prisons. One study noted that every dollar spent on drug treatment results in an overall $3 social benefit (including less crime and more employment). One alternative is the *Treatment Alternatives to Street Crime* (TASC) project, which places drug offenders in drug treatment programs under community-based supervision rather than incarcerating them.[28] Similarly, *drug courts* oversee court-ordered treatment in a community drug treatment program. The offender is assigned a primary counselor, a specific treatment plan is developed, and frequent appearances in drug court are required to help monitor the offender's progress.

California voters passed Proposition 36 in 2000, which mandated that some drug offenders be sentenced to drug treatment rather than prison. The Justice Policy Institute conducted a comprehensive study, issuing the following findings.[29]

- The rate of incarceration for drug-possession offenses has gone from 89 per 100,000 California adults in December 2000 to 58 in December 2005—a 34.3% decrease.
- While opponents of the initiative warned that Proposition 36 might lead to an increase in violent crime, California's violent crime rate has declined since 2000 at a rate higher than the national average.
- Since 2000, spending on drug treatment in California doubled.
- Since 2000, California has experienced a larger increase in drug treatment clients than the rest of the country.
- Proposition 36 and drug court completion rates are comparable.
- The effectiveness of using incarceration to prevent drug use and treatment relapse is not conclusive.
- Proposition 36 is saving the state hundreds of millions of dollars.

Innovative individuals have developed other alternatives to save individuals from the damages of incarceration. David Kennedy had watched a failed pattern repeat itself in distressed neighborhoods from Boston to Houston to Los Angeles. Police would arrive in force, kicking down doors to arrest suspected drug dealers, or they would make undercover buys.[30] His research showed that very small numbers of people cause the violence in distressed inner cities. People wanted a safe place to live, but they viewed the police and the heavy-handed tactics as an occupying army and would not "snitch" on fellow residents.

In 2004 Kennedy convinced the police in High Point, North Carolina, to try a new method of removing drug dealers from the streets. They would bring young dealers into the station house, show them a videotape of themselves dealing drugs, and proceed to prepare the cases for indictment, which would mean prison if convicted. They would then release the suspects and work with their families to find job training and mentors. The message? Police would give youths a second chance—but pursue them aggressively if they didn't take it. In four years, drug dealers were no longer on street corners, and violent crime in the area dropped 57%.[31] Kennedy has trained police in more than 30 cities in the methods. Crime in one Nashville neighborhood dropped 91% in 2008. As Kennedy explains,

> We've been in this cycle in which law enforcement pushed harder and harder and harder, which drives the community further and further away. That creates additional space for the relatively few bad guys to operate, which makes law enforcement push harder and makes the community step further back. We're in this spiral of decline, and the great revelation of the High Point work was that we can consciously step out of that spiral and, in fact, reverse it.

Paul Butler, a former federal prosecutor, notes that the war on drugs has put hundreds of thousands of nonviolent offenders in prison—and that prison is the most expensive and least effective means of stopping drug crimes. The social organization of neighborhoods has a greater impact on community safety than police strategies or prison terms.

> Incarceration breaks up families, destabilizes neighborhoods, creates too many unemployable young men and breeds disrespect for the criminal justice system in the communities that most need its protection. Moreover, it produces young adults that come out of prison angry, violent, and more contemptuous of the law than when they went in. . . . When we lock up young, nonviolent drug offenders with hardened murderers, rapists and robbers it's like sending them to a finishing school for criminals. Mass incarceration has not only made us less safe, it has dramatically changed the way that people think about crime and punishment. Young men expect that at some point they are going to do some time and, statistically, they are correct. The deterrent effect of the criminal law has disappeared and instead has become a self-fulfilling prophecy.[32]

He states that the economic crisis presents a unique opportunity to think about the impact of current policies—from putting nonviolent offenders in prison for drug offenses to inflating prison populations by revoking parole or probation for minor violations.

Expanding Diversion Programs, Avoiding Net Widening

Frank Tannenbaum in 1938 was the first to explain how society creates the criminal by defining what behavior is acceptable based on preferred habits and values. He primarily looked at the effect of society's disapproval on juveniles, although his observations hold for other deviant groups as well.

> American criminal activity must be related to the total social complex. The United States has as much crime as it generates. . . . The amount of crime in the United States responds to all the factors and forces in American life. . . . The relationship between the criminal and the community is a total relationship and not a partial one. He is the product of the sum of our institutions and the product of a selective series of influences within them, as are the best and the worst of the non-criminal population. The community does not set out to make a saint, and yet it does occasionally. It does not set out to make a criminal, and yet it does, more than occasionally.[33]

Anyone who deviates from prescribed behavior challenges society, which then sets the deviant apart so that its order isn't threatened. Tannenbaum termed the process of societal reaction to disapproved behavior "the dramatization of evil" (a precursor to labeling theory). Casting youthful misbehavior (such as shoplifting a candy bar) as deviant begins the process. "The process of making the criminal, therefore, is a process of tagging, defining, identifying, segregating, describing, emphasizing, making conscious and self-conscious; it becomes a way of stimulating, suggesting, emphasizing, and evoking the very traits that are complained of." Tannenbaum believed the solution was to refuse to dramatize the evil. He saw the processes of arrest, trial, and conviction as a drama that pushed the individual further in the direction of crime and believed alternatives to punishment would be more effective.

Edwin Lemert refined labeling theory with his concepts of primary and secondary deviance.[34] Individuals committing primary deviance do not consider their deviance fundamental to their identity—rather, the deviant acts are spontaneous responses in particular situations. With secondary deviance, the individual links deviance with his or her self-identity. A stolen candy bar is an adventure if primary deviance; if the individual defines him- or herself as a thief, the stealing becomes secondary deviance. The change from primary to secondary is usually the result of multiple negative reactions by others over time. Howard Becker refined the concept that deviance is not a quality of the act the person commits but rather the label applied by society.[35] Social groups create deviance by making the rules. When someone breaks those rules, society labels them outsiders and applies sanctions. The deviant individual is one to whom the label has been successfully applied.

The labeling perspective provides the theoretical foundation for programs that divert individuals from juvenile detention, jail, or prison. Legal interaction by the criminal justice system may actually perpetuate delinquency or crime by processing cases that might otherwise be ignored, normalized in their original settings, or better dealt with in more informal settings within the community.

In 1967 the President's Commission on Law Enforcement and Administration of Justice called for the creation of youth services bureaus to develop alternative programs for juvenile offenders in local communities and many different programs for adult offenders. The establishment of these youth services bureaus began a move toward diverting youths, especially status offenders and other nonserious delinquents, away from the juvenile court. These bureaus were quickly established in virtually every community regardless of size.[36] Proponents of diversion programs cite numerous studies showing that diversion programs successfully reduce subsequent deviance.[37] The most successful diversion projects have been those that provide comprehensive services and experienced workers.[38]

Diversion programs have raised concerns about net widening. Ideally, a true diversion program (and the original concept behind diversion) takes individuals who would ordinarily be processed through the criminal justice system and places them into some alternative program. *Net widening* occurs if the alternative programs capture individuals whose cases would have been dismissed rather than prosecuted. Most of the research on diversion programs centers on juvenile offenders.

However, the same concepts can easily apply to adults. The key is the provision of needed services and keeping as many offenders out of the criminal justice system as possible.

A Model Program: The Detention Diversion Advocacy Project

The Center on Juvenile and Criminal Justice (CJCJ) in San Francisco started the original Detention Diversion Advocacy Project (DDAP) in 1993.[39] The program differed from other diversion projects that targeted first-time offenders. CJCJ was aware that 70% of first-time offenders never offend again and decided to concentrate funding and rehabilitation services on repeat offenders.[40] They targeted the highest-risk youths and offered intensive case management and a comprehensive range of community services. DDAP workers generally have caseloads of 12 youths or less. In 2007, they served 149 youths, with an 85% success rate. DDAP has been replicated in Baltimore, Oakland, Philadelphia, Washington DC, and most recently in Boston.

Clients are primarily identified through referrals from the public defender's office, the probation department, community agencies, and parents. Admission to DDAP is restricted to youths currently held, or likely to be held, in secure detention. Because the project deals only with youths who are awaiting adjudication or final disposition, their appropriateness for the project is based on whether they can reside in the community under supervision without unreasonable risk and their likelihood of attending their court hearings. This is similar in principle to what often occurs in the adult system when someone is released on bail pending court hearings (e.g., arraignments, trial).

The author conducted an evaluation of this program, which consisted of comparing a group of youths referred to DDAP with a similarly matched control group that remained within the juvenile justice system.[41] After a three-year follow-up, the recidivism rate for the DDAP group was 34%, compared to a 60% rate for the control group. Detailed comparisons holding several variables constant (e.g., prior record, race, age, gender) and examining several different measures of recidivism (e.g., subsequent commitments, referrals for violent offenses) showed that the DDAP youths still had a significantly lower recidivism rate. An evaluation of the program in Philadelphia found that only 6% of DDAP clients were rearrested and only 4% missed a court date while under DDAP supervision.[42]

Gender-Responsive Strategies for Female Offenders

Chapter 6 described the characteristics of women in prison. Included here is a brief summary of the factors that must be considered in devising effective strategies for female offenders. The number of mothers in prison has increased substantially. About 72% of the women in prison have at least one child under the age of 18. This is an important fact, as research has demonstrated that one of the strongest predictors of chronic delinquency is having one or more parents with an arrest record.[43] Women offenders are primarily nonviolent; drug offenses account for most of the growth in the number of women in prison. Half of the women in prisons and jails are black or Hispanic. Drug and alcohol abuse were prevalent in the families of women offenders, and many have substance abuse problems themselves. They have often experienced sexual and physical abuse. The physical and mental health of incarcerated women is much worse than in the general population.

Most prison programs take a "gender-neutral" approach, which in reality means programs designed for white males. Classification, screening, and assessment techniques have not been validated for women and minorities. Research by Barbara Bloom and her colleagues found the following specific areas where men and women prisoners needed to be treated differently: (1) pat-search and strip-search procedures; (2) commissary items, especially health and beauty items; (3) allowable personal property; (4) transportation and restraint policies for pregnant women.[44] One key finding from their research is that a number of "collateral consequences" of imprisonment are gendered. For instance, the Adoption and Safe Families Act (ASFA) of 1997 mandates the termination of parental rights if a child does not have contact with their mother for 15 or more of the past 22 months. As noted in chapter 8, assistance to needy families is denied to those convicted of a felony involving the possession or sale of drugs. This means that a disproportionate number of minority women and their children are consigned to a lifetime of poverty.

Bloom and her colleagues strongly recommend what they call "trauma-informed services," which entail taking the trauma in women's lives into account when creating criminal justice policies, avoiding triggering trauma reactions (e.g., strip searches), adjusting the behavior of counselors and other staff members, and helping women manage their trauma symptoms. They also recommend a holistic health model to treat women's addictions. This model allows clinicians to treat the problem of addiction while also addressing the complex issues of addicted women: genetic predisposition, health consequences, shame, isolation, and/or a history of abuse. In essence, addicted women are in a relationship with the substances they abuse: "a relationship characterized by obsession, compulsion, nonmutuality, and an imbalance of power. . . . Women often use substances to numb the pain of nonmutual, nonempathic, and even violent relationships."[45] Integrating trauma theory, addiction theory, and relational theory (women develop a sense of self through connections with others) is important when developing substance abuse services for women.

Broad-Based National Strategies to Reduce Crime

There are limitations to any individual proposals that are offered as an alternative to using the criminal justice system as a response to crime if they do not address the root causes of crime. There is only so much tinkering with the justice system that can be done. Without changing basic premises, we will continue to confront a "revolving door" system where, under the best circumstances, we rehabilitate one offender and release him or her only to repeat the process with a new offender. Most crime policies are *reactive*. It is time to make a serious attempt to be *proactive*—that is, to ameliorate criminogenic influences before crime happens.

Over the years, many researchers have offered versions of how such responses should be structured. More than ten years ago, Elliot Currie suggested five general categories for a national strategy to address the general problem of crime.[46] The first is early educational interventions (such as Head Start). Delinquency is related to poor school performance and dropping out, which in turn are related to lack of preparedness for school, especially among lower-class minorities. Second, the United States should expand health and mental health services (including pre- and post-natal care), with a special focus on high-risk youths. Most violent youths suffer from childhood traumas of the central nervous system, exhibit multiple psychotic symptoms, and have experienced severe physical or sexual abuse.[47] Third, Currie suggests family support programs, especially for families dealing with child abuse and other forms of domestic violence. Abused children are far more likely than nonabused children to become abusers themselves. Some recent research indicates that the majority of prison inmates, especially violent ones, experienced severe physical, emotional, or sexual abuse or some combination of all three. Fourth, Currie recommends doing something constructive with offenders after they have broken the law. In other words, do not merely warehouse them in a correctional setting. He notes that an ingredient found in virtually all successful rehabilitation programs is improving skills—work skills, reading and verbal skills, problem-solving skills, and so on. His fifth recommendation is to make drug and alcohol abuse treatment programs readily available.

Currie suggests that we as a society need to reduce racial inequality, poverty, and inadequate services. We also need to prepare the next generation better for the labor market of the future—perhaps the most important challenge. He outlines the following four goals for the decades ahead: (1) reduction of inequality and social impoverishment, (2) an active labor market policy that aims at upgrading job skills, (3) a national family policy to strengthen that institution (for instance, a family leave law), and (4) economic and social stability of local communities. We need to prevent the frequent moving of capital and employment opportunities, which has forced so many families to relocate in order to seek better jobs. The relocation has weakened the sense of community and the development of networks that would provide support. In addition, he suggests the need for a national research agenda to study the effectiveness of these policies in order to find what works.

Two decades ago, Mark Colvin advocated the need for national strategies grounded on the concept of social reproduction—the process engaged in by institutions (primarily families and schools) that socialize children and prepare them for productive roles in society.[48] One of his assumptions was that these institutions have largely failed to help young people develop the social bonds necessary to pursue legitimate avenues to adulthood and employment. The failure to invest in human development and human capital has resulted in increasing expenditures for welfare and prisons. There is a need for a "national comprehensive program aimed at spurring economic growth, human development, and grassroots, democratic participation in the major institutions affecting our lives and those of our children."[49]

Colvin argues that neither conservative deterrence approaches nor liberal approaches to rehabilitation have been very effective, mainly because they are reactive policies. Some prevention programs do not work because of a lack of funding or a failure to address the larger problems in society, or because they often appear to target specific groups (e.g., high-risk, poor children) at the expense of middle-class taxpayers. A comprehensive approach must aim at broader economic and human development programs that affect large segments of the population (e.g., the Social Security system versus welfare for the poor). The United States must do what other industrialized nations do and consider seriously the need to develop human capital for the continued overall well-being of society. In the United States the system is so privatized that public or social needs are often undermined by private investment decisions that result in moving capital all over the world, eliminating jobs at home.

He further argues for the need to redirect our focus away from the question of "what to do about crime" to "what to do about our declining infrastructure and competitiveness in the world economy." Further, there is a need to establish an educational-industrial complex to replace the already declining military-industrial complex. Today, our national security threat comes from within, a result of our domestic decline.[50]

Colvin notes that education must be more than what the term has traditionally meant—namely, formalized public schooling leading to a diploma. He says that education "must include families, schools, workplaces and communities." The educational-industrial complex must "reduce the marginalization of young people." Colvin offers eight specific proposals:[51]

1. *Short-term emergency measures* to reduce immediate problems such as joblessness and human suffering. Colvin stresses the importance of comprehensive programs that reach more people who need help.

2. *Nationwide parent-effectiveness programs* required in the senior year of all high schools and also offered as adult education classes for new parents.

3. *Universal Head Start preschool programs* have been effective in preventing delinquency. Certified preschool programs should also include free day care programs.

4. *Expanded and enhanced public education* should include several interrelated proposals: (a) increase teachers' salaries; (b) change certification to open up the profession to non-education majors so specialists (especially in math and science) can teach; (c) increase the school year to 230 days (from the 180-day average) to compete with Germany and Japan (which average 240 days per year); (d) focus on problem-solving skills; (e) offer nontraditional courses such as "outward bound" and apprenticeships; (f) use peer counseling and student tutoring; (g) eliminate tracking; (h) award stipends for attending school and bonuses for good grades to eliminate the need for students to work; (i) establish nonviolent conflict resolution programs; and (j) invite students to be more active in developing school policies (good preparation for participating in democracy as adults).

5. *National service programs* for high school graduates offer youths the opportunity to complete two years of national service with educational and vocational stipends. This service could include health care, nursing, environmental cleanup, day care services, care for the elderly, and so on. This program could provide much-needed labor for public works projects. It would be good for young people to participate in the improvement of their communities, and communities could take advantage of the energy of youths to help rebuild.

6. *Enhancement of workplace environments* so that young people have hope that they will find a good-quality job. Labor laws that emphasize workplace democracy in noncoercive work environments will attract creative individuals who are needed to compete in a global economy.

7. *Programs for economic growth and expanded production* should target the general public, including investment in research and industrial techniques.

8. *The progressive income-tax system* should return to the graduated rates prevalent before 1977.[52]

Margaret Phillips offers a variation on the proposals by Currie and Colvin.[53] She elaborates on the importance of unemployment as a key factor related to crime. Her thesis is that the stress associated with poverty and feelings of powerlessness (which are correlated) results in the tendency to be present oriented—that is, unable to plan for the future because of a belief that your life is out of control.

She uses the following case to illustrate her theory. In the mid-1980s, the Hormel Meatpacking Company in Austin, Minnesota, broke a strike by hiring workers from outside the town. Many local workers were left jobless, and the rates of crime—especially domestic violence—rose noticeably. After plant closures, a ripple effect is common. Suicides, stress-related illnesses, drug and alcohol abuse, and crime increase. There is also a corresponding decrease in citizen participation in civic activities, which results in less informal social control. Phillips notes that there is abundant evidence that poverty and economic dislocation play an important role in crime, as well as in the lack of self-control.[54] Phillips's theory combines the role of environmental (especially socioeconomic) factors with individual responsibility and powerlessness.[55]

We Need a New Paradigm

After writing and teaching about the subject of crime and punishment for almost 40 years, I feel frustrated. Most of the research is generally ignored. We report on the failures of all the following to reduce crime: simplistic programs (Scared Straight, DARE, Just Say No); expenditures on advanced technology for police departments; and policies like mandatory sentencing, truth in sentencing, repressive drug laws, and the death penalty. Yet policy makers continue funding such programs and passing similar legislation. I am reminded of a famous comment by Ben Franklin: "The definition of insanity is doing the same thing over and over and expecting different results."

We are a reactive society. We have established an elaborate system to respond to crime but very little to improve conditions to prevent crime. As noted in chapter 2, punishment (which by definition comes after the crime) is a big business. Unfortunately, punishment does not address the *causes* of crime, since punishment is essentially a *conservative response* to crime. As noted in the introduction, the conservative view of crime (and the entire criminal justice system) is based on deterrence. But everything has a cause, and the causes will remain regardless of the actions of the criminal justice system.

The criminal justice system can be succinctly summarized with a line from *Rawhide* (a television series about a cattle drive starring a very young Clint Eastwood). At the end of each show, the trail boss gets on his horse and calls out, "Head 'em up, move 'em out." Similarly, in the criminal justice system the emphasis is on processing one case after another, with no end in sight. One offender leaves a jail or a prison, only to be replaced by another.

Thomas Kuhn wrote *The Structure of Scientific Revolutions* in 1962.[56] He argued that paradigms—a collection of general agreements, models, or theories about how problems are to be understood and resolved—guide those who practice the scientific method. However, anomalies that do not fit the commonly accepted models can create a crisis and a dramatic shift in how scientists think about a phenomenon. Classic examples include: the discoveries of Copernicus that challenged the conventional paradigm of viewing the sun as revolving around the earth; Darwin's work on evolution; the work of Isaac Newton and Galileo; the work of Noam Chomsky in linguistics; and the Human Genome Project. When the prevailing paradigm hits a brick wall, a scientific revolution occurs. Answers to troubling anomalies require a new way of thinking—a totally different paradigm.

The prevailing model of how to solve the problem of crime is derived from the paradigm of positivism. More specifically, the dominant view comes from the branch of positivism that locates the causes and hence solutions to the problem of crime and delinquency within the individual. This model focuses on the need to change the individual in some way—their psychological development, their general attitudes, their worldview, and/or their behaviors. It typically includes some form of punishment to force this change.

What I am suggesting here is a revolution not just in the way we frame the problem—the paradigm we use—but also in the way our social and economic system operates. What the prevailing paradigm does, in effect, is take offenders, place them under the guardianship of some program (often within the walls of a prison), and focus on changing them in some way. Then we let them go, only to return to the same social circumstances that brought them into conflict with the law in the first place, never doing anything to change those circumstances.

I am not saying that various reforms are not needed within the criminal justice system; this book has addressed a number of issues that certainly require change. Efforts to make the existing justice system more "efficient" (as many recommend) miss the point. If the current system were more effective, there would be more arrests of the poor and racial minorities and more people in prison. In order to achieve "justice," we need to confront and overcome failures in the current system. Because crime is still very much with us, we should be looking elsewhere for answers. The recommendations in this chapter look at broader issues to help reduce the crime problem.

One example of a paradigm shift is the work of several criminologists grounded in philosophy and various religions, including Buddhism and the beliefs of Native Americans.[57] The latest works of Richard Quinney point us in the direction of peacemaking—seeking peace within ourselves and through various nonviolent and noncoercive alternatives to crime.[58]

The goal of *restorative justice* is to end the pain and suffering of the victims of crime—not just the victims of "normal" crimes but the victims of all crimes and all forms of human rights abuses. The usual response to crime—especially violent crime—is a desire to "get even" by seeking "just deserts" against offenders. But this response has always proved to be counterproductive. In fact, it goes against virtually every religious tenet. As Gandhi and Martin Luther King Jr. taught and demonstrated, the only way to end violence is *not* to reciprocate in kind. In other words, we must stop the violence in order to end the cycle. King, in his acceptance speech for the Nobel Peace Prize in 1964, said: "The choice today is not between violence and nonviolence. It is either nonviolence or nonexistence."[59]

The idea that forgiveness is the only way to rid oneself of hurt and anger has a long history. Alexander Pope (1688–1744), an English poet, wrote, "To err is human, to forgive divine."[60] Unfortunately, forgiveness seems out of step in our current political/economic system. Forgiveness would be more in line with a political/economic system "that sees acknowledgment of a harm done, and apology for it, and forgiveness offered in return, as processes that are personally healing for all involved and simultaneously restorative of community."[61]

David Friedrichs argues that the positivistic focus of mainstream criminology privileges discovery, explanation, and prediction over a concern with developing the concept of justice.[62] It views crime as a legal concept and discounts the political-economic context that defines what crime is and how it should be punished. Criminal justice focuses on street offenders rather than victims or the communities within which crime occurs. Mainstream criminology views crime as the violation of state law. Restorative justice looks for objectively identifiable harm and violations of human rights—removing the exclusive right to define crime from elite groups in society. "Rather than ceding to the state monopolistic control over the historically potent term, 'crime' in a humanistic approach is best defined as activity that is demonstrably harmful to human beings and their environment, regardless of the status of these activities under law."[63]

The underlying aim of restorative justice is to cease further objectification of those who have been involved in the violent act—the victim, the offender, the families connected to those individuals, and the community at large. Restorative justice lets all of the individuals involved engage in a healing process through traditional mediation and conflict resolution techniques—dissolving fears, hate, and resentment in order to return to their former selves prior to victimization. Through this process the person most directly harmed "is able to achieve a greater sense of inner-healing and closure for any traumatic loss of trust, self-worth, and freedom . . . [while] the harmed person might also achieve a modicum of reparation for his or her losses as well as be able to reduce his or her fears of being harmed."[64]

Todd Clear compares and contrasts restorative justice with community justice. "Restorative justice is a deeply penetrating critique of formal justice processes and a profound challenge to the adversarial due process model of criminal justice."[65] Community justice advocates are equally dissatisfied with traditional criminal justice but focus on how the astounding growth of the criminal justice system has failed to make communities better, safer, or more livable. Proponents of community justice argue that the prosecution and punishment of felons should not be an end in itself; rather, it should be to make communities better places for people to live and work.

> The claim is that the growing criminal justice system has, in the end, done more damage than good, and that its strategies need to be recalibrated to take account of what communities need rather than merely what wrongdoers deserve. . . . What we need is not strategies to deal with individuals who engage in misdeeds but those that target places where these misdeeds concentrate.

Restorative justice began with a concern about the victims of crime, and community justice started with a concern about impoverished communities.

Proponents of restorative justice know full well what a difficult sell it is within a capitalist society. As Dennis Sullivan and Larry Tifft observe, the change needed "transforms all of our conceptions of political economy, that is, how we view power and money, and how we assess human worth."[66] But we come to see the "money-surplus complex" for what it really is—namely, a game of power and control over others.

As noted above, part of the new paradigm is redefining the problem. We need to make fundamental changes in the way we think about crime and society before we will see any significant decrease in problems. In discussing delinquency, for example, the rhetoric primarily centers on how young people need to change their attitudes, their behaviors, their lifestyles, their methods of thinking, and so on. A new paradigm might help us see that perhaps *we* need to change.

We could begin by rethinking the labels we use to describe people who violate the laws as currently written. Jerome Miller discussed the evolution of labels applied to young offenders. We began with "possessed" youths in the seventeenth century, then moved to the "rabble" or "dangerous classes" in the eighteenth and late nineteenth centuries, and to the "moral imbeciles" and the "constitutional psychopathic inferiors" in the early twentieth century. We continued with the "psychopaths" of the 1940s and the "sociopaths" of the 1950s and the "superpredators" of the 1990s. In the twenty-first century, the labels

include: "compulsive delinquent," the "learning disabled," the "unso-
cialized aggressive," the "socialized aggressive," and the "bored" delinquent. Miller argues that labels allow us to "bolster the maintenance of
the existing order against threats which might arise from its own internal contradictions." Labeling reassures us "that the fault lies in the
warped offender and takes everyone else off the hook. Moreover, it
enables the professional diagnostician to enter the scene or withdraw
at will, wearing success like a halo and placing failure around the neck
of the client like a noose."[67] Miller warns that juvenile justice reform
has always been essentially rhetorical. While the talk swings from rehabilitation to incapacitation, "juvenile justice has always been, and continues to be, neglectful, demeaning, frequently violent, and largely
ineffective. Permissive treatment of delinquents is reserved for middle-
and upper-class adolescents who are not likely to enter the juvenile justice system, which is reserved for the children of the poor."[68]

We might start the process of change by looking in the mirror. We
should begin by asking ourselves: Is there anything that I can do differently? Is there something wrong with *my* attitudes, *my* beliefs, *and my*
actions that may contribute to the problem? If we want some answers,
we can begin by searching *within ourselves*. This is the message from
many who espouse Eastern philosophies. Thich Nhat Hanh, a Vietnam-
ese Zen master and poet, advises:

> When you plant lettuce, if it does not grow well, you don't blame the
> lettuce. You look into the reasons it is not doing well. It may need
> fertilizer, or more water, or less sun. You never blame the lettuce.
> Yet if we have problems with our friends or our family we blame the
> other person. But if we know how to take care of them, they will
> grow well, like lettuce. Blaming has no positive effect at all, nor
> does trying to persuade using reason and arguments. That is my
> experience. No blame, no reasoning, no argument, just understand-
> ing. If you understand, and you show that you understand, you can
> love, and the situation will change.[69]

Later in his book, Hanh describes young prostitutes in Manila:

> In the city of Manila there are many young prostitutes; some are
> only fourteen or fifteen years old. They are very unhappy. They did
> not want to be prostitutes, but their families are poor and these
> young girls went to the city to look for some kind of job, like street
> vendor, to make money to send back to their families. Of course this
> is true not only in Manila, but in Ho Chi Minh City in Vietnam, in
> New York City, and in Paris also. After only a few weeks in the city, a
> vulnerable girl can be persuaded by a clever person to work for him
> and earn perhaps one hundred times more money than she could as
> a street vendor. Because she is so young and does not know much
> about life, she accepts and becomes a prostitute. Since that time,
> she has carried the feeling of being impure, defiled, and this causes

her great suffering. When she looks at other young girls, dressed beautifully, belonging to good families, a wretched feeling wells up in her, a feeling of defilement that becomes her hell.

But if she could look deeply at herself and at the whole situation, she would see that she is the way she is because other people are the way they are. . . . No one among us has clean hands. No one of us can claim that it is not our responsibility. The girl in Manila is that way because of the way we are. Looking into the life of that young prostitute, we see the lives of all the "non-prostitutes." And looking at the non-prostitutes and the way we live our lives, we see the prostitute. Each thing helps to create the other. . . . [T]he truth is that everything contains everything else. We cannot be, we only inter-be. We are responsible for every thing that happens around us.[70]

Before we can achieve peace on earth, which includes a world without crime and suffering, Hanh believes we have to develop peace within ourselves. How else can we make the world a better place, unless we make our own lives better? How can we tell the "criminals" in our midst how to live their lives if we do not set good examples? As Richard Quinney has written: "If human actions are not rooted in compassion, these actions will not contribute to a compassionate and peaceful world. If we ourselves cannot know peace, be peaceful, how will our acts disarm hatred and violence?"[71]

There are many great challenges ahead for Americans and the entire world. I have begun every class during the last forty years by writing two words on the blackboard: *power* and *control*. This seems to be part of the dominant paradigm we have lived under for more than 150 years. Its ultimate source is the "positivist" tradition in social science. One of the founders of the positivist school of thought was the French sociologist August Comte (1798–1857). According to Comte, the positive or scientific method is the highest or final stage of knowledge, allowing humans to discover regularities among social phenomena and to accomplish *predictability and control*.[72]

While this orderly search for regularities might sound reasonable, the positivist orientation can also embody frightening implications. Two nineteenth-century criminologists, Enrico Ferri (1856–1928) and Raffaele Garofalo (1852–1934), became supporters of fascism. For Ferri especially, the positivist orientation justified elevating the authority of the state over the "excesses of individualism." As Vold and Bernard note, one of the problems of positivistic theory is "the ease with which it fits into totalitarian patterns of government. . . . There is an obvious similarity between the control of power in society advocated in positivism and the political reality of centralized control of the life of the citizen by a governmental bureaucracy indifferent to public opinion."[73]

Like the classical school, positivism is primarily concerned with the *control* of crime, rather than with the amelioration of the social conditions that foster crime. Although positivism does pay lip service to the causes of crime, positivists have been most interested in the offender and how he or she can be controlled or changed. Far too often, change is forced on an individual. This is evident in the way we punish individual offenders and also in the current approach to entire groups of people, such as gangs. On a much larger scale, we can see this way of thinking in the behavior of nations, such as the invasion and occupation of Iraq by the United States and the shelling of the Gaza strip by Israel. In both cases, the punishing actions have only made matters worse, creating hatred for the perpetrators.

Some Concluding Thoughts

A full understanding of crime and the criminal justice response requires a critical perspective.[74] This perspective, as the reader might guess, involves critical thinking, which is essentially a process whereby one practices the scientific method in asking questions that challenge authorities, traditional beliefs, and received dogmas. Critical criminology, a perspective that has been growing in popularity in recent years, uses this kind of critical thinking to argue that crime stems from oppressive conditions that are most likely to impact the poor, women, and minorities—a result of class, gender, and racial inequalities.[75] The elimination of crime and the achievement of justice cannot be done without the elimination of these inequalities. Henry David Thoreau once wrote that: "There are a thousand hacking at the branches of evil to one who is striking at the root."[76] The elimination of inequalities might seem a forbidding challenge. Yet society eventually eliminated slavery; women and blacks achieved the right to vote; and segregation ended in the South. Change may be slow, but it begins with individuals reframing their own views and working to make societal changes. George Bernard Shaw once said: "Some men see things as they are and ask why. Others dream things that never were and ask why not."[77]

NOTES

[1] Parenti, M. (February 18, 2007). "Mystery: How Wealth Creates Poverty in the World." Znet. http://www.zmag.org/content/showarticle.cfm?SectionID=10&ItemID=12151

[2] For a summary of this literature see Shelden, R. G., *Delinquency and Juvenile Justice in American Society.* Long Grove, IL: Waveland Press, 2006, chapter 7.

[3] An excellent brief history of the past three decades is provided by Baker, D. *The United States since 1980.* New York: Cambridge University Press, 2007.

[4] Hutchison, E. D. *Dimensions of Human Behavior: Person and Environment* (3rd ed.). Thousand Oaks, CA: Sage Publications, 2008, p. 305; Central Intelligence Agency. World Fact Book. https://www.cia.gov/library/publications/the-world-factbook/fields/2172.html

[5] Hutchison, *Dimensions of Human Behavior*, pp. 307–308.

[6] Hartman, C. "By the Numbers." http://www.demos.org/inequality/ByNumbersMay31.pdf

[7] G. William Domhoff (September 2005; updated May 2009). "Wealth, Income, and Power." http://sociology.ucsc.edu/whorulesamerica/power/wealth.html

[8] Hartman, "By the Numbers."

[9] Western, B. *Punishment and Inequality in America*. New York: Russell Sage Foundation, 2006.

[10] Krugman, P. *The Conscience of a Liberal*. New York: W. W. Norton, 2007. Others have made the same suggestion. See Dodd, R. (April 16, 2008). "Politically Incorrect Solutions: What about a New Deal-Style Jobs Program?" *Dollars and Sense*. http://www.alternet.org/story/81921/.

[11] The Obama administration included elements of the New Deal in its economic stimulus package. See these stories: Calmes, J. and C. Hulse (January 3, 2009). "Obama Considers Major Expansion in Aid to Jobless." *New York Times*. http://www.nytimes.com/2009/01/04/us/politics/04stimulus.html?_r=1; Associated Press (January 3, 2009). "Obama Urges Quick Passage of Stimulus." http://articles.latimes.com/2009/mar/05/nation/na-obama-czars5

[12] "LA Needs a Marshall Plan to Stop Gangs." (January 13, 2007). http://www.ftpmoore.com/sisbad/gangstudy.pdf; Bischof, G. (October 17, 2005). "Katrina Journal: What We Need Is a Marshall Plan in Reverse." History News Network. http://www.hnn.us/articles/16874.html; Pogrebin, R. (November 6, 2007). "Rebuilding New Orleans, Post-Katrina Style." *New York Times*. Economic aid from the United States to help Europe rebuild after World War II was officially called the "European Recovery Program." It was more commonly called the Marshall Plan, after Secretary of State George Marshall. For more details see the following Web site: http://usinfo.org/docs/democracy/57.htm

[13] Bureau of Labor Statistics. The Employment Situation—July 2009. http://www.bls.gov/news.release/pdf/empsit.pdf

[14] Browne, M. and D. Muhammad (February 16, 2009). "White Recession, Black Depression." *Counterpunch*. http://www.ips-dc.org/articles/1080

[15] Reiman, J. *The Rich Get Richer and the Poor Get Prison* (8th ed.). Boston: Allyn & Bacon, 2007, pp. 4–5.

[16] Ibid., pp. 12–59.

[17] Gray, M. *Drug Crazy*. New York: Routledge, 2000, p. 189. See also the following: Newman, T. (January 13, 2009). "Five Essential Things We Must Do to Stop America's Idiotic War on Drugs." Alternet. http://www.alternet.org/story/119061/.

[18] An excellent analysis is provided by Miller, R. L. *Drug Warriors and Their Prey: From Police Power to Police State*. Westport, CT: Praeger, 1996.

[19] Shelden, R. (December 31, 2008). "Drug War Update, the Year 2008 in Review." Center on Juvenile and Criminal Justice. http://www.cjcj.org/post/drug/policy/drug/war/update/year/2008/review/0; for more details see the following Web site: http://www.drugsense.org/html

[20] Reiman, *The Rich Get Richer*, p. 43.

[21] Moffett, M. (August 26, 2009). "Argentina Eases Rules on Marijuana." *The Wall Street Journal*, p. A11.

[22] Stevenson, M. (August 21, 2009). "Mexico Decriminalizes Drug Possession for Small Amounts as It Battles Big-Time Traffickers." *Chicago Tribune*, p. 14.

[23] Moffett, "Argentina Eases Rules."

[24] Shelden, "Drug War Update, the Year 2008 in Review."

[25] Armentano, P. (March 22, 2007). "It's Been an 'All Out War' on Pot Smokers for 35 Years." AlterNet. http://www.alternet.org/story/49597/

[26] One of the best books concerning the legalization of drugs is Miron, J. *Drug War Crimes: The Consequences of Prohibition*. Oakland, CA: The Independent Institute, 2004.

[27] Burke, P. *Policy-Driven Responses to Probation and Parole Violations*. Washington, DC: National Institute of Corrections, 1997.

[28] http://tasc.org/preview/researchpubs.html

[29] Ziedenberg, J. and S. Ehlers. (April 13, 2006). "Proposition 36: Five Years Later." Washington, DC: Justice Policy Institute. http://www.justicepolicy.org/images/upload/06-04_REP_CAProp36FiveYearsLater_DP-AC.pdf

[30] Smalley, S. (February 9, 2009). "Always on My Mind." *Newsweek*, vol. 153, no. 6, p. 53.

[31] Ibid.

[32] Butler, P. (June 11, 2009). "Smarter Punishments." *Chicago Tribune*, p. 31.

[33] Tannenbaum, F. *Crime and the Community*. New York: Columbia University Press, 1938.

[34] Lemert, E. *Social Pathology*. New York: McGraw-Hill, 1951.

[35] Becker, H. S. *Outsiders: Studies in the Sociology of Deviance*. New York: Free Press, 1963.

[36] President's Commission on Law and Administration of Justice. *The Challenge of Crime in a Free Society*. Washington, DC: U.S. Government Printing Office, 1967.

[37] Pogrebin, M. R., E. D. Poole, and R. M. Regoli. (1984). "Constructing and Implementing a Model Juvenile Diversion Program." *Youth and Society* 15: 305–324; see also Frazier, C. E. and J. K. Cochran (1986). "Official Intervention, Diversion from the Juvenile Justice System, and Dynamics of Human Services Work: Effects of a Reform Goal Based on Labeling Theory." *Crime and Delinquency* 32: 157–176.

[38] Dryfoos, J. *Adolescents at Risk*. New York: Oxford University Press, 1990; Feldman, R. A., T. E. Caplinger, and J. S. Wodarski. *The St. Louis Conundrum*. Englewood Cliffs, NJ: Prentice-Hall, 1983.

[39] This section is a revision of a publication of the Office of Juvenile Justice and Delinquency Prevention published in 1999. See http://www.ncjrs.gov/html/ojjdp/9909-3/det.html; see also the discussion in Shelden, R. G. and D. Macallair, eds., *Juvenile Justice in America: Problems and Prospects*. Long Grove, IL: Waveland Press, 2008.

[40] Center on Juvenile and Criminal Justice. "Detention Diversion Advocacy Program: Overview." http://www.cjcj.org/detention_diversion_advocacy_program

[41] Shelden, R. G. (September, 1999). "Detention Diversion Advocacy: An Evaluation." *OJJDP Juvenile Justice Bulletin*. http://www.cjcj.org/files/ojjdp_ddap.pdf

[42] Feldman, L. B. and C. E. Jubrin. *Evaluation Findings: The Detention Diversion Advocacy Program Philadelphia, Pennsylvania*. Washington, DC: Center for Excellence in Municipal Management, George Washington University, 2002. http://www.cjcj.org/files/ddap_philly.pdf

[43] See Dryfoos, *Adolescents at Risk*.

[44] Bloom, B., B. Owen, and S. Covington. *Gender-Responsive Strategies: Research, Practice, and Guiding Principles for Women Offenders*, 2003, p. 12. http://www.nicic.org/pubs/2003/018017.pdf

[45] Ibid., pp. 61–62.

[46] Currie, E. (1989). "Confronting Crime: Looking toward the Twenty-First Century." *Justice Quarterly* 6: 5–25. See also Currie, E. *Crime and Punishment in America*. New York: Metropolitan Books, 1998.

[47] See also Dryfoos, *Adolescents at Risk*.

[48] Colvin, M. (1991). "Crime and Social Reproduction: A Response to the Call for 'Outrageous' Proposals." *Crime and Delinquency* 37: 436–448.

[49] Ibid., p. 437.

[50] Ibid., pp. 439–440.

[51] Ibid., p. 446.

[52] Reich, R. B. (1991). "The Real Economy." *The Atlantic* 267: 51.

[53] Phillips, M. B. (1991). "A Hedgehog Proposal." *Crime and Delinquency* 37: 555–574.

[54] Ibid., p. 558.

[55] She defines powerlessness and its linkage with irresponsibility in the following manner: The essence of powerlessness is the feeling that nothing one does matters; taking responsibility for one's acts assumes the understanding that one's acts have consequences. Taking control of one's life implies the understanding that one can have some control over the future. Thus, empowerment is a prerequisite for taking responsibility, and the most basic kind of empowerment is economic—the ability to support oneself and a family. Ibid., pp. 558–559.

[56] Published by the University of Chicago Press and subsequently revised in 1970.

[57] An example of using Native American culture is seen in the following: Brendtro, L. K., M. Brokenleg, and S. Van Bockern. *Reclaiming Youth at Risk: Our Hope for the Future*. Bloomington, IN: National Education Service, 1990. A summary of this perspective is found in Shelden, *Delinquency and Juvenile Justice in American Society*, chapter 15.

58 Quinney, R. and J. Wildeman. *The Problem of Crime: A Peace and Social Justice Perspective* (3rd ed.). Mountain View, CA: Mayfield, 1991; Quinney, R. *For the Time Being.* Albany: State University of New York Press, 1999; Quinney, R. *Field Notes.* Madison, WI: Borderland Books, 2008.

59 Quoted in Seldes, G., ed. *The Great Thoughts.* New York: Ballantine Books, 1996, p. 253.

60 Ibid., p. 376.

61 Sullivan, D. and L. Tifft. *Restorative Justice as a Transformative Process.* Voorheesville, NY: Mutual Aid Press, 2000, p. 6.

62 Friedrichs, D. O. "Restorative Justice and the Criminological Enterprise." In D. Sullivan and L. Tifft, eds., *The Handbook of Restorative Justice: A Global Perspective.* New York: Routledge, 2006, pp. 439–451.

63 Ibid., p. 441.

64 Sullivan and Tifft, *Restorative Justice as a Transformative Process*, p. 9.

65 Clear, T. "Community Justice versus Restorative Justice: Contrasts in Family Values." In Sullivan and Tifft, eds., *The Handbook of Restorative Justice*, pp. 463–472.

66 Sullivan and Tifft, *Restorative Justice as a Transformative Process*, p. 34.

67 Miller, J. *Last One over the Wall: The Massachusetts Experiment in Closing Reform Schools* (2nd ed.). Columbus: Ohio State University Press, 1998, p. 234.

68 Ibid., p. 3.

69 Hanh, T. N. *Peace Is Every Step.* New York: Bantam Books, 1991, p. 78.

70 Ibid., pp. 97–98.

71 Quinney, R. "Socialist Humanism and the Problem of Crime: Thinking about Erich Fromm in the Development of Critical/Peacemaking Criminology," p. 26. In K. Anderson and R. Quinney, eds. *Erich Fromm and Critical Criminology.* Chicago: University of Illinois Press, 2000, pp. 21–30.

72 Bottomore, T., L. Harris, V. G. Kiernan, and R. Miliband, eds. A *Dictionary of Marxist Thought.* Cambridge, MA: Harvard University Press, 1983, p. 382.

73 Vold, G. and T. Bernard. *Theoretical Criminology* (2nd ed.). New York: Oxford University Press, 1993, p. 42.

74 See Shelden, R. G., W. B. Brown, K. Miller, and R. Fritzler. *Crime and Criminal Justice in America.* Long Grove, IL: Waveland Press, 2008, chapter 3.

75 A good source for this perspective is the critical criminology Web site: http://www.critcrim.org/

76 The quotation is from *Walden* and is found in Seldes, ed., *The Great Thoughts*, p. 455.

77 This was found on the following Web site: http://www.flickr.com/photos/charlaneg/ 2753553426/. Robert F. Kennedy quoted Shaw in one of his speeches while running for president in 1968.

Index